"There Is No Alternative"

"There Is No Alternative"

WHY MARGARET THATCHER MATTERS

Claire Berlinski

BASIC
BOOKS

A MEMBER OF THE PERSEUS BOOKS GROUP
NEW YORK

Books published by Basic Books are available at special
discounts for bulk purchases in the United States by
corporations, institutions, and other organizations. For more
information, please contact the Special Markets Department
at the Perseus Books Group, 2300 Chestnut Street, Suite
200, Philadelphia, PA 19103, or call (800) 810-4145, ext.
5000, or e-mail special.markets@perseusbooks.com.

Designed by Timm Bryson

Library of Congress Cataloging-in-Publication Data
Berlinski, Claire.
    "There is no alternative" : why Margaret Thatcher matters
/ Claire Berlinski.
        p. cm.
    Includes bibliographical references and index.
    ISBN 978-0-465-00231-3 (hardcover : alk. paper) 1.
Thatcher, Margaret. 2. Great Britain—Politics and
government—1979–1997. 3. Conservatism—Great Britain. I.
Title.
DA589.7.B47 2008
941.085'8092—dc22
                                        2008024595

10 9 8 7 6 5 4 3 2 1

FOR

MISCHA *and* CRISTINA

Boudicea, with her daughters before her in a chariot, went up to tribe after tribe, protesting that it was indeed usual for Britons to fight under the leadership of women. "But now," she said, "it is not as a woman descended from noble ancestry, but as one of the people that I am avenging lost freedom, my scourged body, the outraged chastity of my daughters. Roman lust has gone so far that not our very persons, nor even age or virginity, are left unpolluted. But heaven is on the side of a righteous vengeance; a legion which dared to fight has perished; the rest are hiding themselves in their camp, or are thinking anxiously of flight. They will not sustain even the din and the shout of so many thousands, much less our charge and our blows. If you weigh well the strength of the armies, and the causes of the war, you will see that in this battle you must conquer or die. This is a woman's resolve; as for men, they may live and be slaves."

—ANNALS OF TACITUS, BOOK XIV

CONTENTS

A Note on Style and Sources ix

Preface xi

ONE The Shrine of Mother Margaret 1

TWO La Pasionaria of Middle-Class Privilege 15

THREE "I *Hate* Communists" 47

FOUR Diva, Matron, Housewife, Shrew 71

FIVE The Sledgehammer 113

SIX For Strategic Sheep Purposes 157

SEVEN Coal and Iron 183

EIGHT Miners Is Miners 237

NINE The Triumvirate 263

TEN No! No! No! 307

CONCLUSION Why Margaret Thatcher Matters 343

Epilogue 361

Photograph Acknowledgments 364

Acknowledgments 365

A Guide to Further Reading 369

Index 373

A NOTE ON STYLE AND SOURCES

Thanks to the Margaret Thatcher Foundation—to whom every scholar of Thatcher is indebted—much of the archival material to which I refer in this book is now online. Many of the speeches and interviews I describe are on YouTube. Where possible, I have tried to guide the reader to original documents, video clips, audio files, and photographs on the Internet. On my Web site, www.berlinski.com, you may listen to samples of my interviews with Thatcher's friends and enemies. I encourage the reader to think of this as a multimedia book and to treat my notes as hyperlinks. This is why I have used footnotes, not endnotes. I don't want to hunt and rifle through endnotes while I'm reading. I don't know why anyone else would.

The use of ellipses in quoted text indicates that I have shortened a quotation, but readers who wish to consult my unedited interviews will be able to do so. Following the paperback publication of this book, I will donate my recordings and transcripts to the Margaret Thatcher Foundation. I will also give them to the Churchill Archives Centre in Cambridge, where they will join the Thatcher Papers.

For consistency, I have changed British to American spelling, even when quoting British source material, although I have not changed proper names (such as the "British Labour Party"). For brevity, and because British honorifics are generally meaningless to Americans, I have mostly eschewed them—I refer, for example, to "Thatcher" rather than "Lady Thatcher," or "Baroness Thatcher" as she has in turn been titled. I mean no disrespect by this, only warm American informality and an eagerness to get straight to the point.

PREFACE

This is not a conventional biography of Margaret Thatcher. I do not chronicle her life from cradle to coffin. Nor is this an insider's memoir. Although I lived in Britain during the latter half of the Thatcher era, I did not know her and have not met her. I have created my portrait of her from biographies, from archival documents, and above all from speaking to people who did know her.

She is one of the most controversial figures of the second half of the twentieth century—worshipped, loathed, feted, mocked, her significance alternately exaggerated beyond reason and scornfully dismissed, sometimes by the same person in the same sentence. Everyone connected to her, it seems, has his or her own vividly imagined and almost supernatural Margaret Thatcher. No two Thatchers are exactly alike. I emphasize in this book the divergence of views about her rather than the similarities. I also emphasize the historiographical challenges of judging her impact upon Britain and the world. I do this not to advance an obscure postmodern thesis, but to illustrate the complexity of her personality and legacy.

My own view? I find her fascinating. I believe she was enormously significant. In fact, I believe she changed the world, and mostly for the better. I am nonetheless skeptical of some of the more hagiographic claims made on her behalf. But if this book is not a single-minded defense of Thatcher, this is in part because there is no need for one. She was, after all—far more than most people—exceptionally capable of defending herself. She has done so very ably in her autobiography. When she passes, the army of her devout will carry the torch and will need no help from me.

My aim instead has been to offer a portrait, seen through a prism, of an extraordinary personality and towering historical figure—a woman whose influence extends far beyond Great Britain and far beyond her moment in power.

I have also attempted to answer two questions. How do some people become larger than life?

And why, in particular, did she?

The Shrine of Mother Margaret

REPUBLICANS FLOCK TO SEE THATCHER IN HOPES OF SECURING THE PRESIDENCY
By TOBY HARNDEN
Daily Telegraph
July 27, 2007

WASHINGTON—Republican presidential candidates are flocking to see Britain's icon of conservatism, Margaret Thatcher, in the hope that her blessing could help to secure them the presidency.

Rudy Giuliani, the Republican front runner, will become the latest 2008 candidate to kiss the former prime minister's hand when he travels to London in September to deliver the inaugural Margaret Thatcher memorial lecture to the Atlantic Bridge think tank. He follows in the footsteps of Fred Thompson, poised to announce his presidential run and already running second in the polls, and Mitt Romney, ahead in the crucial early states of Iowa and New Hampshire.

Mr. Thompson, a former senator and Hollywood actor, dropped in on her in London last month, saying he wanted "to remind her of America's affection for her and pay our respects." Mr. Romney took the opportunity to burnish his conservative credentials with a Lady Thatcher audience last fall. It is Mr. Giuliani, however, who is perhaps best placed to capitalize on nostalgia in America for Lady Thatcher and her close friendship with Ronald Reagan, who is still lauded for winning the Cold War and restoring hope and confidence in the country.

—◌ ⧫ ◌—

Several weeks before the article above was published, I too was in London, chatting with Sir Bernard Ingham about his memories of Margaret Thatcher. Sir Bernard spent the years from 1979 to 1990—almost all of her time in power—as her chief press secretary at 10 Downing Street. He saw everything.

I joined him for coffee at the Institute of Directors on Pall Mall, a street of elite gentlemen's clubs in the heart of London. Most of these clubs now admit women, but this is a recent development. Nearby, the archly Tory Carlton Club maintains its traditional gentlemen-only policy. Its members were in an awkward position when Margaret Thatcher was elected, for London's preeminent Conservative club could hardly exclude a Conservative prime minister, but conservatives—in the technical sense of the word—couldn't rush about changing things with every passing fad. At last they settled upon a solution. They declared her an honorary gentleman.

The Institute of Directors is a grand, flag-waving London landmark. Its marmoreal Doric and Corinthian columns sprout arrisbeads of laurel leaves; gas-flambeaux lamps line up like solemn soldiers along its stone balustrades. These days, the members of the club are, as its name suggests, captains of industry, but the Institute was once the United Services Club, and its membership, according to Dickens's *Dictionary of London*, was restricted to "officers not under the rank of commander in the navy, or major in the army." Inside, the marble busts of long-forgotten noblemen commune quietly with oil portraits of their long-forgotten friends, reminiscing about the Crimean War, appalled by the sight of businessmen scuttling about the club with their ghastly cell phones, looking as if they'd have no idea which end of the rifle to shoot from.

Sir Bernard and I are sitting in the Morning Room, where we chat for a while about Britain before Thatcher (*"totally* shabby") and the privatization of British industries (*"astonishingly* successful"). He is a bluff, meat-featured man who becomes passionately exercised at the thought of the British Left—"a nasty, scheming lot, crawling out of their holes in the *grrrrrrround!"*—and when he says this his voice booms and his brandy jowls shake and his Rs *rrrrrrroll* in the manner of a Yorkshire clergyman on the pulpit. He was and is Thatcher's devoutly loyal friend. But he hardly strives to conceal the degree of her current infirmity.

Bernard Ingham: Her memory is *so* unreliable now—
[*Waiter interrupts*]
Waiter: There we are, Sir!
  BI: Thank you very much. I mean, she doesn't *have* a short-term memory anymore!
  CB: Is that so? Because I've heard conflicting accounts of this—
  BI: No, she doesn't.
  CB: That's very sad.
  BI: Yes. [*To waiter*] Thank you. Do you take milk or not?
  CB: I do. Thank you. I suppose that's why she doesn't give interviews . . . she's really not—
  BI: She's *not* up to it.
  CB: I had heard from, I don't know if you know Ambassador Middendorf,[1] who was a friend of hers, the American ambassador to Belgium during her time in power; he spoke to her last year and reported that she was in wonderful form,

---

1. John William Middendorf II, U.S. diplomat, telephone conversation, March 9, 2007.

so I had hoped that perhaps the reports of her incapacity were exaggerated, but I guess—

BI: Well, she can be in wonderful form, if you only have her for five minutes! HAH! HAH! HAH!

I believe Sir Bernard. He has no reason to exaggerate. Others who visit her regularly told me the same, in so many words. When I called her office at the House of Lords to see if it might be possible to meet her, her secretary politely told me I shouldn't even dream of it.

Thatcher has now had several strokes. On good days, say her oldest friends, she remembers who they are. Sir Bernard visits her faithfully, and when he does he pretends to brief her on the issues of the moment, the way he used to when she was the most powerful woman in the world. She enjoys this but often can't remember how the conversation began.

Given this, you have to ask: What could Rudy Giuliani hope to gain from a discussion with her? I have been told that she does at least *recognize* Giuliani, but I can only imagine that her response to the sight of Fred Thompson would be mystification. Was he accompanied by his spectacular young wife, the one who is always photographed in plunging décolletage? Thompson used to be an actor, like Thatcher's great friend Ronald Reagan. Perhaps he mentioned this to her, hoping to suggest that he, like Reagan, could readily slip into the role of leader of the Free World. I cannot imagine he got very far. Thatcher, said the satirists, stood for a Britain that was "proud, profitable and ever so prim." Whatever one may think about Nancy Reagan, she did not inspire jokes about pole dancing.

No, I doubt these meetings are greatly edifying to any party concerned. So why are they taking place? Why do the most ambitious men in America traverse the ocean to kiss her hand? Why is it *she* who grants *them* an audience? Why is her answer to the question *Who, in your opinion, should lead the most powerful nation in the world?* not only important to Americans, but somehow sanctified in a way no other living person's could be?

Why has Margaret Thatcher become a living shrine?

_ᗒ ᗒ ᗒ_

The answer to this question has three parts.

First, Margaret Thatcher was one of the most vigorous, determined, and successful enemies of socialism the world has known.

There are as many species of socialism as there are species of insects, and Thatcher loathed them all. I use the word "socialism" here as a shorthand for a system of government in which property is largely owned or controlled by the state, rather than by individual citizens, and in which wealth is redistributed to create a more egalitarian society. Equality is the *ideal*, coerced redistribution the *means*, the state the *agent*. I also use the word "socialism" to compass both weak and extreme versions of this system. Britain before Thatcher was a weakly socialist nation in that many of its major industries and utilities were nationalized and rates of taxation high— and by "high" I mean *really* high, with top rates of 98 percent—but most private property rights remained. In the Soviet Union, almost no private property rights remained. I use the word "communism" to refer to the latter system, which I classify as a species of socialism.[2]

It is almost hard to remember now, but it must be remembered that when Thatcher came to power, in 1979, socialism, communism, and doctrinal Marxism were still taken extremely seriously,

---

2. One could argue for quite some time about these definitions, and many do. Karl Marx did *not* classify communism as a species of socialism; socialism, as he defined it, was the stage between the inevitable proletarian revolution and the emergence of communism. These doctrinal debates are interesting, if you like that sort of thing, but they are not my point. My point concerns the locus of property rights: If they tend to reside with the state, I define the system as socialist. So did Thatcher.

not only in the Eastern bloc but in much of the West and the developing world. The Soviet Union presided over a vast, miserable, subjugated empire. The 1970s had been a banner decade for international communism: In Southeast Asia, communist regimes had seized Cambodia, Laos, and South Vietnam; pro-Soviet factions had captured Afghanistan, Angola, Ethiopia, Grenada, Mozambique, Nicaragua, and South Yemen. Spain and Portugal were lurching leftward.

Britain's Labour Party, which since the inter-war period had either been in power or been by far the largest party in opposition, remained committed to Clause 4 of its constitution:

> 4. To secure for the workers by hand or by brain the full fruits of their industry and the most equitable distribution thereof that may be possible upon the basis of the common ownership of the means of production, distribution and exchange, and the best obtainable system of popular administration and control of each industry or service.

I repeat: *common ownership of the means of production, distribution and exchange.* Although these words were written in 1918, they are not ancient history. Clause 4 was not abandoned until 1995, two years before Labour Prime Minister Tony Blair took power. Unless you are still in elementary school, you were alive when this was the official platform of what is now Britain's ruling party.

The final decade of the twentieth century was marked by a dramatic, global disenchantment with Marxist theory and experiments. This disenchantment had many causes, not least among them the poverty of the theory and the failure of the experiments, but Thatcher's anti-socialist revolution in Britain, combined with the impact of her personality on the international stage, contributed to it significantly. By setting a domestic example of socialism reversed, she proved a point: The forces of history did *not* inevitably lead to socialism, as Marx had predicted, nor was it true that once socialism arrived, there could be no going back. She thus prompted observers around the world to ask a crucial question: Why must *we* have socialism? After all, Britain got rid of it.

The Soviet Union collapsed in 1989. The Warsaw Pact countries adopted broadly capitalist forms of government. By the end of the 1980s, more than fifty countries on every inhabited continent— Jamaica, Japan, Malaysia, Mexico, New Zealand, Pakistan, the Philippines, Sri Lanka, Singapore, Turkey—had set in motion privatization programs. Countries that remained nominally committed to socialism, such as China and Vietnam, discreetly reduced their public sector. Even the United States took its cues from Thatcher, embarking on schemes to denationalize public monopolies. In 2001, Peter Mandelson, a Labour MP closely associated with Tony Blair, famously said, "We are all Thatcherites now." The current Labour prime minister, Gordon Brown, once her sworn enemy, has recently decided that in fact he is a politician in her mold.[3]

Thatcher's role in the great disenchantment was not limited to setting an example in Britain and encouraging others to follow suit. What she managed to do, more effectively than any other politician in history—including Ronald Reagan—was convey a very particular message about socialism. It was not only that socialism was an economically inefficient way to organize human societies. It was not only that communist regimes had in the twentieth century drenched the world in blood. It was that socialism itself—in all its incarnations, wherever and however it was applied—was morally corrupting. Socialism turned good citizens into bad ones; it turned strong nations into weak ones; it promoted vice and discouraged virtue; and even when it did not lead directly to the Gulags, it transformed formerly hardworking and self-reliant

3. "I'm a Conviction Politician Like Maggie, Brown Taunts Cameron," *Evening Standard*, September 5, 2007.

men and women into whining, weak and flabby loafers. Socialism was not a fine idea that had been misapplied; it was an inherently *wicked* idea. This was Thatcher's signal contribution to the debate. It was a point she emphasized again and again: "In the end, the real case against socialism is not its economic inefficiency, though on all sides there is evidence of that. Much more fundamental is its basic immorality."[4]

Now, this point had been made before and made by many. Of course it had. It has its intellectual origins in classical liberalism; among political philosophers it was most famously expressed by Friedrich von Hayek. But it had never before been made by a politician with Thatcher's skill at conveying *this aspect* of the case against socialism or by a politician with her dramatic presence and magnetism. Nor had it been made by a politician who was not American and whose message was not therefore inextricably conflated with what many imagined to be the American imperial project. Nor had it been made—most importantly—by a politician with her ability to project something unique onto the world stage: a radiant aura of unswerving moral certainty. Reagan shared her convictions about socialism, of course, and led a vastly more powerful nation. But Reagan's was a relaxed and genial personality; hers was an intense and wrathful one. He was thus unable to convey something she conveyed in full: a scorn and fury of Old Testament proportions with socialism and the moral corruption it wrought.

How much precisely did she contribute to the world's disenchantment with socialism? The answer to this question cannot be quantified, but roughly speaking, *a lot*. In doing so she affected the lives of billions, literally billions, of men and women.

---

4. Speech to Grantham Conservatives, March 4, 1977, Guildhall, Grantham. Thatcher MSS (digital collection), doc. 103329. All documents from this collection may be consulted at www.margaretthatcher.org.

Second, she matters because she is widely perceived to have reversed the terminal decline of Britain. To understand the significance of this claim, it is necessary first to grasp what Britain once was: the rump of the greatest empire in history, the cradle of capitalism (in Max Weber's phrase), and from roughly 1815 to 1870 the world's only industrialized power. In 1870, Britain produced nearly a third of the globe's industrial output. In the words of the historian Eric Hobsbawm,

> An entire world economy was thus built on, or rather around, Britain, and this country therefore temporarily rose to a position of global influence and power unparalleled by any state of its relative size before or since, and unlikely to be paralleled by any state in the foreseeable future.[5]

He is, by the way, not celebrating these circumstances; Hobsbawm is the world's greatest living Marxist historian, an unrepentant communist to this day. But about this he is quite right. Even America's dominance at the end of the Cold War pales by comparison. At the height of the Pax Britannica, a quarter of the world's population and land mass were under British rule. Let us not concern ourselves with the debate over whether this is a fact to be celebrated or lamented; important as this question may be, it is immaterial to the argument. The point is that for good or ill, Britain was by far the most powerful and influential nation on the globe. It was the world's undisputed premier naval power; it controlled the world's raw materials and markets; it had long been the world's leading scientific and intellectual power; it was the financial center of the world and the premier merchant carrier; it had invented the Common Law; it had invented modern parliamentary democracy. This list could be extended for pages; suffice to

---

5. E. J. Hobsbawm, *Industry and Empire: The Making of Modern English Society, 1750 to the Present Day* (Pantheon, 1968), p. 1.

say that for most of the nineteenth century, Britain excelled its fellow nation-states in virtually every category of economic, military, and political endeavor.

Although the process of decline was in evidence by the beginning of the twentieth century, until the close of the Second World War it could fairly be said that if Britain was no longer the greatest power on earth, it was at least a pivotal one. But in 1945, bankrupt, bled white, and exhausted after fighting two world wars, Britain retreated into itself. Undefeated by Hitler, Churchill was defeated in Britain. Clement Attlee, an earnest socialist who promised to reward the nation for its sacrifices by building in Britain a New Jerusalem, won the 1945 general election. His Labour government was by no means one of Bolshevik extremism, but it nonetheless radically changed the character of Britain, nationalizing major industries and public utilities and introducing both the welfare state and the culture to which such a state gives rise. This transformation—known as the postwar consensus—was accepted by Britain's Conservative Party and remained unchallenged until Thatcher's ascendancy.

Britain retreated from the world stage. The United States and the Soviet Union now dominated the world. The Empire commenced inexorably to dissolve. In 1956, the humiliation at Suez made it clear that Britain was no longer even a great power, no less a superpower. It is not an accident that British literature of this century is known for such titles as *Decline and Fall*, not *Rise and Shine.*

By the mid-1970s, Britain was widely regarded—choose your favorite cliché—as the Sick Man of Europe, an economic basket case, ungovernable, and a living warning to Americans that the wages of imperial sin is death. "Britain," Secretary of State Henry Kissinger remarked to President Gerald Ford in 1975, "is a tragedy—it has sunk to begging, borrowing, stealing." It was "a scrounger." "A disgrace."[6]

---

6. January 8, 1975, Ford Library (NSC NSA Memcons Box 8).

In the year before Thatcher came to power, Britain, upon whose empire the sun once rose and set, endured the Winter of Discontent. Labor unrest shut down public services, paralyzing the nation for months on end. At the height of the crisis, Thatcher, as leader of the Opposition, delivered an acrid speech to the House of Commons. Although obviously partisan, it is also accurate in every particular:

> . . . basic food supplies are being stopped. The Road Haulage Association confirms that picketing is affecting the supplies of essential goods. The Freight Transport Association also reports a new problem—shortage of diesel fuel, particularly in the South-West, because of picketing at the oil terminal at Avonmouth.
>
> British Rail reports quite simply: "There are no trains today."
>
> The British Transport Docks Board, the nationalized ports sector, says that, on average, traffic at its ports is down 40 percent in and out of Southampton. The rail strike has added to the burden.
>
> The report from the Confederation of British Industry is that many firms are being strangled. There is a shortage of materials. They cannot move their own products. Exports are being lost. It says that secondary picketing, picketing of firms not in dispute, is very heavy all over the country. It is particularly affecting such items as packaging materials and sugar and all vital materials necessary if industry is to keep going. Lay-offs known to the CBI are at least 125,000 already, and there are expected to be 1 million by the end of the week. There are telegrams and telexes from many companies saying that their exports are not being allowed through and that they might lose the orders forever . . .
>
> The strikes today are not the only ones we have experienced recently . . . We have had the bread strike, hospital strikes, strikes at old people's homes, and strikes in newspapers, broadcasting, airports and car plants . . . nearly half

our factories [have] had some form of industrial conflict,
stoppages, overtime bans and go-slows in the past two years;
and nearly one-third suffered from all-out strikes.

This is the picture in Britain today.[7]

Britain had recently become the first country in the OECD to
supplicate for a loan from the International Monetary Fund.[8] This
was an almost unimaginable indignity, hinting that Britain was now
in the category of nations to which UNICEF donates mosquito nets.

Rubbish was piled high on the streets of Britain that winter, and
so, at one point, were human corpses.[9] The Soviet trade minister
told his British counterpart, "We don't want to increase our trade
with you. Your goods are unreliable, you're always on strike, you
never deliver."[10]

This was what had become of the world's greatest trading
power.

Sometime in this period—the date is unclear and varies according to the source, but the story is almost certainly true—a gray,
timorous functionary delivered a paper on economic policy to a
gathering of British Conservatives. Britain, he argued, must take a
pragmatic middle path. In the middle of his speech, Margaret
Thatcher, leader of the Opposition, interrupted. She stood up. She
reached into her handbag, extracted a copy of Hayek's *Constitution of Liberty*, held it up before the audience, then slammed it on
the table. "*This*," she said, "is what *we* believe!"

---

7. January 16, 1979, Hansard HC [960/1524–61].

8. The OECD, or Organization for Economic Cooperation and
Development, is a club for rich countries.

9. "Come on, there weren't *that* many corpses," Thatcher's detractors tend
to respond when this point is raised. Readers may decide for themselves how
many corpses would need to be piled on their streets before the situation
struck them as a legitimate cause for concern. My own view is that even one
would be a corpse too many—unless it belonged to one of my enemies,
obviously—but perhaps I'm excessively fastidious.

10. PBS interview with Cecil Parkinson, trade minister in Thatcher's first
government, for *Commanding Heights:* www.pbs.org/wgbh/commanding
heights/shared/pdf/int_cecilparkinson.pdf.

Britain is now the richest country in Europe, and London once again the world's financial capital. Thatcher is widely perceived to be the reason for this.

I use the word "perceived" for a reason. I do not propose that anyone accept at face value the claim that Thatcher single-handedly reversed Britain's trajectory. The story of Britain's economic and geopolitical decline is exceptionally complex; it is not sure that it has been permanently reversed; and even if it has been, it would be, as Chou En-lai said of the French Revolution, too soon to tell. My own view is that the claim is at least partially true, and this is enough to ensure Thatcher's place in history. But I do not need to prove this beyond all doubt. The widespread perception that it is true is also a critical element of this story. Given the grip Thatcher retains over the world's collective political imagination, this legend matters because contemporary leaders—including yours—hope to emulate her example and appropriate her prestige.

This point is connected to my first. Without saying so explicitly, Thatcher conveyed through her words and actions a thesis: Britain's decline was not an inevitable fate, but a punishment. It was not, as many believed, a punishment for the sin of imperialism. It was a punishment for the sin of socialism. Thatcher proposed that in 1945 the good and gifted men and women of Britain had chosen a wicked path. They had ceased to be great because they had ceased to be virtuous. In ridding Britain of socialism, she intimated, she would restore it to virtue. She would make it once again worthy of greatness.

To a Western world preoccupied with guilt, decline and decay, Thatcher's message has a particularly significant resonance. It is hardly a secret that many of us are still wondering whether capitalism is the right path. It is the *only* right path, says Thatcher, and the only one men and women of virtue—not greed, but *virtue*— should take.

Third, she matters because she is a woman. She achieved things that no woman before her had achieved, and she did so in a remarkable fashion, simultaneously exploiting every politically useful aspect of her femininity and turning every conventional expectation of women upside down. In doing so, she refuted several millennia's worth of assumptions about women, power, and women *in* power. She is for this reason not only an important figure, but an immensely interesting one, so much so that she has passed into mythological status even before her death. And this point is related to the two before: The myth she created of herself is what enabled her so completely to capture the world's imagination and present her case to such transformative effect.

No other living politician can claim these achievements, and none enjoys this stature.

This is why the hopefuls are visiting her, even if she is not quite sure who they are.

La Pasionaria of
Middle-Class Privilege

*Let me give you my vision. A man's right to work
as he will. To spend what he earns. To own property. To have the state as servant and not as master. These are the British inheritance.*

— THATCHER'S FIRST SPEECH
TO THE CONSERVATIVE PARTY
CONFERENCE AS PARTY LEADER

To place the rest of this book in context, we must take a biograph-
ical detour. Don't skim this part! You must understand where she
came from to understand what she accomplished.

Margaret Hilda Roberts was born in 1925 in Grantham, Lin-
colnshire, above her father's grocery shop. If you look at a map of
England, Grantham is about a third of the way between London
and the Scottish border, slightly to the east of Britain's midline.
Isaac Newton, too, was raised in Grantham, and in between, nothing of note happened there. Grantham was twice voted Britain's
most boring city in national polls. It is known for its production of

diesel engines and road rollers. I was on a train that stopped there once. It is a flat, featureless town of red-brick houses, all roughly alike. As the train idled in the station, I wondered for a moment if I should get out to take a closer look. I peered from the rain-streaked window at the dreary expanse of low-slung brick buildings. In the distance lay a food-processing plant. I looked up at the slate-colored sky. I stayed in my seat.

Hers was a lower-middle-class, piously Methodist family of no distinction. During her time in power, rumors circulated persistently that somehow, through some ancestral illegitimate dalliance, nobility had slipped into her bloodline. No evidence for it at all. The rumors themselves are significant, though, for they suggest the depth of Britain's obsession with breeding and class. Never were there rumors, by contrast, that Bill Clinton's grandmother had trysted with a Kennedy; no one in America believed it *literally* impossible for a leader of his stature to have surfaced from an Arkansas trailer park milieu. Americans don't think that way.

Her father, Alfred Roberts, was a town alderman and for a short time Grantham's mayor, so she was exposed to politics from her earliest childhood, but he earned his living as a grocer. He was a Wesleyan lay preacher. This is a significant point. Lay preaching was one of the few ways a man of his epoch and class background could acquire ease and fluency as a public speaker. He thereby inherited a famously eloquent oratorical tradition and passed it on to his daughter. Margaret Thatcher's speaking career began in childhood, on Sundays, when she read from the high pulpit.

Her mother was a dressmaker. Thatcher revered her father and spoke of him often; she almost never spoke of her mother. No one knows why she didn't, but everyone thinks it significant. It is a clue, it is said, albeit an opaque one, to understanding her ambition and the nature of her interactions with men.

Margaret Roberts spent her youth, according to the legend she later assiduously promoted, carefully weighing flour and counting change in the family shop, learning the housewifely principles of industry and thrift that subsequently informed her economic policy. Clearly this legend is not the whole story; there is no obvious path between measuring flour and championing monetarism. But like many legends it contains elements of truth. Even if her political philosophy clearly emerged from other influences as well, her class background—that frugal, industrious, Methodist upbringing—was crucially important to informing her worldview.

Britain's aristocracy tends to be educated at public schools, such as Eton and Harrow, which are not public schools in the American sense, but rather exclusive private ones. Margaret Roberts went to the local grammar school, a public school in the American sense. She was an exceptionally hardworking student and self-righteous, even as a child, about her unnatural discipline. At the age of nine, she was congratulated by her school headmistress for her luck in winning a poetry-reading contest. "I wasn't lucky," she replied. "I deserved it."

Through her diligence she earned a place at Somerville College at Oxford University. Oxford's self-governing colleges, of which there are now thirty-nine, are united in something like a federal system. At that time only a small number of these colleges admitted women; Somerville was an all-women's college.

By the time I arrived at Oxford, roughly half a century later, all of its colleges admitted women. My college, Balliol, had done so for only a decade, however, and the ratio of men to women at the graduate level was still about five to one. It is commonly assumed that being a woman in this largely male environment must have been a terrible disadvantage for her, and I am sure that at times this was so. She was unable to join the Oxford Union, for example, the debating club that is the traditional first step to a parliamentary career. But from personal experience I can say that for a woman of the right temperament, this environment was a huge advantage. "Largely male" need not mean "male-dominated." If you were one of only a handful of women among a group of young men who have barely seen a woman before in their lives—sex-segregated schools were and still are common in Britain—it was almost trivially easy to stand out from the crowd, terrify your peers, receive special attention from your tutors, and be the cynosure of any social gathering. It was a clearly observable law that the more bitterly a woman could be heard complaining of the university's institutional sexism, the more likely it was that she was ugly, hopelessly passive, or not all that bright. If Thatcher subsequently had no patience with feminists—"Some of us were making it before Women's Lib was even thought of," she once snapped—I would wager it was because she made precisely the same observation.

Politically, she did well for herself at Oxford, becoming president of the university's Conservative Association. Academically, she did less well; she took a Second Class degree in chemistry. Oxford degrees are classified into Firsts, Seconds, and Thirds; they are awarded based on a student's performance in a single set of exams at the end of a three- or four-year study period. That she received a Second might be seen as evidence for a claim commonly made about her, to wit, that she was a woman of relatively modest intellectual gifts. On the other hand, when she subsequently decided to become a lawyer, she qualified after only two years of part-time study, all the while working full-time as a research chemist *and* assiduously seeking election to Parliament *and* getting pregnant—with twins, no less. She passed the bar exam only weeks after giving birth. However hardworking you are, I doubt you can do that without being quite fast on the draw.

But we are getting ahead of ourselves. After graduating from Oxford, she worked in an Essex plastics factory while immersing herself in politics. She ran for a seat in Parliament twice, in 1950 and 1951, both times unsuccessfully. She had not been expected to win. The contested constituency was a Labour safe seat; running an inherently doomed campaign or two is a political rite of passage in Britain. But she gave her opponent an unexpectedly vigorous workout. Her uncommon energy in campaigning was widely remarked.

She was only twenty-three when she made her second attempt. In the same year she became engaged to Denis Thatcher, whom she met while campaigning. He was the heir to a prosperous chemicals business. Here the story of Margaret Roberts, the middle-class girl from a background of no special privilege, comes to an end. She believed in earning money the old-fashioned way, she always averred, and she earned hers in the most old-fashioned way of all: She married it. Her subsequent career *might* have been possible without her husband's money, but it wouldn't have been easier. This marriage was one of her shrewdest political decisions. It appears to have been a genuine love match, too; by all accounts the Thatchers were utterly devoted to each other. As mothers the world around have traditionally reminded their daughters, it is just as easy to love a rich man as a poor one.

Let us take a detour within a detour and return to Sir Bernard Ingham, to whom we have been speaking at the Institute of Directors. Ingham is the man who, more than anyone except Thatcher herself, invented the Margaret Thatcher legend. As her press secretary, Ingham was responsible for managing her image in the media, and in Thatcher's own words, "He never let me down."[1]

Ingham is a convert, and like many converts, uncommonly devout. He was a member of the Labour Party and in his youth ran, unsuccessfully, as a Labour candidate for the city council in Leeds. Before joining the civil service in 1967, he worked as a journalist for the *Guardian*, Britain's leading organ of socialist sanctimony. After winning the 1979 general election, Thatcher met him, took an instant liking to him, and plucked him from his obscure position as a civil service under-secretary. It was a curious decision,

---

1. Margaret Thatcher, *The Downing Street Years, 1979–1990* (HarperCollins, 1993), p. 20.

particularly because she was later known for sniffing out and at the soonest feasible opportunity extirpating the ideologically suspect from her inner circle. But as usual, her political instincts proved shrewd. Ingham became the truest of the blue believers, serving her faithfully until her downfall.

His views about Thatcher are important. Why? Because they represent the Party line. This is how Thatcher wanted herself to be understood. And because her press secretary was good at his job, this is widely how she *was* understood.

He describes the background from which she emerged thus:

> **BI:** We should not forget her upbringing . . . You're not going to get anywhere unless you work like *stink*, there are no prizes in this world for not working, you know, and *you really will have to apply yourself, girl*, and I suppose the unspoken words were, "and especially since you *are* a girl." You could also say it comes from this non-conformist Methodism in which she was brought up. And they are an identifiable people, they're no longer really identifiable except among my generation, but they were identifiable then. And of course she wasn't part of a privileged upbringing, like so many members of her cabinet . . . I think she got the resolution from her father, who if he taught her anything, it was to stand up against the herd, *never go with the herd if you think the herd is wrong*, he told her. And she never went with the herd.
>
> **CB:** What I'm trying to understand is the iron confidence that she projected, did that—
>
> **BI:** *Projected?*
>
> **CB:** Exactly. How deep did it go? Was it a compensation for an underlying sense of insecurity?
>
> **BI:** I do *not* think you should play up the insecurity in her character. I think there was a basic insecurity there in her class and upbringing and sex. I think that is what caused her to

be very careful and deliberate in what she did. But it was not allowed to undermine her determination to do what she believed to be *right*. Her father had told her that she must do what she knew to be *right*. And she revered her father. She was in many ways her father's son.

CB: You just said that she was her father's *son*.

BI: Well, I mean, she *was*.

She did what was *right*, she did what was *right*, she did what was *right*. She did it because her father told her to. She repeated those words over and over until through the hypnotic power of repetition they appeared at last to blaze from her forehead. If it is also true that she did what was practical and politically expedient—in fact, she was a master of the art of the possible, particularly gifted at fighting only the battles she could win—this was not the part of her personality she showcased.

Alderman Roberts's "son" won a seat in the House of Commons in 1959. The Conservatives were in power under Harold Macmillan. At thirty-four, she was the youngest woman in the House. In 1961, she became parliamentary under-secretary for pensions and national insurance. She was known in this position for her extraordinary mastery of economic statistics and for her good looks. "I have the latest red hot figure," she once announced to the House, inadvertently parodying herself on both scores. She was momentarily baffled by the ensuing hilarity.

The Tories were ousted in 1964 and spent the next six years in opposition. Thatcher served in a number of shadow cabinet posts, and again her reputation was for diligence and a remarkable memory for statistics. I have neither heard anyone say nor read anywhere that during this period anyone recognized in her the leader she was to become. Said one colleague: "We all smiled benignly as we looked into those blue eyes and at the tilt of the golden head.

Margaret Thatcher is unveiled as the new leader of the Conservative Party on February 11, 1975. This photo captures what one of her speechwriters, the playwright Ronnie Millar, referred to as the "senior girl-scout freshness about her." Many men commented upon this ("golden"—"girlish"—"trusting"—"innocent") as she rose up through the Commons. These qualities, said Millar, were "rather appealing . . . as though she had stepped right out of *The Sound of Music.*" *(Courtesy of Graham Wiltshire)*

We, and all the world, had no idea what we were in for."[2]

It *was* said of her, remarkably often, that she was pretty. If you have seen unflattering photos of her in late middle-age you may find yourself puzzled by this. But the young Margaret Thatcher was in fact blonde, clear-skinned, pleasantly round, and, of course, young. This was all the more striking because Britons of the postwar era generally looked awful. The stereotype of the Englishman with bad teeth does not come from nowhere. Wartime and postwar rationing had taken a nutritional toll; health care, while provided by the state, was also rationed by the state, and cosmetic dentistry was not the state's priority. If it is now quite common for women in London to spend a hundred pounds to have their hair colored, at that time only women married to very wealthy men, as Thatcher was, could afford the luxury of good grooming. Her grooming was always immaculate.

By the end of the 1960s, unemployment was steadily rising, and so was the tempo of trade union disputes. During the 1970 general election campaign, the Conservatives, led by Edward Heath, proposed a healing elixir of free-market economics, trade union re-

---

2. Peter Rawlinson, *A Price Too High: An Autobiography* (Weidenfeld & Nicolson, 1989), pp. 246–247.

form, tax cuts, and spending restraints. They won. Heath named
Thatcher secretary of state for education and science, and it was in
this position that she first gained national notoriety. She abolished
a program to provide free milk to schoolchildren, earning the nickname "Thatcher the Milk-Snatcher." The slogan "Ditch the Bitch"
also became common currency and remained so until she resigned
from the leadership of the Conservative Party in 1991.

When unemployment passed the million-man mark in 1972,
Heath retreated from the Party's platform in what has infamously
been termed a series of U-turns. He poured money from the taxpayer coffers into flagging British industries and retreated from
confrontation with the unions. This served only to embolden
them. In 1973, directly after the announcement of the Arab oil
embargo, Britain's electricity and coal workers declared an overtime ban. It is only slightly hyperbolic to imagine this analogy:

The New York Times
Tuesday, September 12, 2001
HIJACKED JETS DESTROY TWIN TOWERS AND HIT
PENTAGON IN DAY OF TERROR
New York's Firefighters Declare Overtime Ban

Heath's government declared a state of emergency, imposing a
three-day industrial work-week to save energy. A two-day week
was in prospect. Power cuts became the norm. In 1974, faced with
the threat of an all-out miners' strike, Heath called a general election. His campaign slogan was *Who governs Britain?* The voters answered. *You sure as hell don't.*

The Labour Party took power under Harold Wilson, and from
this defeat, Thatcherism was born.

_⌀ ⌬ ⌀_

The Conservative politician Keith Joseph was the intellectual
force behind Thatcherism. Joseph was Thatcher's mentor; he in

turn was strongly influenced by Friedrich von Hayek and Milton
Friedman. In 1974, Joseph delivered a speech at Upminster that
may be taken as the first public expression of full-throated
Thatcherism. The title itself—"This Is Not the Time to Be Mealy-
Mouthed: Intervention Is Destroying Us"—embodied what would
come to be Thatcher's thematic signature: aggression, a sense of
emergency, a contemptuous rejection of conciliatory language, the
association of government intervention with such words as "destroy." Intervention in this semantic landscape is not "unhelpful" or
"doing more harm than good"; it is *destroying* us. And it is destroying *us*, mind you, the British people: Never was nationalism far
from the surface.

Joseph delivered this speech in response to plans unveiled by
the Labour government's industry secretary, Tony Benn, to extend
public control over the most profitable areas of British industry. "It
is not enough just to stave off Benn's preposterous proposals,"
Joseph intoned:

> The question we must all ask ourselves is how Mr. Benn was
> able to come within striking distance of the very heart of
> our economic life in the first place. How could it come
> about that the suggestions could even be made by a minister
> of the Crown after a generation's experience of state owner-
> ship of a fifth of our economy? How could anyone expect
> that the idea of "more of the same" which has nearly
> brought us to our knees could be seriously entertained?
>
> We must find a satisfactory answer to these questions if
> we are really concerned with our survival as a free and pros-
> perous nation.
>
> Of course, there is more than one answer. But an impor-
> tant part of the answer must be that our industry, eco-
> nomic life and society have been so debilitated by 30 years
> of socialistic fashions that their very weakness tempts fur-
> ther inroads . . .

There is no good reason why this country should continue to fail. We have ample talent, the same kind of talent that made Britain great and prosperous a hundred years ago, the envy of the world . . .

We are now more socialist in many ways than any other developed country outside the communist bloc—in the size of the public sector, the range of controls and the telescoping of net income.

And what is the result? Compare our position today with that of our neighbors in northwest Europe—Germany, Sweden, Holland, France. They are no more talented than we are. Yet, compared with them, we have the longest working hours, the lowest pay and the lowest production per head . . .

We have achieved what seemed impossible. We have poured never-ending flows of real resources into coal, rail and shipbuilding, among others, yet after 30 years they are as ailing and problematic as ever . . .

These are the lean kine which, as in Pharaoh's dream, are eating the healthy cows—the productive sector of the economy—and yet remain as hungry as ever.[3]

The biblical allusion is particularly significant; not only does it suggest the origins of Joseph's nickname—the Mad Monk—but it foreshadows Thatcher's preoccupation with socialism as *sin*. Indeed, in a 1978 speech concerning Christianity and politics, she specifically described the core of socialism not merely as a folly, but a heresy:

. . . there is one heresy which it seems to me that some political doctrines embrace.

It is the belief that Man is perfectible.

---

3. Keith Joseph speech at Upminster, June 22, 1974, Thatcher MSS (digital collection), doc. 110604.

This takes the form of supposing that if we get our social
institutions right—if we provide properly for education,
health and all other branches of social welfare—we shall
have exorcised the Devil. This is bad theology and it also
conflicts with our own experience.[4]

Her fluent command of both the Old and the New Testaments
was a notable aspect of her political personality. She held, she said,
a "personal belief in the relevance of Christianity to public policy."[5] Not only was she intimately familiar with the prophets of
yore, she was prepared to associate herself among their ranks. "The
Old Testament prophets," she remarked in a campaign speech,

> didn't go out into the highways saying, "Brothers, I want
> consensus." They said, "This is my faith and my vision! This
> is what I passionately believe!" And they preached it. We
> have a message. Go out, preach it, practice it, fight for it—
> and the day will be ours![6]

It is said that she once began a speech with the words "As God
once said, and I think rightly," but the story is, alas, apocryphal.
That these words are so often attributed to her nonetheless suggests the nature of the woman.

Although widely considered Thatcher's intellectual superior, the
Mad Monk was a political incompetent who destroyed his own
chances of becoming prime minister by delivering an ill-considered

---

4. Speech at St. Lawrence Jewry, City of London, March 31, 1978. Oxford
University Press CD-ROM of Margaret Thatcher's Complete Public
Statements, 78/039.

5. Speech to the Church of Scotland General Assembly, May 21, 1988,
Thatcher MSS (digital collection), doc. 107246.

6. Speech to Conservative rally at Cardiff, April 16, 1979, Thatcher MSS
(digital collection), doc. 104011.

speech, in 1974, urging poor British women to take more care with their contraception. To many this sounded suspiciously like a call to solve Britain's economic problems with eugenics. Thus did Thatcher inherit his legacy, and thus did his legacy come to be given her name.

In the early 1970s, Joseph and Thatcher founded the Centre for Policy Studies, a think tank devoted to promoting Joseph's distinct form of conservatism, now termed Thatcherism. What Thatcherism is, precisely, is a matter of some debate, even if Bernard Ingham finds it a simple concept:

CB: If you were asked to define Thatcherism—as opposed to Conservatism—would you have a ready definition at hand?

BI: Common sense.

CB: Common sense?

BI: *Resolute common sense!*

The words "common sense" featured largely in her campaign literature and speeches. They were on the first page of her 1979 election manifesto: "This manifesto points the way . . . it sets out a broad framework for the recovery of our country, based not on dogma, but on reason, on common sense."[7]

Obviously the phrase "common sense" was a crowd-pleaser, but beyond suggesting something about her populist appeal, it doesn't tell us much about the specifics. Alone among British prime ministers, Thatcher's name has become synonymous with an ideology—there is no Churchillism, there is no Attleeism. Thatcherism admits of no easy definition, but certain core principles are clear: She believed in free markets, popular capitalism, property ownership, privatization, monetarism, firm control over public expenditure, low taxation, and

---

7. Conservative Party Manifesto, April 1979, Conservative Central Office, THCR 2–7–1–23 (4). All documents prefaced by "THCR" may be consulted among the papers of Baroness Thatcher at the Churchill Archives Centre, Cambridge.

individualism. She was an ardent patriot and nationalist. She deplored socialism and considered welfare spending and collective bargaining to be forms of it. She particularly despised powerful trade unions. She was leery of international organizations. She saw nothing to admire in the Soviet Union and much to admire in America.

But there is a distinctly emotional component to Thatcherism as well, one expressed quite well by Ingham's table-thumping animadversions:

> **BI:** Thatcherism says to hell with all your pesky ideas, *this* is the way you must run a country! You must run it so you protect the value of people's money, so that you protect the weak, the disabled, the infirm, and whatever, so that you defend the realm, and then you let people get on with it! And you organize things for their benefit, not for the government's benefit, or for the benefit of narrow sectional interests! That's *common sense!*

Thatcher had been convinced by Joseph that the Conservatives had lost the last election because they had failed to stand their ground. She was equally convinced that she was the only one left in her party who would defend that ground. She stood against Heath for the party leadership in 1975. When she went to Heath's office to tell him her decision, he did not bother to look up. "You'll lose," he said. "Good day to you."[8]

To his astonishment, and to the even greater astonishment of the nation, she won.

_⌒. ⌒⇒ .⌒_

---

8. There are many versions of this story; it seems reasonable to conclude that if these are not precisely the words he used, they are close enough and certainly convey the mood of the encounter.

CONFIDENTIAL

PAGE 01 LONDON 02415 01 OF 02 161633Z

O R 161602Z FEB 75

FM AM EMBASSY LONDON

TO USMISSION GENEVA IMMEDIATE

SUBJECT: MARGARET THATCHER: SOME FIRST IMPRESSIONS

. . . MARGARET THATCHER HAS BLAZED INTO NATIONAL PROMINENCE ALMOST LITERALLY FROM OUT OF NOWHERE. WHEN SHE FIRST INDICATED THAT SHE INTENDED TO STAND AGAINST TED HEATH FOR LEADERSHIP OF THE CONSERVATIVE PARTY, FEW TOOK HER CHALLENGE SERIOUSLY AND FEWER STILL BELIEVED IT WOULD SUCCEED. SHE HAD NEVER BEEN A MEMBER OF THE INNER CIRCLE OF TORY POWER BROKERS, AND NO POLITICIAN IN MODERN TIMES HAS COME TO THE LEADERSHIP OF EITHER MAJOR PARTY WITH SUCH A NARROW RANGE OF PRIOR EXPERIENCE. NOW SUDDENLY, AFTER WHAT HAS BEEN DESCRIBED AS HER "DARINGLY SUCCESSFUL COMMANDO RAID ON THE HEIGHTS OF THE TORY PARTY," SHE HAS BECOME THE FOCUS OF UNUSUALLY INTENSIVE MEDIA AND POPULAR INTEREST . . .

THERE IS GENERAL AGREEMENT AMONG FRIENDS AND CRITICS ALIKE THAT SHE IS AN EFFECTIVE AND FORCEFUL PARLIAMENTARY PERFORMER. SHE HAS A QUICK, IF NOT PROFOUND, MIND, AND WORKS HARD TO MASTER THE MOST COMPLICATED BRIEF. SHE FIGHTS HER CORNER WITH SKILL AND TOUGHNESS, BUT CAN BE FLEXIBLE WHEN PRESSED. IN DEALING WITH THE MEDIA OR WITH SUBORDINATES, SHE TENDS TO BE CRISP AND A TRIFLE PATRONIZING. WITH COLLEAGUES, SHE IS HONEST AND STRAIGHT-FORWARD, IF NOT EXCESSIVELY CONSIDERATE OF THEIR VANITIES.

CIVIL SERVANTS AT THE MINISTRY OF EDUCATION FOUND HER AUTOCRATIC. SHE HAS THE COURAGE OF HER CONVICTIONS, AND ONCE SHE HAS REACHED A DECISION TO ACT, IS

UNLIKELY TO BE DEFLECTED BY ANY BUT THE MOST PERSUA-
SIVE ARGUMENTS.

SELF-CONFIDENT AND SELF-DISCIPLINED, SHE GIVES
EVERY PROMISE OF BEING A STRONG LEADER . . .

EVEN BEFORE HER GREAT LEAP UPWARD, MRS. THATCHER
HAD BEEN THE PERSONIFICATION OF A BRITISH MIDDLE CLASS
DREAM COME TRUE. BORN THE DAUGHTER OF A GROCER, SHE
HAD BY DINT OF HER OWN ABILITIES AND APPLICATION WON
THROUGH, SECURING SCHOLARSHIPS TO GOOD SCHOOLS,
MAKING A SUCCESS OF HER CHOSEN CAREER, AND MARRYING
ADVANTAGEOUSLY. IT IS NOT SURPRISING THEN THAT SHE ES-
POUSES THE MIDDLE CLASS VALUES OF THRIFT, HARD WORK,
AND LAW AND ORDER, THAT SHE BELIEVES IN INDIVIDUAL
CHOICE, MAXIMUM FREEDOM FOR MARKET FORCES, AND MIN-
IMAL POWER FOR THE STATE. HERS IS THE GENUINE VOICE OF
A BELEAGUERED BOURGEOISIE, ANXIOUS ABOUT ITS ERODING
ECONOMIC POWER AND DETERMINED TO ARREST SOCIETY'S
SEEMINGLY INEXORABLE TREND TOWARDS COLLECTIVISM.
SOMEWHAT UNCHIVALROUSLY, DENIS HEALEY HAS DUBBED
HER "LA PASIONARIA OF MIDDLE CLASS PRIVILEGE."[9] . . .

UNFORTUNATELY FOR HER PROSPECTS OF BECOMING A
NATIONAL, AS DISTINCT FROM A PARTY, LEADER, SHE HAS
OVER THE YEARS ACQUIRED A DISTINCTIVELY UPPER MIDDLE
CLASS PERSONAL IMAGE. HER IMMACULATE GROOMING, HER
IMPERIOUS MANNER, HER CONVENTIONAL AND SOMEWHAT
FORCED CHARM, AND ABOVE ALL HER PLUMMY VOICE STAMP
HER AS THE QUINTESSENTIAL SUBURBAN MATRON, AND
FRIGHTFULLY ENGLISH TO BOOT. NONE OF THIS GOES DOWN
WELL WITH THE WORKING CLASS OF ENGLAND (ONE-THIRD
OF WHICH USED TO VOTE CONSERVATIVE), TO SAY NOTHING
OF ALL CLASSES IN THE CELTIC FRINGES OF THIS ISLAND . . .

---

9. The Labour politician Healey was at the time favored to win his party's
leadership election.

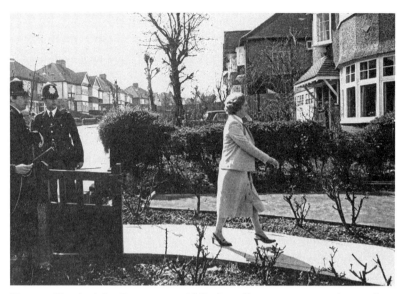

Margaret Thatcher's bustling, proper, middle-class officiousness prompted astonishing effusions of snobbery among Britain's elites. When asked why intellectuals loathed her so, the theater producer Jonathan Millar replied that it was "self-evident"—they were nauseated by her "odious suburban gentility." The philosopher Mary Warnock deplored Thatcher's "neat well-groomed clothes and hair, packaged together in a way that's not exactly vulgar, just low," embodying "the worst of the lower-middle-class." This filled Warnock with "a kind of rage." *(Courtesy of the family of Srdja Djukanovic)*

> THESE ARE STILL EARLY DAYS THOUGH . . . THE ODDS ARE
> AGAINST HER, BUT AFTER HER STUNNING ORGANIZATIONAL
> COUP D'ÉTAT THIS PAST MONTH, FEW ARE PREPARED TO SAY
> SHE CAN'T DO IT.[10]

Prime Minister Harold Wilson resigned in 1976, succeeded by the new leader of the Labour Party, James Callaghan. As leader of the Opposition, Thatcher immediately began to attract international notice, particularly for her coruscating attack on the Soviet Union, delivered at the Kensington Town Hall:

10. U.S. Embassy in London to State Department, "Margaret Thatcher: Some First Impressions," U.S. State Department Archives, February 16, 1975. www.margaretthatcher.org/document/E85DA4E0A8144A278F350BCF08F7F80A.pdf.

The Russians are bent on world dominance and they are rapidly acquiring the means to become the most powerful imperial nation the world has seen . . . They put guns before butter while we put just about everything before guns. They know that they are a superpower in only one sense— the military sense. They are a failure in human and economic terms . . . If we cannot draw the lesson . . . then we are destined, in their words, to end up on the scrap heap of history.[11]

This speech led the state-controlled Soviet press to give her the name by which she has since been known: the Iron Lady. It tells you something about the way Britain was perceived at the time that the communist apparatchiks who coined this phrase presumably believed this would be understood in Britain as a hurtful insult, one that would damage her prestige, not enhance it. It also suggests how divorced those apparatchiks were from the sentiments of their own citizens, many of whom from then on worshipped her as primitive man worshipped the sun.

Like the rest of the industrialized world, Britain endured throughout the 1970s the reverberating effects of the 1973 oil price shock. Inflation soared, reaching a peak of 27 percent in 1975. If real wages were diminishing, Britain's labor leaders concluded, this was more than a hardship for the working man, it was an injustice perpetrated against him by the ruling classes. The remedy, they concluded, was workers' solidarity and the blunt weapon of industrial action. Labor leaders of greater wisdom, or at least ones in possession of a more sophisticated economic model, might have concluded that strikes and work stoppages were the last thing Britain now needed, and indeed the one thing guaranteed to deal a death blow to an already faltering economy. Wisdom was not their forte.

---

11. Speech at Kensington Town Hall, "Britain, Awake," Chelsea, January 19, 1976, Thatcher MSS (digital collection), doc. 102939.

During the Winter of Discontent, the question raised by Heath—*Who rules?*—hung over Britain like a cold cloud. That question was understood to be *the* question, and it was a question to which Britain's powerful unions had a ready answer: *We do.* They had, after all, with contemptuous ease brought down the Heath government. The labor barons were persuaded that although they would never lead Britain, it was within their power to run it, and they proposed to run it for their benefit, embedding in both law and custom practices that everyone beyond the union halls could see would in the end destroy Britain as a competitive economic power.

When the 1979 general election brought the Conservatives back to power, there was no widespread expectation that Thatcher could change this situation, and there has been no attempt retrospectively to suggest that there was. Her election, according to her friends and enemies alike, was not personal: It was a rebuke to the Labour Party and the embarrassing diminishment of Britain over which it had presided.

BI: She won by a contempt, really, for the Labour Party's inability to cope with the trade unions. But no great expectation that she would be any better at it. They felt she ought to have a chance. I think quite a lot of people thought that she couldn't do any *worse* than the men . . .

CB: How would you describe the economic climate, the moral climate in Britain back then?

BI: Let me try to make the point this way. Just as I believe people in this country, the most *stupid* people in our country, most of whom can be found in our government, do not understand the nature of the trauma that hit the United States with 9/11, so the United States—and people in this country have forgotten—so people in the United States will have no understanding, really, of the dire nature that British society had reached by 1979. It wasn't quite so bad that people felt that society was breaking down, but it was bad

enough for people to wonder whether they would go into
work that day, whether they would get into work that day,
whether their rubbish would be cleared, where the next
strike—railway or whatever—would happen. And it was a
poor society. I've never been as poor in my adult life as I was
in the mid '70s. Devaluation [of the currency] and all that
kind of thing. I felt, even though I was a civil servant, I felt
impoverished. Because of the shabbiness. The way Britain
had become, it felt totally shabby. In the hands of a many-
headed dictator called—

CB: What did "shabby" look like?

BI: It was a fairly primitive society. People living in council
houses, under the thumb of local authorities, large areas of
working-class houses that had long since seen their best . . .
It was shabby.

Britain *was* shabby, I can testify to this. In fact, I moved to
Britain in 1988, at the tail end of the Thatcher era, and it was still
shabby. Before this, I had been working in Paris as a *fille au pair*.
The difference between Paris and London—even after nearly ten
years of Thatcher—was shocking. Paris was gay, bright, renovated;
London was dreary and sullen. Throughout Britain, people looked
ragged and worn-down. The food was inedible. Standards of customer service were appalling. Nearly twenty years later, the transformation of Britain is undeniable. London is now pristine and
gleaming, packed with superb restaurants, purveyors of flat-screen
televisions and organic linens, upscale aromatherapists. There has
been a transformation in the appearance of the British people:
They look healthier; they have better skin and glossier hair; they
are well-dressed. To take the Eurostar from London to Paris is now
to have precisely the opposite reaction from the one I had two decades ago. Getting off the train, one notes immediately that by
comparison with London, Paris is shabby.

Prior to the 1979 election, the British ambassador to Paris,
Nicholas Henderson, sent a dispatch to the Foreign Office. It was

leaked several weeks later to the press during the general election campaign and immediately became an iconic document, a detailed and devastating dissection of British shabbiness and all that it entailed.

"I myself," he wrote,

> was able to observe Churchill, Attlee and Bevin dealing on equal terms with Stalin and Truman at the Potsdam Conference when no German or Frenchman was present . . . in the mid '50s we were still the strongest European power, economically and militarily . . . It is our decline since then in relation to our European partners that has been so marked, so that today we are not only no longer a world power, we are not even in the first rank as a European one . . .
>
> Indeed in France we have come nowadays to be associated with malaise as closely as in the old days we were associated with success.[12]

Contemporary readers of this document will be struck by another remark. "Apologists," wrote Henderson, ". . . will argue that the British way of life, with ingenuity and application devoted to leisure rather than work, is superior to that elsewhere and in any case what people want." If that argument sounds familiar, it should: It is what is now said about France.

There is a point that should be emphasized here. In terms of key economic indicators, Britain was not declining in absolute terms; in fact, the economy had grown at a slow but steady average of 2 to 3 percent per annum since the end of the Second World War. What Ingham and Henderson are lamenting is Britain's relative decline. Once the world's foremost power, it had now been outpaced by Germany.

---

12. Sir Nicholas Henderson, "Britain's Decline: Its Causes and Consequences," March 31, 1979, Diplomatic Report No. 129/79, Thatcher MSS (digital collection), doc. 110961. Almost all of this document was published in the *Economist* on June 2, 1979.

And why? This is a key question. One hypothesis is that the economic policies Britain pursued after the Second World War destroyed Britain's natural genius for greatness. A second is that Britain simply followed a natural economic pattern: It experienced rapid growth at the onset of industrialization, but slower growth thereafter. If Germany was, in the 1970s, growing faster than Britain, this was because Germany had begun the process of industrialization later than Britain. More to the point, having been leveled in the Second World War, Germany was starting from zero, which severely skews any statistical analysis.

I mention this argument to Sir Bernard, who agrees that yes, Britain's decline was only a relative decline. But his reply—and again, this may be taken as the official Thatcherite view—was that even this relative decline needn't have occurred.

> **BI:** The big difference was, after the war, the Germans let *rip*, and we didn't. I mean, we had controls, we had—we were a semi-socialist society. Not with the apparatus of the Soviet Union or anything like that, but we were a semi-socialist society with all kinds of restrictions and controls that held back enterprise. Whereas they let it go. Much quicker. I mean, I remember that during the '50s—*Why don't they have rationing, and why do we?* I mean, we *won* the bloody war!

We won the bloody war. To understand Thatcherism, start with this sentiment. We won the bloody war, and we used to run the world. Now we have rubbish and dead bodies piled on our streets, and compared to German cities, gleaming and rebuilt with Marshall Aid (never mind that the trees in those cities are exactly the same height, one of the most chilling sights in the world, when you consider what it means), we look *shabby*.

This sense of humiliation was Thatcher's fuel.

At the age of fifty-three, Margaret Thatcher became the first female prime minister in the history of Britain. At the age of fifty-
four, she became the most unpopular prime minister in the history
of Britain. By no standards could her first years in office be termed
a success. Zealously embracing the monetarist prescription, her
government attempted to control inflation by raising interest rates.
To her dismay, inflation rose, and unemployment quickly doubled.

In 1980, at the Conservative Party conference, Thatcher made
one of her most famous speeches. This would not be Heath re-
dux. "To those waiting with bated breath for that favorite media
catchphrase—the U-turn, I have only one thing to say. *You* turn if
you want to—"

Dramatic pause.

"The Lady's not for turning!"[13]

A punch line perfectly executed. A roaring crowd. The words
came from the title of Christopher Fry's play *The Lady's Not for
Burning*, and even those who did not understand the reference understood the drama.

Ronald Reagan took office in 1981. Britain was now in a severe
recession, with unemployment at its highest rate since the Second
World War. According to Keynesian orthodoxy, the government
should have been stimulating demand, even if this created inflation. Instead, it continued to attempt to curb inflation by controlling the money supply. Thatcher's chancellor, Geoffrey Howe,
unveiled another counter-Keynesian budget, raising taxes. Keynesian economists throughout Britain were aghast; 364 of them sent
an open letter to the *Times* arguing that this policy would "deepen
the depression, erode the industrial base of our economy and
threaten its social and political stability." Thatcher ignored them.
She purged her cabinet of those who agreed with them. In this respect, she had not been kidding; there was no turning.

---

13. Speech to Conservative Party Conference, October 10, 1980, Brighton,
Thatcher MSS (digital collection), doc. 104431.

But on the other critical battlefront, she turned straightaway. Faced with the threat of a miners' strike and unprepared for it, she capitulated immediately to the National Union of Mineworkers.

> **BI:** You can imagine her, how *devastated* she was . . . Nothing had been *prepared*! Now—
>
> **CB:** She was devastated?
>
> **BI:** Yeah.
>
> **CB:** What did she say?
>
> **BI:** Well, they'd never *prepared* anything!
>
> **CB:** Did she say, "I am devastated," or are you inferring from something she—
>
> **BI:** No, no, I don't remember her saying, "I'm devastated," but I do remember her saying, "No preparations have been made, what on earth is going *on*?" . . . When I say she was devastated, I think she was *mortified*, certainly—
>
> **CB:** Well, it really required years of preparation, how could she have been—
>
> **BI:** *Two years*, they'd had *two years* by then. But what does that tell you? It tells you that there was a *palsy of will* in the government machine . . . It was like a rabbit in the headlights! They knew trouble was there, but they thought they had to find a way of living with it, rather than beating it.

Ingham is arguing—as he would—that the failure to prepare for this absolutely predictable challenge wasn't Thatcher's fault. It was the fault of the "government machine." But Thatcher was the head of the government, so this is an impossible distinction to sustain. The failure to prepare was Thatcher's failure and was widely understood to be so.

Thus the achievements of the first years of Thatcherism: Her economic policy was ostensibly a disaster, and far from taming the unions, she had proved herself, as the union leaders claimed, a bitch, to be sure, but *their* bitch. Had her time in power ended here, she would have been noted by history as a footnote and a minor curiosity.

⸻ ❧ ⸻

By 1982, unemployment had reached 3.6 million—a conservative estimate, in both senses of the word, since the government kept finding new ways to define unemployment to make this statistic come out lower. Heath had caved in and reversed his policies when unemployment reached *one* million. Inflation was beginning slowly to drop, but British manufacturing had shrunk by a quarter. Rioters took to the streets; British cities burned. No one believed Thatcher would survive, and indeed she might not have survived, had she not been blessed by extraordinary luck—as so often she was.

That luck came in two forms: the utter disarray of the Labour Party, riven by factional infighting, and the fecklessness of the leader of the Argentine military junta, Leopoldo Galtieri, who chose this moment to seize the Falkland Islands. Thatcher dispatched a naval task force to recapture them, winning a spectacular military victory. The Labour Party fragmented, its members at each other's throats. Thatcher won the 1983 general election in a landslide.

It was now that the Thatcher revolution really began. Britain's economy began not only to recover but to grow. The Tories introduced legislation to curb the power of trade unions and stockpiled coal, preparing to withstand a miners' strike. The government began selling off nationalized industries and public utilities at a brisk clip, and continued selling state-owned council houses to their tenants, an enormously popular policy.[14] With Thatcher's support, Reagan announced the Strategic Defense Initiative and stationed cruise missiles on British soil.

---

14. When you see the words "council houses," think "housing projects."

In 1984 came the defining moment of Thatcher's tenure: the battle for the coal mines. The story of the miners' strike is so gripping it might be fiction, but it is entirely true. It involves two great personalities: Thatcher herself, and Arthur Scargill, coal miner and communist, one of the most powerful orators in the annals of the Left. It is a story of two ways of looking at the world, and the contest that would determine whether Britain would be a capitalist society or a socialist one.

Previous mining strikes had been over in a matter of weeks. Not this one. Over the course of a year, as all of Britain watched, horrified, waiting to see who would break first, Thatcher proceeded to crush her enemies with a calculating, ruthless violence that stunned the British public. Neither labor nor the unions ever recovered. For a brief moment of clarity, power politics stood revealed in all its stark drama. The unions had made a bid for power. They lost. They were doomed. No longer was there any doubt what kind of country Britain would be. No longer was there any doubt who ruled.

In late 1984, Mikhail Gorbachev visited Britain. Thatcher declared him a man she could do business with. One year later, the West did business with him at the Reykjavik summit, and the year following, Reagan and Gorbachev signed the Intermediate-Range Nuclear Forces Treaty. In 1987, Thatcher won a third term in office, becoming the only prime minister in the twentieth century to serve three consecutive terms.

In 1989, the Berlin Wall fell. Just as communism's prehensile grip on power began to loosen, so did Thatcher's. The introduction of the poll tax—a uniform, fixed charge for community services—was intended to reduce the hold of the Labour Party on local councils by exposing its profligacy, but instead sparked protests and riots. Inflation began again to rise. Her cabinet fractured over the terms of Britain's entry into Europe.

In 1990, her longest-serving minister, Geoffrey Howe, resigned. Thatcher was challenged for the Conservative Party leadership by her former defense minister, Michael Heseltine, who gained sufficient votes in the first round of balloting to force a second one. Persuaded by her cabinet colleagues that she had lost the support of her party and could not win, she resigned.

She was never defeated at the polls.

Leave aside for the moment the question of credit for the vibrant state of Britain's economy now—is it the consequence of Thatcher's policies, or New Labour's, or both, or neither? We will come back to that. Let us instead ask what seems to me the obvious question to ask of the man who managed Thatcher's image. Given that the economy *is* now so vibrant, why is Thatcher still so often reviled in Britain? For if it is often said that the American people would elect her in a heartbeat, this is not so in the country she ran. Thatcher's name to this day inspires in a remarkable number of her countrymen profound vitriol, even among people who have clearly been the beneficiaries of her policies. What was it about her that so rubbed people the wrong way?

Needless to say, Ingham does not believe the animus to be fair.

> **BI:** First of all, I don't think people really understand the *viciousness* of the Left in this country. Okay, you may say that the Left is infinitely more vicious in France, where they riot at the drop of a hat and all that, but this lot are *really* nasty.
> **CB:** What do you think is the source of that viciousness?
> **BI:** Well, I think, because we are a fairly intemperate lot. The British pride themselves on being a wonderfully even-tempered and decent people, but once they embrace a doctrine, they can become quite, quite extreme. And the Left, they're a nasty bunch. And they're a nasty, *scheming* bunch, too . . . Then there was the affronted self-regard—you remember, do you, the 364 economists who wrote to the *Times?*

CB: In 1981, yes—

BI: Good. Well, they don't like being proven wrong. And they were proved comprehensively *wrong!*

In one sense, Ingham has a point. Awkwardly for the signatories, immediately after the publication of their letter, Britain's economy entered an uninterrupted eight-year period of growth. Yet it is also true that the industrial base of the economy was not only eroded, as they had predicted, but gutted. The growth rate reflected the expansion of the services sector; the manufacturing sector contracted sharply in those early years and never recovered. The prediction that her policies would threaten social stability was borne out: Britain was taken to the brink of civil war during the miners' strike. I note what Ingham said not because it is the unalloyed truth, but because it nonetheless contains an important insight about the nature of Thatcherism and the grievances of her critics.

BI: The British establishment was in the grip of a sort of pale-pink socialism. There are still a lot of them around now who believe, who have this sort of naive, this *romantic* view of the working classes—from which I come! I mean, I said, to Eric Morley, "What's he like, Tony Benn?" "Oh!" he said. "The only thing you need to know about *Wedgie* is that he thinks the *sun* shines out of the working classes—!" And then he said to me, "And you and I know better, don't we?" It's this romantic notion of—I mean, it's horridly condescending.

Anthony "Tony" Neil Wedgwood "Wedgie" Benn, a prominent figure on the Left wing of the Labour Party—the man whose proposals Keith Joseph savaged in his Upminster speech—was the grandson of First Baronet Sir John Benn and the son of the secretary of state for India, First Viscount Stansgate. Benn was educated at one of Britain's top-flight public schools. Ingham grew up in the West Yorkshire Pennines. His father was a cotton-weaver. Although many of Thatcher's intimates came from the traditional British ruling class, a notable number did not. Some had not even graduated from university. Many came, like Ingham did, from a working-class background, or, like Thatcher herself, from a lower-middle-class background. A surprising number were Jewish, among them Keith Joseph. It was a government, in many respects, of outsiders, and this must be understood to appreciate both its revolutionary character and the hostility it inspired.

> **CB:** Where does this romantic notion come from? What are the origins of that?
>
> **BI:** Oh, I would have thought the origins are in the Fabians, you know, that *we must do good*. *We* know how to *do good*, and we have the money to *do good*, and we have the security and we will *do good*. And that inevitably became, and *you* will be *done good to*!

The thought of the Fabians and their quest to do good makes Ingham bulgy-eyed and red-faced; he punctuates this comment with table-pounding, then lapses, winded, into phlegmy coughing, prompting in me the slight concern that he is about to suffer a fit of apoplexy and keel over. The Fabian Society was the precursor to the Labour Party. Founded in 1884 to advance socialism by reform, rather than revolution, it took its name from the Roman general Quintus Fabius Maximus, the Cunctator, who proposed to exhaust the Carthaginians through a strategy of harassment and attrition. None of the Fabians' founding members came from a working-class background, and most came from money and privilege.

I have remarked that being a woman in a man's world was not necessarily the disadvantage it is often imagined to be. Nor was being a grocer's daughter in a world of guilty aristocrats. In the way only a Republican could go to China, Thatcher was able to pursue an anti-socialist agenda precisely because her class background lent her an ideological imprimatur. She and Ingham found each

other so sympathetic in part because they shared a thorough re-
vulsion with the condescension of people who wanted to *do good*
to them and people like them, when they felt themselves *quite
good enough* as they were.

> BI: It is an attitude of mind toward ordinary people that they
> are not capable of leading their lives without direction. And
> Mrs. Thatcher was essentially saying, "Oh yes they *are*, let's
> set them free." And of course when they were set free, quite
> a lot of them didn't do well—of course they didn't. But
> quite a lot of them prospered *enormously*, and have never
> looked back since they got their hands on their council
> houses! . . . But she really challenged notions—well, she
> challenged notions of class!

She challenged notions of class. This is an absolutely key component
of Thatcherism, and critical to understanding the emotions she inspired and still inspires in Britain.

> BI: So, does that explain British society?
> CB: Well . . . yes and no.
> BI: Well, tell me where you are *desperately* uninformed. What
> do you think is missing?

There is not much that is missing at all, if you are looking for an
account of the way Thatcher and her supporters saw themselves
and what they told the world.

There are, of course, other perspectives.

⸙ ⸎ ⸙

Sir Bernard escorts me from the Morning Room and back to the
streets of London, holding the doors open for me with a courtly
flourish. The city is sparkling; the restaurants are full; the sushi

carousels are turning; the Chablis is flowing; the boutiques are selling bath salts made of organic lavender and crystallized kelp. "She stopped the *rot* in the old colonial power," Sir Bernard offers as his parting thought. "She stopped the country from going to the dogs. And it was not in the best interests of the world that Britain should go to the dogs, because it had so much more to contribute to the world."

I say good-bye, and I thank him for his time. I mean it sincerely. Anyone who has not spent a morning with Sir Bernard has missed one of life's great experiences.

As I head for the Tube, a man of about thirty passes me, walking purposefully, pecking at a Blackberry while simultaneously barking orders down his cell phone. "Still struggling with the flat refurb . . . yeah, brilliant . . . no, need the car at the *airport* . . . that's *utter* bollocks . . . Hong Kong that weekend, client meeting." From his accent, I cannot precisely discern his class background, but clearly his parents did not live in a castle or hunt foxes.

A great many Britons found—and still find—such insights unnecessary, mad, and odious challenge to the natural order of men.

3

"*I Hate Communists*"

*Economics are the method; the object is to change
the soul.*
                    — Margaret Thatcher, 1981

In the mid-1980s, the prime minister was urged by her foreign office, against her better judgment, to receive a notorious Congolese
communist at 10 Downing Street. No sooner had the hapless
Marxist seated himself in her drawing room than she fixed him
with an acid glare. She introduced herself with these words: "I *hate*
communists."

Mortified, the translator stammered, then rendered Thatcher's
comments thus: "Prime Minister Thatcher says that she has never
been wholly supportive of the ideas of Karl Marx."[1] One trusts that
the visitor nonetheless guessed from her expression where he stood.

Hatred of communism, *hatred* of Marxism, *hatred* of socialism—
and an unflinching willingness to express that hatred in the clearest
imaginable terms—was the core of Thatcherism. It was absolutely

---

1. Interview with Baron Charles Powell, June 15, 2007, London.

sincere. It was absolutely personal. If American Cold Warriors deplored the tyranny imposed by communist regimes overseas—in faraway countries of which, frankly, they knew little if not nothing—Thatcher was affronted by the effects of Marxist dogma on her *own* country, an entirely different order of outrage.

The key theme of the election campaign that brought Thatcher to power in 1979 was the decline and humiliation wreaked upon Britain by socialism. In virtually every strategy document and public pronouncement from this campaign, we see the very deliberate association of socialism with wickedness and decay. "This election," the 1979 Conservative Manifesto announced,

> is about the future of Britain—a great country which seems to have lost its way. It is a country rich in natural resources, in coal, oil, gas and fertile farmlands. It is rich, too, in human resources, with professional and managerial skills of the highest caliber, with great industries and firms whose workers can be the equal of any in the world. We are the inheritors of a long tradition of parliamentary democracy and the rule of law. Yet today, this country is faced with its most serious problems since the Second World War. What has happened to our country, to the values we used to share, to the success and prosperity we once took for granted? . . .
>
> Our country's relative decline is not inevitable.
>
> We in the Conservative Party think we can reverse it, not because we think we have all the answers but because we think we have the one answer that matters most. We want to work with the grain of human nature, helping people to help themselves—and others. This is the way to restore that self-reliance and self-confidence which are the basis of personal responsibility and national success.[2]

---

2. 1979 Conservative Manifesto, p. 6.

Socialism, Thatcher emphasized again and again, was against the grain of humanity's God-given nature. The manifesto bears her signature on the first page; the two Ts in her last name are crossed high above the stem of the letter. Graphologists would say this is the mark of an exceptionally ambitious, self-confident, optimistic person. For once those frauds would be right.

—◦ ⟫ ◦—

I bring up her handwriting because we are about to spend an afternoon in the Thatcher archives. Dull? Not at all. This is where we actually see and smell and touch the fossil record of history, the documents stamped CONFIDENTIAL and SECRET—words that always give me a pleasurable *frisson*, even if the documents in question are tables of inflation statistics, long-since declassified. This is where we see her handwritten notes on speech drafts and policy memos— mostly illegible, alas, let the graphologists make of that what they will—but some of them perfectly clear. This is where we snoop through the notes and memoranda passed to her by her advisors under cover of that SECRET stamp, the documents that say the things politicians wouldn't dream of saying in public. This is the good part.

The Thatcher papers are housed in Churchill College, Cambridge.[3] They are curated by Andrew Riley, a man whose welcoming warmth and enthusiasm for all things Thatcher calls to mind Willy Wonka's pride in his chocolate factory. *I, Andrew Riley, will*

---

3. Why Cambridge? After all, *Oxford* was her alma mater. But Oxford failed to award her an honorary degree, a deliberate snub to protest her parsimonious funding of higher education. Every previous prime minister educated at Oxford had been given one. She was neither the sort to forgive this kind of insult nor fail to return it; many years later, delivering a memorial to Keith Joseph, she was still furious enough to take a nice swipe at "those raging, spitting Trotskyite crowds at our great liberal centers of learning." So Cambridge got her papers. Churchill College was the obvious choice; Churchill, after all, was the figure with whom she most wished to be associated.

conduct you around the archives myself, showing you everything that there is to see, and afterwards, when it is time to leave, you will be escorted home by a collection of large CD-ROMs. These CD-ROMs, I can promise you, will be loaded with archival documents to last you and your entire household for many years!

Andrew whisks me off for several cups of strong coffee, then takes me up the modern stairs and down the modern hall to tour the paper collection. To enter the manuscript room he spins a huge steel dial—something manufactured by a military contractor, I suspect—and puts his whole weight against the heavy, reinforced door. The manuscript room feels like the interior of a spaceship: sterile, climate-controlled, not a mote of dust, unnaturally silent but for the mechanical hum of the air conditioner. Like an accordion, the shelves whoosh apart and re-whoosh shut at the twirl of a Meccano wheel. Hyperactive motion sensors control sliding glass partitions leading to an elevated overpass; they open if you even breathe too close to them, suggesting that they have a will of their own. Andrew shows me the stacks that contain the documents that are yet classified and will remain so for another generation. "Oh, can I just take a peek?" I ask.

Whoosh-whoosh, the shelves glide shut. "Nope! Not for you."

"Oh, come on. I won't tell anyone. It will be our little secret."

"No, no, no! But come on, I have something even better to show you, " he says cheerfully, ushering me along. I leave the forbidden section, looking reluctantly over my shoulder. The stacks go on for rows and rows; the archive contains over a million documents, 2,500 boxes, 300 meters of shelves, tens of thousands of photographs, a vast collection of press cuttings, audio tapes, video tapes. Andrew shows me what I'm allowed to look at, explains how the catalog system works, then, spinning smartly, beckons me to the back of the room. "Look!" he says, bouncing on his heels with excitement, pointing to a gunmetal-grey box on a raised platform.

The box appears to be made of something bombproof.

"What *is* it?" I ask.

"Come closer!"

I approach. The strange vessel appears to be emitting an aura. Andrew leans over, shielding from my glance the trick he uses to open it. It flips open noiselessly. He stands aside. *"Ta-da!"*

There it is: *her handbag.*

The thing is almost alive and pulsating. I half expect it to whiz up and begin soaring about the room. Thatcher famously opened a ministerial meeting by thumping that handbag on the table and announcing, "I haven't much time today, only enough time to explode and have my way."

"Smell it," says Andrew. He is flushed with sly delight.

"Can I? Really?"

"Go on."

I lean over and sniff, gingerly. There is a faint odor of talcum and lily. I look at him, surprised. "It smells—"

"My grandmother wore a perfume that smelled *just like that.*"

He's right. The handbag smells like a nice old lady.

I'm taken aback. I had been expecting it to smell like napalm and gunpowder.

Now we'll look at the documents. Have you washed your hands? Stored your belongings in the locker? You must place each paper flat on the table. Only one file at a time. Use a pencil to take notes, absolutely *not* a pen, and for God's sake, don't get the papers out of order.

Many of the documents are useless and mind-numbingly boring. "Tourism is an important growth industry in Wales," that sort of thing. We'll skip those. The good stuff is in the pre-election strategy documents, the documents that show us just what Thatcher and those around her proposed to do and how their minds worked. This one, for example:

Britain under Jim Callaghan is far from an ideal society. Yet
already the normal rosy hues that proceed [sic] an election
are being painted by the Labour Government. Even the IMF
are springing to their aid. We must counteract this propaganda. We shall do this by painting what we believe to be the
true picture of "Jim's Britain." This is a very ugly society and
we believe the following words characterize it: selfish, cruel,
irresponsible, evil, unjust, unfair, dishonest, secret, frightened,
cowardly, lacking nerve, stupid, illogical, dull, unthinking, unreasonable, erratic, simplistic, hostile, hateful, ignorant, confused, poor, hesitant, short-sighted, blind, apathetic, bored,
tired, pessimistic, unfulfilled. In other words we have an im-
mature society where individuals deny responsibility to each
other. Both they and their country seem to have lost faith in
themselves. There is no appearance of personal growth, no

Thatcher was particularly gifted at spotting opportunities subliminally and overtly to
convey that she was above all a thrifty housewife who did the family shopping, knew
how much groceries cost, and understood how deeply rising prices affected the ordinary British family. (Contrast this with the elder George Bush, who was reportedly
baffled by the sight of a supermarket scanner.) Her policies, she intimated repeatedly, were nothing more than common-sense household economics writ large.
(Courtesy of the family of Srdja Djukanovic)

fulfillment of satisfaction for self, children or indeed the whole family. No sense of pride, no sense of patriotism.

We shall contrast Jim's Britain with the normative model of Britain's ideal society that Tory values will create. By contrast this society would evidence concern for others, law and order, justice, fairness, honesty, integrity, openness, courage, a preparedness to take risks for fair rewards, enterprise, invention, intelligence, thoughtfulness, freedom, good sense, concern, knowledge, underlying convictions, mature restraint, self-confidence, loyalty, responsibility for others, self-respect, pride, vision, vibrancy, patriotism, inspiration and interest. Above all, a willingness to support one's country, the best for oneself and one's family. An optimism, a sense of fulfillment, a desire to reach maturity so that one is at peace with oneself and the world, and in a natural state of grace.[4]

A natural state of grace. Clear enough?

This passage comes from the draft of a critical document, the 1977 "Stepping Stones" report, written by the future head of her policy unit, John Hoskyns. "Stepping Stones" was the blueprint for the Thatcher Revolution.

In 1977, Hoskyns collaborated with Thatcher's adviser Norman Strauss on a plan for the Tory Party's communication strategy. Hoskyns sent Thatcher the following memorandum summarizing their recommendations:

> The objective is to persuade the electorate that they must consciously and finally reject socialism at the next election . . . Before voters will do this they must feel:
>
> a) A deep moral disgust with the Labour-Trades Union alliance and its results—the "sick society." (Disappointment with the material results is not enough.)

---

4. John Hoskyns, "Stepping Stones," draft, undated (circa 1977), THCR 2–6–1–247 (6) and (7), p. 46–47.

b) A strong desire for something better—the "healthy society." (The hope of better material results is not enough.)[5]

To this end, the author advises, Thatcher's speeches should

Show how the Labour-Trades Union alliance "power at any
price" has corrupted the union movement and impoverished and polluted British society.[6]

Later, in a review of the "Stepping Stones" plan, he notes:

Relative decline makes little impact on ordinary people until it has gone so far that it is almost too late . . . We therefore suggested that the key to changing attitudes would be
people's emotional feelings, especially anger or disgust at socialism and union behavior.[7]

Note again: The point is not that socialism has made people worse
off, materially. It is that Britain is corrupt, immoral, disgusting, and
polluted. It must be returned to a state of grace. This is a much
more ambitious program, and there is no doubt that it was, indeed, Thatcher's program.

Nothing less.

_⌐꒱ ⌐☙ ꒰⌐_

"Stepping Stones" is an essential artifact, the document that best
expresses a core precept of Thatcherism: British decline was a
punishment for the sin of socialism. Conservative policy was developed around the strategy set out by Hoskyns in this paper,

---

5. Memorandum from John Hoskyns to Thatcher, October 3, 1977, THCR
2–6–1–247 (410), p. 1.
6. THCR 2–6–1–247 (411), p. 2.
7. John Hoskyns, "Stepping Stones Review," November 8, 1978, THCR
2–6–1–247 (442), p. 2.

which not only helped Thatcher achieve victory, but led directly to almost every key Thatcherite reform.

Thatcher's inner circle was famously divided between the wets and the dries. The wets resisted the radicalism of her program. The dries were true believers. Hoskyns was drier than a Churchill martini; indeed, he resigned from government service in 1982, exasperated, having decided that Thatcher herself was a bit damp.

Hoskyns joined the military at the age of seventeen, one week after VE day, and served in the army for a decade, helping to quell the Mau Mau rebellion. He went on to be an extremely successful software entrepreneur. Like many of the men close to Thatcher, he was an outsider; not only was he not educated at Oxford or Cambridge, he did not have a university education at all.

At the time Thatcher came to power, very few prominent figures in government had any kind of background in business. Many still don't. "You get a tendency to think," Hoskyns says to me over lunch, "that 'business is a sort of unskilled labor for people who aren't as clever as I am,' you know, 'I got a First in PPE and therefore I'm naturally going to be in the cabinet, and I'm going to be running the world, even though I've never *done* anything.' I mean, David Cameron is a classic example of this."[8] It maddened Hoskyns that the men determining British economic policy had no idea what managers and entrepreneurs actually *did*, what it really took, day by day, to create wealth.

Parenthetically, Bernard Ingham's reaction when I described Hoskyns's views was priceless:

CB: He was extremely critical of the civil service, and felt that it was stacked by people who knew nothing about business, nothing about economics, had no experience of running a

---

8. David Cameron is the current leader of the Conservative Party. PPE, short for Politics, Philosophy, and Economics, is a famous degree course at Oxford.

company, and felt this was one of the great liabilities that
Thatcher confronted—what do you say to that?

BI: It is in my view a load of *bunkum!* They aren't there to run a
business, they're there to run the government machine!
That's rather like the press telling me that the government
didn't know anything, and this sort of thing, and I said, "You
dare!" I mean, I *exploded*, in a very early encounter, I said,
[*shouting and banging table*] "You *dare* to tell me that you
know how to run *any* bloody business when you people
were playing Mickey Mouse on a Friday night on Fleet
Street!" I mean, people made up identities in order that they
could be paid! I said, "*Get stuffed!*" I said. "*Go away!*" I mean,
I got *so* angry with them. [*Calming down slightly*] But *no*, I
don't think you have to be a businessman to know how to
run Britain, especially in those days, when businessmen had
made a complete *hash* of managing their businesses. They
couldn't manage them without the government! I mean, the
number of times that I was—I just—I was reduced to *groan-
ing*, quietly, in meetings, when these *businessmen* came in,
stormed upon her, said what a *brilliant* Prime Minister she
was, but we need more incentives! And I *cheered* when she
said, "You realize that 'incentives' means more taxation, do
you?" I mean, they were *totally* insecure, *totally* insecure in
their ideology, and they were *pure* opportunists! . . . In any
case, how many businessmen have got *any* experience in
government? *Bah!* . . . *Maybe* life is a bit more *complicated*
than *Mr. Hoskyns* thinks!

Back to Hoskyns, who in fairness would actually be described as
the Thatcherite who *best* appreciated the complexity of life. In the
1970s, contemplating the intensely hostile business environment
in which he was obliged to operate, he began thinking obsessively
about the etiology and dimensions of the British sickness. "It was,"
he writes, "like one of those puzzles from a Christmas cracker that

you can neither solve nor leave alone."[9] His analysis of this sickness, which he details in his memoirs, is one of the most comprehensive extant.

> One could start the discussion at almost any point: trade union obstruction, inflationary expectations, the tendency of the best talent to keep away from the manufacturing industry, fiscal distortions, high interest rates, an overvalued pound, stop-go economic management, the low status of engineers, poor industrial design, the anti-enterprise culture, illiterate teenagers . . . Almost everything turned out to be a precondition for almost everything else, and trying to solve one problem in isolation would probably make the other problems more intractable.[10]

In his efforts to delineate the constituent parts of the sickness, Hoskyns produced what has come to be called the wiring diagram, a labyrinthine pictorial description of the British Disease *(overleaf)*.

This is not, I think you will agree, the work of a man who fails to see that life is complicated.

Having constructed the diagram, Hoskyns concluded that Britain's postwar settlement had produced an entirely dysfunctional economy and society. It would have to be completely rewired. In other words, Britain needed a revolution. For a revolution, you need fervor. In "Stepping Stones," he supplied the vocabulary with which to rouse that fervor.

> Events continue to reveal the true morality of collectivism. But the real point—that socialism is *less* moral than capitalism,

---

9. John Hoskyns, *Just in Time: Inside the Thatcher Revolution* (Aurum Press, 2000), p. 8.
10. Ibid., p. 11.

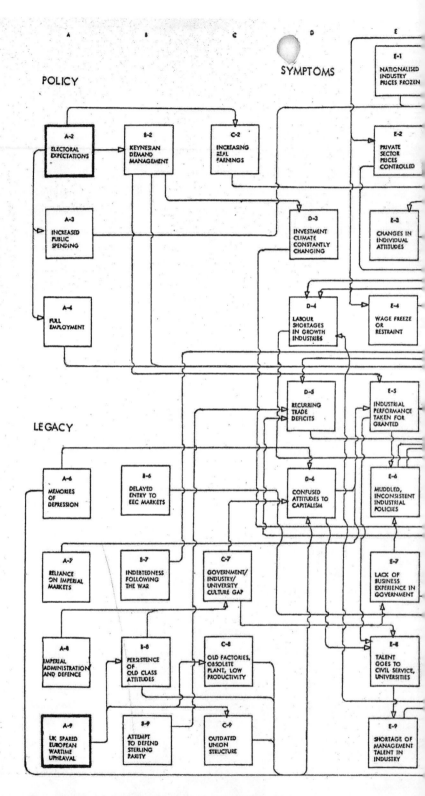

POLICY

SYMPTOMS

LEGACY

Reproduced with John Hoskyns's kind permission.

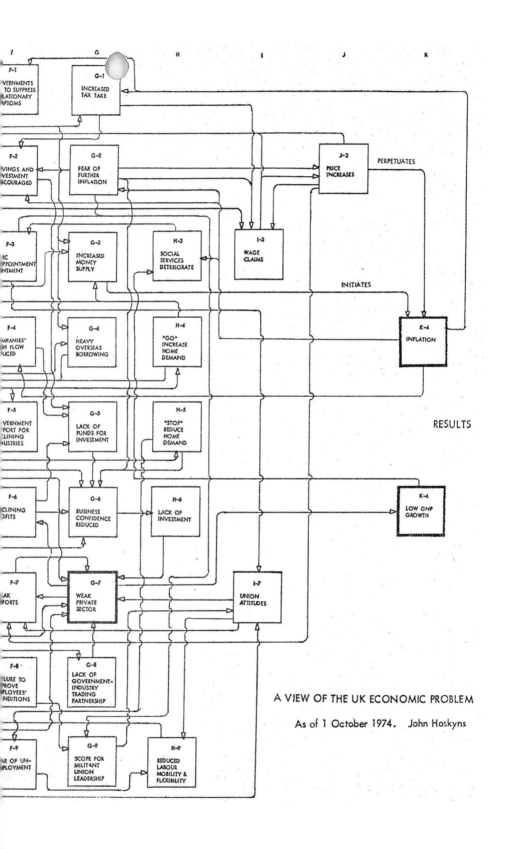

A VIEW OF THE UK ECONOMIC PROBLEM

As of 1 October 1974.   John Hoskyns

rather than *as* immoral—has not been made.[11] [*Emphasis in original*]

How was that point to be made, precisely? He proposed that the electorate might be divided among "Doers," "Thinkers," and "Feelers." Thatcher's message, he held, should be tailored to appeal to all three groups, but to all, one message would be repeated over and over: *Shame.*

> TRIGGERING THE DOERS
>
> We believe this should concentrate on people's place of work . . . This is the behavior we wish to cause people to question. Are people really not *ashamed* that they enter into strike action which, they all know, has no concern whatsoever for their fellow humans, let alone workers? They must be *ashamed* but they do it because they are frightened and bewildered and because no political party has identified a society which can give them hope for the future and reason to behave as the science tells them they ought . . .
>
> They know that there are massive hidden economies, i.e., fiddles and thefts that go on at work. Yet no one has made them feel *ashamed* of this, no one has pointed out that it would be far better if morality and integrity were reintroduced into society so that all could *hold their heads up with pride* . . . [12] [*My emphasis*]

Thatcher, he advised, must demand that the electorate not merely change its government, but reject socialism root and branch.

> To achieve this it is necessary to instill into the emotional majority (the "Feelers") . . . a sense of *shame* and *disgust*

---

11. John Hoskyns, "Stepping Stones Review," November 8, 1978, THCR 2–6–1–247 (447), p. 7.
12. "Stepping Stones," November 14, 1977, THCR 2–6–1–248 (237), p. 55.

Thatcher with Conservative politician Neil Thorne at the Ilford Conservative Club, presenting her case during the 1979 general election campaign. The journalist John Biffen once described the prime minister as "a tigress surrounded by hamsters." *(Courtesy of Graham Wiltshire)*

with the corrupting effects of socialism and union power—class war, dishonesty, tax fiddling, intimidation, shoddy work[13] . . . [*My emphasis*]

The Labour Party, argued Hoskyns, must be identified clearly with this shame:

To regain the initiative, we therefore have to explain to the Feelers that Labour really does stand for Clause 4 Socialism, and the dictatorship of unsackable union leaders; a partnership which has led to a "Sick Society" which is materially impoverished, dishonest, stupid, arbitrary, unfair, and finally

---

13. THCR 2–6–1–248 (32), p. 18.

frightened; so that it is *pitied*, as *childish* and backward, rather than *respected* by other countries.[14] [*My emphasis*]

Above all, the voters must be made to understand the meaning of socialism:

> Spell out Clause 4, printed on every party members' card
> . . . This is what they're determined to get, in the end. . . .
> The union-Labour link is unique to Britain; so socialism al-
> ways has the real power, whatever people thought they had
> voted for. That is why we are now the most socialist, as well
> as the poorest country in the Western world except for
> Italy . . .

Socialism—and the Labour Party—must be shown to be inextrica-bly linked with the overweening power of the trade unions:

> In order to attack an adversary, one must first identify his
> weak points or Critical Links. For the Labour Party this is
> obviously their relationship with the unions . . . We must
> both attempt to defeat the Labour Government in its own
> right, and also the unions in their own right. If we succeed
> in bringing down one, we bring down both.[15]

But the message must not, he repeated, be confined to promising people that they will be better off, economically, under the Tories. "*Morality* in the end counts for more than personalities; an *appropriate value system* counts for more than 'correct' economic policy."[16] My emphasis, again.

Stern stuff.

14. THCR 2–6–1–248 (254), p. 29.
15. "Stepping Stones" draft, THCR 2–6–1–247 (6) and (7), pp. 46–47.
16. "Stepping Stones," November 14, 1977, THCR 2–6–1–248 (257), p. 37.

I meet John Hoskyns for lunch at the Travellers Club, the oldest of the gentlemen's clubs on Pall Mall. You might think, from the documents above, that Hoskyns would be rather a grim and self-righteous personality, but nothing could be farther from the truth. He is jolly and charming, quick to laugh, and touching—grandfatherly, almost—in his concern that I enjoy my meal and order the richest items on the menu. I order the Dover Sole, and to please him, the buttery mashed potatoes. Then we discuss the famous wiring diagram.

John Hoskyns: What the diagram really said is that if you're going to change anything, you've got to change *everything*. Not because that sounds like a good, *Hurrah!* sort of thing to say, and we want to be revolutionaries, and we want to do big things, but because actually, in terms of logic, the causal connections are such that you cannot say, "Let's just do *that*," because—you can't! Because actually, there are five *other* things that are causing that.

[*Waitress interrupts*]

Waitress: Would you like to look at the dessert cart?

JH: What would you like? A large slice of chocolate cake?

CB: I'll have a look—

Waitress: We have a strawberry cheesecake, chocolate truffle cake, and then we have a trifle, and strawberries in red wine with orange—

CB: I'll try a trifle.

JH: *There* we are! . . . I think the wiring diagram satisfied me, and I know I had to explain to Keith [Joseph], "This is not a magic gadget which tells us how to do it. What it does is it says, 'At last, we have an imperfect but very rough and ready picture of the problem, well, really, of the *answer* to the question, *why is this country such a mess?*'" And the answer goes right back to the end of the war, the challenges of the peace, and the policy responses to those challenges . . . which with hindsight, very easy to make that mistake at the time, probably if one had been in his forties or fifties as a politician in those days, one would have done the same thing. One would have gone with the New Jerusalem. The Thatcher remedy started, I do think, with the wiring diagram. Then, the next step is you say, "Only a revolution will do any good." And you don't have revolutions for fun, they're very uncomfortable, very unpleasant, a lot of people get hurt, and—*You shall have a war.* It's going to be very unpleasant, and we're going to be hated, and the better the things we do, the more hated we will be. I remember all these thoughts were in my mind when I was working for her, and I thought, "We're not likely to bring it off. But if we do, she will be a historic figure."

CB: When you first met her, did you sense any particular political charisma? Or was that something that only emerged later?

JH: [*Long silence*] I didn't particularly. I think that grew as time went on. I was interested, having already met her through Alfred Sherman [initially one of Thatcher's political advisors], a tough, rude, multilingual, seven-languages or something, brilliant East End Jew, built like a sort of 5'2" gorilla—*lovely* man, very funny man, too—absolutely fearless, tremendous mental energy—and I thought, if she can realize what *he's* got to offer, compared with some of these Beta-minus, Beta-plus intellects in the Party machine, and doesn't safely settle for another public schoolboy, but takes this fellow instead, well then—and that Keith and Margaret, those two people, could forge such an unlikely bond, and both listen to this completely from-outer-space *brainbox*, it did make me think, when I came to meet her, "She's not your ordinary, world-weary, pompous, self-important, thinking-inside-the-box, slightly defeatist, pragmatic, cautious, Tory politician." You know, she's *not*. She's actually realizing that something *terrible* has got to be done.

$$\_\curvearrowleft \; \mathrel{\rightleftharpoons} \; \curvearrowright\_$$

Something *terrible* had got to be done. The battle would be bloody, and they would be hated. Hoskyns knew it, Sherman knew it, Joseph knew it, Thatcher knew it. So did everyone who managed her ascent to power. Even the wringing-wet Chris Patten, then director of the Conservative Party's research department, uneasily sensed it. He drafted a paper titled "Implementing Our Strategy" in 1977, outlining the themes to be stressed in the coming election campaign.

> Labour's record is appalling. What has happened is their own fault. They cannot blame us, or world factors. They virtually doubled prices, more than doubled unemployment, doubled the tax burden and doubled public spending? Why? Because when they came in they gave us a double dose of Socialism.[17]

Nigel Lawson, who was later to become the most famous member of Thatcher's cabinet as her chancellor, reviewed this memo and heartily concurred with this sentiment, writing in response that "<u>A well thought-out scare campaign is a must</u>."[18] The words are underlined in Thatcher's hand, I believe.

Lawson appended to this note an earlier memo he had written titled "Thoughts on the Coming Battle":

17. Chris Patten, "Implementing Our Strategy," December 11, 1977, THCR 2–6–1–246 (13), p. 2.

18. Note from Nigel Lawson to Thatcher, "Thoughts on 'Implementing Our Strategy,'" January 15, 1978, THCR 2–6–1–246 (27), p. 1. Lawson is now even more famous for having fathered Nigella Lawson, the voluptuous television chef.

The Socialists have avowedly adopted the most extreme Left propaganda and posture in their Party's history. This central fact, and its detailed implications, should be the ever-present theme of our propaganda war . . .

Linguistics. The semantic battle is an important aspect of the overall battle. We need what newspapers call a "house style," circulated to all concerned, to ensure that Socialist policies are always referred to by words with unfavorable emotive overtones, and our policies by words with favorable emotive overtones.[19]

The minutes of a 1977 meeting of Thatcher's Strategy and Tactics Committee emphasized, again, the semantic linking of socialism, guilt, and sin:

SECRET
NOTES ON THEMES

Destruction of our opponents:

Guilty men. Hypocrisy of individuals, damaging failure as Government. Label them with failure. *Link failure/decline of Britain inextricably with Socialism.* . . .

"Doubled" theme—spending, unemployment, but particularly prices. Doubled Socialism/nationalization. Juxtapose doubled nationalization and doubled prices. . . .

Labour and the Trade Unions will turn us into an Eastern European state. What's moral about locking up your enemies? . . .

Free Enterprise. *Moral case for freedom.* Choice, dignity, responsibility, worth of the individual.

Let the individual control his own life. Right to property.

---

19. Memorandum from Nigel Lawson to Sir Michael Fraser, "Thoughts on the Coming Battle," October 15, 1973, THCR 2–6–1–246 (34), p. 1 and (35), p. 2.

Open up debate on what sort of society we want in the late 20th century. The right approach to society/social policy . . .

The courage and the real concern to *do what is right*. [*My emphasis*][20]

Shortly afterwards, Alan Howarth, a member of the inner sanctum of the Conservative Research Department, wrote a paper for Thatcher's benefit titled "Some Suggestions for Strategic Themes." He hoped, he wrote to her, that it might serve as "raw material" for "the philosophical case that you have been contemplating making."[21] The paper is much in the same vein, and I suspect that it did indeed provide raw material—or at least rhetorical inspiration—for Thatcher's case.

Labour's failure. Fantastic economic mismanagement. Prices doubled in three years, production at level of five years ago, unemployment more than doubled, colossal debt. A humiliated and impoverished Britain. . . .

The Guilt of the Socialists. They are guilty of fraud. Remember "Back to work with Labour" and look at the unemployment. Look at the social services, the dereliction of Labour controlled cities and the crime and violence. [*Underlined in original*]

It is the Socialists who are guilty, not the British people (or world economic factors).

Their Guilty Men. Their hypocrisy.[22]

---

20. Memorandum from Alan Howarth to Thatcher, December 16, 1977, THCR 2–6–1–250 (16) and (17), pp. 2–3.

21. Memorandum from Alan Howarth to Thatcher, January 4, 1978, THCR 2–6–1–250 (26).

22. Alan Howarth, "Some Suggestions for Strategic Themes," January 4, 1978, THCR 2–6–1–250 (32), p. 4. The end of this section of the document is mildly puzzling. Howarth concludes by calling for "an end to the depressing politics of guilt"—words rather at odds with all the words preceding them. But the word "politics" has been altered, by hand, to read "policies." Whose hand did the altering? I don't know. Is it significant? I don't know. Archives are like that, sometimes.

An interesting aside: In 1993, Howarth defected to the Labour Party. It seems he changed his mind.

—⟨ ⟩⟨ ⟩⟨—

This culminates in Thatcher's own voice, rallying her troops in 1976. The speech anticipates and embodies all of these themes:

> I want to speak to you today about the rebirth of a nation: our nation—the British nation.
>
> . . . Economically, Britain is on its knees. It is not unpatriotic to say this. It is no secret. It is known by people of all ages. By those old enough to remember the sacrifices of the war and who now ask what ever happened to the fruits of victory; by the young, born since the war, who have seen too much national failure; by those who leave this country in increasing numbers for other lands. For them, hope has withered and faith has gone sour. And for we who remain it is close to midnight.
>
> . . . the world over, free enterprise has proved itself more efficient, and better able to produce a good standard of living than either socialism or communism. [But] . . . The Labour Party is now committed to a program which is frankly and unashamedly Marxist.
>
> . . . let's not mince words. The dividing line between the Labour Party program and communism is becoming harder and harder to detect. Indeed, in many respects Labour's program is more extreme than those of many communist parties of Western Europe.
>
> . . . Between the pair of them, Sir Harold [Wilson] and Mr. Callaghan and their wretched governments have impoverished and all but bankrupted Britain. Socialism has failed our nation. Away with it, before it does the final damage.
>
> . . . We can overcome our doubts, we can rediscover our confidence; we can regain the respect of the rest of the

world. The policies which are needed are dictated by common sense.

. . . Of course we're not going to solve our problems just by cuts, just by restraint. Sometimes I think I have had enough of hearing of restraint. It was not restraint that brought us the achievements of Elizabethan England; it was not restraint that started the Industrial Revolution; it was not restraint that led Lord Nuffield to start building cars in a bicycle shop in Oxford. It wasn't restraint that inspired us to explore for oil in the North Sea and bring it ashore. It was incentive—positive, vital, driving, individual incentive. The incentive that was once the dynamo of this country but which today our youth are denied. Incentive that has been snuffed out by the socialist state.

. . . Common-sense policies must, and will, prevail if we fight hard enough.

. . . I call the Conservative Party now to a crusade. Not only the Conservative Party. I appeal to all those men and women of goodwill who do not want a Marxist future for themselves or their children or their children's children. This is not just a fight about national solvency. It is a fight about the very foundations of the social order. It is a crusade not merely to put a temporary brake on socialism, but to stop its onward march once and for all.

. . . As I look to our great history and then at our dismal present, I draw strength from the great and brave things this nation has achieved. I seem to see clearly, as a bright new day, the future that we can and must win back. As was said before another famous battle: "It is true that we are in great danger; the greater therefore should our courage be."[23]

---

23. Speech to Conservative Party Conference, October 8, 1976, Brighton, Thatcher MSS (digital collection), doc. 103105.

The last line is from Shakespeare, whose achievements, as she points out, were not the product of restraint. The words are spoken by Henry V on the eve of the victorious Battle of Agincourt.

Shakespeare, the Crusades, great and brave things, the fruits of victory and common sense—all of this, she claimed, was her rightful inheritance. They were Britain's rightful inheritance. But the Marxists were scheming to cut her children out of the will.

They would not succeed.

_⊶ ⧚ ⊷_

It is all like this, in the archives. *Guilt, shame, decay, decline, immorality, wickedness, a once-great nation brought to its knees, doubledoses of socialism.* These words are counterpoised against descriptions of Thatcher as a woman of old-fashioned virtue and common sense who will do what is *proud, patriotic, self-respecting, honorable, and right.*

Do you find the language of these documents shocking? I confess that I do. I completely agree that socialism is corrupting. I hate communism, too—I loathe it. But to see these overwrought sentiments emerging from a people famed for their reserve, irony, and understatement leads me to suspect that Bernard Ingham was on to something when he remarked that "the British pride themselves on being a wonderfully even-tempered and decent people, but once they embrace a doctrine, they can become quite, quite extreme."

4

Diva, Matron, Housewife, Shrew

Pierre, you're being obnoxious. Stop acting like a
naughty schoolboy.
— THATCHER TO CANADIAN PRIME MINISTER
PIERRE TRUDEAU, 1981

It is all very well to hate communists, but self-righteousness and rage are not politically appealing qualities in and of themselves. Thatcher had charisma, too—feminine charisma—and this is what made her message effective.

If history is any guide, it is exceptionally hard to make femininity work to advantage in a political career. Several strategies are available to those who try. Hillary Clinton, for example, intimates that whereas she may have no obvious feminine qualities to speak of, a vote for her is a vote for feminism itself, a principled stand in favor of sexual equality. Some, like the French politician Ségolène Royal—or the woman she so resembles, Eva Perón—play the role of the mystical hysteric. Some exploit their status as wives or daughters of prominent politicians—Hillary Clinton and Eva Perón, again, or Indira Gandhi, Nehru's daughter. It helps considerably if the husband or father has been martyred. Sonia Gandhi followed her martyred husband. Benazir Bhutto followed her martyred father—and followed him, sadly, all the way to martyrdom.

In her success in capitalizing upon her femininity, Margaret Thatcher had no equal. Yet she adopted none of these strategies. She had no use for feminism and no use for women, either—only one served in her cabinet, and only very briefly. By my count she inhabited, shiftingly and at will, at least seven distinctly female roles:

1. The Great Diva
2. The Mother of the Nation
3. The Coy Flirt
4. The Screeching Harridan
5. Boudicea, the Warrior Queen
6. The Matron
7. The Housewife

These roles deserve a close inspection. They were the tools she used to make her revolution happen.

I am visiting Charles Powell, Thatcher's foreign and defense advisor from 1983 to 1990, at his tastefully appointed Georgian mansion on Queen Anne's Gate, overlooking St. James's Park. Powell descends from one of the knights who carried out Henry II's orders to assassinate Thomas Becket. Like his ancestor, Powell is a knight. His full title is the Baron Powell of Bayswater of Canterbury in the County of Kent. He is a member of the House of Lords. Some people in Britain take these titles very seriously; some don't; some make an ostentatious point of pretending not to. I am not sure which category he falls under, so when I introduce myself, I hesitate.

His last name presents another challenge. I have been told that he pronounces it *Pole*, but his brother Jonathan pronounces it *Pow-*

ell, to rhyme with *towel*. His brother was Tony Blair's chief of staff. I am not sure what to make of this but suspect it is evidence for the claim that they are all Thatcherites now. Left-leaning British newspapers, unable to find much to distinguish between the brothers politically, have fixated on their names; they declare the pronunciation *Pole* pretentious. As I offer him my hand, I worry that I've gotten it mixed up. Which is the pretentious pronunciation again, and which one is he?

"So nice to meet you," I say.

"And you," he replies.

The interchange offers no clues about his name. His part of it suggests that he may well be uncertain of mine.

Powell was Thatcher's closest advisor, "the second most powerful figure in the Government," writes her biographer John Campbell, "practically her *alter ego*."[1] Powell and American National Security Advisor Brent Scowcroft shared a secure line to each others' phones. Scowcroft called Powell directly when he needed to talk to Britain. Powell was, according to Scowcroft, "the only serious influence" on Thatcher's foreign policy.[2] Powell's status as the prime minister's pet was greatly resented. Alan Clark, Thatcher's defense minister and an infamously indiscreet diarist, recalls the vexation of another close Thatcher advisor, Ian Gow, who lamented "the way the whole Court had changed and Charles Powell had got the whole thing in his grip."[3] The ever-irritable Nigel Lawson, Thatcher's chancellor, was equally dismayed by Powell's overweening influence: "He stayed at Number 10 far too long."[4] Everyone—whether or not they liked him—agrees that Charles Powell is a highly intelligent man.

---

1. John Campbell, *Margaret Thatcher*, vol. 2: *The Iron Lady* (Jonathan Cape, 2003), p. 258.

2. George Bush and Brent Scowcroft, *A World Transformed* (Knopf, 1998), p. 31.

3. Alan Clark, *Diaries: In Power, 1983–1992* (Phoenix, 2001), p. 319.

4. Nigel Lawson, *The View from No. 11: Memoirs of a Tory Radical* (Corgi, 1993), p. 680.

Given the descriptions I have read of him, I am expecting to encounter a suave, gregarious personality, but instead I find him a man of subdued affect. He is correct and courteous, but as we speak, I worry that I am failing to draw him out. Only later, when I transcribed the interview, did I realize that the language he used to describe the former prime minister was passionate.

"Tell me about your first impression of her," I say. "I understand that you first met her when you were waiting with your wife for the by-election results in Germany—"

"That's right, yes—we were in the embassy in Germany. She came out to see Schmidt and Kohl.[5] She was quite recently elected in the Opposition. Well, I think it was of this tremendous energy and zest, we'd got pretty used to this procession of rather dispirited politicians, of all three parties, trooping through Germany lamenting Britain's decline and so on, and here, suddenly, there was this woman, of whom we knew little at the time, who seemed to believe it could all be changed. It just needed *her* to be in power to bring about this tremendous change. It was invigorating."

Energy, zest—everyone uses those words. She famously required no more than four hours of sleep at night. "She hated holidays," Powell recalls. "She *loathed* holidays; she didn't like weekends, because they were a bit of an interruption, but that was all right because she could pretend they didn't exist by continuing working at Chequers, and making some of the rest of us work at Chequers, but holidays, after two days she was on the telephone, looking for excuses to come back to London."[6]

"Would you describe the environment around her as tense?"

"The environment around her was *boiling.* A permanent state of everything sort of red hot. Like some kind of lava coming out of a volcano. It really was."

---

5. The two Helmuts—Helmut Schmidt, then chancellor of West Germany, and Helmut Kohl, then chairman of Germany's Christian Democratic Union.
6. Chequers is the prime minister's country residence.

This image of Thatcher, visiting the White House in 1979, conveys the old-fashioned movie-star glamour she could project when it suited her purposes. If you did not know this was the new prime minister of Britain, you could easily imagine this woman sweeping regally into the Kodak Theater to collect an Oscar for lifetime achievement.

"Did you like being around that?" The man before me is sedate, his hands folded primly in his lap. It is hard to imagine that a boiling environment would be to his taste.

"Well, it was pretty invigorating, but really tiring."

I'll bet.

I ask him to tell me more about the way Margaret Thatcher looked to him, back in those early days. "Her posture was always upright," he says. "She was very, very stiff-backed and upright, and she was always very tidy as well. A lot of British politicians are very sloppy, in their dress and so on—I don't want to actually name any names or be discourteous, but you can probably think of quite several, female as well as male. But she was always meticulous in her dress, and perhaps some of her earlier styles look a bit fussy now, but once she got into the power-suit dressing it was all part of it. She was really—you've got to think in terms of Margaret Thatcher Productions, almost, I mean there were the policies and the rhetoric, but there was also the hair, the dress, the lighting, and everything. She could have tremendous dramatic effect on the platform, whether at a party conference speech or a speech to a joint session of the U.S. Congress. It was all packaged. It was almost like a great diva, giving a performance."

He is right. Margaret Thatcher often seemed like an exceptionally gifted actress playing the role of Margaret Thatcher. On television, she fills the screen. The eye is ineluctably drawn to her, so that everything and everyone else in the frame is dwarfed by comparison. Hollywood executives call this quality *It*. Marlon Brando had *It*, and so did Marilyn Monroe. But neither of them had nuclear weapons.

Let's look at one of those Margaret Thatcher Productions in slow-motion. Part of it is on YouTube, in a clip titled "Margaret Thatcher Talking about Sinking the *Belgrano*."[7] During the Falklands War, Britain declared a two-hundred-mile exclusion zone around the islands, warning that any Argentine ship within the zone was subject to destruction. The Argentine cruiser *Belgrano* was outside this zone, sailing away from the islands. Thatcher or-

---

7. www.youtube.com/watch?v=1aZdAyHVjzQ.

dered it sunk nonetheless. The attack killed 323 Argentine sailors. An outcry over the carnage ensued, in Britain and abroad; some charged that this was a war crime. Whatever you may think about the sinking of the *Belgrano*, do note this: The Argentine navy thereafter refused to leave port.

Here is Thatcher, responding to critics who have charged her with obfuscating the circumstances leading to the decision to sink the *Belgrano*. She is in the television studio with interviewer David Frost, an ordinarily articulate man who is not known for backing away from power but who in her presence appears oddly goofy. Her hair is sprayed into a stiff golden helmet; not a strand is out of place. Her rouge is flawless. Pale lipstick highlights a mouth that on another face might be described as sensuous. She is wearing pearl earrings; the broach on the lapel of her stern navy suit complements her blouse. The effect, as Powell said, is immaculately tidy.

David Frost: On that day, when the Government said it changed direction many times, it only changed direction once to go back home and a 10-degree difference to get closer to Argentina—

Prime Minister: A ship is torpedoed on the basis that *if* wherever she is she can get back to sink your ships in reasonable time, you do not just *discover* ships on the high seas and keep track of them the entire time. You can lose them. You can lose them. I would far rather have been under the attack I was for the *Belgrano* than under the attack I might have been under for putting the *Hermes* or *Invincible* in danger, and if ever you think that governments have to reveal every single thing about ships' movements, we do not! And if I were tackling—

DF: No, but I mean, the reason people get—

Prime Minister: —in charge of a war again, I would take the same decision again . . . Do you think, Mr. Frost, that I spend my days prowling round the pigeonholes of the Ministry of

Defense to look at the chart of each and every ship? If you
do you must be bonkers!

DF: No! Come back to the—

Prime Minister: Do you think I keep in my head—

DF: —when you said to Mrs. Gould[8]—when you said to Mrs.
Gould on the election program before the election in '83
that it was not sailing away from the Falklands, you had
known from November '82 that it was!

Prime Minister: What I said to Mrs. Gould was, "If you think that
I know in detail the passage of every blessed ship I cannot
think what you think the Prime Minister's job is!"[9]

You may tune in on YouTube to see the rest. Study the voice: Like
a trained stage actress, she projects from the chest and uses the full
range of her vocal register. Her body remains still; she does not
fidget or shift or even gesture. Note the varied rhythm of her
speech—one moment slow and deliberate, the next insistent and
percussive. "What I know, Mr. Frost," she says—and she pronounces his name, *Mr. Frost*, as if a *Mr. Frost* is some thoroughly
disgusting species of bug—"is that the ministers have *given* the information to the House of Commons. They said that *one* thing was
not correct. I was the *first* to say, 'Right, *give the correct information*.' And the correct, and *deadly* accurate information was given."
The word "deadly" flows easily from her tongue. She is leaning for-
ward, intense, alert. Her eyes are blazing. You are looking at a
woman who has given the order to kill 323 young Argentine men,
and her glowing complexion suggests that this has not troubled
her sleep one bit. Indeed, she looks as if she has had an exceptionally good night's rest.

---

8. Diana Gould was a British housewife who on BBC TV in 1983 attacked
the prime minister's decision to sink the *Belgrano*. This exchange too may be
viewed on YouTube: www.youtube.com/watch?v=rWOy23MLY1I.

9. TV Interview with David Frost for TV-AM, June 7, 1985, London.
Transcript from Thatcher MSS (digital collection), doc. 105826.

"But *I* do not spend my days," she continues—in response to a question he has not asked—"*prowling* around the pigeonholes of the Ministry of Defense looking at the precise course of action." She says *I* as if the *I* in question is something magnificent, and the very hint that such a vital magnificence—*Prime Minister Margaret Thatcher*, the human embodiment of the British people and their destiny!—would do something as lowly as *prowl* (never mind that Mr. Frost never said this) is contemptible. There is now something like a bat squeak from Mr. Frost. "One moment!" she pronounces, lifting an imperious finger. "*One moment!*"

Mr. Frost tries haplessly to get a word in, fumbling with his papers. "Woodrow Wyatt says you only respect people who—"[10]

"One moment," she demands.

"Yes," he says meekly and falls silent. Her voice is lower now, and all the more menacing for it. Given her expression you would not be entirely surprised to see laser beams shoot from her eyes and vaporize this disgusting Mr. Frost, bringing the death toll to a salutary 324. "That ship"—she says this slowly, her mouth narrow, her voice full of controlled fury and contempt—"was a danger to *our boys.*"

Our boys: These are in fact *men* she is talking about, every last one of them over the age of majority and armed with fearsome weapons, and the use of the word "boys" sounds at once fiercely maternal—a tiger protecting her cubs—and intensely patronizing. *Those* boys are our heroes, as all right-thinking men and women know, and you, Mr. Frost, are not fit to shine their shoes. But they are still *boys*, just as you, Mr. Frost, are a silly stripling. The lot of you—*boys*. But you are *my* boys, and that is why despite your childish foolishness, I shall protect you and set you on the right course. "*That's* why that ship was sunk," she says. "I *know* it was right to sink her." A pause. Mr. Frost has gone mute. "*And I would do . . . the same . . . again.*"

---

10. Wyatt was a Labour MP and journalist who became an admirer of Thatcher.

Fade to black.

She did not rehearse this speech; there was no speechwriter or teleprompter; it was live and impromptu. The performance is a miracle of menace, rhythm, dramatic timing. It is impossible to watch without thinking that you would not trade places with the miserable Mr. Frost for all the world.

_____

I now take the train from London to Oxford, where I have an appointment to speak with the Master of Balliol College, Andrew Graham, about his memories of Margaret Thatcher. The Master is a man of the Left. From 1966 to 1969, he was an influential economic advisor to Labour Prime Minister Harold Wilson; he worked again for Wilson between 1974 and 1976 at the policy unit attached to 10 Downing Street. In the early 1990s, he advised the leader of the Labour Party, John Smith. After Smith's death, he fell out spectacularly with the New Labourites: *You* may all be Thatcherites now, he told them, but count *me* out.

I am seeing him because I want the other side of the story. I have met a series of Thatcher's cabinet ministers and her most ardent defenders. Now I want to hear the best and most serious case *against* Thatcher's economic policies (which we will not get from New Labour, because they are all Thatcherites now). He will not disappoint, but we will come back to that later.

I am early for my appointment, so I stroll slowly through the streets of Oxford. Oxford is two cities, sharply divided. The poets ignore the outskirts of the city—the menacing townie pubs with their tattooed patrons, places students know better than to enter, the seedy bedsits over the Cowley Road where the stairwells smell of urine and turmeric, the rows of kebab vans, all named *Ali's*, parked outside those stairwells and reeking of ancient mutton. The poets write about the city center—a rook-racked, river-rounded city of dreaming spires, they call it, and they are right.

The Master of Balliol was my economics tutor when I was an undergraduate, many years ago. I had last seen him when I was in my early twenties. I was very fond of him—he was warm, lively, unstuffy, a wonderful teacher. I had feared as I walked to our meeting that I would find him much older and that this would remind me that I too am much older, but to my delight he is unchanged.

He's running a few minutes late. He darts through the sitting room in the Master's lodge, spots me, beams broadly in welcome, then dashes up the staircase. "I'll just be another minute, Claire. I'm sitting for my portrait!" How lively and spry he looks, I think! Could it be that in the portrait he is stooped and wrinkled?

When he returns he escorts me to his office, with its high ceilings and heavy brocaded curtains framing a picture window overlooking Broad Street. Haphazard stacks of papers cover the floor, the tables, the chairs. We chat for a while about economics, then we turn to the subject of Thatcher's political presence. We are trying to put our finger on what it was about her that kept the electorate coming back for more and more and more, despite—in his view, of course—her disastrously misguided policies. What was the source of her charisma, I wonder aloud?

"Well," he says, "I didn't think this, I never felt it, but—quite a lot of people, some men—found her quite—*sexy*!"

"Mmmm," I say. "I've heard this. Who was it, Mitterrand, who called her Brigitte Bardot with Caligula's eyes?"

"Exactly! And I think some of it was the sex that goes with power, and I, you know, I just can't get on that wavelength. I won't say I don't find power interesting, I do, but I just can't get there with Mrs. Thatcher *at all*, I can't even get to square one! But I've heard it from people I was surprised by."

"Perhaps you'd care to say who?"

He won't name names. "I mean, a colleague of mine in Balliol, who is now dead, was a professor of physics, went along to a seminar in All Souls, incredibly impressed by her, just sort of swept off his feet by how articulate and how clear she was, and by her general demeanor um—this, she had—*I* wouldn't say, because *I* never

Thatcher addressing a conference on foreign policy in London, in 1989. "It was as if there was a sort of electric glow about her," recalls the conservative MP David Ames. "She seemed to overshadow everyone." Graham Wiltshire, who took this photograph, remembered that "the effect she had on these events was almost hypnotic." *(Courtesy of Graham Wiltshire)*

felt it—she had, somewhere in there—there is something more interesting than just a domineering personality. There is a degree of magnetism that somehow all big leaders have. I didn't see it, couldn't *remotely*—"

I get it, I get it. He wasn't attracted to Margaret Thatcher, no how, no way. I do note that it wasn't *me* who suggested he might be. "*I've* seen it," I say. "And I'm still trying to figure out how to describe what it was that I see—I mean, sex appeal is one aspect of it, but it's not just that, it's—it is an *utter* confidence which is unbelievably rare in women."

"Yeah, I mean, going back to what—I mean—I'm not a pacifist, I think war is sometimes essential, but I wasn't—you know, most people in the UK were sort of gung-ho about the Falklands War, I thought it was absolutely unnecessary, but I think she deserves enormous credit for that. I mean, one Exocet on one of those destroyers and the whole thing would have been a completely different story. Just a completely different story."

In fact, the HMS *Sheffield* did take a direct hit from an Exocet missile. It was blasted apart. This did not for a moment cool the prime minister's ardor. But I agree with the point he is expressing. I have thought of it often, what it must have felt like to be her at that moment, of the enormous risks she took. The outcome was not at all guaranteed. "So," the Master wonders aloud, "is that foolhardiness or is it courage?"

"In terms of psychological typing," I say, "probably it would be described as a touch of narcissism—"

"Yeah, yeah," he agrees, nodding.

"And perhaps a bit of hypomania, as well—"

"Yeah, but—" He pauses. "It's also a kind of guts."

Armchair diagnosis can be taken only so far, but the words "narcissism" and "hypomania"—and "guts," for that matter—do fit her uncannily well. Take the Mayo Clinic's description of the narcissistic personality style, for example:

> People who have a narcissistic personality style . . . are generally psychologically healthy, but may at times be arrogant, proud, shrewd, confident, self-centered and determined to be at the top. They do not, however, have an unrealistic image of their skills and worth and are not dependent on praise to sustain a healthy self-esteem. You may find these individuals unpleasant or overbearing in certain social, professional or interpersonal encounters . . . [11]

Check, check, check. And hypomania? Without a doubt:

> Some traits of hypomania: . . . filled with energy . . . flooded with ideas . . . driven, restless, and unable to keep still . . . often works on little sleep . . . feels brilliant, special, chosen, perhaps even destined to change the world . . . is a risk taker . . . [12]

As for "guts," I trust no definition is needed.

11. Mayo Clinic Staff, December 19, 2005, Mayo Foundation for Medical Education and Research (MFMER), www.edition.cnn.com/HEALTH/library/DS/00652.html.

12. John T. Gartner, *The Hypomanic Edge: The Link between a Little Craziness and a Lot of Success in America* (Simon & Schuster, 2005).

"I do think," I say to the Master, "that men tend to be more certain in their convictions. This tends to be a male trait. Which is one reason why Thatcher is so unique."

He nods. "Ah, she's interesting, yes."

"I mean, you keep seeing comparisons of, say, Ségolène Royal with Thatcher, and that's absurd, they've got nothing at all in common, they're a completely different species. And the comparisons between Hillary Clinton and Thatcher seem to me not only from a policy point of view, but a personality point of view, completely ridiculous. Hillary conveys none of that absolute, rock-solid *authority*, which I think was the source of Thatcher's charisma—"

"Yeah. Yeah."

"Thatcher's wasn't a Bill Clinton kind of charisma at all." I met Bill Clinton once at a reception held for him at Oxford—his alma mater—during the first years of his presidency. His charisma was just as it is always described. He shook my hand and did that thing for which he's famous: one hand holding mine, the other on my elbow, looking deeply into my eyes, and for one moment, just that moment, the clicking cameras stopped, the crowds faded to a blur, and I *knew* that the leader of the Free World was more interested in me, more interested in what I thought and felt, than anyone— including my own mother—had ever been before. His eyes told me clearly that if only this annoying Secret Service detail would stop hurrying him along, we would just talk and talk and talk, he and I; I would tell him about my thoughts about health care, and Social Security, and . . .

"No. Not remotely," agrees the Master.

"It's the charisma of someone who is absolutely certain she is right—"

"And with some of us, drives us completely *bonkers*, because we think she's so wrong!"

"I think that's the source of the passionate emotions about her," I agree. Bernard Ingham attributes it to the sheer viciousness of the Left, but the Master of Balliol is anything but a vicious man. Thatcher's brand of certainty was fascinating and maddening in equal measure, and if you happened to think her wrong, it was enough to make you *bonkers*. "So there's that utter certainty in herself," I continue, "and there was something sexy about her, in a traditional way, especially as a young woman—she was not a raving beauty, but she was attractive—"

"Yes, yes."

"But also a maternal archetype—she reminded people of their mothers or their schoolteachers—"

"Yeah, but, you know, I've never had that, you know, doesn't remotely work at all for me, not at all, so you'd have to find—but you know, some people find that very—*attractive*!"

Margaret and Denis Thatcher stand outside No. 10 Downing Street directly after her 1979 election victory. Two days later, she arrived to address a meeting of Conservative backbench MPs. "She was flanked only by the all-male officers of the committee," recalls Geoffrey Howe. "Suddenly she looked very beautiful—and very frail, as the half-dozen knights of the shires towered over her. It was a moving, almost feudal occasion. Tears came to my eyes . . . this overwhelmingly male gathering dedicated themselves enthusiastically to the service of this remarkable woman." *(Courtesy of Graham Wiltshire)*

Back to London. "She was always very conscious of being a woman," says Charles Powell. "This was a tremendous part of her political personality, and she played it for what it was worth—which was a lot. Here was the first woman leader of Britain, first woman head of government in Europe, a whole host of things, and she took advantage of that, and it was very sensible to do that—after all there were enough strikes against her as a woman to justify making the most of the advantages of it."

There is a framed photograph of Thatcher in her prime right above his chair. Flaxen-haired, rosy-cheeked, and power-suited, she is staring at me intently. It is one of those curious portraits in which the subject's eyes seem to follow you no matter where you move. It reminds me of a line from her autobiography:

> I took a close interest in the physical as well as the diplomatic preparations for our big summits. For example, I had earlier had the swivel chairs around the big conference table at the "QE II" replaced by light wooden ones: I always thought there was something to be said for looking at your opposite number in the eye without his being able to swivel sideways to escape.[13]

I think momentarily of the campaign for the French presidency and of Nicolas Sarkozy's final debate with the lustrously beautiful Ségolène Royal. Royal's handlers had presumably urged her to try to make Sarkozy lose his famously volatile temper, which was— supposedly—his great electoral liability. Sarkozy was too sly to fall for it. The more she tried to provoke him, the more unctuously polite he became, until finally the frustrated Royal became nearly hysterical with rage. At this point Sarkozy contemplated her with infinite solicitude and told her patiently that *Madame*, you lose your temper too easily, and a presidential figure must learn to be *calm*. Royal was left spluttering, on the verge of tears. Everyone who watched this sensed what Sarkozy managed to insinuate while of course never saying it outright: *How extremely attractive you are*, ma puce. *It is a pity that you suffer so from your menopausal hormones.* That was the end of poor Ségo. "How *exactly* did Thatcher manage to use her femininity without having it turned against her?" I ask Powell.

---

13. Thatcher, *The Downing Street Years*, p. 557. She is talking about the conference center, by the way, not the cruise ship.

"Well, for one thing, she was extremely shrewd. She could read the character of the English public schoolboys who made up the majority of her cabinet, and she knew they'd been brought up to be polite to women, also to, you know, treat them in a sort of patronizing way, and she would rock them to their foundations by screeching at them and yelling at them and arguing with them and generally treating them very badly in order to get her way. And she knew they would not easily fight back."

A screeching, yelling, arguing woman—*oh!* It is every man's nightmare. Yet her ability to be an utter harridan was somehow one of her great strengths, and only one of her many distaff weapons. "Most of them would become defensive," Powell recalls, "Geoffrey Howe above all, you know, and just withdraw into their shells, and not really punch back, and then they'd go off and cry and complain and moan to the deputy prime minister, Lord Whitelaw, about how awful she was . . . "

It was Geoffrey Howe, her longest-serving and longest-suffering cabinet minister, who ultimately put the knife in her back. It is a matter of near-universal consensus that in a court of law he would be acquitted for this crime on a battered-minister defense.

Neil Kinnock, the leader of the Labour Party for the better part of the Thatcher epoch, was unhinged, utterly discombobulated by the simple fact that his opponent was a woman.[14] He had no idea how to deal with this.

Kinnock happens to be a man of spellbinding charm. I was astonished to discover this, for this is not his reputation. He was mocked as "the Welsh windbag" in the press, continually derided as a weak and ineffectual debater in the House of Commons. But

14. He is now Lord Kinnock, but the man is, after all, a socialist (a "crypto-communist," even, if you take Thatcher's word for it), so the title seems a bit ridiculous. In fact, I finally just asked him, "What would you like me to call you?" He said, "Neil."

when I spoke to him he was superbly articulate, and his mellifluous baritone voice, with his melodic Welsh accent, made me want to keep him on the phone for hours. I would gladly have spoken to him about anything—philately, maritime law, animal husbandry— just to keep listening to him.

The odd thing about him is that his face doesn't match his voice. Had I been given the chance to vote for him while speaking to him on the phone, I would have pulled the crypto-communist lever. His voice was just that charming, just that authoritative. After hanging up I looked again at photos of him. His head is a bit pigeon-like, with a beaky nose and a glabrous skull skirted by thin wisps of pumpkin-orange hair. There is something smirky and schoolboyish about his expression. That beautiful baritone voice is the voice of a leader, but that face? No, not quite. Would history have been different, I wonder, if Kinnock had had a full head of regal silver hair, a square jaw, and a Roman nose?

History is what history was, and the record shows that Kinnock was not much of a match for Thatcher. "Even in Margaret Thatcher's weak moments," recalls Charles Powell, "he was quite unable to capitalize; he just didn't have the ability. He was absolutely petrified of her, too, because she destroyed him every week in Prime Minister's Questions." Powell is of course biased, as he freely admits, but Kinnock's own account is not all that different.

I ask Kinnock what it was it like to square off against Thatcher during Prime Minister's Questions. "Well," he says, "the immediate problem I had—I had two immediate problems. One was, she's a woman seventeen years older than myself. And there were punches I could throw against, say, John Major, who's a man of my age, that I just couldn't throw against a woman seventeen years older."

"Like what?"

"Well, you know, there's a form of language that—you know, I could accuse Major of hypocrisy, of evasion—"

I'm puzzled. If you consult the parliamentary record, you will find no shortage of examples of Kinnock accusing the prime minister of hypocrisy and evasion.

Mr. Kinnock: Is she innumerate, or simply mendacious?[15] . . .
Mr. Speaker: Order! Mr. Kinnock: Is she an Iron Lady or is
she a closet flexi-toy?[16] . . . Mr. Kinnock: Will the Prime
Minister then answer the question, which she evaded yesterday?[17] . . . Mr. Kinnock: Will she admit that last night
she was up to her usual tricks of fabrication?[18] . . . Mr. Kinnock: Is it the case . . . that her cynicism and vindictiveness
have overwhelmed all sense of duty?[19] . . . Mr. Kinnock:
What is she trying to evade now?[20] . . . Mr. Kinnock: Is it
not a fact that the Prime Minister's selfish pride has reached
such depths as to require her to threaten the careers of loyal
civil servants in order to impose her selfish will?[21] . . . Mr.
Kinnock: The Prime Minister's answer will be regarded
both inside and outside the House as complete humbug—[22]
Mr. Kinnock: The Prime Minister's refusal to give a straight
answer to a straight question will be noted by the whole
country—[23] . . . Mr. Speaker: Order! Order! . . . Mr. Kinnock: Why does not the Prime Minister, just for once, answer the question on the subject raised?[24] . . . Mr. Kinnock:
Is the right hon. Lady copping out on this one again?[25] . . .
Mr. Kinnock: Why will the right hon. Lady not answer
straight questions on these matters? Why is she still such a
twister?[26] . . . Mr. Kinnock: Frankly, I do not believe the

15. June 4, 1985, House of Commons PQs, Hansard HC [80/149–54].
16. July 11, 1985, House of Commons PQs, Hansard HC [82/1256–60].
17. January 16, 1986, House of Commons PQs, Hansard HC [89/1203–08].
18. November 12, 1985, House of Commons PQs, Hansard HC [86/422–28].
19. January 22, 1985, House of Commons PQs, Hansard HC [71/855–60].
20. June 13, 1985, House of Commons PQs, Hansard HC [80/1007–12].
21. Ibid.
22. November 15, 1984, House of Commons PQs, Hansard HC [67/791–96].
23. June 13, 1985, House of Commons PQs, Hansard HC [80/1007–12].
24. January 17, 1985, House of Commons PQs, Hansard HC [71/506–10].
25. May 21, 1985, House of Commons PQs, Hansard HC [79/851–56].
26. April 30, 1985, House of Commons PQs, Hansard HC [78/133–38].

right hon. Lady— **Hon. Members:** Withdraw! . . . **Mr. Speaker:** Order! The right hon. Gentleman is in order![27]

"Well," I say, "you *did* use some pretty strong language with her."

"Yeah, sure, but Christ, nothing like *that*. Nothing like I *could* use. You know. So, I'm not complaining about that. That's the way I was brought up, and, the fact is, it wasn't my instinct to be vile to a lady who was seventeen years older. Secondly, in any case, the public would see fellows my age standing toe-to-toe and knocking the hell out of each other and think, 'Well, that's what happens,' but if I did it to a woman, a whole segment of society, for understandable reasons, would say, 'That's so disrespectful. That wasn't political antagonism, that was *disrespect*.' And so, both because it was my instinct and because of political reality—"

I interrupt: "You say you really felt put at a disadvantage by her femininity, and yet she was willing to use that when it—"

"True. Yeah, yeah, yes."

"Let's talk about the kind of femininity that she used. I keep hearing various accounts of this."

"Yes—"

"You know, that she was fully capable of flirting and flattering to get her way. Did you see that in action?"

"Um." He manages to convey an arctic tundra of distaste in that syllable. "I saw her doing it with others." He snorts. "Not *my* type o' lady."

Kinnock remembers her trying it on him, though, in meetings about Northern Ireland. "You were meeting with her one-on-one?" I ask.

"Yeah, well, there would be some civil servants. Maybe a soldier there, or a security expert. And if she had some difficult requirement, some way where she really wanted cooperation, and they thought I might have interpreted it as a political step too far—I

---

27. February 12, 1985, House of Commons PQs, Hansard HC [73/161–66].

never did—she'd take her shoes off, and sort of curl her legs under her on an easy chair, and offer me whiskey. And I used to think, 'This is bloody *pathetic*.' I mean, here's a woman in her *sixties*. I mean, I know why she did it—because it worked with other people, you see—"[28]

"That's the odd thing," I break in. "I've spoken now to a number of people, a number of men, all said, '*Other* men found her attractive.' But not one will admit, '*I* found her attractive.' So who was it who found her attractive?"

"Well, you know, there are people who wrote about it, you know—Mitterrand."

"Yeah," I agree. "And Alan Clark. Yeah." ("But goodness," wrote Clark, "she is *so* beautiful; made up to the nines . . . quite bewitching, as Eva Perón must have been. I could not take my eyes off of her and after a bit she, quite properly, wouldn't look me in the face."[29]) Of course, there is no sexual desire to which Alan Clark wouldn't have admitted. This was the man who in his diaries—not published posthumously, but while he was still alive and married—describes with priceless gusto bedding a South African judge's wife and her two daughters. At the same time.

"Well," Kinnock says, "a couple of people have written about it. And, you know, I saw her being what I suppose you'd call coquettish to other people at receptions and whatnot."

---

28. I've heard variants on this story from a number of Thatcher intimates. One of her civil servants remembered desperately trying to finesse a compromise between Thatcher and her chancellor during a dispute over the budget. His delicate diplomacy was upended when Thatcher came back from the Commons, apparently quite drunk, and discovered her chancellor holding a secret strategy meeting behind closed doors. She strode in uninvited, kicked off her shoes, tucked her heels under herself, and declared, "Well, gentlemen, let's just settle this now, shall we?" She "held court like a Queen Bee," and what do you know, they settled it. Afterward, the other civil servants could be heard muttering among themselves, "*Phwooarh*, wasn't she sexy tonight?" Mitterrand, according to the same civil servant, was "visibly moved" in Thatcher's presence.

29. Alan Clark, *Diaries: Into Politics 1972–1982* (Phoenix, 2000), p. 147.

"It's not just sexiness," I say. "It was also the maternal archetype. I keep getting the sense that people responded to her as a stern mother, a stern schoolmistress—"

The *matron*. We should linger for a moment on this image; the full dimensions of it may be obscure to the American reader. Men of Margaret Thatcher's generation who attended the public schools were apt to have grown up under the matron's influence. George Orwell described the matron thus in *Such, Such Were the Joys*:

> I think it would be true to say that every boy in the school hated and feared her. Yet we all fawned on her in the most abject way, and the top layer of our feelings towards her was a sort of guilt-stricken loyalty . . . Whenever one had the chance to suck up, one did suck up, and at the first smile one's hatred turned into a sort of cringing love.[30]

Neil agrees. "Yeah, yup. No, honestly, she had that characteristic, so that there was a very widespread feeling, at many times, that 'She was wrong, but she was strong.'"

Why, I ask him, were the British so susceptible to that characteristic? I don't venture a theory, but he seems to think I'm advancing one. "I think that's pop psychology went mad," he says. "I think that's complete bullshit. I think there's a certain amount of—"

"You think *asking* the question is bullshit, or—"

"I don't think that countries, mature countries have national moods like that, looking around, sucking our thumbs, waiting for cuddlesome old mothers. That's just not the way it works."

Now, I haven't said anything of the sort, and the fact that he spontaneously injects the word "mother" into our discussion of Thatcher—and then dismisses the relevance of the word he introduced with such disproportionate indignation—strikes me as re-

---

30. George Orwell, *Such, Such Were the Joys* (Harcourt Brace, 1953).

vealing, not about Thatcher or about the British nation, but about Kinnock himself. In fact, I encountered among almost all the male politicians to whom I spoke an almost violent antipathy to what seems to me an obvious psychological observation, one that anyone with the remotest degree of insight into human nature would accept: The way people react to a very powerful, middle-aged woman is apt to suggest something about their relationships with their mothers. I am not exactly casting a laser-light of fresh psychoanalytic acumen on the situation by suggesting this. Yet every time I even hinted so, the man to whom I was speaking reacted as if I had just said that I sensed a blockage in his heart chakra. I am not sure what to conclude from this, except, perhaps, that men who rise to the top of the power game tend to be men of action, not introspection.

"There *is* a segment of the Conservative Party," Kinnock concedes, "whose main contacts with females in their formative years was with a matron at their public schools, and I don't think you'd be stressing psychology too far to say that there were some who regarded her as Maggie the Matron, and were consequently *exceedingly* joyous if she showed them any kind of favor or even notice. Now, I wouldn't say it was more than a segment, and I certainly wouldn't say it was true of all the ex–public schoolboys. But some."

"Yes," I agree. "I've noticed that among some of the men I've spoken to, some of them are still nursing wounds, still nursing injured pride about slights from her, how she didn't notice their brilliant report or whatever—"

"Yeah, it's poisonous. I'm almost relieved by the fact that my dislike of her was absolutely constant. It never varied. I never needed a damned thing from her."

Several more times during our conversation, he tells me that he simply couldn't figure out how to attack a middle-aged woman without looking like a cad. He says this as if menopause were an illegal weapon. "The feeling I'm getting," I say to Kinnock, "is that you did not feel that she played fair."

"Oh, Christ, this is politics!"

"I know."

"No, this is not boxing under the Queensbury rules, and it's not association football! This is a blood sport!"

"Well, then, how come you weren't willing to really *stick* it to her? I mean, you're saying, 'I didn't want to use discourteous language, I didn't want to be seen attacking a woman older than me,' but if this is a blood sport, why didn't you?"

He sighs. I feel a bit cruel now, as if I'm not playing fair myself, but I really do want to know how he explains this to himself. "Well, like I said," he answers at last, "it would have been politically disadvantageous—but in any case, it would have bloody *demeaned* me to have done that. If you're doing it, you know, toe-to-toe with a fellow about your age, or even if he'd been a bit older than myself, that would have been—"

"So you're basically saying, 'I couldn't hit a girl.'"

"Well, I *know* I couldn't hit a girl—"

"Yeah, but you know, she happened to be the *prime minister*. And you felt that you couldn't hit back? Because she was a *woman?*"

"Not that I couldn't hit back, I mean, I did hit back!"

I am left, in the end, with two images—a small boy of about three, red-haired, pink-faced, hiccupping as he fights back tears, staring into the looming face of an impossibly large woman in an apron. *If you don't eat your meat, you can't have any pudding! How can you have any pudding if you don't eat your meat?*

And then, the image of a beleaguered middle-aged man with a thin fringe of wispy pumpkinish hair, lying on the psychotherapist's couch.

"My mother," he is saying, "was a *formidable* woman."

⁓ ⁂ ⁂⁓

Let's return now to John Hoskyns—remember him, the wiring diagram? We have been talking about economics and the miners' strike over lunch at the Travellers Club, but it is time to repair to the tea room, where his wife, Miranda, has arrived to join us. I have spoken to many men who knew Thatcher, but thus far no women: Miranda is the first. She is also the only interview subject to show even the remotest curiosity about me. She wants to know about my family, how I came to be a writer, why I live in Istanbul. Her feminine curiosity makes her to my mind an interesting witness. It suggests that she might pay attention to things in a way powerful men tend not to do.

I tell Miranda that I am so glad she joined us. I had been hoping for a woman's perspective on Thatcher. She laughs, seeing right through me, and turns to her husband. "She's hoping to get some *gossip!*"

"Gossip?" says John, as though it would never have occurred to him.

"Yes!" says Miranda.

John raises an eyebrow. "We never used to talk about anything except economic theory, did we? The Laffer Curve featured largely."

Miranda permits herself a Mona Lisa smile. "If you're occasionally allowed amongst these august presences," she says, "you can be a fly on the wall, as it were, as a wife. Which is awfully useful."

"Let's start with your first impressions of her."

"Well," she says, "I was very left-wing, in the early '70s. John and I used to argue. I was an artist, and all of my friends—"

"I'll absent myself while she makes these confessions," says John, chastely sipping his coffee. "I mean, she was an absolute *Marxist.*"

"No, I *wasn't* a Marxist. Well, we used to have these violent arguments about politics . . . John and I used to argue at breakfast, and unfortunately his logic was so much stronger than mine that he eventually talked me out of it. So when he sold his company and decided he wanted to go into politics, I was appalled. Because a lot of people wanted him to get a seat. And I was horrified, because I didn't know how I was going to explain it away to everybody. But I was beginning to understand what he was talking about. And I suppose it was after you met Keith Joseph that I first became aware of Maggie—it must have been about 1975, was it? I think I had seen pictures of her—she was known as Thatcher the Milk-Snatcher. I became aware of her and thought she was pretty awful. I really did. She wasn't my kind of woman at all—"

"'Pretty awful' how?"

"She represented everything having to do with my own parents' generation. To do with middle-class values, behaving properly, wearing hats—all the kinds of things that I was longing to throw away. Because the '60s—although I was already married and having children—in the '60s, I was *thrilled* with everything being overthrown, you know, all the terrible fuddy-duddy stuff. I didn't want a royal family anymore, you know, freedom for everybody—I really thought it was wonderful! I wasn't involved in it very much, but seen from the outside I thought it was a very good thing. And she represented, as she did to everybody on the Left, the absolute antithesis of that. She had nothing to do with that world of the '60s. And I was in a very uncomfortable position, because I was beginning to see that John was right about what he was saying, or at least my brain told me he was right. My emotions told me he was all wrong, and he didn't *understand*. He kept saying, 'How do you think somebody like me, who's an entrepreneur, can possibly make his way in the world with taxes and everything like that,' and I kept arguing back, 'Well, it's your choice, you do it because you like doing it, you don't mind about profits, they don't matter,' you know, all that sort of stuff. I mean—I was pretty silly."

John nods wisely.

"But he was beginning to persuade me that he was right," she continues. "So I was in this position of seeing this *awful* woman, knowing that she thought the same sorts of things as he did, and I had to be gradually converted over—and by the time she was likely to win in

1979, I was a terrific fan! I thought she was the most courageous and wonderful woman, and I was *longing* to get to know her."

"Was there a moment in particular where your feelings began to change?" I ask. "Was it something that she said while campaigning, or—"

"I can't remember exactly what it was, but there was a moment when I realized that she had a courage that nobody else seemed to have. And I admired the courage more than anything. I still deplore some of the things she stood for, but I admired her courage more than *anything.*"

"What do you deplore?"

"She's—quite narrow-minded. She doesn't like women. She doesn't like women who—um—*impinge* on her life in any way. She's absolutely charming to women who work for her, who, you know, waited on her in Chequers, in London. She was delightful with children, delightful. Absolutely charming to children—"

"Genuinely sweet—" says John.

"Oh, genuinely!" she agrees.

"Completely un-self-conscious, not—"

"Oh, absolutely!"

"Not knowing she was being observed, or—"

"Yes!"

"Very touching, that way."

"One of my biggest memories," says Miranda, "was this very touching way that she took this little boy, and I was just standing nearby, and she said"—Miranda's voice becomes gentle and coaxing, like Mary Poppins—"'Now, come along, shall we go to the kitchen? What's your *favorite* food?' And she walked out of the reception, and apparently got his favorite food, whatever it was. It was really lovely."

"Lovely," John agrees.

"But she didn't like women," she says. "And I wasn't the only one to feel it. Nearly all the wives—I mean, I remember Peter Hennessy saying, 'Those wives are going to get out their knitting needles one day!'"

"Why do you think she didn't like women?" I ask.

"Because they were a threat to her. Because on one level, she was an attractive woman—"

"Yes," agrees John in the slightly abstracted way of a man who hadn't really thought about it before.

"I mean, there were some men, William Whitelaw, for instance, who found her dazzlingly attractive, and apparently when drunk made passes!" William Whitelaw was Thatcher's deputy prime minister. She found him an invaluable source of support, famously announcing that "every prime minister needs a Willie." She apparently said this in perfect innocence and had no idea why everyone found it so funny.

"Who did?" says John, suddenly curious.

"William Whitelaw!" she replies, pleased with herself.

"Oh, *really?*" says John.

"He supposedly said to her, 'I'm in love with you!'"

John looks surprised. "Did you have a long conversation about it with Willie?"

"This is gossip! This is gossip! I didn't, no."

"Certainly, he got terribly emotional about her," says John.

"Terribly emotional!" agrees Miranda.

"Saying, 'She is the *only*—'"

They are talking over one another now, and I can't catch what they're saying. No matter. We have a a solid piece of unsourced gossip: Willie Whitelaw was in love with her. So was her parliamentary private secretary, Ian Gow, according to Alan Clark, who describes Gow's devastation at being supplanted by another in the prime minister's affections. "How ruthless women can be," Clark laments. "Far worse than men. Ian was completely in love with the prime minister and utterly devoted to her."[31]

Miranda too was utterly devoted to the prime minister, and she too suffered her share of indignity. "I mean, I really came to the

---

31. Clark, *Diaries: In Power*, p. 35.

point where I really would have done anything for her. I thought she was so marvelous, and she just simply treated me like dirt." She says this with no rancor—she seems to suggest with her voice that it was just one of those peculiar things about Margaret Thatcher, and nobody's perfect. "And I came to the conclusion at the end that it was because at some of these gatherings and parties, I'd been in a group, with one or two other people, and we were all having a lot of fun. And she thought *she* wanted that fun, with the men, but she didn't want the women there. It was something like that, some peculiar thing—"

"One of those female types," I say, "and we all know them, who likes to be the center of male attention—"

"Absolutely!" says John.

"*That's* it," says Miranda simultaneously.

"*Absolutely,*" agrees John again, nodding vigorously.

"And there was one occasion," Miranda recalls, "when she literally, when I was saying good-bye, literally—she used to do this to a lot of people—she'd take your hand to say good-bye, and you were just hoping to have a word or two, to say thank you—and she'd just *sweep* you out, and wait for the man to come—it's very, very weird."

"Like some old-fashioned Hollywood diva," I say.

"Yes! Yes!" agrees John.

So what was it like, I ask, when this diva entered the room?

"She'd always be very correctly dressed," Miranda says, "with all the jewelry in the right place."

"*Quick,*" adds John. "A quick, funny, shuffling walk. Comes in through the door at very high speed and immediately shows off like mad to show she's arrived—"

"Yes, *shows off*! She was a great shower-off. I mean, at the end of parties, when you were invited to stay and have a drink with her before she went off to the House of Commons, she would throw off her shoes, and sit down on the sofa with her feet up, and everyone would sort of cluster 'round her—which I used to feel very uncomfortable about—you know, everyone looking at her with worship. And she just showed off. Non-stop. Again, back to the diva, you know. Very much that sort of thing. But I'm thinking back to when I actually met her. John—I was hoping I would have met her the night of the election, when we were around at—um— Central Office?"

"Central Office," he agrees.

"Once it became clear that she was in, and she was going to be elected, John came 'round and said, 'OK, let's go home and watch it on television.' And I said, 'But I've never *met* her!' He said, 'I don't care, I've *got* to get out of this.' And as we left, all the newspapermen outside the door, saying, *'She's coming! She's on her way!'* And I couldn't get back in again! I had to go home and watch it on television! I missed the whole thing. So I didn't meet her until well after that. And she took hold of my hand, in a very friendly way, and said"—here Miranda breaks into a perfect impression of Thatcher's imperious, regal voice—"'Oh, well, I *do* hope you can spare your husband. You've got *lots* of things you like to do yourself, haven't you.' She didn't *ask* me whether I had, she *told* me!"

Miranda is too charitable to dwell for long on these memories. "She was devoted to Denis," she adds. "She *adored* him—"

"Yes, yes—" John nods vigorously.

"She was delightful. Now, you would expect someone like that to have a henpecked husband, who she was always telling what to do. Not a bit of it! She was very, very considerate and sweet to him. Really delightful."

"Did she have a sense of humor?" I ask.

"She did," says John, "but it only showed up every now and then . . . the only time I remember making her laugh was when we were sitting in the long library at Chequers, trying to write a speech. And there'd been a great scandal about a Labour shadow minister who'd been caught up in some enormous affair with a married woman, which had upset his political career, and there was a picture of him at an air display at Farnborough sitting next to the queen." John begins laughing—in fact, he begins laughing so hard that the next part of his story is unintelligible. "And of course there was the implication of all journalism, that, you

This photograph of Denis and Margaret Thatcher immediately puts me in mind of columnist Julie Burchill's wonderful description of their marriage: "Denis was so supremely self-confident/drunk that he didn't give a fig about being seen as an alpha woman's consort; with the quiet, amused, ceaseless tolerance of the little woman's little ways typical of the real man, he was a tower of strength disguised as a bumbling buffoon—never the cretinous yes-man caricature portrayed by some weird lefties who, while paying lip service to feminism, seemed decidedly uncomfortable at the sight of a man walking behind a woman." *(Courtesy of the family of Srdja Djukanovic)*

know, he'd been shagging this bird, and was absolutely . . ." Now they are *both* doubled over with laughter. I have no idea what's so funny. "And I was there with the paper, saying, you know, 'This man must go!' And she absolutely fell about! And I remember her being fairly obvious and saying he needed a quick forty winks, you know! And to my astonishment—she really thought that was funny!"

I later listened to this part of the transcript several times, trying to figure out what he was talking about. I'm still not sure. Perhaps you had to be there.

"Yes," says Miranda, "she quite liked—"

"Slightly raunchy humor," he finishes for her.

"Yes, she quite liked raunchy humor with the *boys*, but again, would never have done with women!"

"No!" he agrees.

"You know, she loved to be thought of as one of the boys, making slightly risqué jokes—"

They are enjoying these memories. As they finish each other's
sentences, their eyes meet and sparkle with affection. One can
never know what another couple's marriage is really like, but they
certainly give the impression that theirs is the very ideal of what
marriage ought to be. This, I think, must be why Miranda is so san-
guine about the prime minister's rudeness to her: Only a very
well-loved woman could be so charitable.

Margaret Thatcher may have liked to think of herself as one of the
boys. The boys, I gather, did not quite think of her as one of them.
But one of the *men*—that's another story. "Reagan, Gorbachev, and
Thatcher," says John, "that triumvirate—just amazing. She could
just walk the world stage by then, looking like a million dollars,
with a fur hat on, in Warsaw, through the snow, and we thought—
this woman was a *star*! And not only that, but unlike the French
people, her economy isn't in trouble. You know, her economy, now
everyone is looking to it, saying, 'Perhaps this is the way we should
do things!' And now here she is, saying, 'This is the way the West
has got to deal with the Soviets!'"

The footage of Thatcher in Poland is indeed unforgettable.[32] In
1988, as the Polish economy was collapsing and the Solidarity
movement was gaining strength, Prime Minister Wojciech Jaruzelski invited Thatcher to visit Poland. He was presumably hoping to
enlist the support of the woman who had vanquished her unions
in Britain; perhaps he expected a cozy tête-à-tête, one union-
crusher to another.[33] He was to be severely disappointed. As a con-

---

32. It may be seen on the PBS series *Commanding Heights*: www.pbs.org/
wgbh/commandingheights/shared/video/qt/mini_p02_09_300.html.

33. For a more complete discussion of Jaruzelski's gambit, see John
O'Sullivan, *The President, the Pope and the Prime Minister: Three Who
Changed the World* (Regnery, 2006), pp. 294–299.

dition of her visit, Mrs. Thatcher demanded the communist government allow her to meet Solidarity leader Lech Walesa. They agreed. "You didn't say no to Mrs. Thatcher," Lech Walesa recalled. "No one refused her."[34]

She sailed into the Lenin shipyard at Gdansk aboard a small ship. The docks were lined with vast throngs of shipyard workers dressed in their drab, oil-stained, Soviet-regulation boiler suits. Defying the police blockade, they climbed the gates and clambered atop the cranes and roofs surrounding the shipyards to catch a glimpse of her. In the video footage she seems literally to be casting light upon the grayness: It is almost as if she has been shot in Technicolor against a black-and-white background. Before the great crowds she passes, slowly, regally. The men and women in the crowd wave and wave and peer at her with hopeful reverence; they chant "*Solidarność! Solidarność!*" and "*Vivat Thatcher!*"

She lays a wreath at the monument to shipyard workers killed in 1970 by the security forces. The crowds roar as she addresses them: "*Solidarity was, is, and will be!*" "*Thatcher! Thatcher!*" "*Send the Reds to Siberia!*" Solidarity workers escort her to a packed church. There the entire congregation—faces cragged and careworn—begins, in unison, to sing the Solidarity anthem. The camera focuses on Thatcher's face. Her eyes are filled with tears.

It was at this point, I imagine, that Jaruzelski realized, his head sinking into his hands with horror, that he was completely and utterly finished.

—◦ ⇌ ◦—

Thinking of that scene, I remark to John and Miranda, "It's a very strange thing, political charisma. It's fascinating to try to understand what it is, and how it works—"

---

34. Transcript from *Commanding Heights, Chapter 9, Poland's Solidarity*: www.pbs.org/wgbh/commandingheights/shared/minitextlo/tr_show02.html#9.

"Fascinating," Miranda agrees. "And you do feel this ability of certain people to transmit it—it is a kind of magical thing."

She had that magic, no doubt. But in the end, they both agree, there was something more than charisma at work. She had guts. John remembers the way she rose to the occasion on October 12, 1984, when an IRA bomb blasted apart the Brighton Grand Hotel. Thatcher and the members of her cabinet were staying there before the opening of the Conservative Party conference. The prime minister and her husband narrowly escaped injury, but five of her friends were killed. Margaret Tebbit, the wife of her cabinet minister Norman Tebbit, was paralyzed.

The bomb went off at 2:54 a.m. The prime minister was—as usual—awake and working on her speech for the next day. "The air was full of thick cement dust," she recalls in her memoirs. "It was in my mouth and covered my clothes as I clambered over discarded belongings and broken furniture towards the back entrance of the hotel."[35] She was taken to the police station, where she changed from her nightclothes into a navy suit. Her friends and colleagues arrived, suggesting she return to Number 10. "No," she said. "I am staying."[36] Then—and this is the detail that makes you realize that this woman is *not* like you and *not* like me—she lay down and took a short nap, so to be fresh for the long day ahead of her. After she woke she took breakfast, she recalls, with plenty of black coffee.

Hours after surviving an assassination attempt, she walked into the conference center at 9:30 a.m., precisely on time. She delivered her speech, partly ad-libbed. "The bomb attack," she began,

> . . . was an attempt not only to disrupt and terminate our conference. It was an attempt to cripple Her Majesty's democratically elected Government. That is the scale of the outrage in which we have all shared. And the fact that we are

---

35. Thatcher, *The Downing Street Years,* p. 380.
36. Ibid., p. 381.

gathered here now—shocked, but composed and determined—is a sign not only that this attack has failed, but that
all attempts to destroy democracy by terrorism will fail.[37]

With that said, she proceeded briskly to defend her government's economic policies.

The weekend following, she described the event thus: "We
picked ourselves up and sorted ourselves out as all good British
people do, and I thought, let us stand together, for we are
British."[38] If anyone was in doubt before this that she could walk
the walk as well as she talked the talk, they were not now.

"I remember writing to her afterwards," recalls John, "saying
what an appalling thing it was and how absolutely right she'd been
to just let it have no effect at all. And she wrote the most marvelous letter back, I mean, full of sort of ranting and raving about,
'The forces against democracy must never be allowed to triumph,'
and that sort of thing. But it was *absolutely* from the heart. And I
think again and again one finds, all the time, that the one thing
that people know—was there was this absolute *lion* heart.
Courage. It really was there."

Miranda nods. This is why she would have done anything for a
woman who showed not a bit of graciousness to her.

_⌒ ⇌ ⌒_

Even Thatcher's detractors concede her courage. Her charisma, on
the other hand, was not a universal emollient. However power-
fully it affected her admirers, it was incomprehensible to her ad-
versaries. Bill Clinton's sworn enemies will usually admit,

---

37. Speech to Conservative Party Conference, October 12, 1984, Brighton,
Thatcher MSS (digital collection), doc. 105763.
38. Speech to her constituency at Finchley, October 20, 1984, Thatcher
MSS (digital collection), doc. 105769.

grudgingly, that there *is* something charming about the man. Not Thatcher's. Kinnock's views are typical.

CB: Did you like Margaret at all?

NK: No. [*Emphatic and cold*]

CB: I see. You *really* didn't like her personally.

NK: No. She didn't like me, and I didn't like her.

CB: If you had met her in another context, a social context, not a political context, what kind of reaction do you think you might have had to her?

NK: Same as most other people.

CB: Which was?

NK: That she was cold, arrogant, patronizing, snobbish—

CB: Do you have an anecdote . . . can you tell me about something she said that would really bring that alive for me?

NK: In the week of the Lockerbie disaster, the terrorist sabotage of the 747, quite naturally both she and I went to the memorial service that was held in the village of Lockerbie. And at the service, we went into the church hall to meet the bereaved relatives. And of course there were United States citizens and British, one or two others, but they were the main passengers on the 747. And she said to me, very unusually, "Would you be good enough to come in with me." Because we'd been to several memorial occasions, and she generally tended to sort of stay apart. Which suited me fine. So I went in with her. She walked up to a group of black Americans. I would say probably servicemen's families—

CB: —yeah, a lot of servicemen—

NK: —six or seven of them. And she sort of walked up to them, and put her head to one side, which was quite characteristic of her, and said [*absolutely perfect imitation of MT's voice*] "And how many did *you* lose." [*Snorts in disgust*] I mean, these people didn't know what the hell she was talking about. Maybe it was her accent. But I was shocked to my roots. I mean, of all the opening questions—*how many did you lose?* When the hairy free enterprise—

CB: I'm sorry, which enterprise?

NK: There was a ship, a ferry, called the *Herald of Free Enterprise,* which was coming out of Zeebrugge harbor in Belgium, and the cargo, the hold doors were opened as the ship started to move, the water came in and the ship rolled over, and 150 people were killed, including several of the crew of the ferry. We went to the memorial which was held in Canterbury Cathedral, down in southeast England near to Dover. And after the service the clergy sent everybody, the grieving relatives and everybody else, down to the crypt of the church for tea, or brandy if we wanted it. And of course, quite naturally, quite a lot of the survivors from the crew, family, working-class people, lit cigarettes. Absolutely naturally. None of the clergy turned their heads. They didn't even notice it was happening, they were busy going around *comforting* people. And I was about two yards away from Margaret Thatcher, talking to people—my wife is from a seafaring family, so we have a natural empathy with these sorts of people on these occasions. Thatcher went up and told them [*voice rises, scolding, mimicking her voice, uncannily accurate*], "You shouldn't be smoking in here!"

CB: Oh, my God!

NK: "*This is consecrated grrrround. You should put those cigarettes out!*"

CB: Oh, God, that's a very telling anecdote. Do you have more like that?

NK: Yeah, yeah. Lots of them. Lots of them—but I've gone far enough. I tell you why. Because these were very, very somber, very sad occasions. I'll only repeat those two. But they're only a sample. Sadly. To show that she just had *no* social skills in those circumstances—

CB: But, come on, how could she have been as successful a
    politician as she was with *no* social skills ? Surely you must
    have also seen a different side of her, a charming side—
NK: No. [*Icy*]
CB: Never?
NK: No. [*Emphatic*]
CB: You don't remember *any* moment when you thought, "Oh,
    that's her charm. *That* must be it."
NK: No. [*Emphatic. A long, cold silence*]

Back now to Charles Powell, in his Georgian mansion on Queen
Anne's Gate. It is late in the afternoon, post-prandial, dozy. The
weather is muggy. The air is still. Powell's hands remain folded in
his lap, and I suspect that he rather wishes I were not there so that
he might shut the door, tell his secretary to hold his calls, stretch
out for a few minutes on the sofa, and close his eyes. Thatcher,
from her picture frame, surveys the scene with what seems by
contrast an almost lunatic vitality. "Is a personality like hers a freak
of nature," I ask him, "or do you think there was something in her
background that created this phenomenon?"

"It's a very good question, and one I've never been able to answer. Because it's quite clear there was this enormous change of
gear, that up until 1974, '75, she had been a talented, able, hardworking, but not particularly distinguished member of a couple of
Conservative governments, and a bright young sort of political
candidate. Something between 1975 and 1978–9 changed her
from that, into being somebody who dug deep into herself and
really thought, 'Look, this can't go on, I'm going to change it, and
I've got the willpower to do it.' I don't know how this sort of
Pauline conversion really happened, but it did. Now, some of it
was certainly under the influence of Keith Joseph, but something

really changed in her character in that time. Did it have roots? Yes, of course it did, it had roots from her upbringing and her father, you know, the sort of Methodist insistence on the virtues of hard work, improving herself, getting herself up from a sort of grammar school girl, pretty undistinguished little town in the Midlands—"

"If you were to just speculate, wildly, about what might have happened between 1975 and 1979, what do you think *might* have happened?"

"Well, part of it was the depth of Britain's condition by that time. I mean, in the latter years of the Macmillan government when she was having her first years on the job you could conclude that Britain wasn't too bad of a place, I mean, you remember the slogan 'You've never had it so good,' the slogan on which Macmillan went into the '57 election. But in the early '70s we were beyond all that, that was certainly an important part of it, but what else changed it—I just don't know, it's almost insane . . . a vision, some sort of lightning striking from heaven, but there was something. Something happened there. I mean, she herself claims, really, she just was forced finally to think why earlier Conservative governments had failed. But I've never been able to explain this. I remember when reviewing her autobiography, I identified this as the greatest mystery about her, really."

"As have I," I agree. "I find myself confronted with statements she made such as, 'I knew I was the only one who could do it,' and the question I keep coming back to is, how on earth does anyone, *anyone* have that kind of self-confidence, no less a woman, at that time, of her background—"

"Yes, well, people do, I suppose. Stalin had it—"

"And people ask the same questions about Stalin—"

"Yes, yes. Is it nature? Of course, it helped, I think, the other factors in her character. She could never see two sides of a question. There was only one side of a question, as far as she was concerned. I mean, most of us are reasonable people, we can see the pros and the cons, but she was not the slightest bit interested in the cons, she—*this is the way it was going to be done, and don't worry about the arguments against it, this is the way.* Now, of course it makes you very vulnerable if you're wrong, but she was right an awful lot of the time, and therefore her self-belief grew to vast proportions, and in the end of course it was part of her downfall. She'd become clearly imperial, by the end. You could say it's a weakness, but it can be a great strength, politically, too, especially in crisis."

"Do you remember ever seeing her in a moment of profound doubt? Ever?"

He pauses for quite some time. "No, I don't think I do. Not profound doubt. Profound doubt about whether she was going to get through, not because she was wrong, but were the odds stacked against her too much? I think you can say, certainly in the early days of the government, on the economy, I think she probably felt that—I think she had some moments of doubt. Certainly on the Falklands conflict, when she took on the extraordinary task of sending out the expeditionary force 8,000 miles—"

"Doubt, or anxiety?"

"Well, doubt, too, I think. Yeah, anxiety, certainly, she got very nervous before big speeches, terrible business trying to keep her sedated, as it were, before she went on stage. She was always convinced at the last moment that she had the wrong text, or it wasn't going to work, or whatever, but that was just a way of pumping up the adrenaline. Lots of fine opera singers, or whatever, suffer the same phenomenon."

A diva, again. The image comes up over and over. So do the others.

_⁊ ⬥ ⁊_

Powell's secretary knocks on the door. Our time is up. I fit in one more question. "Why does she matter?"

"I think," he says, "the overall message would be that you *can* change a country—a lot of people think *you can't; you can run a country, you can administer it, but don't be silly, governments come and go, life goes on, you can't change it.* Now, you have Mr. Sarkozy saying he can change France—and it will be very interesting to see if he does—but she shows that it *can* be done. I think that's a very important lesson. And from the point of view of the rest of the world, well, I think she did a better job than anyone of exposing socialism and really destroying it. I mean, there's no socialism left in this country and there's not much left in Europe. No one believes in socialism anymore."

5

The Sledgehammer

The Russians, who are lucky to have such a mar-
velous sense of humor, if only because they've had
so little to laugh about, recount a story about
Leonid Brezhnev's arrival at the pearly gates. St.
Peter tells him that he has not exactly led the sort of
life that would qualify him for heaven, but that he
can choose between a capitalist and a socialist hell.
To St. Peter's surprise the former Soviet leader
replies that he would prefer a socialist hell. St. Peter
tells him to think carefully: This is no time for prop-
aganda! But Brezhnev repeats that he chooses the
socialist hell. St. Peter grants his wish but, greatly
puzzled, asks for an explanation. "Ah," replies
Brezhnev. "It is because I know that in a socialist
hell they will always be short of fuel!"

— ONE OF MARGARET THATCHER'S
FAVORITE JOKES[1]

---

1. She told this version of the joke while giving a speech in Bermuda on
August 7, 2001, Thatcher MSS (digital collection), doc. 109301. It pops up
elsewhere; it seems to have been a staple of her repertoire.

Margaret Thatcher was not an economist. Her views about economics were not original. Her critics often note this with derision.
"Thatcherism," sniffs the economist Frank Hahn, "as represented
by Mrs. Thatcher herself, is intellectually without interest. It con-
sists of homilies on the virtues of work and ambition and on providing the carrot and stick to elicit these virtues."[2] Hahn appears to
be suggesting that there is something wrong with this, but I am
not sure why. It is hardly a politician's job to be intellectually interesting. It makes no more sense to criticize Thatcher because her
ideas were unoriginal than it does to criticize Adam Smith because
he was not a good politician.

Thatcher herself was exceedingly proud of the unoriginality of
her economic opinions. She held it to be a measure of their value.
She did not invent Thatcherism, she claimed; she merely rediscovered it, in much the way doctors have recently rediscovered the
medical value of leeches—both are tried-and-true, old-fashioned
cures only latterly obscured by high-tech faddism, and if both
cures are rather unpleasant, well, when a patient is dying it is no
time to be squeamish. (This is my analogy, not hers, although she
did once liken herself to a tough nurse who refused to coddle her
patients lest their muscles atrophy.)

"When people spoke about the 'Thatcher experiment,'" she remarked after her resignation, "they missed one very important
point. I am a trained research chemist. I know what experiments
are. And I never confused my country with a bacterial culture. The
proof that the theory worked was, I knew, already to be found in
the economic progress of the West."[3]

As these remarks suggest, there is a theory behind Thatcherism.
Nigel Lawson, Thatcher's chancellor of the exchequer from 1983
to 1989, correctly insists that Thatcherism is not "whatever Mar-

2. Frank Hahn, "On Market Economies," in *Thatcherism*, ed. Robert
Skidelsky (Chatto & Windus, 1988).

3. Speech in Korea, "The Principles of Thatcherism," September 3, 1992,
Thatcher MSS (digital collection), doc. 108302.

garet Thatcher herself at any time did or said."[4] Rather, as he puts it, Thatcherism is "a mixture of free markets, financial discipline, firm control over public expenditure, tax cuts, nationalism, 'Victorian values' (of the Samuel Smiles self-help variety),[5] privatization and a dash of populism."[6] He is right, but his phrasing might suggest that these ingredients are independent or equally weighted. In fact, all but nationalism and populism, which are not economic policies, derive from the first on the list: free markets.

Free-market economics and Thatcherism are often held to be synonymous. This is nearly true, but there is an important additional dimension to Thatcherism—a faith in the morally redemptive power of the free market that goes well beyond standard economic claims. Generally, free-market economists favor free markets for two reasons: because they believe free markets are efficient, and because they are, by definition, free. (To make the latter point non-trivial, add the suppressed premise: *freedom is good.*) Thatcher believed both these assertions to be true. But equally importantly, she believed that free markets not only served but *created* robust, self-sufficient, and moral citizens, and vice versa.[7] "We must not focus our attention exclusively on the material," she declared in 1977,

> because, though important, it is not the main issue. The
> main issues are moral. In warfare, said Napoleon—the moral

---

4. When I spoke to Lawson about the definition of Thatcherism, he noted pointedly that Thatcher "was very much the captain of her team," but her policies "were made by a team, and not just by her alone." Of course they were. When I speak of Thatcherite reforms, I am using a shorthand for the reforms made by Thatcher and her team. Thatcher was the *prime* minister, however, so I think it fair to call the reforms that took place while she was in power "Thatcherite reforms."

5. Samuel Smiles was the Victorian author of *Self-Help,* as well as the similar page-turners *Character, Thrift,* and *Duty.*

6. Lawson, *The View from No. 11,* p. 64.

7. For an excellent discussion of this point, see Shirley Robin Letwin's *The Anatomy of Thatcherism* (Transaction Publishers, 1992).

to the material is as three to one. You may think that in civil society the ratio is even greater.

The economic success of the Western world is a product of its moral philosophy and practice.

The economic results are better because the moral philosophy is superior.

It is superior because it starts with the individual, with his uniqueness, his responsibility, and his capacity to choose.

Surely this is infinitely preferable to the Socialist-statist philosophy which sets up a centralized economic system to which the individual must conform, which subjugates him, directs him and denies him the right to free choice.

Choice is the essence of ethics: if there were no choice, there would be no ethics, no good, no evil; good and evil have meaning only insofar as man is free to choose.[8]

Free markets, she emphasized again and again, forced individuals to take responsibility for the outcomes of their choices. "People must be free to choose what they consume, in goods and services," she told the Greater London Young Conservatives:

Choice in a free society implies responsibility on the part of the individual. There is no hard and fast line between economic and other forms of personal responsibility to self, family, firm, community, nation, God. Morality lies in choosing between feasible alternatives. A moral being is one who exercises his own judgment in choice, on matters great and small, bearing in mind their moral dimension, i.e. right and wrong. Insofar as his right and duty to choose is taken away by the state, the party or the union, his moral faculties, i.e. his capacity for choice, atrophy, and he becomes a moral cripple in the same way as we should lose the faculty of

8. Speech to Zurich Economic Society, "The New Renaissance," March 14, 1977, Thatcher MSS (digital collection), doc. 103336.

walking, reading, seeing, if we were prevented from using them over the year.

. . . The Socialists would take away most or all of these choices. A man would do what he was told by the state and his union, work where work was "found" for him, at the rate fixed and degree of effort permitted. He would send his children to school where the education authority decided what the children are taught and the way they are taught, irrespective of his views, he would live in the housing provided, take what he could get, give what he was obliged to give.

This doesn't produce a responsible or a moral society.

This does not produce a classless society; on the contrary it produces the most stratified of all societies, divided into two classes: the powerful and the powerless; the party-bureaucratic elite and the manipulated masses.

And are these rulers better fitted to make choices on our behalf or to dispose of resources? Are they wiser, less selfish, more moral? What reason have we for supposing that they are?[9]

It is critical fully to appreciate that Thatcher's enthusiasm for free markets can't be reduced to an enthusiasm for economic efficiency—this is a charge often made, but it simply isn't so. A *moral* society, not an efficient one, was her ultimate goal.

～❀ ❀ ❀～

Almost everyone—no, everyone—has heard the phrase "free market." But try asking the next five people you meet to explain what a free market is and why it might be desirable. My own admittedly casual research suggests that few people have given the matter

---

9. Iain Macleod Memorial Lecture, "Dimensions of Conservatism," July 4, 1977, Thatcher MSS (digital collection), doc. 103411.

much thought. This is surprising, because more than any other concept in economics, and perhaps more than any other idea in history, the concept of the free market has had a direct—a vital—influence on the lives of billions.

The argument for free markets involves a beautiful, fascinating, counterintuitive theory. It is one of the great achievements in human thought. It is also, basically, simple. A free market is one in which the prices of goods and services are determined by individual sellers and buyers, not by the government. It differs from a planned or command economy in that no centralized authority makes decisions about resource allocation.

The central claim of the theory is this: Free markets allocate resources efficiently because the decisions men and women make about what to buy, what to sell, and how much to pay or charge for those goods convey critical information about what people really want and how much they really want it—as opposed to what the government believes they want, or worse still, what the government believes they *should* want. I use the word "efficient" because economists are partial to it, but I am aware that the word carries cold and technocratic overtones. You may substitute "an allocation of resources that makes people happier." That is what we really mean. Or more bluntly, you can put it this way: "an allocation of resources such that fewer people starve to death."[10]

A free market is more efficient than a controlled one because in a free market, prices convey critical economic information—information about the relative scarcity of goods. This in turn

---

10. Economists will quibble with my rephrasing. They will note that the First Theorem of Welfare Economics predicts only that given certain initial conditions, viz, that (1) there are markets for all the goods and services that people want to trade and (2) that economic agents act as price takers, a free market will generate a Pareto-efficient outcome. The theorem does not specifically predict that fewer people will starve to death. I added that part. I added it because it's true, and we wouldn't give a damn about Pareto-efficiency if it weren't.

guides the myriad decisions of individual actors in the economy about what to produce and what to consume. This point tends to be abstruse in the abstract but intuitively obvious in the specific. Why, for example, are Hawaiian pineapples cheaper than Alaskan pineapples? They are cheaper because they cost less to grow. They cost less to grow because light, in Hawaii, is abundant. Why is Hawaiian seal blubber more expensive than Alaskan seal blubber? It is more expensive because seals, in Hawaii, are scarce.

Suppose that the Alaskan pineapple farmer—who grows his pineapples under halide lamps and thus pays a high monthly electricity bill—is finding it tough to stay afloat in a market flooded by cheap Hawaiian pineapples. Rather than selling the hothouse and buying a seal-spear, he persuades the federal government to give him farm subsidies on the grounds that without them, he will go broke. This is hardly a far-fetched example; the federal government dishes out billions of dollars every year in farm subsidies on precisely these grounds. The Alaskan farmer can now charge less for his pineapples than they cost to produce. At the supermarket, however, the price of Alaskan pineapples and the price of Hawaiian pineapples will now be similar. Perhaps the Alaskan farmer will even be able to undercut the Hawaiian one. *Ceteris paribus*, the consumer will pick the cheaper pineapple.

This state of affairs disguises an important truth: The Alaskan pineapples do not really cost what the Hawaiian ones do. The government subsidy comes from money taken from taxpayers. The consumer is not, in fact, paying the same price for Alaskan pineapples as he is for Hawaiian ones—quite the contrary. He is paying more for them, but doing so indirectly. Since the true cost of Alaskan pineapples has been obscured from him, he is apt to buy more of them than he would if he knew how much they really cost. But he has not been offered the information he needs, in the form of a price, to express his preference, in the form of a purchase.

I, for one, would not want Alaskan pineapples enough to pay their real price. I would rather keep the money that has been taken from me, buy a Hawaiian pineapple, and spend the difference on the latest issue of *Public Choice*. But it is clearly absurd to imagine that any government functionary, however well-meaning and prescient, could predict that this is how I would prefer to spend my money. It is even more absurd to imagine that the government could predict the preferences of every actor in a large economy with this degree of precision. In a free market, the government does not have to predict anything of the kind—the price mechanism does the work for them.

Consider another hypothetical scenario. Imagine the government has decided that the price of pineapples is simply too high. It decrees that all pineapples must now be sold for a dollar each. This will ensure that everyone, even the poor, has equal access to pineapples.[11] Thanks to the Fair and Compassionate Pineapple Program, pineapples of every provenance will appear, at the supermarket, to be cheap. If they are cheap enough, I will buy more of them. I may well buy every last pineapple in the store: I have been known to do this when something I like is on sale.

There is obviously a problem with this. If I buy all the pineapples, there will be none left over for anyone else. And if the government has capped the price of pineapples, no one will voluntarily start growing more of them, because *in reality* it costs two dollars to grow a Hawaiian pineapple and twenty to grow an Alaskan one. Pineapple farmers are not charity workers, and pineapple farming has now become not only unprofitable, but a form of personal economic suicide. Very quickly, you will have a pineapple shortage. Now apply this example across the board, to all food items: Soon you will have food queues. Ultimately, you will have starvation.

---

11. Again, this is *not* a far-fetched example. This is taking place right now. Food prices are rising precipitously, and governments around the globe are responding with price caps.

Is my example simplistic and far-fetched? Try putting that question to anyone who grew up in the Soviet Union. Gorbachev, apparently, struggling to solve precisely this problem, once asked Thatcher how she made sure the British people got enough food. She didn't, she told him tartly. *Prices* did. By extension, anything that distorts the information conveyed by prices is harmful to the market's functioning and leads, sooner or later, to oversupply of things that people do not want and shortages of the things they do want—as Soviet planners discovered. "It was a shame," recalled Gorbachev in 2001, "and I continue to say that it was a shame, that during the final years under Brezhnev, we were planning to create a commission headed by the secretary of the Central Committee, [Ivan] Kapitonov, to solve the problem of women's pantyhose. Imagine a country that flies into space, launches Sputniks, creates such a defense system, and it can't resolve the problem of women's pantyhose. There's no toothpaste, no soap powder, not the basic necessities of life. It was incredible and humiliating to work in such a government."[12]

The free market is a simple concept, and the empirical evidence that it provides goods and services more efficiently than a command economy is about as strong as we can hope to have in the social sciences. Command economies everywhere have resulted in waste, shortages, poverty, and immiseration. That is why the great command economies of the twentieth century collapsed and the free-market economies are still here. Of course, the free market is a model, and like all models, it can only be approximated in reality. But it can be approximated to greater and lesser degrees, and those degrees matter. A freer market, Thatcher believed, is almost always a better one.

Despite the manifest failure of any number of command economy experiments, the concept of a free market continues to arouse

---

12. "Heresy in the USSR," *Commanding Heights,* PBS, April 23, 2004.

great suspicion. Many people who are in no doubt that they favor freedom of religion, free speech, free assembly and free elections feel no such instincts about free markets. Likewise, many people who claim to believe in free markets think that free markets are fine for the widgets they talk about in the textbooks, but not for food, water, medicine, energy, or, indeed, jobs. After all, they think, you can't trust that essential goods will be provided by impersonal market forces. No, the government had best step in to make sure there's enough of those to go around. But if you accept the argument that free markets work better than ones that are not free, then logically, the essential goods are the ones you least want the government allocating by decree. The more you need the commodity in question, the more you must hope it is being produced and sold in the most efficient way possible.

No one in his right mind believes free markets will function smoothly with no government intervention at all. Even the most enthusiastic free-marketer willingly concedes that governments must make and enforce the laws that permit a free market to operate: You may not sell your widgets at gunpoint, for example, and if you promise to deliver fifty widgets on the first of January, you must do just that—you must not take your customer's money and decamp for the Caymans. No one believes you should be allowed to buy or sell anything; not even the late, great Milton Friedman would have said that parents should be allowed to sell their children's eyeballs to the highest bidders. To prevent people from doing these things, you must have a legal system; to have a legal system, you must raise taxes. Enthusiasts of free markets accept this but believe that government intervention should be the exception, not the rule. The government's role, in other words, should be confined to the smallest possible sphere.

Yes, but how small is the "smallest possible sphere"? Those on the Left side of the spectrum often ask this in a sly, knowing way, as if the question is basically unanswerable and the optimal size of government thus a matter of taste. In fact, the question is not unanswerable at all, and the answer is quite precise. The answer is 14 percent of GDP.[13]

＿ᴄ⟩ ⟨ᴇᴈꞋ ᴄ⟩＿

From a commitment to free markets, Thatcher believed, certain policies followed logically: monetarism; financial deregulation; reducing controls on prices, wages, and exchange rates; lowering taxation; reducing government spending; privatization; and curtailing the power of trade unions to set wages that did not reflect market demand for labor. These were the policies Thatcher put in place, with varying degrees of success.

Let us look first at monetarism because this is where Thatcher's critics usually start. Those who are inclined to sneer when they say the name *Thatcher* are likewise inclined to pronounce the word *monetarism* much as they would the words *pervert* or *pathogen*. Often the criticism reflects a conflation of monetarism with the rest of Thatcher's policies and personality. In fact, monetarism was only one component of Thatcherism, and not the most significant one. But because it is so widely held to be *the* defining Thatcherite dogma, it warrants our attention.

So what is monetarism, really?

---

13. Beyond this, the economist Georgios Karras has suggested, the drag on productivity begins to outweigh the benefits. See "The Optimal Government Size: Further International Evidence on the Productivity of Government Services," *Economic Inquiry* 34 (April 1996). In developing, rather than developed, countries, the optimal size is larger. When governments cost more than this surprisingly small percentage of a nation's gross domestic product, you do *not* tend to see commensurate improvements in critical social indicators such as life expectancy, infant mortality, or school enrollment. See, e.g., E. A. Peden, "Productivity in the United States and Its Relationship to Government Activity: An Analysis of 57 Years, 1929–1986," *Public Choice* 69 (February 1991). This research was done after Thatcher's rise to power, of course, but would have come as no surprise to her.

The story begins with the Phillips Curve. If you took Economics 101 as an undergraduate, you may remember it. In 1958, the economist A. W. Phillips described a relationship between inflation and unemployment. Simply put, he argued that when unemployment falls, workers interpret this, correctly, as a sign that there is now a greater demand for what they are selling—labor. They therefore increase the price of labor by demanding higher wages. Employers then pass on the cost of these higher wages to the consumers in the form of higher prices. Rising prices, inflation—same thing. The Phillips Curve implied that you could have low inflation or low unemployment, but not both. It also implied that there was a reasonably simple cure for unemployment: Create inflation.

It is not hard to create inflation. All you need to do is increase the quantity of money in an economy, otherwise known as the money supply. The value of money, like the value of any other commodity, depends upon the relationship between the supply of that commodity and the demand for it. If the supply of money increases, its value will diminish. That is the very meaning of inflation.

A government can pursue an *expansionary* policy—which often leads to inflation—in one of two ways. It can control the supply of money directly, through what is called monetary policy. For example, it can lower interest rates. This increases aggregate expenditure, because when interest rates are low, people save less and spend more. Investors invest more, because they can get cheap loans.

Alternatively, it can use fiscal policy: By taxing less, or by spending more, the government directly increases aggregate expenditure, leading to an increase in output. The use of fiscal policy to combat unemployment is commonly associated with the economist John Maynard Keynes—this is broadly what is meant by the term "Keynesian economics"—and until the late 1960s, Keynesian policies were held to be the state of the art. No one likes inflation, but the assumption underpinning an expansionary policy is that at times of unusually high unemployment, a controlled rise in the inflation rate is a reasonable tradeoff for getting people back to work.

Controlled is the operative word.

The state of the industrialized world in the 1970s led to a crisis of faith in the Phillips Curve. Stagflation—high rates of inflation *and* unemployment—forced economists to develop a competing idea: the *natural* rate of unemployment. If unemployment fell below this natural rate, they speculated, prices would not rise in a stable and proportionate way. Instead, inflation would gallop.[14]

Now why would that happen?

In 1975, the economist Milton Friedman famously proposed this answer: At any given time, constraints placed upon the economy's efficiency create barriers to full employment. These constraints include, for example, the degree to which it is easy to relocate to find work, the degree to which the price of labor is artificially elevated (by, for example, mandatory minimum wages or collective wage bargaining), and the degree to which options other than working—such as collecting unemployment benefits—seem attractive. If these constraints are not lifted, then no matter how high the rate of inflation, unemployment cannot be completely eliminated.

Now suppose, said Friedman, that despite these constraints, the government, seeking to reduce unemployment below the natural rate, accepts the logic of the Phillips Curve and pursues an expansionary policy. This pushes up prices. Real wages fall, leading firms to increase their demand for labor, which is now cheaper. Employment rises. In the short run, the policy seems to work. Happy employees enter the marketplace; the government wins the election.

The problem, said Friedman, is this: The workers agreed to supply their labor at Wage W assuming that prices would remain stable. But the workers aren't stupid: They notice that prices are rising, and they notice that the real value of Wage W is falling. They expect that this trend will continue. They demand higher wages. When labor becomes more expensive, employers buy less

---

14. It is often said that inflation *accelerates* under these circumstances, but this is technically wrong. Acceleration refers to the rate of change. The inflation rate is the rate of change in prices. What is accelerating here is the rise in prices, not inflation. To say that inflation "accelerates" would better convey the drama of the problem, however, as in, *This inflation is like a truck with failed brakes careening down a steep hill.*

of it. Unemployment returns to its previous level. You have therefore raised inflation and gained nothing.

Now the government, which unlike the workers *is* stupid, again
pursues an inflationary policy to correct unemployment. The
workers respond by demanding higher wages still. This cycle continues, each time more rapidly. Voilà, skyrocketing inflation, and
still no commensurate rise in employment.

If you accept this analysis, you will conclude that policymakers cannot attempt to choose between high unemployment and
high inflation. Instead, they should steer the economy toward a
growth rate such that prices remain stable, and accept the level
of unemployment consistent with this. This target is called the
Non-Accelerating Inflation Rate of Unemployment, or NAIRU.[15]
To treat unemployment, the government should fix the underlying
problem—the structural flaws in the economy that are increasing
the NAIRU. Over the long run, argued Friedman, unemployment
simply *cannot* be cured by pushing up the inflation rate, so there is
no point in trying. What's more, by stimulating runaway inflation,
the government will serve only to raise the overall level of misery.

During the 1970s, this argument looked extremely persuasive. Britain was suffering from acute stagflation. Thatcher's
predecessors—both Labour and Conservative—had attempted to
control inflation through fiscal policy and by implementing wage
and price controls.[16] These efforts had failed. Moreover, wage and
price controls were ideologically abhorrent to free-market economists. Thus did Thatcher determine

- to target inflation, *above all*
- through monetary policy, *alone.*

---

15. Again, the term, strictly speaking, should be non-*increasing* inflation
rate of unemployment—but for some reason that's not what economists call it.

16. Thatcher's predecessor, Jim Callaghan, also tried to control inflation
through monetary policy. It is incorrect to imply, as some do, that Thatcher's
was the first British government to try this. But Callaghan didn't last long
enough in office to be widely remembered for it.

It is important to stress that Thatcher viewed inflation not only as a problem, but, like socialism, an *evil*. And if inflation is evil, skyrocketing inflation is more evil still. But why was inflation so wrong? First, because it punishes the thrifty: If inflation is rising unpredictably, it is pointless to save. If you have not saved, to whom will you turn in your needy old age? You will turn to the government. Inflation, Thatcher believed, thereby encouraged citizens to adopt a dependent, infantilized posture toward the state.

Moreover, inflation distorts price signals. If the cost of goods and services rises quickly and unpredictably, the information conveyed by prices becomes gibberish. Who can plan or invest when they have simply no idea what things will cost in a year's time or ten? The price mechanism is the key to the free market. If prices fail to convey meaningful information, the market will not function efficiently. This is why monetarism, for Thatcher, devolved from a commitment to free markets. Just as contract law is necessary to ensure the smooth functioning of the free market, so, she held, was the control of inflation.

If you believe, as Thatcher did, that free markets are morally ennobling, you must of necessity view inflation as no mere macroeconomic problem: It is, in fact, a *moral* problem. Thus did Thatcher describe inflation as an "insidious moral evil to whose defeat everything must be subordinated." In her famous "The Lady's Not for Turning" speech, she called the defeat of inflation her "prime economic objective":

> Inflation destroys nations and societies as surely as invading armies do. Inflation is the parent of unemployment. It is the unseen robber of those who have saved. No policy which puts at risk the defeat of inflation—however great its short-term attraction—can be right.[17]

---

17. Speech to Conservative Party Conference, October 10, 1980, Brighton, Thatcher MSS (digital collection), doc. 104431.

Contractionary economic policies appealed intuitively to Thatcher, for they seemed consonant with a key Methodist value: *thrift*. The Keynesian idea that a government could make an economy grow by spending more money seemed to her not only contrary to common sense, but a serpent-in-the-garden species of temptation. That way lay the wickedness of profligacy. "For many years," she said,

> we have been told that a little bit of inflation is good for you. Many economists assured us—indeed some still do so assure us—that inflation is necessary to maintain full employment, to facilitate growth and to keep the economy moving. The message was: spend your way to prosperity, and when the economy faltered, spend and spend again.
>
> Of course it was difficult for governments to resist such siren voices. Britain was among the first large economies in the West to pursue these policies. We learned a hard lesson— monetary expansion stimulates only a brief and temporary growth. Decay soon sets in. But such monetary expansion does have a permanent effect—albeit an unfortunate permanent effect. It raises the rate of increase of the price level. Inflation comes to stay.
>
> With the hindsight of this sad history, we can easily see how the inflation rate rose persistently throughout these decades. But more strikingly, the average level of unemployment has also risen. The average unemployment was less than 2 percent in the 1960s, 4.1 percent in the 1970s and 6.8 percent in 1980. Our higher inflations have merely brought lower growth and rising unemployment.
>
> The lesson is clear. Inflation devalues us all.
>
> But the erosion of the currency not only has insidious effects on the health of the economy; it also breaks a trust between the government and the governed. The fabric of faith on which so much of our life depends rests on the maintenance of money values. A reliable and safe currency is a cen-

tral responsibility of government. Once the people lose their trust in money the freedom of men and women in society will be diminished or even, eventually, destroyed.

That is why my administration has put the permanent reduction of inflation as its first economic priority. In a free society this can be achieved only by reducing permanently the rate of growth of the stock of money. We knew that the transition could not be painless and smooth. After these many years of inflationary drift the costs of recovery have to be paid.[18]

A *siren voice, decay,* and ultimate *destruction*—we all know this story, although it is usually not a fable of fiscal policy. From the analogy to the Fall, it is obvious that redemption will require, as it always does, pain.

Even less subtle was the language used in 1981 by her then energy secretary and future chancellor, Nigel Lawson, who publicly asked critics of the government's tight money policy to "drop their high moral tone, because there is really nothing that is moral or compassionate in prescribing policies that would engulf this country in a holocaust of inflation."[19] His use of the word "holocaust" is noteworthy: Lawson is Jewish, and obviously no word conveys greater moral horror to a Jew. The use of the word in this context is grotesque, but at least it makes it quite clear just how much the Thatcher stalwarts hated inflation and why they were willing to bear any price to kill it.

What Thatcher hoped to do, by maintaining strict control over the money supply, was return the economy to the point of zero—or at least low and stable—inflation. She imagined this would necessitate a slight period of higher unemployment, after which unemployment rates would return to their starting point.

---

18. Speech at Georgetown University, Washington, D.C., February 27, 1981, Thatcher MSS (digital collection), doc. 104580.
19. Lawson, *The View from No. 11,* p. 137.

That is not what happened—at all.

—⟨ᵒ⟩ ⟨≡⟩ ⟨ᵒ⟩—

Within two years of Thatcher's monetarist ministrations, British unemployment soared to rates exceeded in the twentieth century only during the Great Depression. A quarter of the British manufacturing industry disappeared—the largest drop in industrial output since 1921. Britain's inner cities went up in flames.

> . . . The latest government figures show unemployment rising from 1.5 million to 2.5 million in 12 months . . . Joblessness among ethnic minorities is rising even faster, up 82 percent in one year . . .
>
> . . . four nights of what Home Secretary William Whitelaw describes as "violence of extraordinary ferocity" . . . Police are forced to withdraw . . . 150 buildings are burnt down . . . 781 police officers are put out of action . . . CS gas is used for the first time on the British mainland . . .
>
> . . . In Toxteth, unemployment has risen to 37 percent, climbing to 60 percent among young blacks, with 81,000 people chasing 1,019 jobs in Liverpool . . . the local careers office has information on just 12 vacancies to offer school leavers throughout the city . . .
>
> . . . New riots in Brixton are accompanied by a wave of disturbances the length and breadth of Britain. Southall, Battersea, Dalston, Streatham and Walthamstow in London, Handsworth in Birmingham, Chapeltown in Leeds, Highfields in Leicester, Ellesmere Port, Luton, Leicester, Sheffield, Portsmouth, Preston, Newcastle, Derby, Southampton, Nottingham, High Wycombe, Bedford, Edinburgh, Wolverhampton, Stockport, Blackburn, Huddersfield, Reading, Chester, Aldershot—all these and other towns and cities report riots . . .

... Margaret Thatcher cancels a planned visit to Toxteth
because her safety cannot be guaranteed.[20]

Unemployment rose and rose and rose. Stores were firebombed
and looted. Imagine this period with a soundtrack by UB40. You'll
recall the band, I expect, but may not know that the name stands
for Unemployment Benefits 40, a form issued by the Department
of Health and Social Security, otherwise known as DHSS, an
acronym you'll also recall if you've ever listened to Wham!

WHAM!

BAM!

I AM!

A MAN!

JOB OR NO JOB, YOU CAN'T TELL ME THAT I'M NOT!

... DHSS ... DHSS ... DHSS ... DHSS ...

All the same, the inflation rate simply refused to come down and
stay down. The government couldn't even achieve the one goal that
was supposed to justify this misery. When Thatcher was elected in
May 1979, the retail price index had risen by 10.3 percent over the
previous year. By early 1980, it had risen above 20 percent.

By the spring of 1983, it had fallen below 4 percent. Much excitement ensued: Had she done it? Had she vanquished inflation at
last? Alas, no. In late 1985, inflation began again to climb. In 1991,
the retail price index rose 10.9 percent—higher even than the
year Thatcher became prime minister. It is not a coincidence that
this was her last year in power.

Why didn't it work? The answer is quite technical, and even a
professional economist who has spent his life explaining these
concepts to hung-over undergraduates would be hard-pressed to
sum it up neatly. I know this for a fact, because I asked the Master
of Balliol to try.

---

20. Various news reports from Channel 4. These were, not at all
incidentally, race riots, very similar to the ones now common in France.

CB: Why wasn't it working?

Andrew Graham: [*Sighs*] Oh, God. This is back to tutorials, isn't it? I'll try and do as best I can. It's a long time since I've given an economics tutorial . . . this is an incredibly *boring* technical argument . . . Um, I wonder if I could put my hands on an article, that would be even better . . . [*Gets up and rummages through files*] What happened is that a whole load of money that had been going out through the banks suddenly came in through the money supply, and ended up counted in the monetary aggregates, whereas before it had been outside the monetary aggregates—and, um, uh, sorry, this is extremely inefficient of me—God, it's amazing what kind of stuff I've got in here, how weird! Um, I could give you, I have more than enough stuff to read—I could probably give you a copy of that—getting warmer . . .

CB: I can't put a bunch of graphs in this book.

AG: Don't worry, don't worry. It doesn't explain it there, that's annoying—um—There are targets for M3, which was a funny old thing we were supposed to measure in those days, and it was supposed to grow by between 7 and 11 percent in that year—

CB: And M3 is?

AG: Current accounts in banks, plus deposit accounts in banks, plus, that's about it, plus cash—M3 is simply a technical number. It was supposed to grow between 7 and 11 percent, and it grew 17 percent.[21] Next year it was supposed to grow between 6 and 10 percent and it grew 14 percent.

CB: And how do you explain the discrepancy?

AG: The abolition in the same year of the corset. The banks had not been allowed to engage in various forms of lending. So what had been happening was companies had been lending direct to one another, and company lending didn't count,

---

21. In fact, it grew 19.5 percent.

since it's not part of the bank lending, so it just didn't appear in the bank figures . . . At the same time as Thatcher
and Keith Joseph were trying to hold down the quantity of
money, they changed the way the quantity of money was
being influenced and took off this administrative control.

Let me rephrase this. Monetarism sounded simple in theory
but in practice proved confusing. This does not mean the theory
was wrong, but it does mean that no one quite understood how to
use it.

The heart of the technical problem is this: To control the money
supply you have to *measure* the money supply. To measure the
money supply, you have to define what you mean by money. Coins
and bills with the Queen's face on them are obviously money. So
you measure those. What about the contents of savings and check-
ing accounts? Yes, that's money too. What about bananas? No, not
money, definitely not. Treasury bills? Well—actually that one's
tricky; you could argue it both ways.

The contents of a PayPal account?

Mardi Gras beads?

Mexican pesos?

Mexican pesos after they've been taken from the mattress
where they've resided for the past five years and converted to
British pounds?

If not, why not?

In principle, as long as you use a consistent definition of money,
you should be able to measure the growth of the money supply
over time—*if* people are using money, as you've defined it, in a
consistent way.

But while it was using an unchanging definition of money,
Thatcher's government was changing the way money was used.
The abolition of foreign exchange controls and the deregulation of
the banking sector were key free market reforms, obviously, and
both led to a radical change in the way people used money *as the
government defined it.* Corporations that had previously lent money

to each other directly to bypass cumbersome bank regulations began using banks—which were now, as intended, more efficient—to
facilitate these transactions. Stuff (to use the term of art) that had
not previously been defined as money went into the banking system, where it *was* defined as money. This severely skewed the government's efforts to measure the money supply, in a meaningful
way, from year to year.

> **AG:** It's just like—imagine that you've got a particular market-
> place. Prohibition in the '30s. You're using all your official
> statistics on sales of alcohol, but alcohol sales are banned, so
> it looks pretty low. But plenty of alcohol sales were going on
> in the '30s in the black market. Take off the controls, sud-
> denly your shops are selling the alcohol, which was previ-
> ously being sold by bootleggers. The banks in this case are
> the shops. Suddenly all this money-lending comes back to
> the banks, because banks are the efficient way to do it, and
> the black market is the inefficient way to do it. So it comes
> back into the banks and it suddenly counts as money.

Here's an even simpler way of looking at it: Thatcher's key economic reforms collided in mid-air and exploded.

And yes, they should have predicted this.

There is a consensus now among economists—to the extent
that there is ever a consensus among economists—that Thatcher's
first government measured money the wrong way and thus chose
the wrong monetary targets. Her last government confused matters inordinately with an incoherent policy toward entering the
European Exchange Rate Mechanism. This is why Thatcher's remedy did not work as quickly or as well as expected, and this is why
British cities went up in flames.

What is fascinating in this story is this: Despite Thatcher's insistence that she was not confusing her country with a laboratory experiment, experimenting is precisely what she was doing.
Obviously she was. That famous article by Friedman was published

in 1975. No one in the world knew if this "monetarism" business would work. No one had really tried it before. As clearly evidenced by her government's inability to figure out what to measure, no one was quite sure how to apply this theory in practice.

CB: Now, were they aware that this [abolishing the corset] would have this effect? Or was it inadvertent?

AG: No, they were aware of it, but they probably didn't understand it.

It is the consensus of everyone, and I do mean *everyone* who knew Thatcher—even her most devoted loyalists—that she didn't understand the technical details of the policy upon which she staked everything. Yet she did stake it all, and she would not relent, because it just sounded *right* to her.

Her policies appeared in these initial years to be an absolutely catastrophic failure. Economists the world over proclaimed Thatcher's government to be the most disastrously incompetent in the history of postwar Britain. When asked in a debate in the Commons whether she could name just two economists who supported her, Thatcher managed to cough up the names of a pair of dogged loyalists who would have agreed with her had she pronounced her allegiance to the theory of phlogiston. Upon her return to Downing Street after this exchange, one of her civil servants apparently said to her, "It's a good job you weren't asked to name three."

Yet she would not relent, even in the face of overwhelming pressure, not only from the public, not only from the Opposition, but from her own party. She believed, with what seemed at the time an almost religious faith, that it would work—because *it just sounded right.*

CB: Where does she get the confidence to do this?

AG: I don't know! I would posit—I think Keith Joseph thought he did understand these things, and he was very enamored with Friedman, so he thought there were explanations as to why this would all work . . . I don't think Thatcher went into these arguments *at all* . . . I think she was a remarkably instinctive politician. I think that she probably sort of at some gut level thought, *I've just got to kill this inflation, I think it will create unemployment, but I think somehow we'll get through* . . . She had no training as an economist, none, no intellectual equipment which would suggest that she would have thought it through . . . Her statements were the statements of somebody who thinks about the economy as—I mean, to put it crudely—as a *housewife.*

Before concluding that monetarism was nothing more than the dimwitted delusion of a demented housewife, however, note this. In 1981, 364 highly trained economists, led by Frank Hahn (the very one who declared Thatcherism to be "intellectually without interest") signed an open letter to the *Times* protesting her economic policies. Not long thereafter, the economy began rapidly to grow, entering the longest sustained period of expansion of the postwar era, and not long after that, unemployment began to come down—and it has stayed down to this date.

Rates of both inflation and unemployment in Britain are now *very* low. In fact, since 1997, Britain has ranked top in both output and inflation stabilization in the Organisation for Economic Cooperation and Development. The prestige of highly trained economists has never quite recovered. Thatcher's first chancellor, Geoffrey Howe, subsequently declared that he had "actually produced a definition of economists as a result: that an economist is a man who knows 364 ways of making love, but doesn't know any women."

One may argue—and many do—that unemployment declined despite rather than because of Thatcher's intransigent adherence to monetarist doctrines, but the fact remains that it did come down—a lot—which at least leaves the matter open to debate.

So was it insanity, or was it uncanny intuition coupled with astonishing force of will?

To be honest, I'm not sure. I think the jury is still out.

Nigel Lawson, predictably, feels the monetarist perspective has been vindicated. Although economists certainly have not converged around the principle that you must control inflation *above all*, there is no longer much doubt that *if* you are attempting to control inflation, monetary policy is the tool of choice. "The Andrew Grahams of this world," Lawson wrote to me,

> believed that you dealt with inflation largely by imposing prices and incomes policies, with perhaps some assistance from fiscal policies. What we said was no; all that is worse than useless, it is actively damaging. You deal with inflation by monetary policy. Since we now have an independent Bank of England, charged with keeping down inflation (and with nothing else), whose only tool is monetary policy, for which it is wholly responsible, I think it can fairly be said that it is game, set and match to us.[22]

About this, he is right. Before Thatcher, there was a debate about the primacy of monetary policy in controlling inflation. There is no debate now. In this respect, the Labour Party did indeed go beyond anything Thatcher ever attempted to do: As Lawson points out, in 1997 it removed the authority to set interest rates from the Treasury and transferred it to an independent monetary policy committee. This is a measure often recommended by monetarists on the grounds that the key to controlling inflationary expectations is credibility: People must be given a good reason to believe that inflation will stay under control. If you take responsibility for controlling inflation away from elected governments—which are apt to manipulate the economy for short-term electoral gain—you are sending a signal: *We're not just yanking your chain. No matter what happens, your money will be good.* I am not sure that I would

---

22. Lawson, e-mail correspondence, September 27, 2007.

describe this development as "game, set and match" for the monetarists, but I agree that it's certainly not an outright loss.

The Master of Balliol is not a great fan of Thatcher's, but he is
fair-minded enough to concede that the relationship between
Thatcher's experiments with monetarism and Britain's now-vibrant
economy is at least an open question. "It's one of the very big
unanswered questions in my mind about economics. She said
there was no alternative."

He hesitates for a moment, then adds, "She might have been
right."

"No alternative to—?"

"No alternative to massive unemployment to stop inflation. I
wrote an article in 1975 which more or less said I thought this
would happen. I didn't believe for a minute this rubbish that it
would be peaceful and easy. I thought it would be difficult, and I'd
much rather we hadn't had to do it. We've had one huge recession
under her and another one under John Major, and it's killed off inflation in the British economy and it needed to be killed off somewhere along the way. I'd much rather we'd found an alternative.
But if we didn't have an alternative—"

He pauses again, then sighs. "She had the guts to push it
through."

— ◌ ⳥ ◌ —

If we see the heart of Thatcherism as an attempt to control inflation *above all* by using monetary policy *alone*, our judgment of
Thatcherism will be ambivalent at best. The high costs associated
with this policy—and her inability to bring inflation down immediately and keep it down—have tended to obscure the success of
her other policies. But they shouldn't. That would be to miss the
point of Thatcherism.

Recall the second part of Friedman's prescription: To treat unemployment, you must fix the underlying problem—the distor-

tions in the economy that are increasing the NAIRU. You must, in other words, target the supply side of the economy. As successive Thatcher governments struggled to bring down the inflation rate, they simultaneously sought to increase economic productivity through a series of dramatic supply-side reforms. The reason Thatcher matters *now*, not the reason she mattered then, is the story of these reforms.[23]

What did Thatcher do, specifically, to affect the supply side? For that matter, what *is* the supply side? When we speak of strengthening the supply side, we are talking about creating incentives for people to produce—in other words, supply—goods and services. When taxes are lower, for example (this is the classic supply-side remedy), people have more incentive to be productive.

Foremost among the things Thatcher did to strengthen the supply side was smash the trade unions. (Economists would describe this as "augmenting labor market flexibility.") When Thatcher came to power, some 70 percent of the British labor force was paid according to the terms of a trade union agreement. By 1998, this figure had fallen to 35 percent. Next in importance were changes made to the welfare benefit system: Prior to Thatcher, welfare payments had been indexed to average wages. Under Thatcher, payouts were linked to the Retail Price Index. Because wages rose faster than prices, over time this reduced payouts. These policies—together with reductions in income tax, the privatization of public industries and utilities, trade liberalization, and deregulation—were designed to heighten the ability of prices to convey information, create incentives to work, and ultimately lower the NAIRU.

They did precisely what they were intended to do.

These terms—supply side, incentives, NAIRU—may sound sterile. The everyday economic realities they describe, however, are

---

23. I am greatly indebted to the economist Martin Davies for helping me to disentangle these policies and their consequences.

nothing of the sort. John and Miranda Hoskyns, for example, recall what they meant in practical terms.

CB: I want to know what the business environment was like in 1979. What does it really mean when you talk about the "British malaise"? I mean, I've heard the anecdotes about garbage piling up on the streets, and corpses going unburied, but let's talk about someone who comes from an average, mid-sized city in Britain and has modest ambitions for himself or herself. What were the obstacles to, say, going into business, becoming a small businessman?

Miranda: Well, you couldn't send things by mail very easily, for a start, could you? I mean, the Post Office was—

John: No, no—

Miranda: A friend was having a baby . . . and all the electricity went off at the hospital. In the middle of giving birth. We had an elderly aunt in a nursing home who was left in pitch darkness because the lights went out. That kind of thing happened *all the time*. Every day.

John: But those were at particularly critical times, like the Winter of Discontent—

Miranda: Yes, but quite a few years—

John: But there's also the question of, sort of, what did people over the years think? I mean, what was their level of optimism—and did they have any ambition? And part of my answer would be, because you remember this in the company, the Hoskyns Group . . . if any of our people went to work in the States, they never came back. They simply couldn't afford to! . . . I mean, I remember the way it was always put. It was, "I can save money for the first time in my life." . . . The general level, the standard of living, the standard of earning, and everything else, was pretty low. Taxes *very* high. And it was just impossible for anybody to save money. You just could *not* do it . . . Not only was I subject to high taxes, but

because I was living on investment income, which was regarded as practically criminal in those days, there was an *ex-
tra* level of tax. So the maximum—so my maximum tax rate
. . . was 98 percent.

Miranda: 98!

CB: 98 percent is *unbelievable*. . . . Is that the highest tax rate
that's ever been imposed on a modern country?

John: I suspect the Emperor Diocletian might have—didn't he
have higher taxes? I think he did.

Miranda: You just felt absolute despair. You felt you couldn't rise
above it.

That is what we're talking about when we talk about the supply
side.

Thatcher's policies resulted, as would be predicted, in what
economists would call "a complete reassignment of resources,"
leading to "an inevitable period of readjustment." Now remember,
many of those "resources" were human beings. Some of them
never adjusted. What we mean, in simpler terms, is this: Thatcher
took a sledgehammer to a dysfunctional semi-command economy,
stepped back, and waited for the rubble to reassemble itself—*sans*
government direction—in a more efficient configuration. It took
many years for the dust to settle, and the collateral damage was
considerable. But in the end, the restructured economy was, as she
had predicted it would be, leaner and meaner. The fact that these
effects were chiefly seen after, and not during, the Thatcher era
should not obscure the fact that they were the consequence of her
policies.

Privatization generally saved the taxpayer a fortune and made privatized industries more competitive and innovative. The privatization of British Telecom resulted in a dramatic lowering of prices

and improvement in service. The sale of council houses was and remains one of Thatcher's most popular policies. But it would be
wrong to describe privatization as an unalloyed success in every
instance. Having taken British trains both before and after privatization, I can report that they were lousy and expensive before, and
they are lousy and expensive now.

Generally—and predictably—privatization was most successful
in industries with natural competitors. As the Master of Balliol
correctly pointed out, "Don't mix up competition and privatization. They're not the same thing."

CB: How would you introduce competition in a non-privatized
industry?

AG: Well, I'd say you have to come at it a different way. You have
to make up your mind, on the basis of analysis, whether this
industry is of the kind where competition is feasible—I
mean, competition between restaurants—drop-dead easy.
Do it. Nobody in their right mind would do anything else.
Competition between electricity-generation stations, one
generating a supply in Scotland, another one generating a
supply in Kent—tricky!

CB: Which do you consider the most successful privatizations, if
any?

AG: Um—probably in the long run, telecoms, but that's—the
rate of technical change in that area has been so huge that
the industry would have transformed itself no matter
what happened. I think that British Telecom was eventually put more on its toes. But British Telecom even in the
old state-run way would probably have been put on its
toes by the mobile phone industry, etc. You just can't
compare telephones today with telephones then. Buses?
Maybe.

CB: And which ones in your view were the least successful?

AG: Railways? Energy, I don't know about.

CB: Well, that's a shame, because that's where I was going
next—

AG: I'm allowed to—much better to just be humble and say you
don't know!

CB: I never thought so. Did you ever hear *me* admit I didn't
know the answer to something?

AG: All that bluffing in my economics tutorials—I *knew* you
were bluffing.

Fair enough, I was, but I am still not persuaded that British
Telecom would have been put on its toes by the growth of the
mobile phone industry. Other nationalized industries, in the face
of technological change and overseas competition, had simply
grown more and more unprofitable. Coal, as we shall see, was a
key example.

If some of the privatized industries, such as rail, were not noticeably better than their nationalized predecessors, nor were they
noticeably worse. And most were noticeably better.

John Hoskyns: And you think, we had a government that had
been making motorcars! Very bad motorcars! I mean, clearly
this is *ridiculous!* Quite extraordinary. The Post Office—for
the customer, this was the most dramatic change. . . . Our
old state-owned Post Office, it was absolutely ludicrous.
You'll have experienced it yourself, when you were at Balliol. Six months to get a telephone line![24]

CB: I never did get one.

John: And what was your telephone? Your telephone had a dial,
and you could have it in one of three colors! Now that the
war's over, they're not black anymore. You can have a pale
cream one, or even a pale green one!

---

24. Before Thatcher, the state-owned Post Office provided *all* of Britain's
telephone, telecom, and postal services.

Miranda: —and also the queues at the Post Office, they did go on *forever*, you could never get anywhere . . . The customer was at the bottom of the pile.

John: The customer just had to put up with—you know, you're lucky to get a pink telephone.

The withdrawal of state support to nationalized industries accelerated the restructuring of the British economy, hastening its transformation from one based primarily on manufactured goods to one based on services. Thatcher's critics often charge that this transformation was undesirable. This criticism, because so often made, requires a response.

When we talk about manufacturing, we are talking about making things, either manually or with machines. When we talk about services—very crudely—we are talking about everything else, save for the direct sale of natural commodities. Doctors, accountants, lawyers, software designers, hoteliers, theoretical physicists, massage therapists, veterinarians, and journalists, for example, all provide *services*, not manufactured goods. Is an economy based on the supply of services really based on anything? Many people instinctively say no. There's no *there* there, they say. You're not making anything; it's all a chimera.

But there is no special reason to believe this. As economies mature, they experience a predictable transformation in specialization: First they are agricultural, then industrial, then based upon services. This is a pattern that has been seen throughout the world, and there is nothing wrong with it—or if there is, most of the First World is now in worse economic condition than most of the Third World, which is an apagogical argument. Services are real economic goods, and civilization depends upon them. If you possess a comparative advantage in service provision, you are clearly better off providing services. The money I make writing books is no more or less real to me than money I might make by building toasters in my basement. However, given my particular set of competitive advantages, it would be ridiculous for me to try to make a living by building toasters.

Britain led the world in its transformation from an agricultural to a manufacturing economy. It then led the world in the next phase of development. Thatcher never publicly proposed to reduce Britain's manufacturing sector and replace it with a service-based economy. But by forcing uncompetitive industries out of business, her policies dramatically accelerated this transition, and because of this, Britain is now far ahead of its rivals.

Recall Sir Nicholas Henderson, the British ambassador to Paris, who sent a telegram to the foreign office in 1979 remarking that "today we are not only no longer a world power, but we are not in the first rank even as a European one." He included in this missive a table: It showed that Britain's per capita income was 46 percent below West Germany's and 41 percent below France's.

As of today, British per capita income is 6 percent higher than united Germany's and 8 percent higher than France's.[25] Britain is Europe's fastest-growing economy now, and the world's fifth largest. (It was not long ago the fourth, but China is now ahead.) If these trends continue, it will soon overtake Germany, becoming Europe's largest economy for the first time since 1959. This would have been unimaginable in the 1970s.

Britain's economic performance since the Thatcher era has been unusual—strikingly unusual. Given that unemployment has fallen, what you would expect to see, at least if you still relied upon the Phillips Curve to make your predictions, is higher inflation. For

---

25. Per capita income of course is not the only measure of a nation's economic health; it certainly proves nothing about a nation's long-term economic prospects—if it did, Germany would still be at the top of the table. Moreover, it is not entirely reasonable to compare British performance with Germany's, given that during this period West and East Germany were reunited. Even with these reservations, these are impressive statistics.

the past decade, Britain has experienced declining unemployment with stable or falling inflation. The NAIRU has fallen, in other words. It has fallen—there is no other reasonable explanation—because Thatcher's supply-side policies have worked their way through.[26]

How do we know that Thatcher's policies are responsible for this, rather than the policies of her successors? The answer is simple: Her successors continued her policies. The changes Thatcher put in place were not reversed. They have now been embraced by every major political party in Britain. The Labour Party has reinvented itself as champions of free enterprise. "Government," Tony Blair told the World Economic Forum at Davos, in 2000, "should have a role that is enabling . . . above all, promoting competition and removing the barriers to business growth . . . I call it a Third Way . . . Supporting wealth creation. Tackling vested interests. Using market mechanisms."

You can call it a Third Way all you like, but the fact of the matter is, it is Thatcher's way.

The remaining controversy about Thatcher's economic policy, then, is not whether she strengthened Britain's global economic position. She did. It is whether she did it at an unacceptable cost, and whether those costs were the inevitable price of transformation. Those costs—two painful recessions, a massive growth in inequality, and the creation of what seems to be a permanent British underclass—do indeed seem to have been high.

---

26. See, e.g., Stephen Nickell and Glenda Qintini, "The Recent Performance of the UK Labour Market," *Oxford Review of Economic Policy* 18, no. 2 (2002). By their estimates, the NAIRU was roughly 9.5 percent during the 1980s. From 1991 to 1997 it fell to 8.9 percent, and thereafter to 5.7 percent. In "Falling Unemployment: The Dutch and British Cases," *Economic Policy* (April 2000), Nickell and Jan Van Ours argue that the weakening of the unions was the most important reason for the decline of NAIRU, followed by changes to the tax structure and changes in benefits policy.

The top income tax rate dropped from 83 percent when Thatcher came to power (and 98 percent for those with "unearned income") to 40 percent when she left. Indirect taxation, however, in the form of Value Added Tax, rose from 7 percent to 17.5 percent. This predictably led to a growth in income inequality. This was a design feature, not a bug. Thatcher aimed to reward those who created wealth and to punish those who did not. Inequality, in her view, was natural and inevitable. "The pursuit of equality itself is a mirage," she said in 1975, in a speech delivered to American conservatives in New York:

> What's more desirable and more practicable than the pursuit of equality is the pursuit of equality of opportunity. And opportunity means nothing unless it includes the right to be unequal and the freedom to be different. One of the reasons that we value individuals is not because they're all the same, but because they're all different. I believe you have a saying in the Middle West: "Don't cut down the tall poppies. Let them rather grow tall." I would say, let our children grow tall and some taller than others if they have the ability in them to do so. Because we must build a society in which each citizen can develop his full potential, both for his own benefit and for the community as a whole, a society in which originality, skill, energy and thrift are rewarded, in which we encourage rather than restrict the variety and richness of human nature.[27]

Thatcher's tax policies, coupled with the radical shift in the economy from manufacturing to services under her tenure, caused some poppies to grow to gigantesque heights. Other fields were simply mown down. Educated professionals in the financial sector

---

27. Speech to the Institute of Socio-Economic Studies, "Let Our Children Grow Tall," September 15, 1975, BBC transcript, Thatcher MSS (digital collection), doc. 102769.

flourished; factory employees went under. Some of those who had lost their jobs in the manufacturing sector found new jobs in the service sector, but often at lower salaries. Many did not find new jobs at all.

The average real income of British families rose 37 percent from 1979 to 1992. The income of the richest tenth rose 61 percent; the income of the poorest tenth *decreased* by 18 percent. Rates of welfare dependency and child poverty, in particular, soared—as did the crime rate. Although Britain as a whole obviously became more affluent, the poorest fifth profited not one bit from Thatcherism.

This is quite striking. An increase in income inequality is not a priori a bad thing, if the rich become much, much richer and the poor become only somewhat richer. But no economic policy can be reckoned a wholesale success if the poor become *poorer* during a time of massive economic expansion. Certainly, by all means let some children grow taller than others. But under Thatcher, a substantial number grew shorter. That was not the plan.

Margaret Thatcher went beyond the economic claim that free markets are an efficient vehicle for allocating scarce goods and resources. She argued that free markets were morally ennobling. Although Britain is on average a far more prosperous society now, it is not clear to me that it is a more moral one—in fact, the ubiquitous British underclass is a degraded, disgusting spectacle. Anyone who reads the British tabloid press, or walks through the streets of a British city on a Saturday night, knows this full well.

In this sense, Thatcher's critics are right.

_ი ☙ ი_

In 1986, Thatcher's government opened the stock market to foreign and domestic traders, an event known as the Big Bang. British investors were now free to seek the best rates of return abroad, just as foreign investors were now free to invest in Britain. Thus did London become, again, the world's center of finance. In 2002, the United States passed the Sarbanes-Oxley Act, regulating corporate accounting practices. Bankers in the City of London smirk that they would like to erect a solid gold statue in honor of the legislators who sponsored the act, for their efforts may well have diminished the likelihood of another Enron scandal in America—it is hard to say—but also, certainly, resulted in shifting a massive proportion of the mergers and acquisition boom to Britain.

While I was in London recently, I stayed with one of these bankers, an old friend of mine. He asked me to withhold his name—his company allows him to say nothing about these things on the record—so I'll call him Harry. I'll call his flat mate, a London restaurateur, William. They are typical children of the Thatcher Revolution, both prospering in sectors that are thriving now because of her policies.

Harry and William share a spacious flat in a newly gentrified neighborhood of London. It is conspicuously expensive and in the manner of all bachelor pads conspicuously uncivilized: Ineliminable red wine stains subtly impregnate the luxuriant meringue of the wall-to-wall carpet; the cupboards are fully stocked with drink-mixers involving Rwandan fever-tree quinine, but the kitchen is empty of anything edible. That weekend, Harry was nursing not a broken heart, precisely, but a mildly indignant one. The woman he had been dating had just dumped him, telling him that she wanted someone who made still *more* money: "That's what all women want, deep down," she had apparently said to him.

We opened a bottle of champagne before going out to dinner, and when the subject of Thatcher came up, I switched on my recorder.

Harry: Why has London become the world financial center? . . . through a combination of multiculturalism, the ability to suck up the most talented from all over the world, and I think it's worked also because of light-touch regulation. I mean, you just have to look at Sarbanes-Oxley in the States, and all the business that's put London's way. . . . The miners' strike's interesting because of its wider significance in the battle against trade unionism, and actually, the freeing up of the economy, and I think that's been thrown sharply into relief by things like France, and Germany, and thirty-five-hour weeks—

William: Yeah, that's madness—

Harry: And you have Sarkozy. And what, you know, he does speak to—it's funny, because they interview people and they say, "Well, what do you think we need, Sarkozy or Royal," and most people say, "We need Thatcher!"

William: —the journalists in France have been saying that for years!

Harry: Yeah, and so they need someone with the balls to do it. . . . But actually I think what is more interesting is the Falklands, you know . . . America, America sat on the fence for long periods . . . it had, you know, it was very much the kind of classic State Department, Defense Department, had a very . . . you know, was it . . . Fritz . . . Patrick, was it Fitzpatrick who was the—

CB: Kirkpatrick. Jeanne Kirkpatrick.

Harry: Kirkpatrick, yeah—

CB: —who was described by Alan Clark as "that Anglophobe harridan"—

Harry: Yeah! Exactly! Utter, *utter* Irish bitch, basically, who was causing us all kinds of issues. Anyway, focusing too much on the economic and the analytic arguments, I think, is a bore.

William: [*bored*] Yeah.

CB: Well, we'll have plenty of time to talk about it, but first we should open that bottle of—

The transcript indicates that we did not, in fact, return to the subject, or if we did, I never turned the recorder back on.

It is not hard to see why unemployed former coal miners who are still living in poverty would fail to see the lifestyle of these two men as evidence that Thatcher created a better world. Now, you know where I stand on Thatcher—I am not saying that I agree with them. I am just saying that if you want to know why they still hate her, look no further.

Was there an alternative? Many people still think there was. Neil Kinnock thinks so, of course.

Neil Kinnock: I mean, the thing is, people say, "Ah, she got the trade unions reformed; she got the restoration of industrial order." What she got was *massive* unemployment, so everybody is scared shitless! I mean—

CB: Yeah, but that forced restructuring, the moving of manufacturing into—

NK: No, no! That was a bloody *disaster!* I mean, there had to be a restructuring, there had to be a shift in the direction of high-tech, and services, and so on, of course there did. And it didn't come from nowhere, either—that expertise was there in substantial part already. But there could have been a different pace, and simultaneously with a reduction—which was necessary—of traditional manufacturing, an *intensive* development of high-tech industry. I mean, if Sweden could, in twenty-five years, turn from a smokestack country into a high-tech country, do it without unemployment ever going above 6.4 percent, and be the most prosperous country in the world—we coulda done that in maybe the same amount, maybe a shorter time, without the devastation of communities and peoples' *lives*, and the destruction of industries, in the way that it happened! But of course they didn't *plan* it. They made the omelet by breaking the eggs on the wall. That's not the most sensible way to break the eggs.

CB: Analogies to Sweden are always unconvincing, because Sweden has—

NK: Hold on, hold on! If you look at Sweden in, say, the mid-'70s, this was an economy with a more outdated industrial employment structure than we had then, even. I mean, this was a *rustbucket* economy. And it got turned around, they spent the same proportion of their GNP on unemployment as we did in the Thatcher years, except that three-quarters of that expenditure went on training and retraining, and the rest went on unemployment benefits, and the proportions were exactly the reverse in the United Kingdom. That was the difference—

CB: Why was there such a reluctance to spend on training and retraining among the Conservatives? Was it just an objection to spending the money, or was it a sense that—

NK: No, they didn't feel that transition in the economy could or should be organized. So they didn't do it.

CB: Right. It was a philosophical problem with *planning* an economy—

NK: Sure. Whereas, when we used to go around saying that we could get unemployment down, and it would require generating X amount of expenditure in the economy, etc., etc., etc., we'd get absolutely bloody hammered by the classicals—

CB: You'd get hammered by who?

NK: By, you know, the classical supporters of the Conservative philosophy . . . Anyway, you know, it depends on what you think a country should be run for, and how you think it should be run. The great thing about the kind of boiled-down Friedmanism that they had is that they didn't think the country *should* be run. Or certainly, the economy. They felt that it should be left to the magic of the market. She said to me, in Prime Minister's Questions, you may have heard the phrase, "You can't buck the market." And this is an incantation, this is—a religious *conviction*, almost, which is bloody *ridiculous!* I mean, there's no serious economist in the world who would offer that as a kind of a *chant* in an economic church—

CB: No, there are *plenty* of serious economists who would say that the best economic strategy is to have as little state planning as is consistent with providing basic public necessities—

NK: Mmmm. Are they the same ones that defend maintaining the biggest defense budget in the world?

CB: Yeah, they are. And for good reason!

NK: [*Laughter*] There you are! They all believe in [*unintelligible*] capitalism, luv. They all believe the bloody system couldn't run by itself!

CB: They all believe in what?

NK: They all believe the system couldn't run by itself—

CB: No, you said something before "capitalism"—

NK: Tension o' capitalism.

CB: The basic tension of capitalism?

NK: No, no, [*unintelligible*]. The kind o' capitalism that, you know, is freebooting, and minimum interference and all the rest of it, but when it gets into difficulty, there's a stretcher—

CB: But that sort of conservative *does* always say, "Yes, there are certain things the state has to provide, and must provide well." Defense, security. But that's where they draw the line. And they say, "The state should *not* provide job retraining, or health care; that's best dealt with by markets." And it's not ideologically inconsistent; it's spelled out—there are certain things that the market can't do—

NK: Well, the trouble with economic models is that the people who make them never live in them. It's a little bit like those office boxes built by architects who are never gonna work in 'em.

Kinnock, as you can see, wouldn't let me interrupt him. But in the end I have the final word. In his view, and he is perfectly clear about this, the alternative to Thatcher was a planned economy.

And the evidence he offers that such an economy can create anything other than a human hell is Sweden. Let me finish the sentence he wouldn't let me finish. Socialists love analogies to Sweden. But they are always unconvincing because they are based on some *fantasy* Sweden, rather than on an actual Nordic country bordered by Norway and Finland. In this Sweden of lore, every single woman is also eighteen years old, blonde, busty, lonely, naked, and waiting for you in the sauna. Kinnock is simply mistaken about Swedish unemployment statistics. In the early 1990s, Swedish unemployment rose to 13 percent, higher than ever experienced in Britain after Thatcher came to power. In the period Kinnock is discussing, Sweden in fact experienced a precipitous *slide* in the prosperity league—from fourth place in 1970 to sixteenth place in 1998.[28] In fact, the policies Kinnock admires nearly ran Sweden into the ground. Only when they were abandoned did the Swedish economy begin to recover. You may as well argue that the command economy has been a splendid success in Narnia.

Over and over again, Thatcher's critics told me that yes, Britain's economic transition was inevitable, but "she didn't plan for it." No, she didn't. That is precisely the point. If the government plans the economy, it is no longer free. And if it is not free, the transitions that do occur tend to lengthen the lines for bread.

So the question remains: Were the costs of the Thatcher Revolution inevitable? Was this the price Britain had to pay as a kind of entrance fee to a true market economy? I'm afraid most of them probably were. The blow of the first years would have been softened had her first governments been more deft in their monetary targeting, but the bulk of the permanent dislocation can't be attributed to this. For the most part, those whose standard of living declined as a result of Thatcher's reforms became poorer because they had previously been the beneficiaries of state support, either

---

28. See, e.g., Urban Bäckström, "The Swedish Economy," Svenska Handelsbanken's Seminar, New York, October 7, 1998, and "Swedish Economic History: Structural Problems and Reforms," *Ekonomifakta* (2008).

in the direct form of welfare payments or the indirect form of state intervention to prop up fossilized and uncompetitive industries.

Had this system of economic redistribution been sustainable, the argument could be made that it was more humane than the one that replaced it and, therefore, that it should have been sustained. But it was not sustainable: Britain was experiencing slow but steady relative decline. Relative decline, over time, tends to become absolute decline, followed by collapse—a pattern commonly observed in command economies.

Britain is now the world's second-largest producer and exporter of services. What remains of its manufacturing sector is highly competitive. In the period since Thatcher came to power, countries such as China have liberalized their economies and transformed themselves into manufacturing superpowers. It is simply not credible to imagine that Britain could have survived as a major manufacturing power in the face of that kind of competition. Attempts indefinitely to prop up Britain's uncompetitive manufacturing sector were doomed to progressively greater failure.

In Thatcher's defense, let this be said: The transition from a command to a market economy tends everywhere to be brutal. For evidence of this claim, look at Russia. The moral responsibility for this is not with those who seek to return freedom to the markets; it is with those who thought it would be a splendid idea to eliminate it in the first place. The alternative to this brutal transition was—*and could only have been*—maintaining a command economy.

And this was no alternative at all.

6

For Strategic Sheep Purposes

*It is wonderful with what coolness and indiffer-
ence the greater part of mankind see war commenced. Those that hear of it at a distance, or
read of it in books, but have never presented its
evils to their minds, consider it as little more than
a splendid game, a proclamation, an army, a battle, and a triumph.*
— DR. JOHNSON, ARGUING AGAINST SQUANDERING
BRITISH LIFE IN THE FALKLANDS, 1771

BRITAIN 6 *(Georgia, two airstrips, three warplanes)*,
ARGENTINA 0
— *The Sun,* 1982

The Falklands—known to Argentineans as the Malvinas—are a
desolate chain of islands in the South Atlantic some 300 miles east
of the Straits of Magellan. Variously disputed by the major colonial powers until 1816, they were claimed by Argentina upon its
independence from Spain, then reclaimed by the British in 1833,

when a British naval force evicted the Argentineans. They were thereafter uninterruptedly settled and inhabited by the British, but certainly in no large numbers: In 1982, the Falklands were home to some 1,820 British subjects, 600,000 sheep, and five species of penguins. The islands were of no geostrategic significance: no arable land, no warm-water ports, no strategic raw materials, no multinational fruit conglomerates, nothing—just sheep and penguins.

For 150 years, the question of sovereignty over the Falklands had been one of those endless, low-level diplomatic conflicts of scant interest to anyone. Only weeks before the outbreak of hostilities, British and Argentinean delegates were negotiating placidly in New York and reporting their discussions to be of "cordial and positive spirit." It is doubtful that at the time the conflict erupted, even one in ten Britons could have located the islands on a map. Britain achieved nothing, materially, by recapturing them. The Falklands victory was of moral and psychological import alone. This is not to diminish the moral and the psychological in history. Without this victory, it is unlikely that the Thatcher Revolution could have occurred—and without the Thatcher Revolution, Thatcher would not matter.

The significance of the Falklands War, Thatcher later wrote,

> was enormous, both for Britain's self-confidence and for our standing in the world. Since the Suez fiasco in 1956, British foreign policy had been one long retreat. The tacit assumption made by British and foreign governments alike was that our world role was doomed steadily to diminish. We had come to be seen by both friends and enemies as a nation which lacked the will and the capability to defend its interests in peace, let alone in war. Victory in the Falklands changed that. Everywhere I went after the war, Britain's name meant something more than it had. The war also had real importance in relations between East and West: years later I was told by a Russian general that the Soviets had been firmly convinced that we would not fight for the Falklands, and that

if we did fight we would lose. We proved them wrong on
both counts, and they did not forget the fact.[1]

Certainly, Thatcher is correct to assert that Britain had come to
be perceived as a nation lacking the will to defend its interests by
force. The seizure of the Falklands is ample proof of this. To invade
the sovereign territory of a nuclear power requires considerable
confidence that your adversary has been psychologically neutered.
Had those islands been claimed by the Soviet Union and continu-
ously inhabited for 150 years by patriotic Russians, no Argentinean
general, however fine he may have believed his nation's moral
claim, would have dreamt of laying a hand upon them. It is no accident that the Japanese never asserted by force their claim to the
Kuril Islands, which were in fact seized in 1945 by the Soviet
Union and remain to this day in Russian hands.

That the low-simmering Falklands dispute became candescent
offers a pointed lesson about the importance of unambiguous sig-
naling as a deterrent to war. Prior to the invasion, the British government appeared to be telegraphing a certain indifference to the
islands' fate. In 1981, facing the severe budgetary constraints imposed by Thatcher's insistence upon reducing public sector spending, Defense Minister John Nott recommended the withdrawal
from the area of the Antarctic supply vessel *Endurance*, the symbol
of Britain's commitment to the South Atlantic. Judging a massive
conventional naval conflict unlikely in the coming decades, he also
proposed—with Thatcher's approval—to scrap an aircraft carrier as
well as two assault ships, and to reduce by one-third the number of
British frigates and destroyers. In the same year, Parliament passed
the British Nationality Act, which denied the islanders British citi-
zenship. The measure was directed at another set of islanders who
would have preferred to stay British, those of Hong Kong. The un-
intended consequence of the act's passage, however, was to suggest

---

1. Thatcher, *The Downing Street Years*, pp. 173–174.

that Britain was no more willing to go to war with Argentina than with China. It is fair to fault the Thatcher government for giving signals to the Argentineans that hinted of irresolution—although it is also fair to note, as Thatcher does, that no one expected them to do something quite so crazy. "Of course with the benefit of hindsight, we would always like to have acted differently," she remarks. "So would the Argentineans."[2]

If Thatcher's domestic political problems in the spring of 1982 were considerable, General Leopoldo Galtieri's were still worse. The Argentine junta, which since seizing power in a 1976 coup had presided over the disappearance of 30,000 of its citizens, faced a tempest in its tinpot: The nation was experiencing hyperinflation; in Buenos Aires, the largest anti-government demonstrations since the coup had prompted a crackdown. It is not surprising that under these circumstances Galtieri noted with fascination what appeared to be signals of a deteriorating British commitment to the Falklands. Nor is it surprising that he gambled that Britain would not respond militarily should he take the islands by force. He assumed this would lend him a magnificent propaganda coup with which to buttress his flagging political fortunes. So certain was he of this outcome that his military made no special plans to repel a British counterattack. Events, however, ran away with him, as events so often do. The invasion proved wildly popular in Argentina, so much so that when Thatcher proved dishearteningly *cojonuda* about keeping them, he could no longer retreat.

_◦ ◦ ◦_

On March 19, 1982, a group of Argentine scrap metal merchants landed without permission on South Georgia, a dependent island to the southeast of the Falklands, and raised the Argentinean flag.

---

2. Ibid., p. 179.

The offending flag was spotted by a British Antarctic Survey team. Having learned of the incident, Thatcher ordered the *Endurance*, with twenty-two marines on board, to sail to South Georgia to remove the scrap metal merchants. The Argentines sent one hundred troops to defend them. Outnumbered, the British forces held fire, watching the Argentines warily. Thatcher was unnerved by this turn of events but decided it was an "awkward incident," rather than a "precursor to conflict."[3]

She was wrong. On March 30, she received word that the Argentine fleet was steaming toward Stanley, the capital of the Falklands.

> I shall not forget that Wednesday evening. I was working in my room at the House of Commons when I was told that John Nott wanted an immediate meeting to discuss the Falklands. I called people together . . . John was alarmed. He had just received intelligence that the Argentinean Fleet, already at sea, looked as if they were going to invade the islands on Friday 2 April. There was no ground to question the intelligence. John gave the MoD's view that the Falklands could not be retaken once they were seized. This was terrible, and totally unacceptable. I could not believe it: these were our people, our islands. I said instantly: "if they are invaded, we have got to get them back."[4]

The official defeatism of the Ministry of Defense, Thatcher writes, was contradicted by the lone voice of the chief of the naval staff, Sir Henry Leach, who told Thatcher in the same meeting that he could have a task force ready to sail within forty-eight hours. "He believed such a force could retake the islands. All he needed was my authority to begin to assemble it. I gave it him, and he left immediately to set the work in hand."[5]

---

3. Ibid., p. 178.
4. Ibid., p. 179.
5. Ibid., p. 179.

It is not surprising that the prime minister ordered him to assemble the task force. Of course she wished to keep every option open. What is surprising is that she used it. The pessimistic view offered by the Ministry of Defense was grounded in a cold reality: The British navy in the early 1980s was not prepared for a major naval battle in the South Atlantic. It was designed to fight, in concert with NATO, against the Soviet Union in the North Atlantic. It was chiefly an anti-submarine force, ill-equipped for conventional surface warfare or amphibious landings. The British would be fighting with minimal air cover and no missile defense shield. The Argentinean navy, on the other hand, was the best in South America. It had for years been preparing for just this kind of battle with Brazil or Chile. The Argentineans enjoyed a tremendous superiority in aircraft and a three-to-one advantage in ground troops. They could sortie land-based aircraft armed with French Exocet missiles. And they did not have to sail 8,000 miles to reach the combat zone.

The British were perfectly right to declare the invasion an outrage. The basis of the Argentinean claim to the islands was geographic proximity. Since every nation is proximate to another, this is a principle that, if broadly applied, would lead immediately to international anarchy. The British could appeal to a point of much greater relevance, both morally and in international law: The Falkland Islanders did not want to be Argentineans, and this was no mere point of ethnic pride, for the Argentinean regime had an unenviable reputation for throwing dissenters from airplanes into shark-infested waters.

However valid the British case, it is easy to understand why prudent minds in the British government hesitated. If it was humiliating to see the Falklands seized by force, losing a war to Argentina would have been vastly more humiliating. Losing a war to Argentina was a very real possibility.

On April 2, as predicted, the Argentinean task force overran the Falklands. After a brief firefight, the symbolic garrison of eighty British marines surrendered. Photographs of the marines, facedown on the ground, appeared later that day in the British press.

The Argentinean troops reportedly were taken aback to discover that the islanders spoke English and did not welcome them as liberators, but the invaders adjusted quickly to the paradigm shift. Using language that appears to have been inspired by the novels of Graham Greene, they proceeded to issue a series of minatory communiqués to the islanders:

COMMUNIQUÉ NO. 1
Malvinas Operation Theatre Command
The Commander of the Malvinas Operation Theatre, performing his duties as ordered by the Argentine Government, materializes heretofore the historic continuity of Argentine Sovereignty over the Islas Malvinas.

At this highly important moment for all of us, it is my pleasure to greet the people of the Malvinas and exhort you to cooperate with the new authorities by complying with all of the instructions that will be given through oral and written communiqués, in order to facilitate the normal life of the entire population.

Islas Malvinas 02 Abril 1982 OSVALDO JORGE GARCIA General de Division Comandante del Teatro de Operaciones MALVINAS

COMMUNIQUÉ NO. 3
Instructions for the Population
As a consequence of all the necessary actions taken, and in order to ensure the safety of the population, all people are to remain at their homes until further notice. New instructions will be issued. The population must bear in mind that, in order to ensure the fulfillment of these instructions, military troops shall arrest all people found outside their homes.

To avoid inconvenience and personal misfortunes, people are to abide by the following:

1. Should some serious problem arise and people wish to make it known to the Military Authorities, a white piece of cloth is to be placed outside the door. Military patrols will visit the house so as to be informed and provide a solution.

2. All schools, shops, stores, banks, pubs and Clubs are to remain closed until further notice.

3. All infringements shall be treated according to what is stated in Communiqué (Edict) No. 1.

4. All further instructions shall be released through the local broadcasting station which shall remain in permanent operation.[6]

Some liberation.

On the following day, for the first time since the 1956 Suez crisis, the House of Commons was recalled for a special Saturday sitting. Thatcher addressed a furious, jeering Parliament. The fury was not only with Argentina, but with the prime minister for having failed to deter the attack.

It is worth listening to Thatcher's speech and her response to the ensuing hostile interrogatory, a session she subsequently described as the most difficult of her career. Manuals on self-defense often suggest that if an adversary's face is red, he poses no immediate threat; a white face, on the other hand, implies that blood has been diverted to the muscles, so watch out: Violence is imminent. If ever a voice can be described as white-faced, it was Thatcher's on that day.[7] This is a voice of cold, controlled, and genuine fury.

---

6. John Smith, *74 Days: An Islander's Diary of the Falklands Occupation* (Century, 1984).

7. You may listen to this speech here: www.margaretthatcher.org/archive/displaydocument.asp?docid=110946.

Prime Minister: The House meets this Saturday to respond to a situation of great gravity. We are here because, for the first time for many years, British sovereign territory has been invaded by a foreign power. After several days of rising tension in our relations with Argentina, that country's armed forces attacked the Falkland Islands yesterday and established military control of the islands.

Yesterday was a day of rumor and counter-rumor. Throughout the day we had no communication from the Government of the Falklands. Indeed, the last message that we received was at 21:55 hours on Thursday night, 1 April. Yesterday morning at 8:33 a.m. we sent a telegram—

Here the House erupts in howls, followed by cries of "order." Thatcher allows the House to spend itself, then continues.

I shall refer to that again in a moment. By late afternoon yesterday it became clear that an Argentine invasion had taken place and that the lawful British Government of the islands had been usurped.

Mr. Speaker, I am sure that the whole House will join me in condemning totally this unprovoked aggression by the Government of Argentina against British territory.

A loud rumbling of "hear, hear." The mood of the house is changing swiftly as Thatcher harnesses the anger toward her and directs it toward Argentina.

It has not a shred of justification and not a scrap of legality.

She concludes her speech thus:

The people of the Falkland Islands, like the people of the United Kingdom, are an island race. Their way of life is British; their allegiance is to the Crown. They are few in

number, but they have the right to live in peace, to choose
their own way of life and to determine their own allegiance.
It is the wish of the British people and the duty of Her
Majesty's Government to do everything that we can to up-
hold that right. That will be our hope and our endeavor and,
I believe, the resolve of every member of the House.

It is not only with hindsight that a listener would conclude that
Thatcher meant what she said. There is no trace of posturing or
womanish hysteria in her voice. Some years later, François Mitterrand's psychotherapist published a scandalous memoir claiming
that Mitterrand had confessed to him, on the couch, that
Thatcher had threatened to use atomic weapons against Argentina if the French failed to supply Britain with the codes to
deactivate Argentina's anti-ship missiles. Supposedly, Mitterrand
said, "To provoke a nuclear war for small islands inhabited by
three sheep who are as hairy as they are frozen! Fortunately I
yielded. Otherwise, I assure you, the metallic index finger of the
lady would press the button."[8] Did she really say this? Did he? I
assume not: This doesn't have the ring of real speech, and I don't
for a moment believe that Mitterrand discussed these things with
his psychotherapist. Nonetheless, if you listen to her voice on that
day, you can easily imagine her not only threatening to push the
button, but pushing it.

—◌ ◌—

That day, after a feverish round of lobbying, British diplomats
persuaded the UN Security Council to pass Resolution 502, calling for the immediate withdrawal of Argentine troops. Thatcher
and her cabinet decided to dispatch the task force. Again, this was

---

8. Ali Magoudi, *Rendez-vous: The Psychoanalysis of Francois Mitterrand,*
translated and reported in "The Sphinx and the Curious Case of the Iron
Lady's H-bomb," (London) *Times,* November 20, 2005.

an obvious decision, if only to strengthen the British negotiating position, and again, the surprise is not that it was sent, but that it was used.

Over the next several days, the aircraft carriers *Hermes* and *Invincible* set sail, followed by amphibious ships, specialist vessels, and some fifty ships requisitioned from the commercial fleet, as well as two rapidly refurbished cruise ships, including the *Queen Elizabeth 2*. The luxury ocean liner famed for its crisp white linens, sparkling crystal, and impeccable but unobtrusive service was swiftly refitted with three helicopter pads. Its lounges were transformed into dormitories and its carpets covered in hardboard.

In total, 110 ships carrying 28,000 men sailed south—all in a matter of days.

Interviewer: Mrs. Thatcher, you've stated your objective very clearly, you've staked your colors to the mast and you are determined to free the Falklands, if you fail would you feel obliged to resign?

Mrs. Thatcher: I am not talking about failure, I am talking about my supreme confidence in the British fleet . . . superlative ships, excellent equipment, the most highly trained professional group of men, the most honorable and brave members of her Majesty's service. Failure? Do you remember what Queen Victoria once said? "Failure—the possibilities do not exist."[9]

Some of the ships were superlative and some of the equipment excellent, to be sure. But when you are obliged to commandeer the QE2 to supplement your fleet, you are most of all talking about "supreme confidence." A violent winter was arriving in the southern hemisphere, with sixty-foot swells and Antarctic gales.

---

9. TV interview for ITN, April 5, 1982, transcript, Thatcher MSS (digital collection), doc. 104913.

The Argentineans were piling men and materiel into the Falklands. Many have suggested that if Thatcher had had any military experience at all, she would not have been so confident.

But she hadn't.

Her Foreign Office was seized with the vapors, warning of a backlash against British citizens in Argentina, the ire of Britain's allies, the risk of Soviet involvement, charges of colonialism. "All the considerations were fair enough," she later wrote.

> But when you are at war you cannot allow the difficulties to dominate your thinking: you have to set out with an iron will to overcome them. And anyway what was the alternative? That a common or garden dictator should rule over the Queen's subjects and prevail by fraud and violence? Not while I was Prime Minister.[10]

This passage would sound vain and boastful were she not describing precisely what transpired.

None of her other problems had meanwhile disappeared. On April 8, this interchange was recorded in the House of Commons:

Mr. Cunliffe: What Easter message can the right hon. Lady give the three million unemployed in this country? How does she suggest that they share the joys of Easter in the unprecedented atmosphere of despair and hopelessness in which they find themselves? In addition, is it not a scandalous indictment that for thousands of Easter school leavers their first job will be to sign on at an employment exchange? Does the right hon. Lady not feel that that is a scandalous state of affairs and that she must bear some responsibility for this shameless episode? Does she still believe and insist that life is better under the Conservatives?

---

10. Thatcher, *The Downing Street Years,* p. 181.

The Prime Minister: The best hope for future job prospects is to continue to try to reduce inflation.[11]

Failure in the Falklands would have been the end of Thatcher, Thatcherism, and the rollback of socialism in Britain. Her confidence under these inauspicious circumstances was, surely, a miracle of Providence. Leaders who become legend almost always display this strain of preternatural confidence. In all of history, the number of women who have both possessed it and achieved the power to exercise it may be counted on one hand.

The United States initiated a frantic round of shuttle diplomacy. On April 8, Thatcher received Secretary of State Alexander Haig and his entourage at Downing Street. Thatcher opened by showing him her portraits of Nelson and Wellington, then steamrollered the nervous, chain-smoking Haig, rejecting entirely his proposal to establish an interim authority in the archipelago under multilateral supervision. It was out of the question, she told him, instantly likening the idea to the appeasement of Hitler. The scene is wonderfully described by the American diplomat James Rentschler:

> La Thatcher is really quite fetching in a dark velvet two-piece ensemble with gros-grain piping and a soft hairdo that heightens her blond English coloring . . . Dinner in the cramped, wood-paneled private dining-room is a very pleasant affair of overcooked British beef and quippy conversation, at least until coffee, when the PM gets down to the nut-cutter nitty-gritty. Thatcher, you see, just ain't buying our "suggestion" for a diplomatic approach to the crisis . . .

---

11. April 8, 1982, House of Commons PQs, Hansard HC [21/1083–88].

High color is in her cheeks, a note of rising indignation in her voice, she leans across the polished table and flatly rejects what she calls the "woolliness" of our second-stage formulation, conceived in our view as a traditional face-saving ploy for Galtieri: "I am pledged before the House of Commons, the Defense Minister is pledged, the Foreign Secretary is pledged to restore British administration. I did not dispatch a fleet to install some nebulous arrangement which would have no authority whatsoever. Interim authority!—to do *what?* I beg you, I beg you to remember that in 1938 Neville Chamberlain sat at this same table discussing an arrangement which sounds very much like the one you are asking me to accept; and were I to do so, I would be censured in the House of Commons—and properly so! We in Britain simply refuse to reward aggression—that is the lesson we have learned from 1938."

"Tough lady," concludes Rentschler with some understatement.[12]

The prime minister concluded the evening on an arch note. "I do hope you realize how much we appreciate and are thankful for your presence here," she said, "and how the kind of candor we have displayed could only be possible among the closest of friends. With everyone else we're merely *nice!*"[13]

Haig and his entourage returned the next day to Argentina, where vast, chanting crowds had assembled in the Plaza de Mayo. "AR-GEN-TIN-A! AR-GEN-TIN-A! THATCHER PUTA! GUERRA! GUERRA!" Rentschler, observing this scene, despaired of Galtieri's position. "Given the pitch of jingoistic sentiment whipped up hereabouts," he wrote, "I can't possibly see how he's going to walk this cat back."[14]

---

12. James Rentschler's Falklands Diary, April 8, 1982, Thatcher MSS (digital collection), www.margaretthatcher.org/archive/arcdocs/Rentschler PDF.pdf.
13. Ibid.
14. Ibid.

Haig delivered the news to Galtieri: Thatcher was intransigent. Galtieri, suspecting for the first time that he had liberated a genie he could not master, played the obvious card. He threatened to turn to the Soviet Union for assistance. Haig sent a cable to President Ronald Reagan from Buenos Aires:

> Galtieri, face-to-face with the prospect of war, leveled with me. He said he could not withdraw both his military and administrative presence and last a week. If the British attacked, he explained, he would have to accept the offer of full support made by the Cuban Ambassador, who just returned after more than a year's absence. The Cubans implied they were speaking for the Russians, and even insinuated that the Soviets had offered to sink the British carrier (with Prince Andrew aboard), leaving the British and the world to believe an Argentine sub had done it. I doubt that such an offer was actually made by the Soviets, but we cannot discount it altogether.[15]

Haig added that the time for Reagan to intervene personally with Thatcher was at hand. "Good luck, Al," Rentschler remarked dubiously to his diary.

The American entourage flew back to London, where Haig relayed the Argentine hard line. Thatcher's home secretary, Willie Whitelaw, chewed his nails with anxiety. A wintry gust of air, Rentschler noted, blew through the room from an open window as Thatcher stared fixedly down the table:

> "I am afraid that this news fully reinforces the correctness of the course on which we are now embarked," sez she—"the fleet must steam inexorably on" . . . the Iron Maiden is really toughening up her already robust talk, especially on

---

15. Ibid., April 11.

the question of the fleet standing off: "Unthinkable, that is
our only leverage, I cannot possibly give it up at this point,
one simply doesn't trust burglars who have tried once to
steal your property! No, Al, no, absolutely not, the fleet
must steam on!"[16]

And the fleet steamed on.

⟋◦ ⟨≋⟩ ◦⟍

The war that ensued was the largest and longest naval battle since
the great Pacific campaign in the Second World War, and one of
the most logistically complex in history. The British fought with
an 8,000-mile logistics pipeline in a combat arena 4,000 miles
from their nearest air base on Ascension Island, halfway between
South America and Africa. It was not a walkover. In the words of
the commander of the task force, Admiral Sir John Woodward, "It
was a lot closer run than many would care to believe. We were on
our last legs. If they had been able to hold on another week it
might have been a different story."[17]

On April 12, as British submarines arrived in the Falklands,
Britain pronounced a 200-mile exclusion zone around the islands,
declaring that Argentine forces found in the zone would be subject to destruction. The main task force departed from Ascension
Island on April 17. British nationals were advised to leave Argentina. A despondent Haig abandoned his shuttle diplomacy.

On April 23, a small British commando force attempted to
land on a glacier in South Georgia. High winds and heavy snow
forced them to abort. A second attempt resulted in two helicopter crashes. When Thatcher was apprised of this news, it was not
yet known if the crews had survived. Not long afterward,
Thatcher was informed that all had been daringly rescued, but

16. Ibid., April 12.
17. "Falklands Victory 'A Close Run Thing,'" *Guardian*, April 3, 2002.

she allows in her memoirs that for a moment, she gave in to despair, wondering "whether the task we had set ourselves was truly impossible."[18]

Her moment of doubt did not last long. On April 25, the commando force retook South Georgia.

INVASION!

The Sun, *reporting the British*
recapture of South Georgia

Thatcher and her defense secretary, John Nott, delivered the news to the press. The conference may be viewed on YouTube.[19] As Nott reads the prepared statement, Thatcher flushes with obvious pride and, one assumes, overwhelming relief, although one would not know from her face that she had ever suffered a moment's anxiety. Nott, in his horn-rimmed glasses and slightly overlarge suit, looks slouched and haggard; it is clear that he is suffering from the strain. Thatcher, impeccable in a navy ensemble and pearls, is ramrod straight, her chest thrust out, glowing, her hair stiff and shining like a bronze carapace. When Nott reaches the words "So far, no British casualties have been reported," her lips curl into a slight, triumphant smile, which she quickly suppresses in favor of a more dignified expression. Nott then reads the text of the cable reporting the recapture: "Be pleased to inform Her Majesty that the White Ensign flies alongside the Union Jack in South Georgia. God Save the Queen." Thatcher cannot contain herself. She beams. Dimples appear in her cheeks.

Thatcher's enjoyment of the moment is spoiled when reporters seem more concerned with Britain's next step than delighted by the news. A journalist quite reasonably asks, "What happens next?"

"Just *rejoice—at—that—news,*" she booms, her voice resonating from the chest, the force of her indignation causing both her defense

---

18. Thatcher, *The Downing Street Years,* p. 204.
19. www.youtube.com/watch?v=rGxsLbK9F0A.

minister and the assembled reporters to step back as if blown by a sharp wind. "And *congratulate* our armed forces and the marines."

A small voice is audible over the clicking of the flash bulbs. "Are we going to declare war on Argentina, Mrs. Thatcher?"

"*Rejoice!*" she repeats, and flounces off.

On April 30, Reagan announced America's support for Britain. On May 1, British forces landed on West and East Falkland, and the naval bombardment of Port Stanley began. British Vulcans— after a flight that required five mid-air refuelings—bombed the runway of Port Stanley airport.

A PUNCH UP YOUR JUNTA!
Sunday People, *reporting raids on Port Stanley*

The Argentines claimed to have shot down British airplanes. When the war cabinet met on the following day, it was advised that an Argentinean cruiser, the *General Belgrano*, was sailing on the edge of the exclusion zone. It was believed to be armed with Exocet missiles. "It was clear to me what must be done to protect our forces," Thatcher recalls.[20] On May 2, the *Conqueror* sunk the *Belgrano*, with the loss of 323 lives, leading the Argentines to order their ships back to port for the duration of the conflict.

GOTCHA!
The Sun, *reporting the sinking of the* Belgrano

It was and remains the only ship ever to have been sunk by a nuclear-powered submarine. Subsequently, the commander of the *Conqueror*, Chris Wreford-Brown, stoically remarked of the event that "the Royal Navy spent thirteen years preparing me for such an occasion. It would have been regarded as extremely dreary if I had fouled it up."

---

20. Thatcher, *The Downing Street Years*, p. 214.

The loss of life shocked opponents of the war out of their torpor, domestically and abroad. Thatcher now came under intense diplomatic pressure to accept a peace plan proposed by the president of Peru and endorsed by Al Haig. But on May 4, an Exocet missile hit the British destroyer *Sheffield* in waters southeast of the Falklands, killing twenty and severely wounding twenty-four more. It sank several hours later. It was the first Royal Navy ship lost in action since 1945. There was no chance, after this, that anything short of complete Argentine surrender could be sold to the British public, not that Thatcher had ever considered such a thing.

STICK IT UP YOUR JUNTA!
The Sun, *urging rejection*
of the Peruvian peace proposal

Three days later, the Argentines bombed the destroyer *Coventry*, which sank with the loss of nineteen of its crew. The *Atlantic Conveyor* was sunk by an Exocet, killing twelve. Thatcher's cabinet ordered the assault to continue. "Steadily but surely we are gaining ground," she assured her countrymen. "Our men and ships are there also that others may mark and learn that land they take by force they shall not hold."[21]

On May 21, under cover of darkness, British paratroopers and marines landed on the western coast of East Falkland. On May 26, British paratroopers headed south from East Falkland to mount a surprise attack on Darwin and Goose Green. The BBC World Service announced, prior to the action, that a British parachute battalion was poised to take Goose Green, destroying the element of surprise. The commander of the battalion ordered his men to attack nonetheless. Outnumbered three to one, they won the battle, although the commander was killed in action. The residents of

---

21. Speech to the Scottish Conservative Party Conference, May 14, 1982, transcript, Thatcher MSS (digital collection), doc. 104936.

Goose Green, who had been imprisoned by the Argentines, were released.

KILL AN ARGIE AND WIN A METRO
—Private Eye

Reagan feared the destabilization of the whole region, leaving it vulnerable to communist opportunism. He tried in vain to persuade Thatcher to embrace a settlement. She could now claim military victory, he told her; her honor had been restored. She scorched the phone lines in response to the suggestion. "Just supposing Alaska was invaded," said Thatcher. "Now you've put all your people up there to retake it and someone suggested that a contact could come in. You wouldn't do it."

"No, no, although, Margaret, I have to say I don't quite think Alaska is a similar situation—"

"More or less so. I didn't lose some of my best ships and some of my finest lives to leave quietly under a ceasefire without the Argentines withdrawing."

"Oh. Oh, Margaret, that is part of this, as I understand it—"

"Ron, I'm not handing over the islands now. I can't lose the lives and blood of our soldiers to hand the islands over to a contact. It's not possible. You are surely not asking me, Ron, after we've lost some of our finest young men, you are surely not saying, that after the Argentine withdrawal, that our forces, and our administration, become immediately idle? I had to go to immense distances and mobilize half my country."

"Margaret, but I thought that part of this proposal . . ." Here Reagan ceases to form complete sentences. "Margaret, I . . . Yes, well . . . Well, Margaret, I know that I've intruded and I know how . . . "

"You've not intruded at all, and I'm glad you telephoned."[22]

Click.

---

22. "Reagan Asked Thatcher to Stop Falklands War," *Sunday Times,* March 8, 1992, citing National Security Council files.

_ᑫ ᑌ ᑫ_

HERE IT COMES, SENORS!
—The Sun, *caption to a photo of a missile*
signed Up Yours, Galtieri!

The final assault began soon thereafter, with heavy bloodshed. A British force of 8,000 men fought their way over the island and the ring of mountains around Stanley in fierce hand-to-hand combat. One by one, the Argentine positions fell. Then, on June 14, with British troops poised to take Stanley itself, the Argentine commander surrendered. The announcement took Thatcher and her cabinet by surprise. The commander of the British land forces immediately sent a message to London. "The Falkland Islands once more are under the government desired by their inhabitants. God save the Queen."

THE EMPIRE STRIKES BACK
—Newsweek

In total, 255 British lives were lost, as well as six ships, thirty-four aircraft, and £2.778 billion. The Argentines lost 649 servicemen, many of them teenage conscripts. Three civilian islanders were killed.

What was gained? Many wondered.

> Yeah. And then it was a case of no empire no longer. So after World War II, the whole world was going, "Come on, Europe, give these countries back. Come on, we just had a bloody war; let's give 'em back. Britain?"
> "Wha'?"
> "What's that behind your back?"
> "Oh, it's India and a number of other countries."
> "Give 'em back."

"Oh, all right. There's that one there, and there's that one . . ."

"Falkland Islands?"

"Oh, we need the Falkland Islands . . . for strategic sheep purposes."

—Eddie Izzard, "Dress to Kill," 1999

Dr. Johnson's remarks about the Falklands conflict of 1771 remained apt: "Let us now compute the profit of Britain. We have . . . maintained the honor of the crown, and the superiority of our influence. Beyond this what have we acquired? What, but a bleak and gloomy solitude, an island, thrown aside from human use, stormy in winter, and barren in summer; an island, which not the southern savages have dignified with habitation; where a garrison must be kept in a state that contemplates with envy the exiles of Siberia; of which the expense will be perpetual."

Defending the interests of the 1,820 British subjects who lived in the Falklands and wished to remain British was a noble goal. Of course it was. But for the cost of the war, every last one of the islanders could have been airlifted to the Welsh countryside and resettled with a stipend so handsome they would never have needed to shear a sheep again. This could have been achieved without the loss of a single life.

Yet there *was* a gain beyond ensuring the self-determination of the Falklanders. The gain was to British credibility and prestige—and to Thatcher's, in particular, both at home and abroad. The words "credibility" and "prestige" may be abstract, particularly contrasted with the real and immediate horror of the loss of young life. But this credibility and prestige prompted events that were momentous.

At the outbreak of the conflict, Thatcher's colleague Enoch Powell had intimated, in the House of Commons, his suspicion that Thatcher was not up for the task:

The Prime Minister, shortly after she came into office, received a soubriquet as the "Iron Lady." It arose in the con-

text of remarks which she made about defense against the
Soviet Union and its allies; but there was no reason to suppose that the Right Hon. Lady did not welcome and, indeed, take pride in that description. In the next week or two
this House, the nation and the Right Hon. Lady herself will
learn of what metal she is made.[23]

In the wake of the victory, the skeptical Powell became glowing ef-
fusion itself:

> Is the Right. Hon. Lady aware that the report has now been
> received from the public analyst on a certain substance re-
> cently subjected to analysis and that I have obtained a copy
> of the report? It shows that the substance under test con-
> sisted of ferrous matter of the highest quality, and that it is
> of exceptional tensile strength, is highly resistant to wear
> and tear and to stress, and may be used to advantage for all
> national purposes.[24]

This was a view widely shared. Great crowds gathered in London to sing "Rule Britannia" and cheer the woman who had led
Britain to triumph. Thatcher's government won a massive victory
in the 1983 general election—a victory that was by no means certain beforehand and indeed unlikely. She was returned to power
with an increased parliamentary majority, empowering her to
sweep ahead with the reforms that have now come to be associated with her name.

The relationship between the United States and Britain became closer—Americans love a winner—resulting in a more con-
frontational policy toward the Soviet bloc, a period known now
as the Second Cold War. On June 23, little more than a week after the surrender of the Argentines, Thatcher traveled to New

---

23. Thatcher, *The Downing Street Years*, p. 184.
24. June 17, 1982, House of Commons PQs, Hansard HC [25/1080–84].

Margaret Thatcher is presented with a commemorative coin
to celebrate the Falklands victory. "We adored her," recalled
Major General Julian Thompson, Brigade Commander during the Falklands war, "and would have done anything for
her. In all my years' service, I have never seen anything like it
. . . we all loved her for her calmness . . . her enthusiasm, and
dare one say it, because she is an extremely handsome lady.
We appreciated that, too." *(Central Office of Information)*

York to address the General Assembly of the United Nations,
which had gathered for a special session on disarmament. "There
is," she said,

> a natural revulsion in democratic societies against war and
> we would much prefer to see arms build-ups prevented, by
> good sense or persuasion or agreement. But if that does not

work, then the owners of these vast armouries must not be allowed to imagine that they could use them with impunity.

But mere words, speeches and resolutions will not prevent them. The security of our country and its friends can be ensured only by deterrence and by adequate strength— adequate when compared with that of a potential aggressor.[25]

These words clearly conveyed to the Soviet Union a great deal more seriousness than they would have had Thatcher not recently proven herself prepared—to the point of recklessness—to live by them.

Galtieri was placed under house arrest on June 18. He was convicted of mishandling the war, stripped of his rank, and imprisoned. The junta collapsed.

In one of those strange twists of fate suggesting that if nothing else, the Master of the Universe has a fine sense of irony, it now appears that the Falklands just *might* be sitting above a hundred billion barrels of oil. Recent technological advances in deep-sea exploration, specifically the development of controlled-source electromagnetic surveying, have led investors to wonder if the Falklands could be rather more valuable than they look. They have found nothing yet, but if their theory proves correct, the islanders will become the wealthiest people in the world. I stress that this was not suspected at the time and could not reasonably have been suspected: The relevant technology had not yet been invented.

There is a nice story about the penguins. Some 25,000 land mines, mostly planted by the Argentineans, remain in the no-go areas of the Falklands. Fortunately, the penguins are too light to set them off. But the presence of the mines has ensured that the area is now a conservation zone, one where harsh penalties await those

---

25. Speech to UN General Assembly, June 23, 1982, Thatcher MSS (digital collection), doc. 104974.

tempted to violate its integrity. The squawking penguins waddle about happily; conservationists are delighted by the protection of lands that had previously been overgrazed by sheep. There is a suspicion that other forms of bird and amphibious life have similarly profited, but no one is quite sure to what degree. As the director of Falklands Conservation, Grant Munro, remarked, "It has really not been looked into, for obvious reasons."

7

Coal and Iron

We had to fight the enemy without in the Falklands. We always have to be aware of the enemy within, which is much more difficult to fight and more dangerous to liberty.

— THATCHER ON THE MINERS' STRIKE

Orgreave, South Yorkshire, June 18, 1984. It is blisteringly hot. Many of the striking miners are shirtless, dripping with sweat. Not so the police, mounted on horseback and dressed head-to-toe in black battle gear.

It begins in a field near the British Steel coking plant. *BBC News: Arthur Scargill called for a mass picket of Orgreave. Today, he got one.* The sky is bright blue. Scargill—King Arthur, they call him—struts past the massed ranks of miners, directing them with a bullhorn. *Maggie, Maggie, Maggie, out, out, out! The miners, united, will never be defeated!*

But MI5 has infiltrated the National Union of Mineworkers, and the police know what Scargill has in mind even before he calls the orders. Ambulances are standing by. The cops pen the picketers away from the entrance to the plant. When the strikers spot the convoy of approaching trucks, a rumble passes through the crowd. Then they surge. *Here we go, here we go!* The air vibrates with the sound of shouting, police whistles, barking dogs. The phalanx of black-clad policemen runs directly into the scrum. They take on the miners in hand-to-hand combat. The horses charge. The miners throw missiles and rip up fencing—they throw that, too. Cloudbursts from smoke bombs turn the air bright red. *London calling to the faraway towns . . . Now war is declared, and battle come down . . .*

The reinforcements arrive, brandishing massive riot shields. They hold the miners back, grabbing miners at random and shoving them into pig buses.

The trucks sweep in procession into the plant.

The pickets counter with a second push. The police call in the snatch squads: Modeled on the colonial riot police—in turn modeled on the Roman legions—the snatch squads have never before been deployed on the British mainland. An officer gives them their orders: *You know what you're doing. No heads, bodies only!*

The picketers begin throwing ball bearings, rocks. They hit an officer in the face; he clutches his bloody nose. The snatch squads bear down on their horses, cantering straight into the mass of men, beating the miners with truncheons. Panic sweeps the crowd. The miners have blood streaming from their *head* wounds: There is no doubt about that.

At last the cavalry drives the miners back behind the police line. The ambulances burn off, sirens warbling. One hour and twenty minutes later, the trucks leave the plant, laden with the coal and scabby labor they came to collect. The picketing miners, helpless behind the police cordon, stand and watch in almost total silence.

After this some of the miners shuffle off to the pub for a beer, dispirited. It is a red-hot day. But the die-hards stay on the lines. By afternoon, the police have been sweltering in the sun for far too long. The remaining picketers have been taunting them; the cops are tired, hot, thirsty—they begin banging their shields with their truncheons. What happens next? No one agrees. Round two is worse than round one—much worse. Police boots smash into the shins of the picketers. *"Get bloody off!"* *"Shut your fucking mouth, or I'll break your fucking neck!"*[1]

Miners flee across the field and the railway tracks, but the cops close in, beating them even after they fall, unconscious, to the ground. Then to the astonishment of the village's residents, the miners run into Orgreave itself and the cavalry gallops right after them. The miners fight back with scrap-metal missiles. Enraged, the cops charge them—as well as the assembled onlookers—through the terraced streets of the town. The miners improvise barricades; they mount a contraption with a stake to impale the horses. One miner is slammed repeatedly against the hood of a car; the cops stamp on his leg, breaking it, then arrest him and drag him back, on one foot, behind the police lines. *London calling, see we ain't got no swing . . . 'Cept for the ring of that truncheon thing . . .* Weirdly, amid the chaos, the Rock On Tommy ice-cream van keeps selling ice cream until it is completely enclosed by the cavalry.

Twelve years before, the miners had forced Ted Heath's government to surrender by picketing the Saltley coke depot in Birmingham. Scargill was a senior figure in the Yorkshire branch of the miners' union then. He innovated the tactic of using flying pickets—dispatching shock troops of strikers from the most militant areas of Britain to the scene of the dispute. Most of the picketers who shut down the Saltley plant were not even employed there. The tactic was devastatingly effective. The event made Arthur Scargill into a hero among miners and a household name. In 1974, using the same tactics, Scargill brought down the Heath government.

Now Scargill is the president of the National Union of Mineworkers. Thatcher is determined that Orgreave will not be a repeat performance—no matter what it takes.

---

1. Bernard Jackson with Tony Wardle, *The Battle for Orgreave* (Vanson Wardle, 1986).

Soon the image will be broadcast from Orgreave to every British household with a television: a disheveled Arthur Scargill, clutching his baseball cap as he is dragged off by the police. He is telling anyone who will listen that Britain has been turned into some kind of Latin American junta. "1984—Great Britain!" he shouts to reporters.

> *BBC News:* This time Scargill seems to have failed—the 34 lorry drivers today managed to make two journeys unhindered and say they are determined to continue the coke runs.

_◦ ⟶ ◦_

The day after, in the House of Commons:

> **The Prime Minister:** However serious the strike—and it is serious—the consequences of giving in to mob rule would be far graver . . . **Mr. Kinnock:** Will the Prime Minister tell us why she wants this chaos, conflict and cost to go on rising? [*Hear! Hear! Rumbling and jeers.*] . . . **The Prime Minister:** The right hon. Gentleman . . . knows full well that what we saw there was not peaceful picketing, but mob violence and intimidation. I am astonished that he should suggest that, because one faction of the National Union of Mineworkers adopts these disgraceful tactics, it should be given what it wants! [*Hear! Hear!*] . . . **Mr. Kinnock:** If the right hon. Lady expended a fraction of the energy that she gives to political posturing on trying to promote a settlement, we would have ended the strike by now! . . . **The Prime Minister:** I note that the right hon. Gentleman referred to mob rule as political posturing. I can say to him only that whatever government are answering from the Dispatch Box, if they gave in to mob rule, that would be the end of liberty and democracy . . . **Mr. Kinnock:** That was

not an answer; it was a recitation of arrogant complacency, an evasion, and a betrayal of the national interest! [*Interruption, roaring.*] **The Prime Minister:** The right hon. Gentleman, who is shouting and posturing, is more accustomed to it than I am. We have seen violence which he has not— [*Interruption, loud shouting.*] **Mr. Speaker:** Order! There is so much noise that the Prime Minister did not hear that I called Question No. 2! . . . **Mr. Redmond:** Will the Prime Minister inform the House when she has sufficient blood on her hands to satisfy her hatred of the miners? . . . [2]

I meet Lord Peter Walker, who served as Thatcher's energy secretary during the miners' strike, for lunch at the Carlton Club in London. This is the club that reluctantly declared Thatcher an honorary gentleman. Thatcher surveys the foyer from her portrait; a massive bronze bust of her head presides above the staircase. When I ask the porter where to find the ladies' cloakroom, he nods in the direction of the bust: "Turn left past Margaret, Madame." Upstairs is the Wellington Room, where members are permitted to entertain their lady friends. This is where I dine with Lord Walker. Beyond is the Churchill Room—for members only— which of course I do not see, for I am not a gentleman, even of the honorary kind.

Walker was one of the leading wets in Thatcher's cabinet. "From the point of view of the right wing of my party, I was a terrible neocommunist myself, you know," he says ruefully. Thus did it come as a surprise to him when Thatcher asked him, in 1983, to take the energy portfolio. Of course, from a public relations standpoint it made perfect sense to assign that responsibility to a

---

2. June 19, 1984, House of Commons PQs, *Hansard* HC [62/137–40].

man known for his lack of radicalism. *We are not the ones causing the problems here. The miners can't even get along with a wet like Walker . . .*

The Wet Lord sinks into the comfortable sofa of the morning room and orders an aperitif. He spots Bernard Ingham across the room; the men bob their heads at each other courteously. The waiter arrives with the Chablis. Walker clears his throat. Thatcher had called him, he tells me, the morning after the 1983 election. She feared a conflict with Scargill. She thought Walker was the man to handle it. She flattered him lavishly, telling him that everywhere she had gone on the campaign trail, the voters had declared him their hero. Walker's feathers ruffle proudly as he recalls this conversation. He accepted the job. "The first thing I did was do an enormous personal study of Scargill," he says. He read everything Scargill had ever written, every word about him that had ever been reported. "I had this enormous volume of papers. And what you discovered was that above all he was a totally committed Marxist."

Walker is not exaggerating. Scargill *was* a totally committed Marxist. This is the first point everyone close to Thatcher stresses when his name comes up, and they are right to stress it. The brutality of Thatcher's response to Scargill can be put in proper perspective only if we appreciate that Scargill was, in fact, committed to bringing about a communist revolution in Britain. Moreover, it was not at all clear at the time that he would fail. A revolution along Bolshevik lines was never likely, but it was entirely realistic to fear that he would permanently establish the unions as the nation's preeminent political power, reverse the outcome of a democratic election by force, and irreversibly cripple the British economy.

"He was, you know, an absolute, outright, complete Marxist," John Hoskyns had said to me several days prior. "I remember a senior union man saying to me, once, 'I'll tell you about Arthur.' I said, 'Tell me about Arthur.' And he said, 'Well, I think you can say that when he's shaving and he's looking in the mirror every morning, he says to his reflection, "One day, you will be the President of the Socialist Republic of Britain."'"

No one who knows anything about Scargill disagrees with this assessment, no matter what their political orientation. They disagree only about whether Scargill's ambition was a laudable one.

Arthur Scargill—King Coal—was born in 1938, just south of Barnsley, in Yorkshire. Scargill is not a *nom de guerre*, much though it sounds like one; it is just one of those oddball literary coincidences that his first name evokes mythical heroism even as his last name metonymically hints of thuggishness and slime. His father was a coal miner and a member of the Communist Party of Great Britain. Scargill too became a miner after leaving school at the age of sixteen; he joined the Young Communist League in 1955. He became leader of the Yorkshire division of the National Union of Mineworkers in 1973. Two years after Thatcher came to power, he was elected president of the national union.

I wanted very much to meet him. I wrote to him to ask whether he might permit me to get his side of the story. I received a reply from a woman by the name of Linda Sheridan. Scargill was, she wrote, "quite adamant that he does not wish to discuss Thatcher or the miners' strike with you, or any other journalist for that matter."[3] When I entered Sheridan's name in Google, I discovered that she represents the Socialist Labour Party in central Scotland. The party, which Scargill now heads, aims "to abolish capitalism and replace it with a socialist system."[4] Those nostalgic for the Labour Party's Clause 4 will be pleased to know that it is not dead. It is merely pining for the fjords in the Socialist Labour Party's manifesto.

I wasn't deterred. I wrote back, saying that I understood that Mr. Scargill's relationship with the Fourth Estate was not a particularly

---

3. Linda Sheridan, e-mail, May 14, 2007.
4. www.socialist-labour-party.org.uk/.

happy one. But I thought it important to represent his point of view accurately, and I couldn't do that unless he spoke to me directly. Would she please ask him to reconsider?

It was out of the question, she replied. I imagine she had looked me up on Google as well; perhaps she discovered that I am no great fan of revolutionary socialism.

> *Dear Claire,*
>
> *. . . Please understand that Margaret Thatcher is hated by many of us here. For every dozen people you speak to who will say she was a wonderful strong Prime Minister who licked the unions into shape and privatized (and ruined) our national industries, you will find hundreds of others, living in communities which were destroyed by her policies, who feel nothing but a passionate hatred for her. The saying is that when Thatcher goes, she is going to a place where there is a lot of coal, hot coal, and when she does go, we'll all be down at the pub raising our glasses, and putting two fingers up to her. I'm sorry but that's how it is.*
>
> *Best regards*
> *Linda[5]*

I liked her spirit, if not her politics. I searched for more information about her and found her photograph online. She looks to be in her early forties. She has skin so pale it is almost translucent and a beautiful mane of wild auburn hair. I wrote again. Was she *quite* certain Mr. Scargill didn't fancy meeting me?[6]

---

5. Sheridan, e-mail, May 15, 2007.
6. The reader who is wondering why I bothered should know that this has worked for me before. You would be surprised how many people will give in and talk to you if only you pester them enough.

Dear Claire

You owe it to yourself to try. As a writer myself I appreciate that only too well.

Sometimes, if the gatekeeper is lazy, going to lunch and leaving the key in the lock, you can creep on tiptoe and softly turn it, pushing the door wide, inch by inch, until you can slip through into the hallowed hall and surprise the dragon sleeping in his lair, or working hard at his desk, as the case may be. This time it didn't work. No hard feelings.

The unvarnished truth about Thatcher is that generally Thatcher has had a free hand as far as the US media and therefore the American audience is concerned. She is held to be the best prime minister since Churchill and because of strong publicity from, for example, Murdoch,[7] this has never been challenged. She is far from well now which is not surprising. When one lives one's life on a narrow path, without compassion and understanding for the deeper issues in life, when temporal power is taken away, one invariably falls into a spiritual abyss of self-doubt and loneliness. Some people call it karma. As you give so you receive.

It has been nice to talk with you Claire.

Good luck.

Best wishes
Linda

---

7. The publishing titan Rupert Murdoch was so close to Thatcher that he was described by critics as "the phantom Prime Minister."

Right, then. From now on, Scargill will communicate with us through Linda, his spirit medium.

_ᴑ ᴖᴥ ᴑ_

If Peter Walker concluded that Scargill was a committed Marxist, this is because no other conclusion is possible. "Capitalism is an obscene system which deserves to be overthrown," Scargill declared forthrightly.[8] Scargill left the Communist Party in 1961 not because he objected in any way to Stalin's excesses—in fact, he approved of the Soviet Union's invasion of Hungary and mourned the removal of Stalin's body from the Red Square mausoleum[9]—but because he had decided that the British Communist Party wasn't powerful enough. "I gradually began to be interested in the unions themselves," he told the *New Left Review* in 1975,

> because it appeared to me that, irrespective of what I did in
> . . . the Labour or Communist Party or any other political
> organization, the real power—and I say that in the best pos-
> sible sense—the real power lay either with the working
> classes or with the ruling classes.[10]

In the same interview, he proposed as soon as possible to "take into common ownership everything in Britain." The first measure would be "the immediate nationalization of the means of production, distribution and exchange. I can't compromise on this." There could be no middle way: "I do not believe compromise with the capitalist system of society will achieve anything." Immediately upon taking power, he stressed, he would bring all organs of the press under state control.

---

8. *Morning Star,* February 3, 1983.
9. *Sunday Times,* January 10, 1982.
10. *The New Left Review,* July/August 1975.

Not only was Scargill a Marxist, there is much evidence for the case that he was a Stalinist, in particular. Stalin briskly dismissed the notion that workers in advanced capitalist nations, whom he denounced as a labor aristocracy, would spontaneously bring about the Revolution; they had drunk too deeply of the wine of bourgeois ideology; they swam in a soporific miasma of false consciousness.[11] Scargill shared this sentiment. "I disagree totally with the concept of workers' control," Scargill told *Marxism Today*:

> It is only by politicizing our membership that we will ever bring about the irreversible shift towards a socialist system in society. Therefore I don't agree that we ought to be putting workers on the boards . . . I am against the whole concept of participation which only serves to perpetuate the capitalist system.[12]

On the radical Left, the word "irreversible" is a common euphemism. It means *no more elections*.

Like Stalin, Scargill sought to foster a personality cult; activists were encouraged to chant his name and pledge their loyalty to him, rather than to the union or a political party. "Arthur Scargill Walks on Water," sung to the tune of "Deck the Halls," and "There's only one Arthur Scargill," sung to the tune of "Guantanamera," were classics of the genre.

In 2000, Scargill just came out with it. At a meeting of the British Stalin Society in London (yes, there is such a thing), Scargill declared himself "sick and tired of listening to the so-called 'experts' today who still criticize the Soviet Union and, in

---

11. One may reasonably argue—and Trotsky did—that in this sense Stalin was not a Marxist: The *central* prediction of Marxism is the inevitability of a spontaneous revolution in the industrialized world, led by the proletarian vanguard. This discussion is beyond the scope of this book; my point is that an important, relevant current of sympathy runs between Stalin's views and Scargill's.
12. *Marxism Today*, April 1981.

particular, Stalin." The meeting was organized by the Committee to Celebrate the October Revolution. The remarks of Comrade Scargill—as he is termed in the minutes—warrant quotation at length, for there are still many who see Thatcher, not Scargill, as the dangerous provocateur in this conflict. "Tonight's event," Scargill declared,

> must be a celebration and not merely a commemoration of that earth-shattering event, and it should be an evening when we pay tribute to those who created the Soviet Union—a Socialist society which not only defeated poverty, ignorance, injustice and inequality but also defeated the mightiest fascist war machine ever seen on the face of the earth . . . it was the Soviets who first put a man into space. They did so without the obscenities of the market economy, including Coca Cola plants and McDonald's fast-food chains, or what some misguided souls believe is 'freedom and democracy.' Following the death of Stalin in 1953, new forces seized control in the Soviet Union, and a so-called 'new realism' began to take the place of Socialist planning. Khruschev, Brezhnev, later Andropov, Chernenko, but, above all, Gorbachev did what the might of the Nazi army had failed to do—they ripped the heart out of the Soviet Union and destroyed its Socialist system.[13]

Despite the Great Betrayal, Scargill remained throughout his union career on exceedingly cozy terms with the Kremlin, making numerous trips to Moscow and Cuba on the Red dime as he worked his way up the union ranks. He airmailed copies of the *Yorkshire Miner* to Castro every month. He denounced the counter-revolutionary Solidarity movement in Poland and refused

---

13. LALKLAR, "Celebrating the October Revolution," January/February 2000.

to condemn the Soviet Union when in 1983 it downed a South Korean passenger plane.

During the strike, Scargill visited the Soviet embassy in London regularly. The Soviets donated a million-odd pounds' worth of cash, food, and clothing to the miners' union.[14] As the strike wore on, miners and their families vacationed on the Black Sea; the USSR picked up the tab. When the details of this Soviet largesse were reported in the news, Scargill didn't deny it: He declared insouciantly that Soviet miners had taken up a collection for their comrades. "And he got away with it, really," Walker marvels. "The public said, 'Ah, you know, that's very nice of these Russian miners—.'"

Walker claims that the Soviet Union delivered cash to a pub in Yorkshire in cases of ten-pound notes. Scargill has been accused of pocketing a great deal of Russian money for his own use. Many column inches have been devoted to the latter charge and to Scargill's denials, but in the end the question is not particularly important. What is important—and a matter of indisputable public record—are Scargill's declared economic and political objectives. During the strike, when asked by a parliamentary committee just how much of a financial loss a pit must run to warrant closure, Scargill replied, "As far as I can see, the loss is without limits." No pit, he argued, should *ever* be closed because it wasn't making

---

14. Seamus Milne, a journalist for the *Guardian,* argues that most of this money never reached the miners. The payment was authorized, he acknowledges, and sent to a Swiss bank, but the Kremlin developed cold feet when British courts ordered the union's assets sequestered and had the money recalled. See Seamus Milne, *The Enemy Within: Thatcher's Secret War Against the Miners* (Verso, 1994). After the fall of the Berlin Wall, well-placed Soviet officials confirmed claims that the Soviet Union had indeed funneled large amounts of cash to the union. Milne says those officials are lying and attributes their mendacity to post-communist factional infighting within the Kremlin. Milne may be right, for all I know. The essential point—which Milne ignores—is not whether the money in fact arrived, or when it arrived, or by which channel. It is that Scargill did not hesitate to appeal to Moscow for help, and Moscow was eager to give it, although understandably reluctant to risk the loss of hard currency and the diplomatic embarrassment should the transfer become public.

enough money. It should be closed only when there was no coal
left in it, even if you had to tunnel to the center of the earth to get
it. There could be no compromise.

Bernard Ingham was characteristically expansive when he recalled Scargill's declaration:

> I mean, it's the economics of the madhouse! But he believed
> that the nation owed the miners a living, and that the min-
> ers did not need to perform economically, all they needed to
> do was *occasionally* dig out coal so that we might *occasion-
> ally* have some electricity. Oh yes, the man was a menace, a
> total menace.

Likewise, Scargill made no secret of his desire to bring down
the Thatcher government, by any means necessary. "Direct action,"
he declared in 1981 to a union rally—on the hard Left, "direct action" is another important euphemism; it means "violence"—"is
the only language the government will listen to."[15] The forthcoming battle, he stressed, "will not be won in the House of Commons.
It will be won on the streets of Britain." After the 1974 miners'
strike, he had explained the strategy of dispatching flying pickets
to the scene of the conflict thus: Trade union members "had a con-
tractual obligation with the working class, and if they didn't honor
[it] we'd make sure, physically, that they did."[16]

The outcome of the 1983 general election, Thatcher writes in
her memoirs, was a devastating rebuke to socialism. She is justified
in saying this. As she put it, fairly, the Labour Party had cam-
paigned "on a manifesto that was the most candid statement of socialist aims ever made in this country."[17] The voters had made their
opinions perfectly clear: They didn't want what the Labour Party
was offering. Thatcher won a landslide victory. Within a month of

15. *Telegraph,* April 13, 1981.
16. *New Left Review,* July/August 1975.
17. Thatcher, *The Downing Street Years,* p. 339.

the election, however, Scargill announced that he did not "accept that we are landed for the next four years with this government."[18]

In other words, to hell with the voters.

Since Scargill refused to meet me, I cannot say what he is like in person. I have heard that he is funny and sharp-witted—although no one has recounted to me a story about his wit that actually made me laugh[19]—and I have heard that he is a powerful, passionate orator. Like Thatcher, he has a reputation for extraordinary industry and personal discipline. Like Thatcher, he is said to have needed little sleep. Photographs of the epoch show a man with a weak chin, thinning red hair, a comb-over, and last-days-of-disco sideburns.

Peter Walker describes him to me as a man who knew how to have a good time: "He loved living the capitalist life, I mean, his suits were made in Savile Row, several thousand pounds at a time. He always had a chauffeur-driven car, and he dined and wined well, so he loved the joys of a wealthy standard of living himself." This, I suspect, is a bit of an exaggeration, perhaps even one of those famous Tory smears. It is true that Scargill had a driver, and others to whom I spoke agreed that the man enjoyed his food, but I have looked at hundreds of photographs of Scargill and can say with confidence that if he paid a thousand pounds for those suits, he was had.

Scargill and Neil Kinnock loathed each other. Kinnock first met Scargill in the late 1960s. "Did you take an instant dislike to him?" I ask.

---

18. *Morning Star*, June 27, 1983.

19. From the annals of the Marxist wit and wisdom of Arthur Scargill: "In an attempt to prevent the movement of coal, Scargill appealed to the Communist General Secretary of the South Wales miners, Dai Francis, to send thousands of pickets to the Saltley coke works in Birmingham: 'Yes, we can organize them,' Francis told Scargill. 'When do you want them?' 'Tomorrow, Saturday,' Scargill answered. Dai paused: 'But Wales are playing Scotland at Cardiff Arms Park.' There was a silence before Scargill replied: 'But Dai, the working class are playing the ruling class at Saltley.'" Patrick Hannan, *When Arthur Met Maggie* (Seren, 2006).

"*Immédiatement.*"

"Why, what was he like?"

"Poseur. Arrogant. Kind of guy that you knew, if anybody would let him, he would bully them."

"Is there anything specific, anything that he said that made you feel, 'This guy, I just don't like him?'"

"No, you only have to look at him *walking* to hate him."

"How did he walk?"

"Well, he's a *strutter*. He *struts*. He *struts*. And you can take a visceral dislike to someone simply on the basis of that, or the color of their tie, or the way they part their hair." I am not sure whether he meant that he *did* take a dislike to Scargill based on the way he parted his hair, but if so, it would have been understandable. "But the whole character of Scargill *extruded*, you know, I felt, '*Christ*, I don't like this guy.' And quite a lot of the fellows I was mixing with among those South Wales miners—including communists— thought that Scargill was, quote, 'too big for his bloody boots.' That kind of attitude."

"Right."

"And quite a few of these were guys whose judgment I valued, because they were gutsy men with a lot of wisdom, whose basic motivation was to try to help people. I mean, they would have liked to have overthrown the existing order, but the main reason they'd taken on responsibilities in the union or in politics or both was that they wanted to help people."

I am struck by the way Kinnock casually dismisses the eagerness of these men to overthrow the existing order. Such an ambition is, he seems to be suggesting, just a harmless political folly, like an obsession with wind farms. This is one reason he never became prime minister. Too many people wondered about his judgment. They just couldn't be sure that Thatcher was dead wrong about his crypto-communism.

"How did Scargill manage to rise so high?" I ask him.

"Well, he *is* a clever man—"

I am not so sure of that. The strike began on March 12. Calling a coal strike with summer coming is like invading Russia as winter approaches. "How clever could he have been to call a coal strike in the *spring?*"

"Oh no," says Kinnock, "that was idiotic and stupid. And treacherous. I'm not saying that—I'm not saying that clever people can't be stupid."

"So when you heard that he'd been elected to the presidency of the NUM, what was your reaction? Did you say to yourself, 'We're on a collision course,' or did you think there was some way it could be finessed?"

"Well, I'll tell you the funny thing. I was talking to the leading officials of the miners in Durham, who were fairly, sort of, by Labour movement standards, on the right wing. I mean, people outside the movement wouldn't think of them like that, but you know, they were moderates. And they'd never voted for the Left candidate in any miners' election. Not since the 1930s. So I was chatting to them, and taking it for granted that they hadn't voted for Scargill. And when they said they had, I said, 'What in the bloody hell did you do *that* for?'"

Kinnock mimics Pitmatic as perfectly as he does Margaret Thatcher.[20] "Oh, he's a canny lad!" they said to him.

"*Canny?* The man's bloody *crazy!* He's mad as a *hatter!*" Kinnock replied.

"Well, yer know, we need a bit o' push."

"Yeah, I know, but he will push the miners to *destruction.*"

---

20. Pitmatic is the now-dying dialect of northeastern coal miners, e.g., "Te these canny lads we'd like to give a wee bit o' advice: Watch yersels, an' dee what's reet an' divvent be pit mice. We waddent like te see any o' yer ivver cum te grief. There's ne carl at arl te smash yersels or Rarfie's perminent Relief." You can listen to a sample, as well as an interesting discussion of the dialect, here: www.bbc.co.uk/radi04/routesofenglish/storysofar/ramfiles/roe1_ray1 .ram.

They tried to reassure him: "Well, when he goes down to London he'll cool down. He'll get more mature."

Kinnock said, "Hey, wait a minute. You're not telling me that you're relying on this guy going to the fleshpots of London to make him a suitable union leader?"

"No, well it's not like that," they mumbled sheepishly.

"That's exactly what you're saying! Well, I hope you don't live to weep over this."

Kinnock's voice returns to the present. "And they did live to weep over it. I mean, the last coal mine in that coal field was closed in the wake of the 1984 strike. Every single pit."

～ઌ ᴂᴅ ᴂ～

I offered Scargill the chance to reply to Kinnock's characterization of him, but he didn't take me up on it. Linda Sheridan, however, held forth with gusto.

Dear Claire

I am glad your researching trip went well.

Neil Kinnock (known as the Welsh windbag) rose to his position on the votes of the working class and when he got there sold out to the establishment and accepted a title which he once asserted he never would. He has worked hard obtaining lucrative jobs for himself (with massive pension) and for his family in the EU. Neil Kinnock sucks. The Welsh can be treacherous bastards. I know, my father was a Welshman. He won't have a good word to say for Arthur.

Arthur once said to me in a conversation that the relentless pressure on him during the strike coupled with vicious attacks from the media and the untrue allegations of embezzlement of funds made him, in retrospect, wonder how he had survived mentally intact. He did so primarily because of his absolute integrity and because of his faith in socialism. As he constantly says, "I became a socialist at fifteen and I will never stop fighting for socialism until the day I die." . . . And he will not. You won't find Arthur Scargill doing what other union leaders have done, jettisoning principles, accepting a knighthood, and kissing arse at celebrity cocktail parties not EVER. And that's for sure.

I still receive rant e-mails, read letters in the press and meet gullible people who have bought a lifetime lease into the lies, slanders and libels perpetrated at the time of the strike. The press only stopped short of saying he ate babies for breakfast. But Arthur has Irish ancestry and the Irish are resilient fighters. The English have always despised the Irish. Maybe, the so-English Maggie Thatcher, the provincial grocer's daughter who used to help her father count the takings in the evenings when the shop was closed, saw in Arthur Scargill something that she recognized and hated. I say "saw" but as I hope you are aware, they never met. . . .

Scratch the skin and you will find Thatcher had many ordinary middle-class prejudices. On the other hand, Arthur Scargill is no ordinary man. Whatever Thatcher and others may say, he had her running scared, so scared that she had to dredge up every dirty underhand trick in the book in order to defeat the miners. Had he not been up against impossible odds, as outlined in "The Enemy Within,"[21] and had the countries' trade union leaders had the backbone to

---

21. She is referring to Milne's *The Enemy Within.* Milne argues that Thatcher and her government went to extraordinary lengths to smear and discredit Scargill. I agree. Milne thinks this was a bad thing.

*support their own class and to come out in support of the
miners, the strike would have been won.*

*And as for what people say about Arthur, he's heard it all
before and won't lose any sleep over it. His enemies will say
what they always say and his friends and sympathizers
will say what they usually say. No surprises there.*

*It's been nice talking to you Claire but I have no further
comments to make.*

Take care.

*Regards,
Linda*[22]

From the eighteenth century to the mid-twentieth century, the
world ran on coal, as George Orwell remarked in *The Road to
Wigan Pier:*

> Our civilization, pace Chesterton, is founded on coal, more
> completely than one realizes until one stops to think about
> it. The machines that keep us alive, and the machines that
> make machines, are all directly or indirectly dependent
> upon coal. In the metabolism of the Western world the coal-
> miner is second in importance only to the man who ploughs
> the soil. He is a sort of caryatid upon whose shoulders
> nearly everything that is not grimy is supported.[23]

---

22. Sheridan, e-mail, July 14, 2007. I have standardized her punctuation.
23. George Orwell, *The Road to Wigan Pier* (1937). The full text is now
available online: www.george-orwell.org/The_Road_to_Wigan_Pier/
index.html.

Deep shaft mining expanded rapidly in Britain throughout the nineteenth and the beginning of the twentieth centuries. The industrializing world's hunger for coal was voracious, so much so that the miners, secure that their labor was irreplaceable, formed the vanguard of the British trade union movement. The Miners' Federation of Great Britain, later to become the National Union of Mineworkers, was founded in 1889. The imperative of ensuring secure energy supplies during the two world wars ensured there could be no serious challenge to the miners' growing political power. South Yorkshire and its environs were during this era the economic and strategic equivalent of the contemporary Persian Gulf. The miners, to continue this analogy, were something like OPEC.

When the commanding heights of the British economy were nationalized in the years following the Second World War, the mines passed into the government's hands. The National Coal Board was established to manage the industry. But the second half of the century saw the emergence of competing energy sources in the form of oil, natural gas, and nuclear power. The increasing globalization of the energy market ushered in competition from coal-rich and comparatively undeveloped nations such as China, where life and labor were cheap. It is, moreover, the nature of coal pits to become progressively less profitable, for the deeper you have to dig for the coal, the more time, risk, effort, and technology it takes to get it out. At the turn of the twentieth century, 1.1 million British men earned their daily bread in the pits. By 1983, the number was only 240,000.

That year, the Monopolies and Mergers Commission reported that some 75 percent of British pits were making losses. It cost £44 to mine a metric ton of British coal. America, Australia, and South Africa were selling coal to the rest of Europe for £32 a ton. British coal was piling up in mountains, unsold. The industry was surviving because, and only because, the government was spending more than a billion pounds a year to subsidize it—and indeed still more, if you calculate the additional costs to the nationalized steel and electricity industries, which were obliged by law to purchase British coal rather than cheaper imported coal or oil. Indirectly, the high cost of energy was passed on to everyone in Britain. It was, in effect, a completely regressive tax.[24] Highly energy-dependent industries were heavily penalized, particularly in the export market, but so were ordinary men and women who heated their homes and turned on their lights. The coal industry had become an expensive welfare program.

And what a cruel welfare program it was.

> The place is like hell, or at any rate like my own mental picture of hell. Most of the things one imagines in hell are in there—heat, noise, confusion, darkness, foul air, and, above all, unbearably cramped space. Everything except the fire, for there is no fire down there except the feeble beams of Davy lamps and electric torches which scarcely penetrate the clouds of coal dust . . . [25]

Obviously, I do not find Scargill a sympathetic character, but it is nonetheless entirely understandable to me that coal miners so often found themselves tempted by the promises of communism. Frankly, I am surprised that any of them weren't communists. I needn't linger overmuch on the horrors of coal mining—they are well-known—but it is worth acknowledging them with a passing nod. Methane explosions. Crushing. Electric shock. Pulmonary tuberculosis, emphysema. The eternal filth, working crouched over, never seeing the light of day. Black lung, black damp, after damp, fire damp, stink damp, white damp, suffocation, drowning.

---

24. Thatcher's proposal to introduce a flat-rate poll tax was widely pilloried; indeed, it contributed significantly to her downfall. But the only difference between the poll tax and the coal tax was that one was out in the open, the other was hidden. Both were forms of taxation that targeted the rich and the poor equally. The unofficial coal tax cost the average Briton far more than the proposed poll tax.
25. Orwell, *The Road to Wigan Pier.*

The safety standards of British mines had much improved—relatively speaking—by the mid-1980s.[26] But improving safety costs money, a lot of it, which is one reason Britain could not compete with countries such as China. And still the pits were Stygian, filthy, backbreaking. If I had spent my life going up and down those mine shafts, I reckon I too would have liked the ring of the words "dictatorship of the proletariat."

All mines close sooner or later. Either all the coal is harvested, or it becomes so difficult to get to the seam that it costs more to mine than the coal is worth—at least, if that worth is measured by the price it fetches on an open market. The National Coal Board had been closing pits steadily since its creation, and every time, miners had been laid off. Under Harold Wilson's first Labour government, a pit had closed every week. When the coal board announced, under Thatcher, that it planned to close another twenty-odd pits, it was proposing nothing more than the continuation of previous policies. Thatcher presented the argument for pit closure in characteristic terms of housewifely thrift. "You do not

---

26. This is only to say that the mines were now very dangerous, rather than unspeakably dangerous. Coal mining in the nineteenth century was an unmitigated horror. To better understand the militant culture of the miners' union, consider the Risca Blackvein Colliery explosion of 1860, which claimed the lives of 146 men and boys. A random sample of names from the Death Roll: "Brimble, Thomas, Aged 12, After Damp. Brimble, William, Aged 13, Burnt . . . Pearce, George, Aged 13, Burnt . . . Saunders, Llew, Came Out Alive, but died later . . . Skidmore, George, Aged 35, After Damp . . . Thomas, Llewellyn, Aged 15, Burnt." It goes on for pages in this vein. The local newspaper reported only the "severe financial loss suffered by the mine owner, with the death of 28 pit ponies at an estimated value of £1,000" (www.welshcoalmines.co.uk/). Only thirty miners were killed in Britain in the year before the strike: This is what was meant by "an improvement." If the cruelty of the mining industry is not enough to sour you on it, the environmental costs should do it. Anyone who believes that global climate change is a manmade phenomenon must of necessity accept that coal is a large part of the problem. Burning coal produces greenhouse gases in such quantities that the Environmental Protection Agency has declared coal-burning power plants to be the single worst air polluters in America. EPA studies suggest that coal emissions kill some 30,000 Americans a year, causing nearly as many deaths as traffic accidents. See Barbara Freese, *Coal: A Human History* (Perseus, 2003). Clean-coal technology has been developed, but it raises the price of producing coal considerably. Bring on the nuclear power, I say.

Alan Clark supposedly told the journalist Edward Pearce that "It's all absolute crap, of course, to talk about liberal market theory. What Margaret is on about is the Class War." This is certainly how the miners' strike was widely perceived, among the miners, at least. But Thatcher herself was *not* from a privileged class background: As this 1979 photo of Thatcher on the campaign trail suggests, she drew considerable support from Britain's middle- and lower middle-classes, who identified with her. She was able to pursue an anti-socialist agenda in large measure because her own lower-middle-class roots tempered the perception that she was waging an all-out class war. *(Courtesy of the family of Srdja Djukanovic)*

go out and buy suits at four times the cheapest price merely to keep people in work. You say: 'No! I have to use my wages and salaries to the best advantage. I must buy best value!'"[27]

There had never before been a strike over pit closures. Previous strikes had revolved around the issue of wages, not closures. Thus the question, at heart, was not the closure of the pits. The great miners' strike was an ideological struggle. For Thatcher, the miners' union and the bureaucrats who managed the coal industry represented everything wrong with socialism: waste, inefficiency, irresponsibility, unaccountability. To the miners, Thatcher represented everything wrong with capitalism: avarice, heartlessness, the privi-

---

27. Interview for Thames Television's *TV Eye,* January 24, 1985, transcript, Thatcher MSS (digital collection), doc. 105949.

tation of profits over human dignity. Thatcher had made her goal explicit: She sought to destroy socialism in Britain. In return, Scargill made his goal explicit: He sought to destroy Thatcher.

And so the strike began.

_ˌ◌ˌ ⌐☜ ◌ˌ_

In September 1979, six months after Thatcher won the first general election, John Hoskyns sent the prime minister a memorandum: *Begin your preparations now,* he warned her. *The miners are going to give you grief.* The received wisdom in the Conservative Party, he tells me over lunch, was that the miners couldn't be defeated. The attitude was "part of that whole postwar malaise, this sort of deep-down defeatist 'we won the war but we can't win the peace, somehow—there may be some way that you can make peace with the miners, so they don't bring you down and they don't cripple the economy, but don't think that you can actually *defeat* them, because they've got the biggest guns, and they'll just bring everything to a halt.'"

In his memo, Hoskyns urged her to challenge this received wisdom. At the time, Joe Gormley was head of the miners' union. Gormley was "an honorable, old-fashioned, democratic trade unionist," Hoskyns recalls. But he would be retiring. And it was increasingly clear that he would be replaced by Scargill. Gormley's interests, says Hoskyns, "were not ours. But there is a big difference between an old-fashioned trade unionist and a raging Marxist, there really is. One's just someone you disagree with, and the other's the enemy."

Despite Hoskyns's warnings, nothing was done at all. Hoskyns wrote, in his memo, that it might well be possible to change the balance of power. Thatcher returned the memo to him with her reply: "Only at the margins, I fear." Hoskyns decided it would be unwise to insist. "I didn't push her on that, because there's a lot of importance, in my view, in the handling of someone who is under enormous pressures. You cannot go on and on banging at them, because eventually they say, you know, 'Who will rid me of this turbulent priest?'"

Thatcher put the issue on the back burner. As a result, when the miners challenged her in 1981, the government was entirely unprepared. Thatcher was forced to capitulate. Hoskyns was disgusted, and while he was too savvy to say "I told you so" explicitly, I expect his sentiments were clear enough. Hoskyns was not invited to the urgent meeting Thatcher subsequently convened to discuss the miners. He suspects this was because she did not want to be reminded that he had, indeed, told her so. "You know, she's only human. And she knew that we'd been right on that." Not long after this, Hoskyns resigned. "Our relationship," he says, "was quite a difficult one. I wasn't part of her sort of feel-good factor, as it were."

But following this humiliation, Thatcher began to prepare for war. "It was that strike threat, which, to put it bluntly, scared the shit out of her," says Hoskyns. "Suddenly the whole of Whitehall was on a war footing." Thatcher instructed the Civil Contingencies Unit, usually charged with preparing for national disasters, to begin studying the possibility of withstanding a strike. Plans were drawn up for stockpiling coal, training the military to drive trains in the event of a sympathy strike by the railway workers, accelerating the development of nuclear power, importing electricity by cable from France, and refurbishing coal-fired power stations to permit them to run on oil.

Thatcher asked Nigel Lawson to be her energy secretary. He too had been appalled that the government was forced to stand down. "I was determined," he writes in his memoirs, "that, if I had anything to do with it, it would never happen again."[28] He was not seeking a strike, he stresses. "But it was clear that Arthur Scargill was, and I was determined that he should lose it when it came."[29]

I believe it to be true that the government was not going out of its way to provoke a strike. But obviously, if these characteristic

---

28. Lawson, *The View from No. 11*, p. 142.
29. Ibid., p. 143.

words are any guide, by 1984 the mood in Downing Street had become distinctly Clint Eastwoodish. *Go ahead. Make our day.*

Lawson appointed the physicist Walter Marshall to head the Coal and Electricity Generating Board. Scargill's ally Tony Benn—remember him? Wedgie?—had sacked Marshall from his position as chief scientist at the Department of Energy. Lawson was well aware of this. Marshall devoted himself with vindictive relish to developing plans to defeat Scargill; Lawson recalls Marshall's "great zest" for devising schemes to smuggle strategic chemicals into the power stations. Those that could not be smuggled would be flown in by helicopter; landing sites were identified near every power station.

Stockpiling coal is no trivial matter. It is costly, and it is tricky: In critically large quantities, coal can self-ignite. It was, moreover, viewed by many of Thatcher's advisors as a risky gambit. "Up went the great defeatist cry of the most useless civil servants," recalls Hoskyns. "'If we start moving coal to the power stations, that's an outright provocation!'" Thatcher's cabinet was divided; Jim Prior, in particular, considered these preparations a dangerous escalation. Hoskyns draws an analogy to the debate about Reagan's military spending: "I've been through exactly the same process that clearly he and his advisers went through about the Cold War. I mean, I felt ratcheting up economic costs and staying in the struggle was the way to destroy the economic union. I mean, the *Soviet* Union. Just the same. If you just do everything bit by bit, and try to avoid any single action that makes their alarm bells ring, there's a habituation to what's going on. I mean, thinking through the eyes of Scargill, 'Oh, they're moving a lot of coal, aren't they, well, you know, yes, but it's not too bad,' six months later, 'Hmmm, really a *hell* of a lot of coal . . . '"

Thatcher ignored the pleading of the wets. The preparation continued. By 1982, trains ferrying coal to the power stations were running twenty-four hours a day, seven days a week.

Meanwhile, her government ushered in significant changes in the trade union law. The 1982 Employment Act made it vastly more difficult, almost impossible, to form a closed shop, a union with mandatory membership. Unions that engaged in sympathy strikes or dispatched flying pickets could now be sued, fined, or held in contempt of court. By making unions liable to civil suits, Thatcher gave the judiciary a more prominent role in labor relations. The judges ultimately proved, as Thatcher had hoped, to be no friends of the striking miners.

In September 1983, Thatcher named Ian MacGregor chairman of the National Coal Board. MacGregor, who was half American and spoke with an American accent, had previously managed British Steel, cutting its workforce by 100,000. "Ian," recalls Lawson, "was widely seen as an overpaid, over-aged, ruthless American whose main achievement at British Steel had been to slash the workforce."[30] What more could you want? Everything was in place.

Then Scargill was elected. "The moment that happened," John Hoskyns remembers, "we basically said, '*There will be a war. Perhaps the last battle.*'"

Yet there remains a great mystery. Clearly, a *hell* of a lot of coal had been stockpiled. Equally clearly, the government was determined to win a strike. So why, given this, did Scargill call for a strike against pit closures, when no such strike had ever been called, no less won, before? And why did he call it in the springtime, in particular? By this point, Scargill could not have been ignorant of Thatcher's nature. General Galtieri had said to the American envoy, Vernon Walters, "That woman wouldn't dare" attempt to retake the Falklands. Walters raised an eyebrow. He recalled Thatcher's willingness—even eagerness, truth be told—to let the Irish hunger strikers perish. "Mr. President," he replied, "'that woman' has let a number of hunger strikers of her own basic ethnic origin starve themselves to death without flickering an eyelash. I wouldn't count on that if I were you."[31]

---

30. Ibid., p. 157.
31. Robin Renwick, *Fighting with Allies: America and Britain in Peace and War* (Macmillan, 1996), p. 230.

Scargill had seen what happened to Galtieri. I simply cannot understand why he thought he would meet a different fate.

Hoskyns shrugs. "He did something quite crazy. I mean, he was actually, I suspect, in strategic terms, a fool. A stupid man."

⸙

Neil Kinnock: They deserved each other. Scargill and Thatcher deserved each other. But nobody *else* deserved them.

CB: Do you see a lot of similarities in their temperaments?

NK: Well, temperament, maybe not, but there are similarities. *Infinite* self-belief. A huge sense of superiority, coupled with some chips on their shoulders. Scargill thought that anybody who wasn't actually kissing his ass was patronizing him. Or plotting against him. And Margaret Thatcher was more conscious than she should have been about being a grocer's daughter, and had changed her accent, her voice—

CB: You know, can you explain that to me? Because this is something—for an American it's a little bit hard—[32]

NK: Yeah, sure.

CB: Can you tell me what she sounded like before? Can you imitate it?

NK: Well, for instance, I'll tell you what, I'll give you a couple o' words whose pronunciations she would've changed. Margaret Thatcher, prime minister, Oxford graduate, millionaire's wife, would say, "graaaahz." With a long "a." Margaret Thatcher, schoolgirl, would say, "grass." With a very short "a."

CB: Do you speak the same way as you did when you were growing up?

NK: Yeah, pretty much . . . I've made absolutely no conscious effort to change it. Whereas I can give you the names of a few

---

32. It's not hard at all; you'd have to be deaf not to hear how her accent changed. But Kinnock's Thatcher imitations are matchless, and I could hardly pass up an opportunity to hear more of them.

Welshmen, roughly of my generation, who have changed
their accent—

CB: I don't know *why* a Welshman would want to lose his accent—

NK: Well, yeah, I . . . I don't *begin* to understand it.

CB: Look, this is fascinating, but I'm losing the thread, which is
Margaret Thatcher, and her changing her accent, and her
class background, which you think she had a chip on her
shoulder about—

NK: Well, yeah. Because it made her acutely conscious of not
picking up the wrong fork, you know? In Britain maybe
more than anywhere else. I don't know, Turgenev wrote
about it in Russia, and I guess there are German writers and
French writers who've noticed the same tendency, but I
think it may have been more pronounced in the United
Kingdom then.

CB: Well, you say that she had "a chip on her shoulder" about it,
but then what you just said suggests that she was quite *right*
to be self-conscious about it.

NK: Well, no, of course she wasn't—I mean, there was never any
danger. I mean, bloody hell, my father was a coal miner, I
was brought up to hold my knife and fork properly and
know which fork to use, and how to eat—

CB: OK. So your point here—is it that she was or she wasn't
right to have a chip on her shoulder? Because you're
telling me on the one hand that there's an incredible attention to these subtle signals of class, and you're also
telling me that this "chip on her shoulder" was somehow
not rational—

NK: 'Course it wasn't! I mean just—first of all, she had nothing
to fear—

CB: But there *was* a lot of prejudice against her because of her
class background. I mean, I've heard it dripping out of the
mouths of her own cabinet members.

NK: Oh, sure. Oh, yeah, yeah, yeah. But that's *their* kind of stu-
pidity. That's *their* chinless delusion. She was in *charge!* She

was in *charge!* She could have said, "I'm me. I'm bright. I'm
Margaret. I'm a Tory. Get out of my bloody way—"

CB: She *did* say that.

NK: Well, she—

CB: I mean, if *anybody* ever said, "I'm a Tory, get out of my
bloody way," it's Margaret Thatcher.

NK: Yeah . . . [*long pause*] Maybe.

Let us return to Peter Walker, who is telling us how he discovered
that Scargill was a Marxist.

Lord Walker: He spoke at loads of Marxist conferences all over
the world. And—

[*Waiter interrupts*]

PW: Now, my guest is having the, um, the halibut and asparagus.
And I will have six oysters please. [*Sound of clock chiming.*]
And then my guest is having the scallops, and I'll have the
Dover sole.

Waiter: Will you have it off the bone, Milord?

PW: Off the bone, yes, I'm a very lazy man. And, um, now,
vegetables.

Waiter: Spinach, French beans, broccoli, cauliflower?

PW: Potatoes?

Waiter: Potatoes, I've got sautéed, new, French fries . . .

CB: What do you recommend?

Waiter: What do I recommend? Well, spinach is fine, and, er,
sautéed potatoes—

CB: Sounds good to me.

PW: I'll have spinach and new potatoes, please, and, um, we'll
have a bottle of the nice Chablis. Fizzy water or still water?

CB: I like what I'm drinking very much, the fizzy water.

PW: And um, when they introduced profit-sharing, he delivered
a speech, with another very hard-line lady communist, that

said, "We must stop profit-sharing. The capitalists are doing this to make capitalism attractive. And if we're going to achieve the Revolution, we don't want capitalism to become attractive." And so he urged unions not to participate in profit-sharing schemes. And right away, anything he could do to bring about the day of Revolution was in all his speeches and all his remarks.

Imagine that.

But before concluding that Scargill may have had a point, you should know this about Lord Walker. He is the son of a factory worker. His father was a union man—a shop steward, in fact. Walker did not emerge from the privileged class of which he is now a member. He, more than anyone, has the right to say that if equality of opportunity is present, the hardworking and talented will rise to the top. *He* did, after all.

In fact, Walker was the miners' great champion. I believe him when he says that he did everything within his power to avert a strike. Prior to the strike, Walker proposed to offer the miners an extremely conciliatory deal. It would not have forced a single miner into redundancy. He offered early retirement, on generous terms, to miners over the age of fifty. Miners working at the pits slated for closure would be offered the choice of a job at another pit or a voluntary redundancy package. Another 800 million pounds of taxpayer money would be invested in the coal industry. Given the losses the industry had been running, it is impossible to see this as anything other than a bribe.

Walker went to Thatcher, alone, to persuade her that the bribe, though costly, was essential. "Look," he said, "I think this meets every emotional issue the miners have. And it's expensive, but not as expensive as a coal strike. And I think we should do it."

Thatcher thought about it.

"You know," she decided, "I agree with you."

It is often held—it is certainly still believed widely among the miners—that Thatcher provoked the strike deliberately to punish them for the humiliations they had inflicted on prior Conservative governments. Walker says this is a myth, and the logic is on his side. "If you'd wanted a strike," he reasonably notes, "the last thing you'd have done was make an offer of that sort—I mean, an offer that was superb. You could have made an offer which was reasonable, and you'd have got a strike, or you might have got a strike. But we made an offer that was absolutely perfect." Since becoming president of the union, Scargill had tried three times to convince the miners to strike; three times the union had voted no. There was no reason to imagine this time would be different: The deal was too good.

Walker was immensely gratified when Thatcher and the rest of the cabinet agreed to his proposal. The wets, he imagined, would save the day. He thought the miners would never reject such a handsome deal. And indeed, they did not.

In principle, the National Union of Mineworkers was a democratic organization. Its charter called for a ballot of all its members, and the agreement of 55 percent of its membership, before the declaration of a strike. "I presumed there was no way he could win a ballot," Walker says, "so there wouldn't be a strike. And I was wrong."

Upon seeing the terms of Walker's package, Scargill presumably realized that in all likelihood, the union would accept it. To Walker's astonishment, he simply decided not to hold a vote. "What he did was—with money from the Soviet Union—he paid miners to go and violently picket against miners who stayed at work. And he got a strike by brute force instead of the ballot."

When the strike began on March 12, miners in the Midlands and Nottingham refused to join. Their pits were profitable. They were not slated for closure. They had cars, mortgages, decent salaries, pension plans—they had no desire to throw themselves on the bonfire of Scargill's vanity. Their lack of solidarity confirmed Scargill's deepest instincts about the unwisdom of the unpoliticized laboring classes: How easily they were tempted by baubles and trinkets! The dissenting miners demanded a national ballot.

Scargill refused. Why, he asked, should a treacherous labor aristocracy be allowed to vote other working men out of a job?

According to Scargill's logic, the union was a federation; therefore, each region should decide independently whether to strike. He assumed that once it had begun, the strike would spread—he would see to it that it did. Defying him, nine constituent unions held a vote, and to Scargill's disgust, eight voted against the strike. In Leicestershire, 89 percent voted nay. In the Midlands, 73 percent. In Nottinghamshire, 73 percent.

It was an appalling display of false consciousness, Scargill concluded. He dispatched flying pickets from Yorkshire to close down their mines—for their own good. This, too, was an extraordinarily stupid decision. The miners of Nottinghamshire, in particular, were enraged. They took vengeance.

_C_ _C_ _C_

Mr. Fields: How does the Prime Minister feel, having attempted to display to the world a caring mother's face and a preparedness to travel anywhere in the interests of her children, when she sees miners' children and families seeking sustenance from soup kitchens and charities? Is she aware of the repugnance felt by millions of people at her attempts to starve miners back to work? Is she not ashamed of herself, and does she agree that she has disgraced her motherhood? Will she consider joining a closed monastic order as quickly as possible to repent of her sins and reflect on her crimes against humanity?[33]

Scargill called at the beginning of the strike for the "total mobilization of the trade and labor movement," and Linda Sheridan is right: Had the call been heeded—had the miners hung together,

---

33. May 22, 1984, House of Commons PQs, *Hansard* [60/822–26].

and had the other unions come out in support of them—the strike would have been won. But the other unions demurred, and this was no accident. Thatcher made sure of it.

I say "Thatcher," but this was not how it was presented. Officially, this was a dispute between the National Coal Board and the miners' union; Thatcher maintained the pretense throughout that it was not her role to interfere. "The government," she said, "will leave the National Coal Board to deal with the matter as it thinks fit."[34] Unofficially, Thatcher supervised every detail of the operations. She established and chaired "Misc. 101," the cabinet committee that debated and determined every aspect of the government's response to the strike. She met her key ministers daily to receive reports on recent developments and guide the government's response. In her memoirs, she recalls that even when she went to Switzerland on vacation, "The telex chattered constantly . . . I sometimes thought at the end of the day that I would look out the window and see a couple of Yorkshire miners striding down the Swiss slopes."[35]

When the railway workers threatened to strike, she offered them a 7 percent raise. In September, the union of mine supervisors—responsible for the maintenance and safety of the pits—threatened to join the pickets. The supervisors had until then been reluctant to strike on the reasonable grounds that mines, when shut, can quickly flood or otherwise become so damaged that they cannot safely be reopened. Showing more foresight than the men they supervised, the supervisors had thus far argued against the strike on the grounds that prolonged closure could physically destroy the mines and put them out of jobs permanently. This is in fact what did happen to quite a number of pits.

A supervisors' strike would have meant the end for the government. "We were in danger of losing everything," Thatcher recalls. Fortunately, this problem had been anticipated. The government

---

34. March 13, 1984, House of Commons PQs, *Hansard* [60/56/276–82].
35. Thatcher, *The Downing Street Years*, p. 362.

had a mole inside the supervisors' union. Thatcher knew the supervisors' bottom line. She bought them off too.

"Scargill," Nigel Lawson says to me, expressing what is distinctly a minority view, "wasn't an imposing personality." (Mind you, this is from one of the few men who was not intimidated by Thatcher, so it may simply be that Lawson is not particularly gifted at recognizing imposing personalities.) "I mean, his resistance to rational argument gave him a strength of a kind, but it was not he who was strong, it was the president of the National Union of Mineworkers who was strong, provided he could count on the loyalty of the mineworkers. And that was why it was very important to try and engineer a state of affairs in which he *didn't* have the complete support of the mineworkers." That is just what Thatcher did. When Lawson was energy secretary, and against the strenuous objections of environmentalists, he had rammed through proposals to sink two new mines in "a lovely stretch of countryside" in Leicestershire.[36] The miners of the Midlands had been itching to get their hands on the coal seam there, which was underneath the Vale of Belvoir.

Lawson: Beaver.
CB: I'm sorry?
NL: It's pronounced "Beaver."
CB: Is it really?
NL: Yes. But English pronunciation is always a bit weird.
CB: Yes, that's definitely weird.

Understandably, the Vale of Belvoir's residents did not wish to see slag heaps rising from their backyards, but Lawson persuaded Thatcher that it was more important to shore up the support of the Midlands miners than to placate a handful of eager Belvoir environmentalists. The deal, he argued, would increase the likelihood that the miners who stood to benefit would defy Scargill: If

---

36. Lawson, *The View from No. 11*, p. 144.

push came to shove, Lawson reckoned, they would shovel, not push. And that is just what they did. During the strike, with the government's *very* active support, those miners broke away from Scargill's union and with miners from Nottinghamshire formed their own union—the Union of *Democratic* Mineworkers. They kept working, and thanks to their output, stockpiles remained high throughout the winter.

In August, two miners from Nottinghamshire took the National Union of Mineworkers to court for failing to hold a ballot. David Hart, one of Thatcher's friends, paid their legal costs. He organized their legal campaign from his luxury suite at Claridge's, where he met miners who wanted to return to work. When finally they did go back to work, he paid for them to be protected by former SAS bodyguards.

In September, the court ruled in the Nottinghamshire miners' favor, finding that the union had indeed breached its own constitution. The union was fined £200,000.[37] The court ordered the union's assets sequestered. Other unions, observing this, came to the conclusion that strike action might be financially imprudent.

Thatcher determined that violent picketers would be met by an equally violent police force, but she feared that local authorities might be hesitant to do the needful. They would, after all, be arresting the citizens of their own hometowns, people with whom they had grown up. Appropriating Scargill's tactic of deploying flying pickets, the government took the unprecedented step of coordinating the police at a national level and bringing in forces from distant counties to confront the picketers. Over the course of the strike, 11,291 miners were arrested; an untold number injured; eleven killed.

Thatcher also had the wisdom to go no further than this. When it was suggested to her that were this America, the National

---

37. It refused to pay. The court then discovered the assets were missing. They had been transferred abroad.

Guard would be called in with tanks, she immediately dismissed the idea as "political suicide."[38]

The dockworkers were told they would be fired if they refused to handle coal.

The steelworkers, likewise.

The electricians' union was so completely co-opted that its leaders supplied the government with intelligence about the miners.

The Special Branch infiltrated a spy—codenamed Silver Fox—right into Scargill's inner circle.[39] This is one of those assertions that is usually prefaced by "allegedly." I'll let you judge for yourself:

FINAL SCRIPT OF "TRUE SPIES"
Archive of miners
Commentary

But it was in the epic showdown between Mrs. Thatcher and the miners that the Secret State was tested to the limit. Could the tide of so-called subversion be stopped?

Commentary

At its secret spy school at Fort Monkton, MI5 planned for the worst—virtually a civil war scenario. [PAUSE] It summoned selected Special Branch officers for advanced training in agent handling.

Curzon street pix
Commentary

To meet the political threat, the Secret State decided that covert means would have to be used to spy on its enemies. At the time, Stella Rimington was Assistant Director of the MI5 division that countered domestic subversion.

---

38. BBC documentary, *The Downing Street Years*, 1993.
39. From script of "True Spies," produced by BBC News, aired October–November 2002.

ASTON
STELLA RIMINGTON
Director General, MI5, 1992–96
Stella Rimington sync

S.R.: The leaders of the miners strike themselves had actually said that one of the purposes of the miners strike was to overthrow Mrs. Thatcher who was the elected Prime Minister of the country and the industrial department of the Communist Party was very involved in all sorts of different ways in the strike and that was of concern to us, that's what we were interested in.

ASTON
ARTHUR SCARGILL
President, N.U.M. 1981–2002
Arthur Scargill sync

A.S.: . . . There were agents planted within the NUM both for a number of years prior to 1984 in readiness, almost like sleepers. I believe that all our offices were constantly bugged . . . I also know that I was under close personal supervision, so to speak, wherever I went and whoever I met.

Orgreave violence
Orgreave, June 1984
Set to BILLY BRAGG
Commentary

The strike became increasingly violent as flying pickets from all over the country converged on Orgreave coking plant. Scargill hoped to repeat Saltley Gate. The dramatic images of that violent day are etched on the memory of the senior officer in charge on the ground.

ASTON
TONY CLEMENT

Asst Chief Constable, S. Yorks Police, 1981–85
Tony Clement sync

There was violence, there was violence on both sides. You cannot expect that sort of situation to arise when police officers are not at times going to lose their temper or lose their cool or their discipline disappears. It would happen to me, I feel sure, if I was in that situation. There were what, 30 or 40 police officers a day being taken to hospital. We didn't have that sort of situation in this country, they didn't attack police officers like that, not at that time, not until our friend Mr. Scargill decided that that was the way to impose his will.

Commentary

Scargill was on the front line, marshalling his troops to confront the police who'd been drafted in from the Met and Forces nationwide.

Tony Clement sync

T.C.: He thought he was going to win. It was symbolic, it was a trial of strength. He said I'm going to close that. We said you're not.

IX OF BARNSLEY
Exterior and interiors
Commentary

Although Stella Rimington steadfastly refuses to be drawn about monitoring Scargill's Headquarters, we can reveal that the Secret State was running a highly placed agent, close to Scargill and the leadership of the NUM. We understand the agent's codename was "Silver Fox."

Tony Clement sync

T.C.: There was a fairly senior man within the NUM who was talking to Special Branch. He was at the level where he would sit round the table with the NUM leadership.

John Nesbit sync
We were in a position to get information, very, very specific
and precise information that was correct every time, as to
where the violent picketing would be taking place, particularly when the miners started to go back to work.

Commentary
"Silver Fox," the Secret State's spy in Scargill's inner sanctum, gave the police the crucial advantage.

ACTUALITY Police control room
Arthur Scargill sync
INTERVIEWER: Did you know that there was an agent
very close to you at your shoulder almost who was feeding
information to his or her Special Branch handler about the
movement of pickets during the '84 strike?
Arthur Scargill: I would be amazed if there wasn't.
INT: Doesn't come as any surprise?
A.S.: Not at all.
INT: Do you know who this person was?
A.S.: I haven't got a clue and I wouldn't like to guess, be-
cause I know from experience that you can always make as-
sumptions that are wrong, and so I rule nobody in, and I
rule nobody out.[40]

"I rule nobody out." Imagine the world of paranoia in which
Scargill lived that year.

The strike wore on and on and on. The miners suffered desperate impoverishment. But the preparations put in place by the government, the output from the Nottinghamshire pits, and the
intelligence "allegedly" provided by the Silver Fox ensured that the
lights stayed on. The other unions stayed sweet. The power stations

---

40. Ibid.

kept running. The steel furnaces kept burning. It was a mild winter. The government, it was now clear, could last until the spring. Springtime is not a striking miner's friend.

_____ ◦◦ ◦◦◦ ◦◦ _____

Mr. Parry: Is the Prime Minister aware that this Christmas thousands of striking miners, workers sacked from Cammell Laird, single-parent families and people on lower incomes will not be able to buy their children food or toys or new clothes and will tell their children that Father Christmas is dead? Is she aware that, in addition to having blood on her hands, she will go down in history as the woman who killed Santa Claus?[41]

Scargill kept telling the miners the coal stocks would run out soon. *Within weeks,* he promised. *Within weeks.* When the press started repeating Scargill's assurances, Walker arranged for journalists to be taken up in helicopters and flown over the power stations to see the size of the stocks.

Neil Kinnock remembers visiting a coal miners' lodge in his constituency: "The boys were pretty frigid at the start, and they're asking me questions, and you know, they'd never be vicious, but obviously, they'd swallowed all this crap about me not supportin' the miners and all that stuff. But nevertheless they asked their questions, and eventually I said, 'Now listen. I wasn't going to do this, because I think you've had enough punishment. But my union, the Transport and General Workers Union, has just sent me last week's figures for coal stocks in several power stations. And I'll read 'em out to you.' And I read them out. And the guys just sort of looked at me. And I said, 'Now, I don't know'—and there were only several hundred men there—'I don't know how many of you

---

41. October 30, 1984, House of Commons PQs, *Hansard* HC [65/1156–60].

are surprised. I guess there are some of you who've been picketing the power stations who are *not* surprised, because you've looked through the fence. And you've talked to the drivers. And you've talked to the guys working in the power stations. *And you know bloody well* that when Scargill said there's three weeks left—there's three *years* left.' And the guys said—*yup.*"

"And if they *knew* that, why didn't they turn on him?"

"Because of loyalty. Because they were isolated, under attack, and they weren't gonna break ranks and turn on their own leadership—"

"So their loyalty was to the union?"

"No, the loyalty was to their own communities and their own comrades. That being said—"

"But what kind of loyalty is it to march together like lemmings off a cliff?"

"That's how wars are fought, luv. If generals couldn't get men to line abreast against machine guns, there wouldn't be any wars."

"Yeah, I understand your point, but I'm still surprised by this—"

"No, this is the thing. Other than people who know the mining communities and miners *very* well, people will receive what I say, and they'll think, 'Well, he doesn't have any interest in bullshitting us about this, and maybe there's some truth in it, but it can't *really* be true.' *Nobody* who comes from a coal-mining community says that. You just say, 'Yeah, that's right. That's what it's like.' And that *is* what it's like. To some extent it's to do with the physical sociology of coal mining. You depend on all the other guys. *Including* the ones you don't like. All rivalries die the moment you go down the colliery. As far as you're concerned, whether you like someone or not, they're lookin' out for you, and you're lookin' out for them."

Bernard Ingham, of course, sees it a bit differently. The miners "were paralyzed. Because they were in the hands of a military junta, in effect. And the discipline that they exercised, the brutality of their message, was really quite remarkable. I mean, this wasn't a democratic institution, this was a menacing institution. I don't think people really understood the depths to which the British trade union movement sank during Scargill's time. He had a private army! The purpose of these flying pickets was to impose his will upon his union, and of course upon the police and the nation. And these flying pickets went far and wide, and I think I'm right in saying they were the only people the union paid during the strike. Those who formed his private army and fought the battle at Orgreave, against the police. Now, *that* is the nature of the man."

Kinnock's loyalties were utterly conflicted. He loathed Scargill and knew he would bring the miners to ruin. But he represented the Labour Party—whose origins are in the trade union movement—and came from a mining town himself. He could not bring himself publicly to condemn Scargill's failure to ballot the union membership.

Walker implored Kinnock to call for a ballot. He persuaded two Labour parliamentarians—"I can't name names, for obvious reasons"—to go to Kinnock with a message: *Look, Kinnock. Obviously I can't ask you to support a Tory government in a miners' strike. All I ask you to do is say, "The miners have always had a ballot. This terrible dispute doesn't have the support of a ballot. I ask you as leader of the Labour Party to now quickly hold a ballot on this strike." It's in your interest: If they ballot in favor of the strike, you'll be supported by the miners, not by Scargill. If they ballot against it, you will be praised for having settled the strike. As party leader, you have nothing to lose.* The envoys did their best to persuade them. "But he said no, he couldn't be seen, you know, bullying the miners' union."

Kinnock told me that he tried, repeatedly, to talk sense into Scargill behind the scenes. Given how much the men loathed each other, I wondered about the tenor of those conversations. Were they acrimonious, I ask? "Did he speak to you disrespectfully, or—?"

"No, no, no, no, no, no. No, no. Nothing like that. I mean, the only time that Scargill would ever have a go at me was when he was surrounded by a couple o' thousand people. I mean, he'd never do it to my face."

"So what was he saying to justify his actions?"

"Well, he just kept dodging around, you know, and moving the goalposts. I'd say something like, 'It's going to be very difficult for you to get any kind of picketing support, 'cause you have no ballot. Sympathetic action is very difficult,' and he'd say, 'Ah, but the coal stocks, there's only a fortnight left!'"

"But that's *nuts*! I mean, he *knew* it was nuts!"

"Of course it's nuts! Of course it's nuts!"

"So why weren't you insisting on a ballot?" I asked.

"Well, if I'd said at that stage, 'Either have a ballot, or go back to work,' then two things would have happened. First of all, I would have been kicking the miners in the face. Secondly, of course, Scargill could always have blamed me for the failure of the strike. So I wasn't going to allow either of those things to happen. So that was the reason."

"In retrospect do you regret that you made that decision?"

"Oh yeah. It was the worst decision I ever made in my life."

"Really? You think that was the *worst* decision you ever made?"

"Oh, *Christ*, yeah. Yeah, yeah."

When I ask Nigel Lawson about Kinnock's odd passivity during the miners' strike, he snorts derisively. "He was a very weak man. He was and is a very weak man."

I don't agree. Kinnock was in fact courageous; it was Kinnock, after all, who after this debacle purged his party of its hard-left wing, paving the way for the rise of New Labour. But I suspect that until the very last, Kinnock, like Scargill, thought the miners would win. After all, Kinnock comes from a mining town; he is a miner's son. He hated Scargill, and he hated Thatcher, but he loved the miners. So he bet on the wrong horse.

—⁃◌ ⊱≈⊰ ◌⁃—

> . . . When a miner is hurt it is of course impossible to attend
> to him immediately. He lies crushed under several hundred-
> weight of stone in some dreadful cranny underground, and

even after he has been extricated it is necessary to drag his body a mile or more, perhaps, through galleries where nobody can stand upright. They are liable to rheumatism and a man with defective lungs does not last long in that dust-impregnated air, but the most characteristic industrial disease is nystagmus. This is a disease of the eyes which makes the eyeballs oscillate in a strange manner when they come near a light. It is due presumably to working in half-darkness, and sometimes results in total blindness . . . [42]

I do not understand the miners' determination to keep the pits open. I understand their rage—a life in the pits would madden anyone, I reckon—but I don't understand its object. Why were they demanding the right to mine coal? Why were they not demanding the very opposite—that the government do something, anything, to shut every last one of those hellishly cruel pits down? The miners chanted, "Coal, not dole." But a lifetime on the dole, it seems to me, would have been preferable to going down the mines. And the dole was the worst alternative in 1984. Unemployment would not have meant starvation, as it might have a century prior.

Peter Walker nods when I say something to this effect. "I used to go down in the valleys, and knock door-to-door on all the rather humble houses. And it was a terrible experience, because nearly always a widow would come to the door. Her husband had either died of mining illnesses, or mining accidents. Or alternatively, she'd come to the door, and you'd hear in the background an elderly man coughing . . . "

The waiter refills Walker's wine glass. "Was there ever a moment when you doubted that the government would win?" I ask him.

"Never. No."

"You were always completely confident? Why was that?"

---

42. Orwell, *The Road to Wigan Pier.*

"If he had found a way of closing all the pits, I would have imported coal. I mean, there's plenty of coal to be imported. And I would have put the army in charge of protecting the lorries. And I knew that in whatever I wanted to do, I was absolutely confident that if I said, 'Look, we've got to import coal, you know, we've got to have the army monitoring the delivery of coal,' I would have had the support of the cabinet, and Margaret. But I was never anywhere near that. There was never a moment when the coal stocks went down. He tried to do other things, like stop spare parts going in to the power stations, and we found ways to smuggle them in."

The dessert cart arrives. I order the lemongrass crème brûlée; Walker opts for the trio of homemade sorbets. I finish the last drop of wine in my glass.

"I mean," says Walker, "it was a strike you *couldn't* lose. If you'd lost, it would have been a total disaster for democratic capitalism. It would have been unbelievable."

⁀ ⌾ ⁀

The miners, increasingly desperate and increasingly humiliated, grew more violent. Working miners were assaulted, their families terrorized. A taxi driver carrying a scab to work in South Wales was killed.

Reports surfaced in the papers that Scargill had taken money from Libyan agents. Not long before, a British policewoman had been murdered by gunfire emerging from the Libyan embassy in London. Scargill did not deny the reports. He argued—characteristically—that the money came from "Libyan trade unions."

In December 1984 an interviewer remarked to the prime minister that people were literally being killed over coal. Was it not time, he asked her, to do something, *anything*, to bring the strike to an end? *No*, she replied. "As far as Government is concerned, never, never, never give in to violence. *Never.* This strike has been sustained by violence and it took a long time for certain people to condemn that violence, and that length of time should never have occurred in a democracy. This strike is sustained by violence and by a refusal to have the democratic right to a ballot. Now, if anyone is suggesting that I appease those: *No*."[43] The words echoed, as they were intended to do, Churchill's: "Never, never, never, never—in nothing, great or small, large or petty—never give in except to convictions of honor and good sense. Never yield to force; never yield to the apparently overwhelming might of the enemy." By December, it was perfectly clear to the nation that no matter the cost, no matter who died, Thatcher would not break. In her rhetoric, the striking miners had now been elevated, by analogy, to Nazis. At the height of this crisis, on October 12, the Brighton Hotel was bombed. As she makes clear in her memoirs, Thatcher held the bombers and Arthur Scargill to be morally indistinguishable.[44]

The miners, desperate to feed themselves and their families, began trickling back to work. By late February, more than half the miners had returned.

On March 3, nearly a year after the announcement of the strike, the delegates of the miners' union at last defied Scargill. They voted—narrowly—to abandon the cause.

They had lost.

___ ___ ___

"It was a pivotal event," says Charles Powell of the strike. "The Falklands were pivotal in restoring Britain's national self-confidence, and that was an important part of it, because the country again felt invigorated, proud, capable of seeing people off, capable of achieving things. That provided a very good psychological environment for subsequent battles on the domestic front. But the miners' strike, which brought us to the very brink of civil war—"

"Do you really mean that? A civil war?"

43. Press conference for American correspondents in London, December 7, 1984, transcript, Thatcher MSS (digital collection), doc. 105810.
44. *The Downing Street Years*, pp. 370–371.

"Yes, I do, yeah, I do. I really mean that. It was close to a civil war situation, and you've got tens of thousands of police battling miners, huge confrontations, the whole trade union movement on the edge, sort of ready to go. It was a very, very fraught and tense time. And it was almost like fighting a war. If you'd been there on Downing Street at the heart of that you'd have felt that, you know, bulletins from the front, and war councils taking place late at night and all those sorts of things. It was a real crisis atmosphere."

"Do you think that level of conflict could have been avoided with a more delicate policy, while still achieving the same ends—"

"No. Certainly not."

"So you place the blame for the extremity of the dispute entirely on Scargill?"

"She knew there had to be a major confrontation. Scargill had to be defeated in battle. It was almost medieval, you know, this idea, a challenge, a joust, whatever it was. She knew he could only win by deploying all these miners, as many as he could, taking her on, taking on the state . . . I think it really was an exceptional situation, it *needed* to be. The symbolism was so important, namely, you had to establish this dominance over the trade unions. Finally. You can't really imagine what it was like, for people of my generation, we used to switch on the television at night, in the 1960s and '70s, and there were the trade union leaders, coming out of Number 10 Downing Street, night after night, having told the government what to do, what they *could* do, what they'd put up with and not put up with, and they'd got their way, time after time."

"You say I can't imagine what it was like. But try to explain it to me."

"It was demoralizing. Seeing this band of men, holding the whole country to ransom. Looking after the interests of their members at the expense of everything and everyone else. They had no broader view of the national interest, or anything of that sort at all, they were intent only on their narrow interest."

"Were there any moments in the dispute when you thought, 'We're not on the right track here, we're not going to win this'?"

"I don't recall thinking we'd ever lose. There were setbacks, there were things we got wrong, you know, there was all this business about the mine supervisors—but no, no, those were tactical errors. I think the strategy, because it had been so carefully prepared, was always bound to succeed. Now, many people will tell you that they were responsible for it as much as she was. Peter Walker, I think, would certainly argue that he was the man who won the miners' strike—"

"I spoke to him, and yes, he does argue that."

"Yes, and there are sort of politics in that—"

"Of course, of course—"

"Well, he did have a very important role, absolutely. But the ultimate willpower was really hers. She became a Boudicea-like figure at the forefront of the battle. That's how it seemed to people in the country, I think. I mean, it was all the Iron Lady and Battling Maggie stuff. I mean, that's how she proceeded."

In 1985, a triumphant Thatcher addressed the Conservative Party conference:

> We were told you'll never stand a major industrial strike, let alone a coal strike . . . But we did just that—and won. It was a strike conducted with violence and intimidation on the picket line and in the villages. Yet Labour supported that strike to the bitter end . . . What do you think would have happened if Mr. Scargill had won? I think the whole country knows the answer. Neil would have knelt.[45]

Linger for a moment on that last line. Consider all of its emasculating, sadistic, and sexual implications. Kinnock says he didn't think it chivalrous to hit a girl. That hardly stopped Thatcher from

---

45. Speech to Conservative Party Conference, October 11, 1985, Thatcher MSS (digital collection), doc. 106145.

kicking him between the legs—even when he was already on the ground. That too is how she proceeded.

_ɔ ᷒ ɔ_

"Was Scargill a megalomaniac, or was he desperate?" I ask Bernard Ingham.

"*Megalomaniac*, in my view. I mean, it was a gamble, no doubt about it, a bad gamble, but he believed that they were *invincible*. I mean, no government that he'd come across would stand up to him, and of course he was *astounded* when Mrs. Thatcher did! I think he felt he was invincible, and that is *fair!* After all, it was a pretty close-run thing!"

"Was it?"

"Oh, yeah, it was closer than people imagined. I mean, without her resolution, they would have caved in a long time earlier."

"Well it's interesting that you say that, because just yesterday, speaking to Lord Walker, I asked, 'Was there ever a moment when you were in doubt that you would win?' and he said, 'Never.'"

"That's *not* true."

"At what point was there a doubt?"

"I mean, if power supplies had faltered, then they would have been in real trouble. And fortunately, they had Walter Marshall, at the seams, who coaxed every bolt that he could find from anything, you know, and kept us going. And also, it wasn't an excessively cold winter. Of course, if he'd have called a ballot, and won that ballot—"

"Would there have been any chance of him winning?"

"Oh, yes, I think he would, because he wouldn't have split the union. And the very act of splitting the union meant that the government had coal production moving."

"But my understanding was that the reason he didn't call a ballot was because he knew he wouldn't win."

"Well, that's what people say. But you never know. You never know when there's a ballot called. I honestly don't know, and I don't think anyone who's honest does know whether he'd have won . . . But I can't agree with Peter Walker that everything was plain sailing. It wasn't."

"He didn't say 'plain sailing.' He said he never had a doubt that there would be victory in the end. He never believed for a second that there was a chance that Mrs. Thatcher would fail."

"Oh, I see. Well, I never believed for a second that Mrs. Thatcher would give in. That's different."

"How so?"

"Well, she could have been stolid to the end, but if the lights went out . . . if British industry were crippled, what do you do *then?*"

As the men trooped dejectedly back into the pits, their wives distributed carnations—the symbol of heroism—at the gates. At many mines, they marched back to the sound of brass bands. But everyone knew this was no victory.

It was the end of the mining industry in Britain. The pits had permanently lost their customers, who sought to acquire fuel sources that would not be held hostage to the manic caprices of Arthur Scargill.

It was the end of the era of widespread strikes in Britain. Six months after the end of the miners' strike, railway workers threatened to strike over the introduction of new trains that could be operated with fewer men. Union leaders put the motion to a ballot. Of course they did; they had seen what happened to Scargill. Members voted against it. Of course they did; they had seen what happened to the miners. In 1979, 29.5 million work days were lost in Britain due to strikes. Five years later, that number had plummeted a hundredfold, to 278,000. Britain now has the most efficient labor market in Europe.

It was the end of revolutionary socialism in Britain. Shortly thereafter, Kinnock triumphed over and marginalized the Trotskyite wing of the Labour Party, transforming the party into one in which men who proclaimed that they were all Thatcherites now could and did rise to the top.

With the miners permanently neutered as a political force, the government accelerated the closure of loss-making pits. The coal industry was entirely privatized in 1994. The Nottinghamshire miners had expected their cooperation would ensure the security of their jobs, but most of their pits closed, too. When the Labour Party came back into power, in 1997, it made no attempt whatsoever to revive the coal industry. By 2005, only eight major deep mines, employing fewer than 3,000 men, remained.

Scargill had always claimed that the government intended to destroy the coal industry. He says now that he has been vindicated. But the industry was dying anyway. The strike was the *coup de grace*, and the strike was Scargill's fault.

> It is a dreadful job that they do, an almost superhuman job by the standard of an ordinary person. For they are not only shifting monstrous quantities of coal, they are also doing it in a position that doubles or trebles the work. They have got to remain kneeling all the while—they could hardly rise from their knees without hitting the ceiling—and you can easily see by trying it what a tremendous effort this means . . . And the other conditions do not exactly make things easier. There is the heat—it varies, but in some mines it is suffocating—and the coal dust that stuffs up your throat and nostrils and collects along your eyelids, and the unending rattle of the conveyor . . . Every miner has blue scars on his nose and forehead, and will carry them to his death. The coal dust of which the air underground is full enters every cut, and then the skin grows over it and forms a blue stain like tattooing, which in fact it is . . . [46]

---

46. Orwell, *The Road to Wigan Pier.*

The rattle of the conveyor has been silenced now. The slag heaps have disappeared from the British countryside, overgrown by hills and meadow dotted with cow parsley and buttercups, smooth-stalked grass and Yorkshire fog.

Good riddance.

8

Miners Is Miners

"The history of the world is but the biography of
great men." Discuss.
— FINAL EXAM IN GENERAL HISTORY,
OXFORD UNIVERSITY

The General History exam at Oxford is just what it sounds like: a
test of the student's general knowledge of history. It's a crapshoot.
Are the grounds for religious persecution always the same? Why have
some societies been more susceptible than others to belief in magic?
One theme does come up reliably, however, year after year: *Is it all*
about great men?

It is now the fashion among historians to reject the great man
theory of history and study what is termed people's history—the
history of mass movements, outsiders, ordinary men and women.
The essence of history, by these lights, is not the story of Thatcher
and the powerful men around her. It is the story of the ordinary
men and women who lived through the Thatcher years.

The student is implicitly invited to compare the two approaches to studying history and offer a judgment. Which one is

better? A strong opinion, one way or the other, is the key to impressing the examiners. *People's history, no contest.* But in truth, they are both good ways of doing history.

With that in mind, I set out to speak to the miners Thatcher crushed.

My train arrives in Yorkshire on a Saturday evening, and although it is still light, everyone is already drunk. The street from the station to my hotel is lined with nightclubs, from which heavy-set women in short skirts emerge, stumbling, displaying acres of goose-pimpled flesh, arguing loudly about who is shagging whom in the bog. Glassy-eyed young men travel up and down the street in menacing packs. Fast-food joints, surrounded by loiterers, pump hot, greasy-smelling air into the twilight.

Some places seem at first impression like happy places. Obviously, Wakefield, Yorkshire, isn't one of them.

Wakefield is in the heart of a district of now-extinct coal mines. I am there to meet Brian Lewis, who is, as he terms himself, the people's historian of Pontefract and Castleford, both towns slightly to the north of Wakefield. He has promised to introduce me to men whose lives were transformed by Thatcher's policies.

Brian picks me up at my hotel early the next morning. He is a courtly gentleman with rosy cheeks and a wild, white beard, which he grew, I later learn, in honor of William Morris, the English poet, artist, and devout socialist. The back seat of Brian's battered Toyota is full of half-opened boxes of reports he has written for the local government about deprivation in the former mining communities and the results of various schemes he is supervising in the hopes of regenerating them.

As we drive through the Yorkshire countryside, Brian points out the artifacts of the mining industry, the hills that once were slag heaps. In the decade after the strike, unemployment in many of these villages reached rates above 50 percent. Suicides rose significantly. In the late 1990s, the European Union declared this region the poorest in Britain and one of the poorest in Europe. Even now, with Britain's economy performing at unprecedented levels, it is possible to find families here entering their third generation on the dole. Rates of teenage pregnancy are high. School performance is poor. Alcoholism is endemic.

As we drive past villages left derelict after the strike, Brian points out their peculiar geography. They are in the middle of nowhere. They are where they are only because of the coal beneath the ground. When the mines closed, the local economies erected around them collapsed. The miners who lost their jobs after the strike could not simply wake up the next morning and look for another job in the village. Their whole lives had to be uprooted and re-created from scratch.

But as Brian himself correctly points out, people around the world often do just that. "You know," he said, "you go to India, and you go into a home, this bloke who was very kind to me, he and his wife are living in a room with a bed, a couch, and a computer—"

I know where he is going with this. "And with that computer, he's going to be taking customer-service calls from Ohio—"

"That is right. That is right. And his daughter is working for an American company, and she's scanning the Internet, and she has an economics degree, and she understands the computer policy of that company, and she's phoning them back. Now, in the mining community, when they get computers, they play computer games. Right? They don't even play *Civilization*, you know, games like that where you're building."

This is Brian's lament, the problem he has not figured out how to solve. The coal mines, he says, created a dependency culture. There is a profound lack of ambition in these former mining towns, an absence of initiative. The men have always been miners. They cannot imagine being anything else.

Brian is not sure whether the closure of the mines was inevitable. He believes coal may yet stage a comeback in Britain. But if the mines had to be closed, he feels, the government had a responsibility to take care of the men and women in these towns, to find some way to cultivate in them the values—the industry, initiative, and ambition—that would prepare them to function in a different kind of economy.

This is a fundamental ideological divide separating Thatcher from her critics on the Left. At the core of Thatcherism is the belief that the best way—the *only* way—for government to inculcate these values in the citizenry is to structure society so that these values are rewarded in the marketplace. The government cannot be in the business of instilling such qualities as initiative. Not only is that a utopian and impossible project, but schemes to do so— particularly if they involve taking money from those already possessed of industry and ambition and giving it to those who are not—are guaranteed to have precisely the opposite effect.

To someone like Brian, it is a cruel and ludicrous fantasy to imagine that free markets are a more powerful social force than generations' worth of local culture and tradition. "Her moral standings were about self-help, but she didn't understand self-help. I understand bloody self-help, you know? If you pull on your bootstraps, your body doesn't fly up into the air, but it does if you're married to a millionaire! So in one sense, she was supported, always, by her wealth. But her morality came from a culture which said, 'You can improve.' I believe in that, I believe in self-improvement. I write on aspiration. I am an entrepreneur, right? But she was—she was a political lady who had listened to her father on how to run a grocer's shop. And you can't run a country like a grocer's shop."

In fact, quite a bit of government assistance was available to these communities during the Thatcher era. In the years following the strike, Brian tells me, the government backed some twenty-odd separate schemes to regenerate the region. "People spent their whole lives applying for government money." Later, the European Union put up money in similar programs designed to assist areas suffering from the demise of a staple industry. "The weakness," Brian says, "was there weren't enough people who were entrepreneurially minded, so they got the money, but they were thinking,

'Whoa! We got a lot of money! And we're getting the money next year!' But they were seven-year schemes. And very few of them set up sustainable elements to retain any community after the money from Europe and after the money from the regional development agency had folded."

I don't wish to misrepresent Brian's views: He is a champion of these schemes and believes many of them to have been successful. The transformation of a culture and an economy is a slow process, he argues; it would be unreasonable to expect otherwise. I sympathize with this argument and don't at all think it specious. But I think we can all read between the lines of the phrase *very few of them set up sustainable elements . . .*

This is just the outcome a Thatcherite would expect. Thatcher believed it was not the government's role to set prices and wages; it was not the government's role to invest in industries or manage them; it was not the government's role to generate or regenerate anything. It was particularly not the government's role to create make-work projects. The proper role of the government was to create the conditions in which self-sufficient people might thrive. If some people failed to thrive, so be it—that is a natural fact of life. Not everyone is born of equal character and talent.

Regeneration schemes, argued Thatcher, served only "to create artificial jobs. We can do training—and we've got the biggest training scheme ever. We do community jobs, and try to get people back into the habit of work. But in the end the creation of wealth has to come from the private sector."[1]

If there were no more jobs in Yorkshire, the government's proper role was to make it easier for people to start new businesses by lowering their taxes, protecting the value of their currency, and removing distortions in the housing markets so that people might move more readily to places where their talents and labor were desired. But the government certainly couldn't create new jobs. "Ministers

---

1. Interview with CBI News, January 10, 1986, Thatcher MSS (digital collection), doc.106299.

and all our excellent civil servants can't pour out of Whitehall one day," she said, "with bowler and brollies, and say now we are going to start sixty new businesses in every new town. We wouldn't know what to do! We are administrators. It is for us to create the right conditions for enterprise to thrive."[2] Government-funded regeneration schemes that injected money into these communities masked critical information: namely, that there was no consumer demand here for the goods and services that people were trying to sell. End of story, as far as Thatcher was concerned.

The problem is this: If Thatcher is right to note that schemes to generate industry by pumping taxpayer money into idle communities tend to fail, Brian is right to argue that here, at least, the unfettered market has also failed. Left to their own devices and liberated from the dead hand of government intervention, the miners and their families—with a few notable exceptions—did not prosper and thrive. Five minutes in Wakefield is more than enough to establish this.

It cannot be said that this is because the miners were inherently lazy. No one who has ever read a description of life in a coal mine would accept this.

So why is there a problem? No one is sure.

What is the solution? No one knows.

It is possible, I suspect, that there simply isn't one.

Brian's own story, by the way, is one of self-improvement and self-help. He has been by turns a foundry worker, a teacher, a van driver, a painter, and the first poet laureate of Birmingham. "I've got several degrees," he said, "but I didn't get one until I was in my thirties. There was no chance for me. My class knew nothing about education. I didn't know what a university was. Yeah? I'm talking

---

2. Ibid.

about the early '50s. I was brought up in a small industrial town in the Midlands and started work in a foundry. Before I went to night school I washed under a tap outside the molding shed. All week I packed sand which was reinforced with glucose around a hundred wooden patterns. On Saturday we poured molten iron, and on Monday, when the casting was cold, we kicked the dry sand away and started again. So, sometimes you thought, 'There must be a better bloody world than this.' Now that will turn you on to ideas. Yeah?"

The ideas that turned him on were those of Karl Marx. "Scargill is partly in that same tradition," he explains. "He's closer to organized communism than I am—I'm just reading me old Karl Marx and you know, doing that bit, but I'm not in a party or anything. I'm just recognized as a bloke who will follow socialist, internationalist ideas."

Brian is now flourishing—he receives "one book commission after another"—and his daughter is applying to study at Cambridge. Brian is not married to a millionaire. He pulled on his bootstraps, and his body flew into the air.

. . . . . .

You would not know that this lush and gentle countryside was once covered in grey mountains of slag and sulphur. "That was the Newmarket Pit," says Brian as we drive, gesturing in the direction of a hill. "Ackton Hall. Gone" . . . "Allerton Bywater. Gone" . . . "Prince of Wales. Gone" . . . "Whitwood Mere. Gone" . . . "Methley Junction. Gone" . . . "Fryston Main. Gone" . . .

We drive down a long lane with a cemetery on one side and a row of bleak brick houses on the other. These were pit houses, says Brian. You can recognize the ones that were purchased by their residents, thanks to Thatcher's determination to sell off government housing. They are the ones that have been renovated.

We are en route to meet Harry. Brian tells me that Harry was a miner who became a painter after the closure of the mines. As we drive to Harry's house, Brian tries to explain the politics of the miners' union to me, the regional factionalism, why the working classes didn't support their own kind. "They are a federation. Take American politics. Oklahoma isn't gonna be the same as New York, right? Seattle isn't gonna be the same as Colorado—"

"Right, right."

"And if you got Utah in the center, bloody hell—"

"Right."

"But that's what it's like. It's a patchwork of unions, all with various attitudes. Right? And that's absolutely significant in the strike. Because in the big strike, what alienates, where the big problem comes from, is the Left, the far Left in Scargill, and some of the ambitious people—the guys who were very angry, the young braves—they *invade* Nottinghamshire and Derbyshire! Nottinghamshire in particular. And they say, 'Come out, come out, on General Strike with Yorkshire!' And Nottinghamshire says, 'Up yours, mate! We're not coming out with you bloody—' That's where the conflict is. And sometimes the conflict will be so complicated because the leadership in Nottingham might be going with Scargill, but the rank-and-file are not. They're saying, 'Those bastards came down and they picketed our pit.' 'Bloody Yorkshire, we're not going in with that lot!' Primitive!"

"So would you say that in the end, clan solidarity proved more powerful than class solidarity?"

"It did in the early stages, but then it became an attack on the working class. Right? And a lot of people would come in. I mean, I went to a meeting in Wakefield, and a young comrade got up, and he said, 'We were just peacefully picketing, and this bloke grabbed me, this copper grabbed me, and he threw me into the back of a Black Mariah, and he beat me up.' And then he said, '*T'ain't right.*' He suddenly saw that. Thatcher had built it up so that the police were seen as absolutely alien to the—you know, he was beaten up in the back of a van! This was a lad who was politicized by brutalism. And he used those words: '*T'ain't right!*'"

We pull up at Harry's house, a picturesque brick cottage in the countryside. When Brian said that Harry had been down the mines for twenty years before the strike, I imagined a stooped emphysemic with blue veins in his nose. When he told me Harry had become a painter, I thought he meant a house painter. But a youthful, pink-cheeked man welcomes us at the door and ushers us past walls decorated with his paintings—mostly acrylics on canvas. They are painted in a style that might be described as post-Impressionist Socialist Realism. There are sculptures, too, and glazed charcoal-and-crayon sketches. They depict men in the mines, rippling with muscles, drenched in sweat, coated in soot, wearing lamps and helmets. Even the color paintings suggest overwhelming grayness. Every image evokes the horrors George Orwell described.

We sit in a drawing room decorated with Harry's sketches and reliefs. Harry's wife, Lorna, a gentle woman quite a few years his junior, comes in to introduce herself. She is scrambling eggs and smoked salmon in the kitchen, she says. Would we like some? I look at her, then look back at Harry. He is clearly healthy and prospering. This is a middle-class home, complete with dried flower arrangements and scented candles. This was not what I had in mind when I asked Brian to introduce me to people who had been affected by Thatcher's policies. I think of asking Brian to introduce me to someone who is suffering a bit more conspicuously, but I can't bring myself to do it. I don't want to sound like the infamous Fleet Street journalist who hopped off the plane in the Congo and bellowed, "Anyone here been raped and speaks English?"

Harry always had a knack for drawing, apparently. He practiced on his father's back as a child, because there was no paper in the house. When the pits closed, he found himself sketching scenes from the mines, over and over. Unemployed, at loose ends, he submitted one of those drawings to a local competition and won first prize. His first exhibition was in a Pontefract pizza parlor. His second was in the Royal Festival Hall in London. His paintings are now prized by collectors and sold for thousands of pounds. All that talent was sitting at the bottom of a coal mine. No one noticed it. No one would have, had Scargill had his way.

_____ ৹ ৹ ৹ _____

Lorna brings us tea. We sit in Harry's living room, talking about his memories of the strike. "It were a glorious summer for me," he says. "It were one of the best years I had."

"Really? Why?"

He looks at me as if this is quite a stupid question—and I suppose it is. "It were marvelous to do no bloody work!" He sips his tea, then asks me if I've ever been down a coal mine. I tell him that I haven't. "Well. You're talking a shit job. It's the worst of the worst."

"What was your feeling about Scargill's declaration that there should be 'loss without limit'?" I asked Harry.

"I suppose we were talking ludicrous economics, I thought."

"You thought so then?"

"Oh, I thought so then. You could see where they were spending money on mines; we spent a million pounds on the canteen at Fryston pit. Fryston were a reasonable-sized pit, but it weren't a big one. The canteen, you couldn't get a bloody Kit-Kat once they upgraded it . . . So they're spending money on a thing because you got national control of it, and if this is going on on that scale 'round the country, then obviously it's going belly-up, as it were."

I wasn't expecting to hear this. I wasn't expecting what he said about the miners' enthusiasm for strike action, either: "We're talking here that people would strike over lots of bloody things. We're talking about pits here that would strike regular . . . There'd be strikes 'cause of conditions, there would be strikes over pay, there would be strikes just 'cause they felt it were a lovely day and wanted to go home. Sunshine pits."

"I'm sorry?" I said.

"You know, *stick it up your ass where—*"

I nodded.

"There were a lot of hard workers," Harry adds, "but also a lot of bloody idle workers. Now, I knew a lot of guys who were influenced by pubs."

"By what?" I ask.

"Drink. The miners tend to be that sort of men, usually. They come from a background of hard workers, hard drinkers. So much of 'em spent a lot of time in the pubs. To the extent that in the '70s, I knew guys that weren't hardly working three days a week . . . There were one guy in particular, he were sacked on fifteen occasions, and the union reinstated him. Basically, you're going to do a job, and you've no bloody help, because everybody's buggered off home . . . You're struggling, because no one will do any bloody work. I'm not saying that—you know, you've a thousand blokes here, and out of that were a reasonable percentage, and most of them would be at the coal face, as it were. But you're basically forgetting that the whole purpose of a bloody coal mine were to get coal out. And without that, you're going nowhere."

Thatcher would have perfectly agreed.

"What do you think your life would be like if you'd won the strike?" I ask.

"Well, that's the crux o' the matter as well, that's something that—I look back with mixed blessings, I suppose, really. I'd still be back at the pit, and most likely still be married to the first wife. There's no way I woulda met Lorna. My life has changed considerably since finishing the pit. Changed a lot. And whether I'd still be walking is another kettle of fish. Whether my health would still be—certainly I'm a different guy than I was twenty years since. In some respects I feel a lot better than I did in my thirties."

Harry obviously understands the logic of Thatcher's policies and benefited from them. He nonetheless maintains that they were wrong. "You're closing people's lives down," he says, "people's culture down, almost. You know, it's almost like you'd go to a country and wipe out their culture. You wouldn't dream of it, would you, nowadays."

I ask, "But do you think that if an industry isn't economical, it's the government that has a responsibility to keep it alive and preserve the culture around it?"

"There's more things than economics comes into it. There's more things than how much does the coal cost, how much can we sell it for. Because once you close the mines down, you're closing a way of life down, that basically people depended on. And how much money did they spend after the strike, keeping communities together? How much money will you spend on welfare, whatever, after the strike because people's whole way of life had gone belly-up, as it were?"

"Do you see it as abnormal that certain industries would cease to be profitable and be replaced by other industries?" I ask.

"That's the way of life, in some respects," says Harry.

"That's bound to happen," Brian agrees.

I ask Harry, "So, if you'd been in power at the time, if you'd been prime minister, and you're looking at a progressively less economical industry, how would you have handled the pit closures?"

"That's a good question," Harry says. "And I've never been in that situation."

"What other options were realistically open to Thatcher?"

"The option that she wanted, it weren't about closing the mines down, for me, it were about taking power away from the unions. That were the prime target, the prime objective. Basically, emancipating the bloody unions."

I suspect he has misspoken—I believe he meant to say "emasculating" the unions. But I can't be sure. Thatcher maintained that she was emancipating the unions, in the sense that she believed she was freeing the worker from the tyranny of the closed shop and insisting the union leadership adhere to democratic procedures. "Emancipating" is the word Harry uses, but "emasculating" is the word his voice and the context convey.

A feeling of emasculation, whether or not that is what he meant, is obviously something Thatcher aroused in many men. The fact that they were defeated by a woman, I would have thought, must have made the insult of losing their jobs particularly hard for these men to bear.

⸺ ◌ ⤳ ◌ ⸺

If Brian and Harry are willing to concede that the economics of nationalized coal made no sense, I ask, why do they continue to maintain that Thatcher's policies were misguided?

Brian suggests that I am looking at it the wrong way: I am prioritizing economic efficiency, a typical American failing. "What I'm saying is," he says, "where Thatcher goes wrong, she sees it in solely economic terms. If the market is all, and the workers are unprotected—there's a feeling about protecting your poor, which you feel fundamentally in the writings of Jefferson, you feel fundamentally in the writings of Thomas Paine, even more, and the inspiration of America, which you don't feel now. You know. So, and Thatcher is of that ilk, I think."

We digress for a while, arguing (in a good-natured way, they are both good sports) about American history and the American trade union movement. Then I steer the discussion back to the impact of Thatcher's policies. "Some of the questions can't be answered," says Brian, "because in one sense, the world is moving on very rapidly. But I don't think she was a long-term planner at all. She was good for a scrap in the Falklands, right? Yeah."

"Yeah. There ain't any bloody planners. I mean, we were good for a scrap in bloody Iraq!" adds Harry.

"We were!" Brian agrees.

"But we're not good at fuckin' 'What do we do after that?'" says Harry. "No exit strategy at all there! If you go down to Airedale now, there's still a similar educational standard to what when I were goin' to the pit, as it were. But there's no bloody pits now, are there? . . . If me father came back and saw that, he wouldn't believe it. He wouldn't believe what had come here before it, and now it were gone, as it were. I'm just wondering, if there's this big change in my generation, how big a change is there going to be in the next generation? Is it gonna be a lot better? You know, it's all right saying there's wealth and prosperity. There's a lot of kids down there that are wealthy and prosperous. You need to be. But there's a lot of kids down there that are stuck, almost like bloody Victorian kids with their faces pressed up against the window. 'Cause they ain't got the bloody money to use it, anyway. But it looks nice. So yeah, if you go down, like I said, down there, there's a lot more crime, corruption, thieving. It woulda been almost unheard of, in my early life. Drug problems. Drink problems."

"To what do you attribute the rise in crime, thieving, drugs, drink?" I ask.

"Lack of work. Lack of vision. Lack of some aim in life."

"Why is there no aim in life?"

"Because aspirations aren't there. It's all right if you're born in a middle-class family that's got aspirations. Education is a thing you get directed at. Education for its own benefit, to start with. But then towards your own future in life. When you're born to a miner that's never worked for the last twenty years, what's your aspiration there? What's your incentive? Where do you get your lead from, as it were? The only place you get it is from outside."

"If the mines were still there, would there be any aspiration other than to work as a miner?"

"Um—there'd a been some. There'd a been some. Not all miners produce miners' sons. A lot of miners advocated, 'You'll work anywhere but in here.'"

"So why isn't that still the case?" I ask. "I'm not convinced yet that this has anything to do with the pit closures. You're talking about lack of aspiration, you're talking about alcoholism. And I can see the alcoholism just getting off at the train station—"

"Yeah, but you're comin' from a direction with no bloody knowledge of such things, I should think."

"Which direction is that?" I ask.

"Well, you're a middle-class, educated person."

In Britain, this line is used as a conversation-stopper. As one British woman from a working-class background put it to me, when it comes to political debate, being from the working classes functions like a Get Out of Jail Free card. The card does not work well on Americans who are indifferent to the British class structure, however, and more to the point, if I were coming from a direction with a lot of bloody knowledge of these things, why would I bother to come all the way to Yorkshire to ask *his* opinion about them? "That's why I'm asking you to explain it to me," I say.

To his credit, Harry laughs. "You got—not just a family, not just an extended family. You got a village, a town, an area that's grown up with a certain aspect in life, a certain thing that is almost set in bloody stone. That's what you do. And all of a sudden it's not. It's not what you do. But the education system . . . it's the same quality, I may be wrong, but I don't think I am. There's nobody from Airedale school going to college. There's certainly none going to bloody university. There's no drive towards getting 'em there. There's no drive to getting anything further than sixteen. You come out of school at sixteen, and you're either looking for a low-skilled, low-wage job somewhere, or you're going nowhere, because your father's not worked for twenty years. He may not have worked for ten years, he may not have worked for five years. But certainly the direction that you're getting from your family would be little."

"How do you fix that?"

"How do you fix that? It's going to take bloody time. And education."

"But how do you get education, if no one in your family is telling you, 'Get an education'?"

"It's true. It's a bloody hard point, is that."

I am sympathetic to the point he is making. Middle-class people tend to value education. But the arrow of causality goes in two directions. People who value education tend to become middle-class.

I don't know what the solution is. No one does, if they are honest. I certainly can see this issue from his side. The men whose fathers and grandfathers powered the industrial revolution in Britain—men who spent their lives crouched in those filthy mines—were told that they were no longer needed or valued. Many of them were close to retirement age, well past the age when people naturally learn new skills, take new risks, become entrepreneurs. They were given incomprehensible speeches about monetarism and market economics. They weren't asking, in their view, for something unreasonable—just for the right to earn a living by their own labor in the only way they knew how.

Which image is more repugnant? Is it that of a middle-aged man, his body wrecked from a life of hard labor, being told that he must now find a new job, a new city, a new way of life far from his friends and from everything he and his family have ever known?

Or is it the image of Harry, at the bottom of a coal mine, tracing images in dust on the wall with his finger?

It has been a pleasant morning, and I have greatly enjoyed speaking to Brian and Harry. But finally I say it: Harry's life hardly seems to me an irrefragable argument against Thatcherism. They have been telling me that Thatcher's policies were a disaster. If they want me fully to appreciate what they mean, I need to meet someone who isn't doing so well.

They decide to introduce me to Johnny. Johnny, Harry explains, was a ripper. The ripper is a ripper of rock. "Basically, you're blowing that rock face, charging it with explosives, you're blowing it down, and you're shifting it with a gang of five, usually, shifting that with shovels. Johnny were a guy with a shovel that shifted this bloody rock every day. *Hated* it with a vengeance. You know, the conditions were the thing that bothered him up. The dust. The water. And the heat, the temperature were . . . tropics with dust, muck. So not very good conditions."

"No," I agree.

"So he hated that with a vengeance. And I'll allus remember when the pits closed, 'cause he were one that would say, 'I wish they'd blow this bloody pit up.' And I bet within six months of 'em closing the pit, the next conversation I had with him: 'If they were openin' Fryston tomorra, I'd dig it out with a bloody teaspoon.'"

Thus did we set out to find Johnny the Ripper in his garden allotment in the Yorkshire countryside.

Johnny, I had to concede after meeting him, is not doing well.

—◦— ◦— ◦—

Yorkshire, Middle o' Nowhere:

CB: Johnny, can I ask you, how old are you?

Johnny: Sixty-five this year.

CB: And so where were you during the miners' strike?

Johnny: Erm, Nottingham, flyin' picketin'.

CB: You were a flying picket?

Johnny: Yeah, we did Orgreave . . . 'Ave you 'eard anything about it?

CB: I've heard a lot about it. You're a legend.

Johnny: Oh, well.

CB: So were you a miner your whole life?

Johnny: Yeah. Twenty . . . thirty-one years at it.

[*Rooster crows in background*]

CB: When you think of the strike, what's the first word that comes to mind?

Harry: Poor.

Johnny: It weren't you know, like, I wouldn't a missed it, it were, you know, like, I saw more o' ta country in that twelve months 'tan I seen in all me life, you know—you know what I mean, I mean, everywhere were different, I mean, we went inta Nottingham, I've never been in Nottingham before—I mean, you know, it's only sixty mile away, innit, you know—

CB: So how did you come to be a flying picket? Who approached you?

Johnny: Well, I were union, you know . . .

CB: Right. And they said, "We need flying pickets. Would you like to be one?"

Johnny: And we went to union meeting, all go'd, all volunteered. Most o' the people went.

CB: And so were you paid to—

Johnny: A pound.

Brian: A pound per day.

CB: And did they pay your expenses, too?

Johnny: Uh, the person that 'ad the car, got the petrol money.[3]

CB: Right. And how long in advance did they tell you where you needed to be?

Johnny: Uh, the mornin'.

CB: In the morning they'd say, "We need you to go to—"

Johnny: Yeah. Because our place and our phones were bugged and everything, yeah.

CB: So you were at Orgreave.

Johnny: Yeah, I were at Orgreave, yeah.

CB: Tell me how you remember that. When did you realize—

Johnny: It were 'airy! You know, it were really, you know—

CB: Were you expecting it to be?

Johnny: Well, we were just, you know, our police, you know they were all tappin' their shields like Zulus, you know?

CB: Like what?

Johnny, Harry: Like Zulus!

---

3. Peter Walker claimed the flying pickets were paid forty pounds a day. My bet is that a pound a day is a lot closer to the truth.

Johnny: You know that film, *Zulu*—you know when all those Zu-lus were all tappin' their shields?

Brian: Their truncheons against their shields—

CB: Right.

Harry: And the police were goin' bom, bom, bom, bom, bom, ba-bom—

Johnny: bom, bom, bom, bom, bom!

CB: And so you were already there, on the picket line, when the police arrived—

Johnny: Police arrived? It were an army!

CB: OK, so the army arrives, but you were there already—

Johnny: They 'ad us penned in a field. We couldn't get out! They were a world round me, just herded us into here, and we couldn't get out, and I mean, summat lunged out, and I didn't see, and I went in the old out-and-bottom, some-un of us jumped out and ran, and there were dogs after 'em, 'orses, and, you know, arrested, and—I were OK, I were in the middle o' it, there were a big lad runnin', Teddy—

Harry: Carl.

Johnny: Carl. Carl, not Teddy. And I mean this copper, you know 'e were a big lad, and [*smacks fist*]—like that. 'E went straight down, everybody cheered! But you know, they just got 'im and arrest 'im. You know, there weren't many, they had it all sewn up—

Harry: They had a plan.

Brian: It was a trap, wasn't it. Orgreave was a trap.

CB: When did you realize it was a trap? Did you think so at the time?

Johnny: No, after. You know, we thought it wouldn't last, you know, a week. I mean, '72 were five week, '74 were seven week, and maybe, nothing as long as that, twelve, or eleven, or—but not twelve months.

CB: At what point in the big strike did you realize something different was happening, when did you start to realize this was really part of history—

Johnny: Never. We just carried on, you know, 'til it were finished. And it kept going.

CB: What happened to you after the strike?

Johnny: Well, I took redundancy, yeah. I handed in my papers, and I didn't want nought to do with it. And I wanted everybody to do the same.

Harry: That were after the pit closed.

Johnny: Ay?

Harry: That were after the pit closed.

Johnny: No, the pit were open.

Harry: Ay.

Johnny: You know when we went back, I handed on my papers. I said, this is no job! Handed 'em in I'd a got sacked, because they said "I want you to go and drive this machine." Says I, I've lost my confidence, I don't want to drive anymore, I wanted everyone to do that—

Harry: That's so right.

Johnny: You know, this other guy said, they said, go put that Airedale up—

CB: Go put that what up?

Johnny, Harry: Air door. Ventilation.

Johnny: You know, he says, "Put that air door up," and I says, "I'm a miner, not a joiner." You know. He says, "If you don't put it up, you got to go home," so I says, so I went home. I'd had enough. That were it for me. But there was only me doing it. One day, I came off the face, they says, they're sending [unintelligible] on, do you remember that, little kid—daft as a bush, 'e were!

Harry: That one were out of it, weren't he!

[*They fall about laughing; I'm lost.*]

Johnny: What were the manager, then? That little bloke—

Harry: Not the bloody one that came from college—a Geordie—

Johnny: No, that weren't him. Belford.

CB: What made Scargill so popular? Why did people follow Scargill?

Johnny: He were a good speaker, weren't 'e?

Harry: He were a good speaker.

Johnny: I mean, 'e told 'em what they wanted to 'ear, but . . .

CB: When you saw him speak, was there something in particular he said that really moved and impressed you?

Johnny: Everything 'e said. 'E was my 'ero.

CB: Pardon?

Johnny: Were my 'ero.

CB: Was he?

Johnny: Yep.

CB: Is he still your hero?

Johnny: I think so.

CB: You don't feel like he let you down?

Johnny: No. I think a lot of people did.

Harry: A lot of people did.

Johnny: But I don't think he did. I mean, they blackened 'is name that much, didn't they, blackened 'is name that much—you know, everybody, the press did it, the media did it. Crikey . . . You want a beer? [*goes to fridge, passes beer around, sound of flip-tabs opening*]

Brian: No more, honestly, I'm alright.

Johnny: You all havin' one?

CB: Thank you.

Harry: Cheers.

CB: Cheers.

Johnny to Brian: Are you sure?

Brian: Yes, yes, thank you.

Johnny: You don't like beer?

CB: When you say Scargill was your hero, did you ever think about his being a Marxist—

Johnny: No.

CB: Did that—were you a Marxist as well? Or was it just not that important?

Johnny: Well I vote BNP now.[4]

---

4. The British National Party—fascists.

CB: You vote BNP now? Why do you vote for them?

Johnny: Eh?

CB: Why do you vote for them?

Johnny: 'Cause I don't like Tony Blair. 'E's give this country away, hasn't he? Don't you think so? 'E's give this country away. Give it away to Muslims.

[*Finds a BNP leaflet, passes it around*]

Johnny: Everything it says in there, I believe in it.

Harry: Yeah?

Johnny: Yep.

CB: But the BNP is—

Johnny: He's gonna sell this bloody country away. What a man. Worst man since Hitler then.

Brian: Tony Blair?

Johnny: Yeah. 'Orrible.

Brian: Worse than Thatcher?

Johnny: Eh?

Brian: So where do you see Thatcher, then?

Johnny: Well, she knackered *us* up.

CB: Do you think she was good for the country overall?

Johnny: Hmmm. I got me own house now through her. Only a pit house, that, but I own it. And I never'd owned if she hadn't got in. I don't think anybody else woulda done it, uh. Maybe they would have. I mean, if I had had a chance, I'd a shot her.

Brian: Every miner would've shot her.

Harry: I'll get drunk when she leaves. [*Gestures at vegetable patch*] I mean, this is what we got left now.

[*Rooster crows*]

Harry: After the strike, after the pit closed, they went from pit to pit, it were. The life we had, weren't it, you know—

Johnny: Yeah.

Brian: Your wife went to Russia, toured about with Scargill to Russia, didn't she—

Johnny: Yeah, she toured around—

CB: With Scargill? To Russia?

Johnny: Yeah, but Mrs. Scargill went.

CB: Mrs. Scargill went with your wife?

Johnny: Well, there were about two or three 'undred of 'em. [*loud belch*]

CB: And when was this?

Johnny: All of 'em worked in kitchens, were kitchen women.

CB: Who paid for that?

Johnny: Miners. Russian miners.

Harry, Brian: Miners. Russian miners.

CB: Well, how did the Russian miners pay for it?

Johnny: Hmmmm.

Brian: Well, union, union fees!

Johnny: Or whatever. I don't know.

Harry: Generous people.

Brian: It would be union fees. I don't think it would be the government.

Harry: No, it weren't the government.

Brian: The union fees—

CB: You seriously think the Russian miners just gave up money, out of their salaries, to—

Harry: Yes, of course.

Johnny: Yeah.

Brian: Of course. No problem. I don't—honestly, Claire.

Harry: We'd a done the same for 'em.

Brian: Miners is miners.

Harry: I mean, miners is not just a national thing, it's an international thing.

Johnny: I mean, the unions paid for it. Playin' fair. You know . . .

CB: OK, look. How, out of Russian rubles, Soviet rubles at the time, which were not convertible—

Johnny: They were sendin' food parcels over.

Harry: Sending food parcels, there's a lot o' bloody food there—

CB: And you really think this was from the Russian miners and not the Soviet government?

All: It was!

Johnny: It wasn't from the government.

Brian: Don't concentrate on Russia. You're concentrating on Russia. Australia did it—

Johnny: Yep.

Brian: You got, anywhere which had got coal mines would be sending union—

Harry: If they could afford it, they'd be sending it—food parcels, or some donation, towards—

Brian: Yes. French miners, Belgian miners—

Harry: German miners—

[*Rooster crows*]

CB: Why did the unions agree to go along with the pit closures before Thatcher? I mean, there were a lot of them under Labour, too.

Harry: There weren't a lot of pit closures under Labour.

CB: Do you think Thatcher wanted to destroy the coal industry?

Brian: I don't think she could bloody understand it.

Harry: She wanted to destroy the unions.

CB: She wanted to destroy the unions so much that she was willing to sacrifice the coal industry—

All: Yes, yes—

Brian: It was the unions [*all talking, unintelligible*]—

Johnny: And at the top of the unions was miners, so once you got miners, you got it—

CB: Why do you think she hated the unions so much?

Johnny: Because o' Ted 'Eath.

CB: You don't think it was because of '79, because of the Winter of Discontent?

All: No.

Johnny: That were a Labour government, weren't it?

CB: Yeah, but that's why she was elected. She was elected because people were fed up with the unions.

Brian: There's something to that. But that isn't the major one. I mean, my problem is, I think she's not very bright, as I've pointed out, but I think she's single-minded, and I think that she saw, as John said, she thought, *Kill the miners' union—kill everything.* And that's what she did.

CB: Do you think Britain's better off because of her?

Harry: That's the problem, isn't it? You can't really know.

Johnny: Not in my opinion. I think this country's knackered now. I think this man that we got in now has give the country away. In ten years, he's give a thousand years' advantage away. 'Orrible man. It's useless. No workers. What do we produce in this country? Nothin'.

CB: But London is the world's financial capital.

Johnny: London is crap. London is just full o' people that do nothing.

CB: They make a lot of money.

John: What for?

Harry: Doin' nothing.

Johnny: For fuck-all.

[*All speak, unintelligible*]

Johnny: There's six million people in this country that shouldn't be here!

Brian: And who are they?

Johnny: Who are they! Crikey, there's thousands of 'em, isn't there?! They're comin' in droves, they're comin' in bloody droves, they shouldn't be 'ere! We don't need 'em. Make 'em work! They made me work! Make their bloody kids work! Fetch conscription back! I don't want to see 'em 'ere, little shits! Bloody kids around 'ere . . .

[*Rooster crows*]

Johnny: Want some raspberries from the garden?

Harry: Ay.

Johnny: Take a raspberry or two.

9

The Triumvirate

I stand before you tonight in my Red Star *chiffon evening gown, my face softly made up and my fair hair gently waved, the Iron Lady of the Western world. A Cold War warrior, an Amazon philistine, even a Peking plotter. Am I any of these things? Well, yes, if that's how they wish to interpret my defense of values and freedoms fundamental to our way of life . . .*

— Thatcher addressing Finchley
Conservatives in 1976[1]

On August 31, 1983, Korean Airlines Flight 007 lumbered aloft from Kennedy airport, refueled in Anchorage, and continued its journey westward toward Seoul. Most of the 269 passengers, I imagine, fell asleep as the plane chugged through the sky; perhaps a few insomniacs listened to show tunes or traditional Korean folk

---

1. The *Red Star* was the Soviet newspaper that gave Thatcher her nickname—the Iron Lady.

music on the audio system. Among them were twenty-three children and sixty-three American citizens, including an American congressman. They were unaware that their pilot had made a navigational error and strayed into Soviet airspace.

Kornukov: Gerasimenko, cut the horseplay at the command post, what is that noise there? I repeat the combat task: Fire the missiles, fire on target 60–65. Destroy target 60–65.

Gerasimenko: Task received. Destroy target 60–65 with missile fire, accept control of fighter from Smyrnykh.

Kornukov: Carry out the task, destroy! . . . Shit, how long does it take him to get into attack position, he is already getting out into neutral waters! Engage afterburner immediately. Bring in the MiG–23 as well . . . While you are wasting time it will fly right out.

Titovnin: 805, try to destroy the target with cannons.

Osipovich: I am dropping back. Now I will try a rocket.

Titovnin: Roger.

Osipovich: Roger, I am in lock-on.

Titovnin: 805, are you closing on the target?

Osipovich: I am closing on the target, am in lock-on. Distance to target is eight kilometers.

Titovnin: AFTERBURNER, 805!

Osipovich: I have already switched it on.

Titovnin: Launch!

Osipovich: *Yolki Palki!* The target is destroyed.[2]

The voices of the pilots who sent the civilian airliner plunging into the Tatar Strait were picked up by a National Security Agency listening station. *Yolki Palki* is a euphemistic rendition of the Russian curse *yob tvoyu mat*, meaning "Your mother has been fucked."

---

2. The transcript, which I have shortened for the sake of economy, comes from the June 1993 International Civil Aviation Organization report.

The black box from KAL 007 was recovered. Suffice to say that the passengers' deaths did not come immediately.

Grey-faced, grim, and unyielding, the Kremlin's apparatchiks refused to admit error. They insisted first that the plane had crashed of its own accord, then admitted that their air force had shot it down, yes, but with ample justification, they said, for it had been a spy plane, dispatched by the United States as a deliberate provocation and a test of their air defenses.

Six days later, Ronald Reagan delivered one of the angriest speeches of the Cold War. Although his "Evil Empire" speech is better known, the text of this speech was in fact more belligerent, and given the context, far more minatory.

> . . . *Massacre* . . . crime against humanity . . . violating every concept of human rights . . . an explosion of condemnation by people everywhere . . . *savagery* . . . the Soviets still refuse to tell the truth . . . [It's] the Soviet Union against the world . . . *barbarism* . . . a society which wantonly disregards individual rights and the value of human life . . . seeks constantly to expand and dominate other nations . . . yes, shooting down a plane—even one with hundreds of innocent men, women, children, and babies—is a part of their normal procedure! . . . *inhuman brutality* . . . Czechoslovakia, Hungary, Poland, the gassing of villages in Afghanistan . . . *unspeakable act* . . . a righteous and terrible anger . . . *monstrous wrong* . . . we will remember [this] for the rest of our lives . . . [3]

Thatcher made no effort to encourage Reagan to temper his rhetoric. Quite the contrary. "My views on the barbarity of this act," she immediately wrote to him,

---

3. Address to the Nation on the Soviet Attack on a Korean Civilian Airliner, September 5, 1983, www.reagan.utexas.edu/archives/speeches/1983/90583a.htm.

are completely at one with yours . . . This incident has
vividly illustrated the true nature of the Soviet regime. Its
rigidity and ruthlessness, its neuroses about spying and security, its mendacity, and its apparent inability to understand,
let alone apply, the normal rules of civilized conduct between nations, have been an object lesson to those who believe that goodwill and reason alone will be sufficient to
ensure our security and world peace . . . [4]

Reagan's speech, responded the Kremlin, was a compilation of
"obscenities alternating with hypocritical preaching."

I remember these events well. I was fifteen years old. I remember our very serious discussions at school. Was this the beginning
of the end? Would there be a nuclear war? Would we be more
likely to survive if we left the city? Would we *want* to survive?
The Soviets were clearly insane: They had just shot a civilian
plane out of the air. But Reagan was insane, too: There was no
way he would let this rest—just listen to him! Maybe we could go
up to Canada? No good, we concluded; we would nonetheless
perish in the nuclear winter. Besides, none of us had our driver's
licenses yet.

Do you realize how close we really came to nuclear war that
autumn? Most people don't. I didn't, until recently. Not long after
the downing of KAL 007, NATO conducted a military exercise
called Able Archer, simulating a nuclear launch. Reagan's response
to the downing of flight 007 had so spooked the Kremlin that Soviet leader Yuri Andropov and his top aides believed Able Archer
to be the preliminary to a genuine first strike. The KGB sent out a
molinya—a flash message—to its operatives in the West, warning

---

4. Thatcher to Reagan, September 15, 1983, NSA Head of State File, Thatcher:
Cables (3), Box 35, Ronald Reagan Presidential Library, Simi Valley, California.
Documents from U.S. presidential libraries cited in this chapter may be consulted
at www.margaretthatcher.com.

them to prepare for nuclear war. Frantic, the Soviets readied their nuclear forces and their air units in Eastern Europe. Soviet fighter-bombers sat laden with nuclear weapons on the runways, on red alert, their engines roaring.

On September 26, Lieutenant Colonel Stanislav Yevgrafovich Petrov sat watch in the Serpukhov-15 bunker on a cold Moscow night. Shortly after midnight, red lights lit up the bunker: According to satellite data, a nuclear missile had been launched from the United States. Petrov stared at his computer screen in incredulity. It made no sense. Just *one* missile? Why? Against his standing orders, he decided not to press the button that would send this information up the chain of command and precipitate the launching of a massive nuclear counterstrike.

Then the satellite spotted a second missile.

Then a third.

Then a fourth.

Then a fifth.

Everyone in the bunker began screaming. Sweat poured off Petrov's face. According to the computer, they would all be vaporized within minutes.

By the grace of God, Petrov decided this *simply couldn't be happening*. He didn't know what was going on, but it just *couldn't* be what it seemed to be. *It just could not be.* He broke his orders outright and refused to press the button. The sirens wailed as the minutes ticked past. The bombs didn't fall.

Petrov was right, of course: It wasn't happening. The signals had been caused by a freak sunlight alignment. A lone Soviet lieutenant colonel prevented the Apocalypse. The Kremlin rewarded Petrov for breaking his orders by demoting him and sending him into exile, where he suffered a nervous breakdown.[5]

---

5. "Nuclear War: Minuteman," *Weekendavisen*, April 2, 2004; *The Red Button and the Man Who Saved the World*, LOGTV Ltd. & MG Productions, www.logtv.com/films/redbutton/video.htm.

"We had entered a dangerous phase," Thatcher recalls in her memoirs.[6] One week after the downing of KAL 007, Thatcher convened a meeting of top-flight Sovietologists at Chequers. She asked the experts to present papers on the state of the Soviet Union's economy, its military doctrine, its power structure.

A recently declassified memorandum, written by J. L. Bullard of the Foreign and Commonwealth Office (FCO), summarizes the papers presented at the seminar. Overwhelmingly, the participants predicted no change of course in the Soviet Union: "The general message seems to be that the Soviet leaders do indeed face problems in a number of areas, but not on such a scale as to compel them to change course drastically, still less change the system." This is underlined in the document, although it is not clear by whom—perhaps by Thatcher. One of the experts argued that "the enormous Soviet effort on defense is a dynamo rather than a millstone in the Soviet economy." There was, apparently, one—and only one—dissenting view among the British specialists: "In a class by itself, it seems to me, is Michael Bourdeaux's paper, with its conclusion that we may one day see the collapse of the Soviet system from within."[7]

A second FCO memorandum recorded that the meeting considered "whether British policy should aim at, in the words used by the U.S. Secretary of State on 15 June, 1983, 'the gradual evolution of the Soviet system towards a more pluralistic political and economic system.' The view was reached that the realistic possibilities of change in the Soviet system were such that it was very doubtful whether in the foreseeable future any substantially greater diversity could be expected."[9]

---

6. Thatcher, *The Downing Street Years*, p. 450.
7. Bullard note on Chequers Soviet seminar, September 5, 1983, Thatcher MSS (digital collection), doc. 111071.
8. John Coles, minutes on Chequers Soviet seminar, September 8, 1983, Thatcher MSS (digital collection), doc. 111075.

"I liked her immediately," Reagan recalled. "She was warm, feminine, gracious and intelligent and it was evident from our first words that we were soul mates . . . " *(Courtesy of the family of Srdja Djukanovic)*

A final FCO memorandum argued that if anything, the Soviet economy was stronger than the seminar's participants reckoned. "Despite its difficulties, the Soviet economy continues to grow . . . it remains immensely rich in natural resources . . . the Soviet Union has a low debt ratio and remains an attractive proposition as far as the Western banks are concerned." The author agreed with the consensus view: Attempting to destabilize Eastern Europe would be profoundly unwise. "Policies aimed at destabilization would probably provoke the Stalinist reflex . . . I see little prospect for Finlandisation . . . I would expect tension and periodic disturbances but no real change in the foreseeable future . . . I also share [skepticism] about the possibility of reformism in Eastern Europe having an influence on the Soviet Union itself . . . The expectation is of minor reform not major change in the Soviet Union."[9]

---

9. September 7, 1983, Thatcher Archive (FCO), D. J. Manning minute on Chequers Soviet seminar.

Let me translate these memos: *Reagan is nuts. Don't listen to him.*

⎯౸ ⇒ ౺⎯

The experts at Chequers were hardly endorsing a minority view. In the year Margaret Thatcher came to power, the Soviet Union appeared to be not only invincible, but ascendant. In 1978, while the Western economies were still suffering the crippling aftereffects of the 1973 oil price shock, the Soviet Union, owing to its rich Siberian oil resources, had become the world's largest oil producer. Backed by the Soviets, the North Vietnamese had expelled American troops. Backed by the Soviets, the Sandinistas had overthrown the Nicaraguan government. Backed by the Soviets, communists had seized power in Angola, Mozambique, Somalia, Ethiopia, and South Yemen.

In the 1970s, the Soviet Union had achieved nuclear parity with the United States, then surpassed it with the deployment of the SS-18 missile, known in the West, aptly enough, as Satan. The Satan, it was believed, was so powerful and accurate that if used in a first strike, it might well succeed in destroying the American retaliatory capacity. The West's strategic doctrine had until then been based upon the concept of Mutual Assured Destruction. There were now serious doubts that the destruction would be mutual.

The Soviets had placed Satan missiles in Eastern Europe, targeting Western capitals. The Warsaw Pact enjoyed a massive superiority in conventional forces over NATO. The Soviet Navy was shadowing the U.S. sixth fleet. West Germany was pursuing *Ostpolitik* in the assumption that accommodation with the East was the only alternative.

The year of Margaret Thatcher's election, 1979, was also the year in which Iranian revolutionaries seized fifty-two American hostages and paraded them, blindfolded, on television. Americans tied yellow ribbons around their trees. Observing this American reaction—and drawing the obvious conclusions—the Soviet Union one month later invaded Afghanistan.

The Central Intelligence Agency, in that year, summarized the situation thus:

> In part because of their own perceptions of declining American power, in part because of more objective considerations, the West Europeans and Japanese increasingly believe that the United States is losing international political-military position to the Soviet Union. For evidence, they point particularly to the narrowing of the strategic gap and to the activity of Soviet proxies in Africa and Southeast Asia. To some degree that development has drawn the allies closer to the United States, because of their heightened fear of the USSR. But it has also led to increased attention, especially in West Germany, to a possible long-term need to forge an independent accommodation with the Soviets . . . the United States' influence over its allies is clearly declining . . . [10]

It was against this backdrop that Ronald Reagan was elected in 1980, insisting that contrary to all appearance and belief, the Soviet Union was not only weak but mortally vulnerable. Because he was right, it is often forgotten that this point of view at the time marked him as a lunatic. Reagan, remarked former CIA director Robert Gates, "seemed not to doubt that he could change the decade-long trend of Soviet ascendancy. Reagan, *nearly alone*, truly believed in 1981 that the Soviet system was vulnerable, not in some vague, long-range historical sense, but right then" (my emphasis).[11]

---

10. "Changing Power Relations among OECD States," October 22, 1979, CIA National Foreign Assessment Center. Carter Library release 2005/01/28 NLC–7–16–10–14–1.

11. Robert Gates, *From the Shadows* (Simon & Schuster, 1997), p. 197.

From 1947, when the American diplomat George Kennan pub-lished his famous *Foreign Policy* article under the pseudonym X, to 1981, the year of Reagan's inauguration, American policy toward the Soviet Union had been *containment*, not rollback. Generally, American policymakers viewed communism as a kind of incurable cancer, one that with costly, painful, and permanent therapy might at best be prevented from metastasizing.

Obviously, the price of the Cold War had been extremely high. Communism had claimed at least a hundred million lives.[12] But the doctrine of containment had been a success in the most critical sense: There had not been a conventional war between the superpowers, nor had there been a nuclear exchange. It is easy to see why Reagan's insistence that it was time to move beyond containment and MAD—indeed, that it was time to *win* the Cold War—provoked, to put it mildly, dissent and alarm among Amer-ica's allies.[13]

___☙ ❧ ☙___

Reagan's rollback strategy rested upon the very policies the ex-perts convened at Chequers said would not work: destabilizing Eastern Europe, particularly by supporting the Solidarity move-ment in Poland; drying up sources of Soviet hard currency; stress-ing the Soviet economy by accelerating the arms race; and raising the cost of Soviet military adventures by supporting anti-Soviet

---

12. When Stéphane Courtois argued for this figure in his 1997 masterpiece, *Le livre noir du Communisme,* many critics believed this number was inflated. It increasingly appears that his estimate was too low. The book was published in English as *The Black Book of Communism: Crimes, Terror, Repression* (Harvard University Press, 1999). The death toll may well have been more than two hundred million by the end of the Cold War. See, e.g., R. J. Rummel, *Death by Government* (Transaction, 1997).

13. Radio interview for British Forces Broadcasting Service, June 10, 1982, transcript, Thatcher MSS (digital collection), doc. 104962.

forces in the world's proxy conflicts. These policies were accompanied by a rhetoric of unprecedented bluntness: The Soviet Union was evil. It would be consigned to the ash heap of history.

Publicly, Thatcher—and only Thatcher, among the leaders of the world—supported Reagan unwaveringly, despite massive domestic and international pressure to do otherwise. "I regarded it as my duty," wrote Thatcher, "to do everything I could to reinforce and further President Reagan's bold strategy to win the Cold War, which the West had been slowly, but surely losing."[14]

Thatcher's support for Reagan, and the intimacy of their friendship, have been so widely remarked that it is easy, retrospectively, to take as given the robust Anglo-American front during the years leading to the Soviet Union's collapse. It was neither given nor even likely. When Thatcher came to power, American analysts did *not* expect her to throw her weight behind the Atlantic alliance. In October 1979, the CIA declared:

> The "special relationship" between the United States and the United Kingdom . . . has lost much of its meaning. The United States is no longer closer to Britain than to its other major allies. Even if the old relationship still existed it would not mean a great deal, given the United Kingdom's now largely secondary political, economic and military role in the EC, NATO and the Third World . . . Insofar as the Thatcher government is interested in expanding that role, it apparently intends to do so more in an EC than an Atlantic framework.[15]

Every word of this analysis was wrong. Within the next decade, the relationship between the United States and Britain would become closer—far closer—than it had been at any point since the

---

14. Thatcher, *The Downing Street Years,* p. 157.
15. "Changing Power Relations among OECD States," October 22, 1979.

Second World War. Britain would prove itself a prime mover in NATO, a prime spoiler in Europe, and a resurgent economic giant.

Had the Labour Party been in power, the story would have been entirely different. Throughout this period, the Labour Party was demanding unilateral nuclear disarmament and the closure of American military bases in Britain. "It's my total objective," said Thatcher, "to stop . . . anyone who shares that kind of view from ever getting in power."[16] But had Britain lost in the Falklands—and remember, it was a very close-run thing—Labour *would* in all likelihood have come to power, no matter what Thatcher's total objective.

It is unimaginable that Neil Kinnock would have had the rapport with Reagan that Thatcher did, or the influence upon him that Thatcher had. Thatcher and Reagan adored each other. They were natural ideological allies. Their relationship was, moreover, colored in romantic hues—he evoked in her feminine admiration; she inspired his chivalry. If you study photographs of Reagan and Thatcher together, you simply can't miss this. There is a reason the satirists of the era depicted the two as lovers. Reagan was portrayed, for example, carrying Thatcher in his arms in a parody of the famous poster from *Gone with the Wind*. "The most EXPLO-SIVE love story ever . . . She promised to follow him to the end of the earth. He promised to organize it!" The poster was funny precisely because Reagan and Thatcher looked perfectly natural in that pose—she *was* always staring at him in that *Oh, Rhett, when I knew I loved you, I ran home to tell you, oh, darling, darling!* way, and Reagan *did* always seem to be on the verge of saying, *I love you, Scarlett. In spite of you and me and the whole silly world going to pieces around us, I love you!* I am not saying that the slightest impropriety ever passed between them. Of course not. I am just saying that this was a friendship not only between a president and a prime minister, but between a man and a woman.

This could hardly be said of Reagan and Kinnock. In 1984, Kinnock visited the United States. He requested a meeting with Rea-

---

16. "An Interview with Thatcher," *Time*, February 16, 1981.

gan. Although it was customary for American presidents to meet the leader of the British Opposition, Reagan hesitated. "I suspect you would not be keen to meet with him," wrote National Security Advisor Robert McFarlane. "In recent years the Labour party has taken stances inimical to our interests, particularly on nuclear, defense, and broader East-West issues. I doubt that even your persuasive powers will change his views." Kinnock, according to a briefing prepared by the State Department, "has made no secret of his opposition to the Administration's policies." He had recently told a visiting congressional delegation that his party was not anti-American: It was just anti-Reagan.[17] These are not the views from which close friendships are forged.

"In a way," says John Hoskyns of Thatcher, "she trail-blazed for Reagan. I mean, Reagan came in, and he followed Carter, and the Carter years were abysmal, really. America was suffering, in a less extreme form, from the same fashionable left-of-center waffle that we had been doing in spades, for years. And everywhere there was the sort of feeling of, *Well, you know, that's not the future. Market economics is just nineteenth-century fantasy. It no longer has a part in the modern world, it's not like that.* But Thatcher was already beginning to show that the impossible was happening—to the worst basket case of all in the civilized world."

Thatcher's economic example was important. But its effects were not immediately visible. Well before the impossible began to happen in Britain itself, Thatcher played a crucial diplomatic role abroad. Repeatedly, Thatcher supported Reagan publicly even when she disagreed with him privately, often at high political cost to herself. Her support for Reagan went well beyond what was required to shore up the NATO alliance. Without consulting her full cabinet, for example, she allowed American planes to use British bases to stage their raid against Libya. Likewise, she refused publicly to express reservations about Reagan's intervention in El Salvador.

---

17. Reagan meeting with Kinnock, February 14, 1984, briefing and background papers, National Security Council Country File, Box 91331, Reagan Library.

Mr. Flannery: Will the Prime Minister turn her mind for a moment away from the fairy tales of Milton Friedman to the serious situation in El Salvador? Although Conservative Members seem to think that this is a joke, will she use her waning influence with President Reagan, who is twirling his atomic pistols in front of the world, and tell him that the last time that the Americans intervened in a small country, by the name of Vietnam, they got a bloody nose, and that the whole world hopes that they will not intervene in El Salvador but will leave the people of that country to determine their own fate, as they are eminently capable of doing if they are left to their own devices, against the brutal tyranny that exists there at the moment?

The Prime Minister: I do not think that the way in which the hon. Gentleman puts his comments is a classic example of how to win friends or influence anyone.[18]

When faced with the choice between strengthening Britain's ties to Europe and strengthening its ties to the United States, Thatcher did not even try to find a tactful middle ground:

Interviewer: I've heard it said by a lot of people that President Reagan appears to be wanting to be seen to be very strong militarily, yet some people have the thoughts that in Europe the feeling is just a little bit softer, with not quite as much determination as President Reagan has. Where do you stand between the two trains of thought?

Prime Minister: Oh, absolutely four-square with President Reagan.[19]

Giant protests erupted in mainland Europe and Britain against the United States' plans to deploy cruise and Pershing missiles in

---

18. March 26, 1981, House of Commons PQs, Hansard HC [1/1073–77].
19. Radio Interview for British Forces Broadcasting Service, June 10, 1982, Thatcher MSS (digital collection), doc. 104962.

response to the Soviet deployment of the Satan. This antinuclear sentiment blossomed into a mass movement financed by the Soviet Union and supported, in Britain, by the Labour Party. "All over Europe," recalled Reagan, "the peace marchers demonstrated to prevent Western missiles from being installed for their defense, but they were silent about the Soviet missiles targeted against them! Again, in the face of these demonstrations, Margaret never wavered."[20]

The first cruise missiles arrived at Greenham Common in December 1983, inaugurating a permanent state of protest at the U.S. air base. Thatcher scolded the protesters: "We are very fortunate to have someone else's weapons stationed on our soil to fight those targeted on us."[21] Although this was perfectly true, she sounded to her detractors—as she so often did—rather like Mr. Bumble informing Oliver Twist that he was very fortunate to have gruel every day with an onion twice a week.

Mr. Faulds: Reverting to an earlier supplementary question on the subject of theater nuclear weapons, will the right hon. Lady contemplate where that intended theater lies? Will each European Government be free to choose or to veto the push on that final button by that incoherent cretin, President Reagan?

The Prime Minister: I greatly deplore the discourtesy and total futility of the hon. Gentleman's remarks.

Mr. Faulds: Answer the question!

The Prime Minister: They do not help when the security of Europe depends upon the support of the United States of America. With regard to the theater nuclear weapons, the SS–20s are targeted on Europe, including this country.[22]

---

20. Ronald Reagan, "Margaret Thatcher and the Revival of the West," *National Review,* May 19, 1989.
21. "An Interview with Thatcher," *Time,* February 16, 1981.
22. October 29, 1983, House of Commons PQs, Hansard HC [10/985–90].

There was one notable moment of dissent: When in 1983 the United States invaded Grenada, a member of the British Commonwealth, without first notifying the British government, Thatcher was furious. She nonetheless held her tongue in public, even while expressing her extreme displeasure with Reagan in private.

> **Mr. Kinnock:** Is it not a fact . . . that the relationship that was said to exist between the right hon. Lady and the President turned out to be not so special? In the chaos and humiliation of the Grenada affair, will the right hon. Lady at least take the opportunity of adopting a new deportment in world affairs and, as a consequence, demonstrate a greater independence in furthering British interests and working for peace throughout the world?
>
> **The Prime Minister:** When two nations are friends each owes the other its own judgment. That does not mean that the other in either case is compelled to accept it. It would hardly be a friendship unless one could tender advice to another country—
>
> **Mr. Foulkes:** And have it ignored!
>
> **The Prime Minister:** —and have it either accepted or rejected. We do not run the sort of Warsaw pact organization that the right hon. Gentleman—[*Interruption*]
>
> **Mr. Kinnock:** I would be the last to suggest the rendering of any alliances, but when the judgment of this Government is apparently utterly cast aside and trampled on by our ally, what obligation does the right hon. Lady then have?
>
> **The Prime Minister:** It follows from what the right hon. Gentleman has said that, as the United States and Britain are allies, we would always have had to accept any advice that the United States gave us. Indeed, it follows that we would not be free to accept or reject the advice of the United States. However, at the beginning of the Falklands affair we did not ask the United States whether we should recapture the Falklands. We took our own decisions.

By publicly supporting Reagan when he was most isolated abroad, Thatcher won Reagan's trust and earned his gratitude. Ultimately, and in large part owing to her sheer, dogged loyalty, her influence on Reagan came to exceed that of most of his cabinet members. That influence proved pivotal when Mikhail Gorbachev came to power.

—·ε· ⇜ ·ᴐ—

In November 1984, roughly a year after the downing of KAL 007, the Soviets walked out of the Geneva talks on intermediate-range missiles. They then walked out of the Strategic Arms Reduction Treaty discussions on long-range missiles, breaking off all contact with the United States. There was now no personal contact between American and Soviet leaders.

This extraordinarily dangerous impasse, Thatcher believed, made it incumbent upon her to take the diplomatic initiative. She rejected Geoffrey Howe's suggestion that she invite the Soviet premier, Konstantin Chernenko, to visit Britain. She was not prepared to be that friendly. Instead, she issued invitations to several lower-ranking members of the Politburo. The Soviet agricultural secretary, a man by the name of Gorbachev, responded with interest.

Thatcher knew little about Gorbachev save that his wife was reputed to be less unattractive than the wives of the other Soviet leaders. In 1984, there was no reason beyond this to expect that Gorbachev would be much different from the other walking corpses of the Soviet leadership. Gorbachev had never visited the United States. He had never met Reagan. Still furious with the Soviets, Reagan had shown no interest in meeting him. But this Gorbachev fellow seemed keen to come to Britain, so Thatcher asked him to join her for lunch, at Chequers, on December 16.

Charles Powell remembers Gorbachev's arrival at Chequers vividly. "It was an extraordinary moment. You won't have seen Chequers, but it's an old English country house, with a great hall at the entrance, a huge fire, a few members of the government

Thatcher walking with Gorbachev at the Brize Norton Air Force base in 1987. "Certainly the two leaders were attracted to each other, relished each other's company," recalled her Foreign Secretary Geoffrey Howe. "But neither Margaret nor Mikhail ever completely lowered their guard." *(Courtesy of Graham Wiltshire)*

standing there—and nobody had *any* clue what to expect. I mean, Gorbachev was not known outside the Soviet Union. He'd once been outside to Canada.[23] Nobody had taken any notice of him. He came into this room, beaming, bouncing on the balls of his

---

23. He had also been to Belgium in 1972 and West Germany in 1975.

feet, this smartly dressed wife with him, and everyone present just simply had to change gear . . . *this is not Khrushchev, this is not Andropov, this is not Chernenko, this is an entirely new sort of person.* He engaged from the beginning in jovial banter with people and ordered a drink before lunch. Then he and Margaret Thatcher sat next to each other at lunch, and neither of them ate a thing. They spent the whole time talking at each other, and arguing about things—"

"Right from the start? Arguing right from the start?"

"Well, arguing was sort of Thatcher's *raison d'être*—"

"It sounds as if he sort of got that right away, understood it, related to it?"

"Oh, yes, absolutely. He *enjoyed* it. And then we retired into another room. It was just him, and her, and me, and the then Soviet ambassador here, and that man from the Politburo who was Gorbachev's great ally, he'd been exiled to be ambassador to Canada, and whose name now escapes me, began with K.[24] And in that small room, they talked for two and a half hours as against the half-hour scheduled. Gorbachev—immediately, again, you *saw* the difference. I mean, the advisors just shut up. He had no briefs, no documents, he had a few little handwritten notes in green ink, which he occasionally produced, the odd newspaper clipping from the *Wall Street Journal* or the *New York Times*—one was about nuclear war, I remember particularly. About nuclear winter. And he talked absolutely self-confidently and assuredly, and he wasn't even leader at the time. Chernenko was still in charge. Gorbachev was still just a member of the Politburo, technically in charge of agriculture. This was new ground . . . I mean, we'd had this succession of geriatrics, Chernenko, and before him Andropov and Brezhnev, who could barely stand up and who just sort of read from bits of paper. Here was a man who talked and argued like a

---

24. I believe he is referring to Alexander Yakovlev, although his name doesn't begin with a K.

Western politician, didn't need briefs and notes and advisors—and he sat there and slugged it out with her! This was somebody you could really *engage* with."

The then Soviet ambassador to whom Powell is referring was a man named Leonid Zamyatin. "This was how it went," Zamyatin remembered. "They sat down in armchairs at a fireplace, Thatcher took off her patent-leather shoes, tucked her feet under her chair and got out her handbag."[25]

I've spoken now to many men who specifically remember Thatcher kicking off her shoes and curling up her feet in that flirtatious way. I have looked in vain for a photo or video clip that shows her doing this. It seems she never did it with a camera present. She was obviously well aware that it was a coquettish and provocative gesture, and well aware, too, that "barefoot and cuddly" was not the image she wished, as a world leader, to project widely.

I have pieced together what happened next from several different accounts—her memoirs, Gorbachev's memoirs, Powell's recollections, Zamyatin's, various official memoranda of the meeting. I am fairly sure that it went roughly this way:

Gorbachev suddenly suggested they both get rid of their briefing papers.

"Gladly!" replied Thatcher, putting her papers back in her handbag.

Gorbachev told Thatcher it was time to end the Cold War.

Thatcher told Gorbachev it was time to end communism.

Gorbachev told Thatcher that communism was superior to capitalism.

"Don't be silly, Mr. Gorbachev. You can barely feed your own citizens."

"To the contrary, Mrs. Thatcher! Our people live *joyfully.*"

---

25. Interview with Zamyatin, *Kommersant*, May 4, 2005.

"Oh, do they? Then why do so many of them want to leave? And why do you prevent them from leaving?"

"They can leave if they want to!"

"That's not what I hear. And by the way, we're not happy about the money you're sending to Arthur Scargill."

"We have nothing to do with that."

"Who do you think you're kidding? You and I both know that your economy is centrally controlled. Not a kopeck leaves without the Politburo's knowledge."

"*Nyet, nyet,* you misunderstand. It's not centrally controlled."

"Oh, no? How does a Russian factory decide how much to produce?"

"We tell them."

Perhaps Thatcher laughed. Perhaps she snorted. I like to imagine that her gifted mimic of a translator laughed or snorted along with her even as the Soviet translator remained a leaden lump. "The Soviet Union and the West," she said, "have entirely different ways of life and government. You don't like ours, we don't like yours. But it is in our common interest—indeed it is our duty—to avoid a conflict."

"But the United States has been targeting us with missiles since the 1950s!"

"Of course it has. You've been trying to export communism by force. Your missiles are aimed at us. What did you expect?"

I can't determine what Gorbachev said next. But something prompted Thatcher to tell him that Reagan was an honorable man. When he took office, he had put his heart and soul into writing a letter to Brezhnev. He had written it by hand. After months of silence, he received only a typed, pro forma reply.

Perhaps Gorbachev was moved. Or perhaps he rolled his eyes—*how just like a woman to be offended because we didn't hand-write the letter.*

Thatcher, recalled Zamyatin, "had a definite womanish feeling towards Gorbachev."

"I found myself liking him," recalled Thatcher.

Gorbachev's Version:

I unfolded a large diagram representing all nuclear arsenals, grouped into a thousand little squares.

"Each of these squares," I told Mrs. Thatcher, "suffices to eradicate all life on earth. Consequently, the available nuclear arsenals have a capacity to wipe out all life a thousand times."

Her reaction was very eloquent and emotional. I believe she was quite sincere.[26]

Thatcher's Version:

At one point, with a touch of theater, he pulled out a full page diagram from *The New York Times*, illustrating the explosive power of the weapons of the two superpowers compared with the explosive power available in the Second World War. He was well versed in the fashionable arguments then raging about the prospect of a "nuclear winter" resulting from a nuclear exchange. I was not much moved by all this.[27]

Obviously, I cannot say exactly what transpired at that meeting. But this much we know for sure: Thatcher emerged from that meeting and declared, "I like Mr. Gorbachev. We can do business with him."

This was one of the great turning points in the Cold War. Margaret Thatcher had met a communist she didn't hate.

_◦ ⟡ ◦_

Later that month, Thatcher visited Reagan at Camp David. She told Reagan that Gorbachev was "an unusual Russian." He was

---

26. Mikhail Gorbachev, *Memoirs* (Doubleday, 1996).
27. Thatcher, *The Downing Street Years*, p. 462.

"much less constrained, more charming, open to discussion and debate." He did not "cry or complain" when she criticized the Soviet record on human rights.[28]

Gorbachev, she told Reagan, had asked her to give him a message: "Tell your friend President Reagan not to go ahead with space weapons." She reported this to Reagan and told him that she had, in turn, told Gorbachev that Britain supported Strategic Defense Initiative (SDI) research. A White House scribe took detailed notes of this meeting:

> **Mrs. Thatcher** underlined that she had told Gorbachev there is no point in trying to divide Britain from the United States. This ploy will never succeed . . . She also told Gorbachev that she and the President have known each other since long before they assumed their current positions and dividing Europe from America is simply "not on."[29]

Reagan responded with great pleasure. He was "simply amazed" by the parallels in their thought; it was wonderful that she had told Gorbachev exactly what *he* would have said. How gratified he was, he added, that Thatcher supported his much-misunderstood SDI program.

Yes, yes, Thatcher assured him. "The wretched press has tried to make out that we have major differences. This is simply not true." Then, very gently, she added that while *of course* her solidarity went without saying, she did have some . . . *concerns*. Nothing serious, mind you. It was just that Mutual Assured Destruction was a doctrine with a proven record. There had thus far been no nuclear war between the superpowers. Was Reagan entirely sure it was wise to tamper with this formula?

---

28. Thatcher-Reagan meeting at Camp David, December 22, 1984, record of conversation, European and Soviet Affairs Directorate, National Security Council, Folder "Thatcher Visit—Dec 1984 (1)," Box 90902, Reagan Library.
29. Ibid.

Mrs. Thatcher noted that the President said earlier that initial indications are that an SDI program is feasible. Mrs. Thatcher said she must admit that personally she had some doubts. In the past, scientific genius had always developed a counter system. Even if an SDI system proved 95 percent successful—a significant success rate—over 60 million people would still die from those weapons that got through . . .

The President said we need to address the points Mrs. Thatcher had raised and to reach agreement on SDI, a program he called worth pursuing . . . He recognized that the Soviets have great respect for our technology. They also must be concerned about our economic strength. It will be especially difficult for them to keep spending such vast sums on defense. Such spending is in neither of our interests.

The President continued that he also recognized the great losses the Soviets suffered in World War II—20 million or more—and accepted their obsession with security. But . . . Common sense tells us that one needs negotiating tools when bargaining with the Soviets, or anyone else for that matter . . . We must deal with the Soviets from a position of strength. But we also know that in a nuclear war there would be no winners.

Mrs. Thatcher interjected that this is why she had emphasized and praised the deterrence system that has worked so well for so many years. Strength is our best deterrence.

The President agreed and said he is trying to convince the Soviets that we mean them no harm . . .

Mrs. Thatcher replied that it is correct to emphasize military balance, not superiority. Balance gives us security . . . Saying she didn't wish to debate strategic theory, Mrs. Thatcher noted that some claim SDI would be an incentive for the Soviets to produce more offensive systems and could encourage the Soviets to launch a preemptive first strike.

From our point of view, said Mrs. Thatcher, deterrence remains our fundamental objective.[30]

From a woman not generally known for her tact, this is an impressively circumspect way of putting it. "Some" claim SDI would encourage the Soviets to launch a first strike. *Yes, yes, of course I support you, Mr. President, we are absolutely as one, SDI is a marvelous idea, simply marvelous, but have you perhaps thought about the 60 million people who would die even if this harebrained fantasy of yours works, which it won't?*

In her memoirs, Thatcher engages in some rather striking revisionism about SDI. "I had no doubt," she writes, "about the rightness of his commitment to press ahead with the program. Looking back, it is now clear to me that Ronald Reagan's original decision on SDI was the single most important of his presidency."[31] It is true that she supported Reagan and defended SDI against its critics both in Britain and America. It is obviously not true that she had no doubts.

Following this meeting, Secretary of Defense Caspar Weinberger sent Thatcher a brief note. "Dear Mrs. Thatcher," he wrote. "I wanted to especially thank you for the opposition [*sic*] to present the technical side of the President's Strategic Defense Initiative. We feel that very substantial progress is being made, although there is a long way to go."[32] Perhaps the substitution of the word "opposition" for "opportunity" was just a typo; perhaps it was a classic Freudian slip.

Although Thatcher did not persuade Reagan to abandon SDI—indeed, he managed at this meeting to persuade *her* that there might be some merit to the idea—she did convey to him a message that proved enormously important when Reagan subsequently met Gorbachev. There was, she pointed out, a certain logic

---

30. Ibid.
31. Thatcher, *The Downing Street Years*, p. 463.
32. Weinberger to Thatcher, January 29, 1985, NSA Head of State File, Box 36, Reagan Library.

to the Soviet Union's suspicions about this program. If Reagan was to insist upon it, he must succeed in convincing Gorbachev that he was a man of peace.

_____ ๑ ๔ ๑_____

Chernenko expired in 1985. Gorbachev became the new general secretary of the Communist Party. Some historians believe that Gorbachev's election was a direct response to the Reagan-era arms buildup; it was this, they argue, that convinced the Soviets they must embrace radical economic reform so better to compete with the West. I do not know whether this is true. It is certainly true that by this time, anxiety within the Kremlin about the state of the Soviet economy was acute. It cannot have helped that both Britain and the United States appeared to be reversing the dire economic trends of the 1970s, which had been hopefully interpreted in the Kremlin (and in much of the West) as capitalism's death rattle. Capitalism now seemed to be up and about and crankily demanding its boiled egg, even as the Soviet Union was frantically creating commissions to solve the problem of women's pantyhose.

In 1985, impressed by Thatcher's favorable evaluation of the new Soviet premier, Reagan invited Gorbachev to Geneva. "Reagan and Gorbachev each spoke in direct and positive terms," recalls Secretary of State George Shultz. "The personal chemistry was apparent."

Expectations matter: If a trusted friend assures you that you'll find a man likeable, you will be more apt to find the likeability in the man. "As we shook hands for the first time," Reagan recalled, "I had to admit—as Margaret Thatcher and Prime Minister Brian Mulroney of Canada predicted I would—that there was something likable about Gorbachev."[33]

---

33. Ronald Reagan, *An American Life: The Autobiography* (Simon and Schuster, 1990). I leave the story of Mulroney's influence on Reagan to the author of *Sleeping Giant to the North: Why Canada Matters.*

Compare the tone of Reagan's speech following the downing of KAL 007 to the letter he sent to Gorbachev immediately after the summit:

> . . . I found our meetings of great value . . . a better understanding of your attitudes . . . struck by your concern that [SDI] is somehow designed to secure a strategic advantage—even to permit a first-strike capability . . . I can understand, as you explained so eloquently, that these are matters which cannot be taken on faith . . . [but] we should find a way, in practical terms, to relieve the concerns you have expressed . . . we will find a solution . . . I can assure you that the United States does not believe that the Soviet Union is the cause of all the world's ills . . . genuinely enjoyed meeting you . . . already looking forward to showing you something of our country next year . . . [34]

When Reagan returned from Geneva, he convened the National Security Council. The head of the American arms negotiation delegation, Max Kampelman, recalls the scene: "Sitting in the situation room, the president began by saying: 'Maggie was right. We can do business with this man.' His reference to Prime Minister Margaret Thatcher prompted nods of assent. Then, in a remarkably matter-of-fact tone, he reported that he had suggested to Mr. Gorbachev that their negotiations could possibly lead to the United States and the Soviet Union eliminating all their nuclear weapons."[35]

I am not saying that Reagan would not have liked Gorbachev if Thatcher had not told him he ought to, nor am I saying that he would not have taken Gorbachev's concerns seriously if Thatcher

34. Reagan to Gorbachev, April 30, 1985, "To the Geneva Summit: Perestroika and the Transformation of U.S.-Soviet Relations," Electronic Briefing Book No. 172, Document 9, National Security Archive, George Washington University, Washington, D.C.
35. Max M. Kampelman, "Bombs Away," *New York Times*, April 24, 2006.

had not taken pains to explain them to him, but—well, yes, maybe I am saying just that. That *is* the kind of influence she had on him.

_ — — —_

Thatcher's friendship with Reagan has been widely described, so I will add only a few more details to the portrait. I was surprised to hear from so many people that she envied Reagan. "More than anyone else," stresses Charles Powell. "She thought he had this incredible ability to get over a very tough message in very gentle language and tones. It was quite true, if you listen to him speak, I mean, the content and the tone were completely at odds with each other. This gentle, avuncular tone about condemning communism to fire and brimstone was remarkable, and she knew she couldn't do that."

"That's right, exactly," agrees Nigel Lawson. "He had all these warm, lovable qualities which she lacked." There is something poignant about this image of Margaret Thatcher, wishing she could be loved as Reagan was loved, and knowing she simply wasn't lovable.

In Lawson's memoirs, he remarks that Thatcher found George Bush—the elder one—a less inspiring figure than Reagan, and as a result, when Bush was elected, simply transferred her affections wholesale to Gorbachev. Lawson seems to be hinting at a compulsion, in Thatcher's makeup, to look up to at least *one* man, a need that clearly could not be satisfied within her own political circle, given that she was *primus inter pares*. If you are inclined to look at people through a certain prism, you might wonder, reading this, if Thatcher felt the need to have in her life a father figure. Given Thatcher's well-known veneration of her father, it wouldn't be a surprise. Was she perhaps reprising in her relationships with Reagan and Gorbachev a familiar family role?

When I ask Lawson about this, he replies that his psychological interpretation is slightly different. "I think," he says, "that people who are in positions of power come very easily, after a time, to value power more highly than anything else. And when they encounter someone who has even more power than they have, they are in awe of it. And I think that was the question with Reagan—though she was very happy to criticize him when she thought he was getting things wrong. But nevertheless, she was to some extent in awe of him." If she found it easy to admire Gorbachev, Lawson believes, it was because "at that time, nobody fully realized the extent of the fundamental weakness of the Soviet Union."

Perhaps. There is no doubt that whatever its psychological roots, Thatcher's love for Reagan was very real and very deep. Charles Powell was present at all of Thatcher's meetings with Reagan. "It was interesting, because of course they adored each other, and they thought very similarly, but their styles could hardly have been more different. I mean, he was a chairman, presiding loftily over world affairs, while also sort of greeting Miss Multiple Sclerosis from Kansas. She was the chief operating officer, deeply immersed in details of policy, and sometimes, there was just the two of them there—just, you know, a hanger-on like me in the background—and she was rather going on, as one might say, and you could see his eyes sort of straining to the clock on the wall, you know, counting the minutes to lunch, when he could decently say, *Maggie—Margaret, let's go and have a drink, and have lunch,* and she would be going into the finer details of the anti-ballistic missile treaty. It was a curious sort of dialogue, though she had *huge* respect for him. She was very respectful of American presidents. She was not at all an informal person, she called him 'Mr. President' 99 percent of the time, very rarely relapsed into 'Ron,' even in very private settings—"

"And did he call her—"

"He always called her 'Margaret.'"

By the time Reagan died, in 2004, Thatcher was already very ill. She was not strong enough to speak at the funeral. She instead sent a prerecorded eulogy to be played at the National Cathedral in Washington. It is a sad thing to watch. Her diminishment is palpable. There is no doubt of the depth of her grief. The voice of this once-indomitable woman is weak; her eyes are bleak and watery. She gasps for breath between phrases.

Recalling the attempt on Reagan's life, she remembers that he had told a priest, after his recovery, that "Whatever time I've got left now belongs to the Big Fella Upstairs." The words "Big Fella" could scarcely sound less natural coming from her mouth. Her attempt to pay tribute by mastering this casual Americanism is touchingly awkward, like an elderly tourist struggling earnestly to order a meal with a Berlitz phrase book.

"For the final years of his life," Thatcher concludes in her funeral oration, "Ronnie's mind was clouded by illness. That cloud has now lifted. He is himself again—more himself than at any time on this earth. For we may be sure that the Big Fellow Upstairs never forgets those who remember Him." She cannot quite bring herself to refer to God as "the Big Fella" a second time. It is obvious that she is aware that her own mind, too, is clouded by illness. The words "we may be sure" seem especially to pain her. She was a woman who was once unsure of nothing. It is clearly no longer so.

In 1986, Reagan and Gorbachev met again, in Reykjavik. Gorbachev proposed the complete elimination of nuclear weapons in exchange for Reagan's abandonment of the Strategic Defense Initiative. To the horror of many of his advisors, Reagan said no.

I would have been one of the horrified, but I would have been wrong. We now know, from both Soviet officials and the Soviet archives, that Reagan's insistence upon pursuing SDI prompted panic in the Kremlin, leading to an expensive increase in Soviet military spending and accelerating the economic collapse of the Soviet Union.

SDI "played a powerful psychological role," claims KGB general Nikolai Leonov. "SDI was a very successful blackmail," agrees Gennady Gerasimov, the Soviet foreign ministry's spokesman during this period: "The Soviet economy couldn't endure such competition."[36] According to Genrikh Trofimenko, a high-ranking official of the Brezhnev era, "Ninety-nine percent of the Russian people believe that [America] won the Cold War because of your president's insistence on SDI."[37]

Thatcher was immensely relieved by the failure of the talks, not because she was profoundly committed to keeping SDI, but because she thought the offer to give up all the nukes was madness. She was in favor of a gradual reduction of nuclear weapons, but their immediate wholesale elimination? Had Reagan lost his mind? It would have "left the Soviets confronting western Europe with a huge superiority of conventional forces, chemical weapons and short-range missiles."[38]

Reagan was well aware of Thatcher's views on this score; she had visited him in Washington the month prior and told him precisely this, in no uncertain terms. "I regarded the *quid pro quo* for my strong public support of the President as being the right to be direct with him and members of his Administration in private," she said of this meeting.[39] As Bernard Ingham says, "She believed in being a candid friend, and when Mrs. Thatcher is candid, she can be *really* candid."

Reagan famously hesitated after turning down Gorbachev's offer. He passed a note to George Shultz asking, "Am I wrong?"

---

36. John Fund, "Freedom's Team: How Reagan, Thatcher and John Paul II won the Cold War," *Wall Street Journal,* June 7, 2004.
37. Lance Morrow, "The Mystery of Ronald Reagan Lives On," *Time,* April 19, 2000.
38. Thatcher, *The Downing Street Years,* p. 472.
39. Ibid., p. 472.

Shultz whispered, "No, you're right."[40] It is clear from memoirs of the meeting that Reagan's concern, above all, was to protect SDI, which he saw as the best hope given to mankind of eliminating forever the threat of nuclear war. But I have to imagine that somewhere in his calculations, too, was the thought that the last thing he wanted to do, upon leaving that meeting, was phone up Margaret Thatcher and explain to her that he had given away the store.

_C₂ _C₂ _C₂

Peter Walker, who takes credit for winning the miners' strike, also takes credit for the success of Thatcher's visit, in March 1987, to the Soviet Union—and again, he may well be right to stress his role. "Listen," he tells me, "the reputation she had of never listening was wrong." He had seen the brief the Foreign Office prepared for the prime minister before her trip. "It said, 'Mr. Gorbachev is a hardline Communist who tries to convince his people that he's not.' So I phoned up and said, 'Would you ask Margaret if I could see her before she goes to Moscow?' And I went 'round, and I said, 'Margaret, I've read this brief, and it's totally wrong.' And I then took her through quotations from him over five years, all following the same argument, and I said, 'This man thinks the system *won't work*. And he wants to change it. The Foreign Office brief prepared for you is totally wrong.'

"And she didn't say, you know, 'I hate the Foreign Office, how right you are.' She said, 'Well, thank you very much, it is very interesting to read all this before I go.' And when she came back on Sunday, from her three-day visit to him, which had been recorded in the press as an enormous success—they really got on well—she phoned me from Chequers at my house in Worcestershire, and said, 'Peter, thank goodness you briefed me on this man. I like him,

---

40. George Shultz, *Turmoil and Triumph: My Years as Secretary of State* (Scribner, 1993).

we got on well, you're absolutely right. Foreign Office, they always get it wrong.'"

Perhaps this is the way it happened. In her memoirs, Thatcher does not refer to Walker's counsel. But it is certainly true that Thatcher's visit to the Soviet Union was a triumph, another pivotal point in the history of the Cold War. Again, Charles Powell recalls the details. "We had this famous meeting in the Kremlin, which—with one break when she had a lunch engagement—went on for thirteen hours, and I was the only other person present—"

"*Thirteen hours?*"

"Yes. A day of meetings which lasted a total of thirteen hours with him, yeah. And I spent my whole night dictating my notes of it to a secretary in the soundproof cellar at the British Embassy—"

"Do you remember any of the dialogue?"

"She launched into a coruscating attack on the record of the Soviet Union, at home, abroad, its failures and so on, what it needed to do to bring itself into the civilized nations. And he actually responded in similar fashion. I mean, he talked about social inequalities in Britain, and the miseries of the miners, and Northern Ireland and all the other problems we had. And it was a real irony—we reached a stage where I was thinking of packing up my briefcase, thinking we were going to get slung out of the Kremlin, we wouldn't even survive, so we might as well have a statement ready for how we were going to explain to the press that she'd been virtually expelled from the Soviet Union—"

"Were you really thinking that, or are you exaggerating now for effect?"

"Well, I'm exaggerating now a bit for effect, but it really was to the point where I thought, you know, that this was going to end in disaster, this meeting."

"At what point were you thinking that, exactly?"

"Well, quite early on, because it started like that. But Gorbachev himself was very good at breaking the tension, and after about a sort of hour and a bit of this, he sort of suddenly, you know, broke into smiles, and sort of relaxed the tension, and moved on to something else, and after another couple hours again it sort of built up, it was rather like British weather, really."

"You don't remember what he said that had everyone smiling, do you?"

"I can't, I'm afraid."

Too bad.

There were only six people in the room: Thatcher, Gorbachev, Gorbachev's foreign minister, Powell, and the two interpreters. The large delegations of advisors and ministers that had assembled for the meeting were kept waiting outside all day. "They just wanted to talk alone. They had the same instinct, that actually the best thing was to talk to each other without delegations. That was characteristic of her diplomacy—she hated having the Foreign Office involved."

"What else did they talk about?"

"Everything from the Soviet and Cuban presence in Africa, to the whole question of intermediate and short-range missiles in Europe."

"The debate was mostly about the actual record of the Soviet Union, as opposed to the philosophical problem of communism?"

"It was both, it was both. I mean, she was trying to persuade him that communism was fundamentally a misguided system, not to be reconciled with human nature—the concept of communism, with the state running everything and so on, was never going to work. She larded it with examples—the Gulag, the people she had met, like Sakharov—"[41]

"Do you remember what his face looked like when she was—"

"Oh, he could be quite angry, he could be quite stern, Gorby. He waved his arms a lot and so on . . . "

"Was there any point during the meeting when you noticed an expression on Gorbachev's face that would have suggested that he felt she was getting the better of him?"

---

41. Andrei Sakharov, the Soviet Union's most famous political dissident.

"Can't say I do, no. Gorbachev was also, you know, very convinced of his rightness. They were two quite similar people in that sense. I think Gorbachev in some ways found her quite useful—I mean, she was an anvil on which he could beat out his own ideas. If you could sort of take your views to destruction testing with Margaret Thatcher, then, you know, if they could survive that, then they were probably worth having. And of course, very few of his views *did* survive that. But I think his belief that he could negotiate with Reagan, that there could be a decent arms control agreement . . . I think, basically, I think he wanted to run his ideas past her, before he tried them on Reagan."

"Was there any flirtation between the two of them?"

"A bit, yes, yeah, at times."

Thatcher did not, in the end, get herself thrown out of the Kremlin. Perhaps that hint of flirtation, and Gorbachev's willingness to laugh, had something to do with this.

"At the end of that thirteen-hour day you must have been exhausted," I say.

"I was in a *total* state of exhaustion."

His bladder, he later told me, was also about to burst. Finally, he excused himself to look for the bathroom, but he couldn't figure out how to get out of the room. Gorbachev, amused, watched him cast about helplessly. "It was one of the most embarrassing moments of my life," Powell recalls. Finally, Gorbachev took pity on him. Beaming broadly, he pushed a button by his chair. A door slid open. Powell escaped.

Didn't *she* need to go, I ask?

No, she did not, says Powell. Not even once. The Iron Bladder held out for the whole thirteen hours.

_⊙, ⌒⇒ ⊙_

"At the end of that day, was anything concluded?" I ask Powell.

"Nothing. Well, there were conclusions I think about arms control and the right way to proceed, and yes, there were some concrete conclusions on individual foreign affairs subjects. But I think something more was concluded: There could be, at last, after all those years, a genuine dialogue with a Soviet leader, in which you said blunt things and criticized each others' systems, but you could bargain with, and come not necessarily to agreements, but to understandings of each others' point of view—which led to the clear horizon in which the Cold War could be ended."

History hinged upon that visit, in both Britain and the Soviet Union. "It was really from that moment that one knew she was going to win the '87 election," Powell recalled, "because it was a huge PR triumph in this country . . . It was very hard for Labour to criticize her, because there she was, dealing with the Russians, dealing very forcefully, but no one could say that because she was the Iron Lady, because she was making these vitriolic speeches, that she was keeping Britain out of discussing the relaxation of tensions, or arms control, or anything like that."

More importantly, her visit was a PR triumph in Russia. Gorbachev permitted Thatcher to get out of her car and mix through the crowds. "These vast crowds had turned out to see her," Powell remembered. "And Gorby treated her very well. When he invited her, she said, 'Look, I'd like to come, but can I do what I want to do?' And he said, 'Yup, anything you want to do, I'll let you do.' This had never happened with a prime minister before. And she said, 'Well, I want to do a television interview. And I don't want it censored.'"

Gorbachev agreed, and kept his word. This interview was broadcast live, as Gorbachev had promised. "She was interviewed by three Soviet generals," Powell remembers, "and she rode right over them."

Hapless Soviet General: Excuse me, I would like to return to the question of nuclear weapons. You just said that nuclear weapons preserved peace for forty years, but many times we were at the verge of nuclear war during those forty years; many times we were saved only by accident, by chance, but with that, nuclear weapons developed. In the beginning, they threatened cities; now they threaten the whole of humanity. How can one speak of nuclear weapons as a guarantor of peace?

Prime Minister: Are you not making my point? If you say that many times we were at the verge of war and we did not go to war, do you not think that one of the reasons we did not go to war was the total horror of nuclear weapons? After all, I think conventional weapons are awful. It did not stop a war, a terrible war, in which the Soviet Union suffered enormously. You cannot just act as if there had never been nuclear weapons. If conventional war started again, the race would be on as to who got the nuclear weapon first. *One moment!* That person would win.

Hapless Soviet General: The thing is that there is a possibility of an accidental outbreak of a nuclear conflict. Time passes, nuclear weapons are improved and more and more sophisticated. There is a great possibility of an accidental—not political, that politicians will decide, but computers. The flight time of a Pershing 2 to the Soviet Union would be only eight minutes. Who will be deciding? Who will be in charge?

Prime Minister: There are more nuclear weapons in the Soviet Union than any other country in the world. You have more intercontinental ballistic missiles and warheads than the West. You started intermediate weapons; we did not have any. You have more short-range ones than we have. You have more than anyone else and *you* say there is a risk of a nuclear accident? *One moment!* . . . [42]

"Taxi drivers in Moscow still speak of it," says Powell. "They really do."

---

42. Interview for Soviet television, Vladimir Simonov, Novosci Press Agency; Boris Kalyagin, Soviet TV; Thomas Kolesnichenko, *Pravda*, March 31, 1987, transcript, Thatcher MSS (digital collection), doc. 106604.

Neil Kinnock has a different perspective on Thatcher's trip. He recalls discussing it with Gorbachev:

NK: First of all, it wasn't thirteen hours.

CB: It wasn't?

NK: No. It was sporadically over a period of about nine hours.

CB: Right.

NK: And it arose because Margaret Thatcher, they went through
the usual discussions, you know, governments do, blah-blah-
blah-blah-blah-blah. And eventually she started to tell Gorbachev what was wrong with the Soviet Union, and what he
should do about it.

CB: Uh-huh?

NK: Now, I think the first part of that is fine, some other people
think that breaks the code, but I think that's bloody rubbish.
I think it's quite right to tell people what you think of their
country. I've done it. But it's very difficult then to say what
they should do about it without inviting them to say, "OK,
OK, fine, I've heard what you said, now this is what you
should do about *your* country." And that doesn't really *get* you
anywhere, you just get an exchange of prescriptions, but—

CB: Well, what I understood, and correct me if I'm wrong, because I've only heard this from one source, is that Charles
Powell was saying that Gorbachev *did* start telling her,
"Look, you've got this problem with the miners, you've
got—"

NK: Yeah, that's just what he did, you see, and Northern Ireland,
and the whole thing. So that went on for some time. Then,
what Gorbachev told me, when I asked him about it a few
years afterwards, he said, "I thought at the time that she so
completely failed to understand Marxist-Leninism, even
though she claimed to understand it, that I should tell her
where her analysis was wrong." So there were exchanges on

that basis, but they *didn't* get on like a house on fire, they had a kind of ideological duel—

CB: Uh-huh—

NK: And it wasn't, at that time, that Gorbachev could have been described as the most profound Marxist-Leninist, although at the time he did think that he could adapt Marxist-Leninism for the purposes of a more open and free society—

CB: When you talked to him about it, did he seem to be describing her warmly?

NK: *No.* I mean, there was a twinkle, and he had—um, he has regard for her strengths, he's a very courteous man, but he thought she was *so* wrong about the central issues and difficulties of Soviet society that—he treated her with some bemusement. He wasn't dismissive, it wouldn't be in his nature to be dismissive, but he thought she was sort of— skidding off the surface. But anyway, the caricature of this series of exchanges is of two immensely earnest people who had a political chemistry, and if a few more hours had been available, they could have probably resolved the problems of the world. That's the impression that's conveyed, but what I've heard from the other side, including from Gorbachev's interpreter . . . that um, you know, it *wasn't* desperately profound.

Kinnock is very passionate on the subject, no doubt, but in the end, his account of the meeting diverges from Powell's in only one substantive way: He claims the meeting lasted only nine hours. Was it nine hours or thirteen? I don't know; it is easy to imagine that it was really nine hours but *felt* like thirteen. Either way, it sounds like a long meeting.

But Kinnock seems otherwise to be describing more or less the same events. I am not sure what his problem is, really. Neither of them gave way? What would he expect? Was he expecting Margaret Thatcher to say, "You know, Gorby, I've thought it over, and there's more to this Marxist-Leninism business than I realized. Do you think you could give me a few tips on shooting my intellectuals and collectivizing my farms?" Was Kinnock expecting the head of the Politburo suddenly to declare, "You know, Margaret, I've seen the light, and you're right, communism will never work. It's time to tear down the Wall"?

The very idea would be risible, were it not for one thing: One year later, Gorbachev said—through his actions if not his words—*exactly* that. Perhaps things would have worked out even better had Thatcher evinced in this meeting a more sophisticated understanding of Marxist-Leninism.

But how, exactly?

_๑ ⨉ ๑_

On December 8, 1987, Gorbachev and Reagan signed the Intermediate-Range Nuclear Forces treaty, eliminating from the planet intermediate-range ballistic and cruise missiles. Reagan kept SDI. The treaty strongly favored NATO, giving it unequivocal strategic superiority over the Soviet Union. It resulted in the most dramatic and significant reduction of nuclear arms in history.

Gorbachev signed the treaty for many reasons, not least among them that he was a great and visionary leader. But it is fair to assume that the personal relationship between Reagan and Gorbachev— and Reagan's success in persuading Gorbachev that he would not use this advantage to launch a first strike—gave Gorbachev the confidence to make this deal. And it is reasonable to assume that Thatcher's friendship with Gorbachev played a large role in this.

There is a great debate, of course, about the extent to which Reagan's policies prompted the Soviet Union's collapse. Many scholars are now inclined to believe that it would have soon collapsed anyway. Gorbachev, many say, is the hero of this story.

The debate is to an extent artificial. Heroism is not a zero-sum game. Gorbachev *is* a hero. I agree. A monumental historical figure. We should not understate his role. I am not seeking the nomination of the Republican Party, so I am happy to say the obvious: Gorbachev was even more significant to history than Reagan.

Would the Soviet Union have collapsed absent Reagan's policies? Absent Gorbachev's ascent? No one knows. We can only guess. Some of the people who now say it would have collapsed anyway are the ones who were saying it would never collapse before.

Peter Schweizer, an analyst of the Reagan doctrine, estimates that Reagan's policies cost the Soviet Union roughly $45 billion a year—a catastrophic burden, given that Soviet hard currency earnings amounted to $32 billion a year. He bases these numbers on Moscow's own estimates. Specifically, Reagan blocked the Soviet's natural gas pipeline to Europe, costing them $7 billion to $8 billion per year in revenues. By financing anti-communist guerrillas from Latin America to Afghanistan, Reagan forced the Soviet Union to spend an additional $8 billion a year in counterinsurgency operations. Following the invasion of Grenada, an anxious Cuba demanded and received an additional $3 billion in Soviet arms. The Soviets lost between $1 billion and $2 billion a year because of the restrictions Reagan placed on technology exports. Aid to Poland, to counter Reagan's sanctions, cost them another billion per year. Reagan cajoled the Saudis into opening the oil spigots, depressing the global price of oil, and thereby depriving the Soviets of billions of dollars in hard currency.[43] Most devastatingly, to match Reagan's defense spending, the Soviets increased their military budget by $15 billion to $20 billion per annum.[44]

---

43. Specifically, he bribed the Saudis with Airborne Warning and Control System (AWACS) planes. If you're curious about this story, you may consult my doctoral dissertation, *Our Common Enemy: The Making of the United States Arms Transfer Policy Towards the Arab-Israeli Antagonists, 1967–1988.* It is available for consultation at the Bodleian Library at Oxford University. You will be the only person ever to have been curious. When last I checked, I discovered that according to the library's records, no visitor to the library—not one—had ever signed it out. *Sic transit gloria mundi.*

44. Peter Schweizer, *Reagan's War: The Epic Story of His Forty-Year Struggle and Final Triumph Over Communism* (Doubleday, 2002).

I can't resolve this debate—and neither can anyone else—but this much we can say with confidence: Reagan's policies did not provoke the Stalinist reflex in the Soviet Union, as the Sovietologists at Chequers had feared. The Soviet economy was not growing, as the Sovietologists at Chequers believed. The destabilization of Eastern Europe *did* have a profound effect on the Soviet Union itself. Soviet defense spending *was* a millstone, not a dynamo. And Soviet leaders *did* face problems of a nature that compelled them to change drastically—and indeed prompted the system itself to collapse. Now that the Soviet archives are open, it is clear that Reagan's policies at the very least hastened the Soviet Union's demise.

Reagan's policies, moreover, did not lead to nuclear war.

To someone who was unsure, in 1983, whether there would be a 1984, this is an impressive record.

In one sense, the end of the Cold War represented the triumph of an idea: The free market and liberal democracy defeated communism and totalitarianism. In another sense, the end of the Cold War was a contingent story of human relationships. Thatcher played a critical role in both senses of this story. It is hard to see how the story could have played out quite as it did without her.

The end, when it came, was swift and vertiginous. In 1988, Gorbachev announced a drastic reduction of the Soviet military presence in Eastern Europe. The Soviet Union, he said, would no longer intervene in the Eastern bloc. Emboldened by this declaration, the Hungarian parliament voted in January 1989 to permit freedom of speech and assembly. It set a date for multiparty elections.

In February 1989, the last Soviet troops withdrew from Afghanistan.

On April 5, 1989, the Communist Party in Poland agreed to permit free elections. On June 4, Solidarity won an overwhelming majority of the vote. When the Communist Party leaders phoned Gorbachev to ask what to do, he replied, "The time has come to yield power."

Shortly afterward, the Hungarian Communist Party renounced communism and opened the border to Austria, allowing thousands of East Germans to flee to the West.

In October, massive demonstrations took place in East Germany. *"Wir wollen raus!"* chanted the protestors: *We want out!* The hard-line communist Erich Honecker wanted to shoot them all. He turned to the Soviet Union for help, but none was forthcoming. The protests grew in number and strength, forcing Honecker and his entire cabinet to resign.

On November 9, 1989, East Berliners breached the Berlin Wall. Fatefully, the Kremlin refused to give the orders to restrain them with lethal force. The overwhelmed border guards opened the gates. Tens of thousands of East Germans surged through the checkpoints. At first disbelieving, then euphoric, they began drilling through the wall, pounding at it with hammers. They dismantled it with chisels and screwdrivers. They lifted slabs away with cranes. They poured through the holes. They scrambled over the top. They flooded across by the millions, emerging, dazed and blinking, into the sunlight.

West Berliners, delirious with joy, met them with champagne. "The Wall is gone! The Wall is gone!"

10

_,ᴄ, ⸝⸜⸝ ᴅ_

No! No! No!

Stoop, then, and wash. How many ages hence
Shall this our lofty scene be acted over
In states unborn and accents yet unknown!
— *Cassius*, THE TRAGEDY OF JULIUS CAESAR

In 2005, the French and the Dutch held referendums on the proposed European Constitution. The constitution—265 handsome
pages, forty times the length of the American Constitution, un-
readable, uninspiring, and an absolute tour de force of bureau-
cratic jargon—would have enshrined such self-evident truths as
these:

> As regards Huta Andrzej S.A., Huta Bankowa Sp. z o.o.,
> Huta Batory S.A., Huta Buczek S.A., Huta L.W. Sp. z o.o.,
> Huta Łabedy S.A., and Huta Pokój S.A. (hereinafter referred
> to as "other benefiting companies"), the steel restructuring
> aid already granted or to be granted from 1997 until the end
> of 2003 shall not exceed PLN 246 710 000. These firms have
> already received PLN 37 160 000 of restructuring aid in the

period 1997–2001; they shall receive further restructuring aid of no more than PLN 210 210 000 depending on the requirements set out in the approved restructuring plan (of which PLN 182 170 000 in 2002 and PLN 27 380 000 in 2003 if the extension of the grace period under Protocol 2 of the Europe Agreement establishing an association between the European Communities and their Member States, of the one part, and Poland, of the other part, is granted by the end of 2002, or otherwise PLN 210 210 000 in 2003).[1]

I am told that visitors to the Library of Congress often find their eyes glistening when they contemplate the yellowed parchment of the American Constitution. I suspect this document might not have the same effect.

A few points to note: Every year, the European Commission produces more than 11,000 new regulations;[2] and every year, according to the commission's own findings, these regulations cost European businesses 600 billion euros.[3] The commission's rulings are intended to supersede those made by the elected officials of the member states. Although the European parliament is elected directly by the citizens of member countries, the vastly more powerful commission is not elected at all.

In both France and the Netherlands, the European Constitution was contemptuously rejected. And for obvious reasons: No matter how many times they have been told by their leaders that they are to cherish the ideal of European unity, ordinary Europeans feel a quaint, persistent attachment to their distinct cultural identities,

---

1. Title VIII, Article 63, The Treaty Establishing a Constitution for Europe.
2. Alberto Alesina and Francesco Giavazzi, *The Future of Europe: Reform or Decline* (MIT Press, 2006), p. 122.
3. "Fighting against Overregulation and Red Tape," *Financial Times,* October 9, 2006.

their legal and educational traditions, and their sovereignty. What's more, they don't *like* all those regulations.

Margaret Thatcher warned that they might not.

_ᴑ ⤙ ᴑ_

The story of Thatcher's downfall is often described, with justification, as a classic tragedy: *a noble hero, a tragic flaw, reversal of fortune, downfall, purgation.* "Ideology, aggression and arrogance grew on her," wrote Anthony Bevins, the political editor of the Left-leaning *Independent.*

> . . . and with each success her image and ego became more and more inflated. She began to believe that . . . if she could conquer the miners, she could go on to conquer Brussels, too . . . She spurned the advice of friends, cast them aside, and retreated increasingly into the bunker mentality that has destroyed so many leaders deluded by visions of immortality . . . [Despite] warnings of impending disaster, Mrs. Thatcher charged ahead regardless . . . The critical weakness was the refusal to listen. Unbending, unyielding, she could only break, and break her they did. To the end, she refused to heed the advice—if, indeed, there was anyone left with the nerve to brave her wrath by telling her the truth.[4]

Neil Kinnock agrees. "After she got the second victory—reduced majority, but not reduced enough—*hubris* set in. And you know the rest of the story."

I do; others might not. Thatcher's reluctance to bring Britain further into Europe divided her cabinet. In September 1990, Geoffrey Howe, her longest-serving cabinet minister, resigned in protest. His

---

4. "Iron Grip Corrupted by Fatal Arrogance," *Independent,* October 8, 1996.

bitter resignation speech set in motion the train of events that led to the revolt of the Conservative Party and her resignation.

Those who see in Thatcher's downfall the plot of *Julius Caesar* are not imagining things. Shakespeare anticipated every line in this story.

_ʘ_ ˜ʘ˜ _ʘ_

Certainly, Thatcher had by the end of her time in power become hostile to Europe. In *Statecraft*, written in 2002, Thatcher laid out the case against Europe with devastating precision:

> You only have to wade through a metric measure or two of European prose, culled from its directives, circulars, reports, communiqués or what pass as debates in its "parliament," and you will quickly understand that Europe is, in truth, synonymous with bureaucracy. It is government by bureaucracy for bureaucracy . . . The structures, plans, and programs of the European Union are to be understood as existing simply for their own sake . . . It is time for the world to wake up to it; if it is still possible, to stop it . . . [5]

Her critics—particularly the members of her party who defenestrated her—do not take this argument at face value. Thatcher, they say, was hostile to the European project for no good reason. She was simply, in her fundament, a profound xenophobe who despised Europeans generally and the Germans in particular.[6]

As the author of a book titled *Menace in Europe*, I can hardly pretend neutrality on this subject. I agree with Thatcher and think

---

5. Margaret Thatcher, *Statecraft: Strategies for a Changing World* (HarperCollins, 2002), pp. 323–325.

6. For example, see Hugo Young, *This Blessed Plot: Britain and Europe from Churchill to Blair* (Macmillan, 1991).

it absurd to believe that the excellent arguments she advances in *Statecraft* are the reflection of nothing more than xenophobia. Permit me the indulgence of quoting myself: "No effort to unify Europe has ever succeeded. Most have ended in blood. The European Union is historically nuts. It reflects neither the will of a single nation-state, nor the will of an Empire, based on the ability of a central political entity to dominate its periphery, nor some form of established European national identity with deep historic roots. . . . The EU is in effect an empty empire."[7]

Thatcher is known to history as the great Euroskeptic. As a Euroskeptic myself, I would be delighted to report that on this matter she has always been constant as the northern star. But this is not the case. The peculiar truth is that for most of her career, she was a passionate advocate of European unification. The charge that her policies represented nothing more than pathological xenophobia simply can't be reconciled with the facts.

It *is* true that Thatcher didn't much care for Germans. I ask Charles Powell whether he believes the claim that at heart, Thatcher simply loathed them. "Well, yes," he says. "I think one has to be very candid, yes. She was antipathetic to Germany. Could never quite accept that it had changed. She had an antipathy above all to the German manner, really. [Helmut] Kohl, who tried very hard to get on to terms with her, had that German manner, had that sort of big booming German—that sense that *Germany pays, and that therefore Germans were entitled to lay down the law.* She just hated that. Now, what does it stem from? It stems from a girl brought up at an impressionable age coinciding with the rise of Nazism and the Second World War."

---

7. Claire Berlinski, *Menace in Europe* (Three Rivers Press, 2007), p. 235.

Of course it does.[8] And not just the Second World War: Thatcher was raised, like everyone of her generation, in the shadow of the First World War. "In our attic," she recalls in her memoirs, "there was a trunk full of magazines showing, among other things, the famous picture from the Great War of a line of British soldiers blinded by mustard gas walking to the dressing station, each with a hand on the shoulder of the one in front of him."[9]

She was not yet fourteen when the Second World War broke out. I have heard that one of her secretaries once asked her what she believed her most meaningful accomplishment to have been. Surprisingly, she replied that it was rescuing her sister's Jewish pen-pal, Edith, from the Nazis. After the 1938 Anschluss, she persuaded her father and his Rotary Club to help Edith escape from Austria and to shelter her in Grantham. This, Thatcher said, more than anything else, was her proudest achievement.[10] Thatcher mentions Edith only en passant in her memoirs: "One thing Edith reported particularly stuck in my mind. The Jews, she said, were being made to scrub the streets."[11]

During the war, German bombing raids on Grantham killed seventy-eight of her fellow townspeople. She carried a gas mask with her to school. When the air raid sirens went off, she did her

---

8. Needless to say, there will always be someone who places the blame on Germany's notorious persecutors. The British diplomat Nicholas Henderson remarked that "People give all sorts of reasons why she became fanatically anti-German, one of which, I don't know whether it's true, is that her constituency was Finchley and it's full of Jews. That may have had something to do with it . . . I don't know." Malcolm McBain interview with Nicholas Henderson, September 24, 1998, British Diplomatic Oral History Programme, Churchill Archives Centre, Cambridge.

9. Margaret Thatcher, *The Path to Power* (HarperCollins, 1995), p. 25.

10. I was told this by Sally McNamara, an analyst at the Heritage Foundation's Margaret Thatcher Center for Freedom. "It wasn't relayed to me by Lady Thatcher herself," she wrote, "but [by] one of her secretaries at a private event I organized with my former organization . . . It was particularly striking to the group we were meeting with because we were honoring her with our organization's 'Pioneer Award' for her services to the advancement of the conservative principles of free markets, limited government, federalism (in the American sense and not the European sense!) and individual liberty." E-mail, January 23, 2008.

11. Thatcher, *The Path to Power*, p. 27.

homework under her kitchen table. Yes, I'm sure this made an impression. The Germany of Thatcher's adolescence—the age at which political prejudices tend to be shaped—was a nation of murderous, jackbooted thugs. Italy was ruled by a preposterous Italian bellowing from a balcony. The French and the Dutch were collaborators; Americans were liberators. It would be understandable if living through this era had persuaded Thatcher to believe that Britain should have no truck with the grand project of European unification. Certainly, this interpretation is often retrospectively imposed on the story.

But in fact it persuaded her—as it persuaded many—that little could be more important than European unification. "We should remember," she said in 1961, "that France and Germany have attempted to sink their political differences and work for a united Europe. If France can do this so can we." In the same speech she argued that if Britain failed to enter the Common Market—the precursor to today's European Community—"We should be failing in our duty to future generations." In response to those who feared Britain would cease to formulate its own foreign policy and lose its separate identity, she replied,

> Sovereignty and independence are not ends in themselves . . . we have entered into many treaties and military alliances which limit our freedom of individual action. More and more we are becoming dependent for our future on action in concert with other nations . . . It is no good being independent in isolation . . . [12]

Not precisely the voice of Euroskepticism, that.

Was this speech a youthful folly? A tactical concession to majority opinion? Not at all. Britain entered the European Economic Community in 1973 under the Heath government. In 1975, with

---

12. Speech to Finchley Conservatives, August 14, 1961, Thatcher MSS (digital collection), doc. 101105.

his own cabinet divided over Europe, Labour Prime Minister
Harold Wilson called a national referendum. "Parliament has decided to consult the electorate on the question whether the UK
should remain in the European Economic Community," said the
ballot. "Do you want the UK to remain in the EEC?"

Both the Labour and the Conservative parties were split. The
left wing of the Labour Party, in particular, was vehemently opposed. Thatcher led the Conservative Party's "Vote Yes" campaign.
"The Community gives us peace and security in a free society," she
intoned, "a peace and security denied to the past two generations."
She pulled out the rhetorical blunderbuss to make her case, invok-
ing the spirit of Churchill, who was, she intimated, looking down
upon the British people from his throne in Paradise and urging
them to vote yes.

> It was Churchill who, at the Congress of Europe in 1948,
> said, "The movement for European unity must be a positive
> force, deriving its strength from our sense of common spiri-
> tual values. It is a dynamic expression of democratic faith,
> based upon moral conceptions and inspired by a sense of
> mission."
>
> It is a myth that the Community is simply a bureaucracy
> with no concern for the individual . . .
>
> It is a myth that our membership of the Community will
> suffocate national tradition and culture. Are the Germans
> any less German for being in the Community, or the French
> any less French? Of course they are not![13]

She *specifically* argued during this campaign that membership
in the EEC militated against the expansion of the frontiers of the
state in Britain. Remember these words:

---

13. April 16, 1975, Speech to Conservative Group for Europe (opening
Conservative referendum campaign), Thatcher MSS (digital collection), doc.
102675.

Anything that the left wing of the Labour Party wants is probably bad for our country. And they desperately want us to leave Europe. Their reasons are clear. They fear that, if we stay in Europe, they cannot have their way. They cannot turn us into a socialist siege state, our society suffocated by a spendthrift government. So if they want us out, I say all the more reason to stay in.[14]

Two years later, she was still embracing this line, positioning herself firmly against those in her party who were voicing doubts about the wisdom of further integration.

. . . the [European] Community needs to strengthen itself. For we face dangers from within as well as from without. Dangers of disunity, dangers of disillusion. Some people are beginning to have doubts about the European idea in practice. At home, there are those, some of them politicians, who blame the Community for all our problems. Others, a small but vociferous minority, would have Great Britain pull out. That is not the position of the party I lead. We are the European party in the British Parliament and among the British people; and we want to co-operate wholeheartedly with our partners in this joint venture.[15]

Let no one tell you that Thatcher never succumbed to the European fantasy—nor that her subsequent hostility to further integration was motivated by nothing more than irrational and petty prejudice. It simply isn't so.

So what changed?

---

14. Speech to Helensburgh Conservative rally, April 18, 1975, Thatcher MSS (digital collection), doc. 102678.

15. Speech at Centro Italiona di Study per la Conciliazione Internazionale, Rome, "Europe as I See It," June 24, 1977, Thatcher MSS (digital collection), doc. 103403.

c꜡ ꜡ꜟꜟꜟ ꜡

Simply put, the romance between Thatcher and Europe soured as so many love stories do: They started to fight when the money got tight. She became progressively more infuriated, Powell recalls, by "the fundamental unfairness of the arrangements for British membership—and the budgetary part above all."

Some 70 percent of the European Community's budget was devoted to agricultural subsidies. Britain's agricultural sector was smaller and more efficient than those of its European counterparts, and moreover its economy was not based upon agriculture. It was unacceptable, Thatcher felt, that at precisely the time she was asking the British public to accept broad public cuts in spending she should also ask them to subsidize inefficient European farmers to the tune of a billion pounds a year.

Britain was receiving only £1 for every £1.50 it contributed to the EEC. It was the second-biggest net contributor after Germany, but one of the poorest member states. So upon taking office, Thatcher demanded a rebate. In November 1979, at the Dublin European Council, Thatcher began an epic argument with her European counterparts. It was to last five long years. "We are not asking the Community or anyone else for money," she said repeatedly. "We are simply asking to have our own money back." She threatened to withhold further contributions to the EEC if she did not get her way. To Europeans who wished to maintain the pretense that Europe was now one happy family, this demand seemed distinctly unfraternal. "Every meeting," Powell recalls, "was turned into a battle about Britain's contribution. It was seen as anti-European to argue about what your contribution was, and half of them pretended they didn't *know* what they contributed."

It did not take long for the members of the new European family to remember that idealistic rhetoric aside, they loathed one another and always had. At a meeting in Strasbourg, French President Valéry Giscard d'Estaing insisted upon being served his meal before Thatcher. When next he visited her in London, she repaid him by seating him beneath portraits of Nelson and Wellington. "I suspect," she purred, "that the distinguished Britons looking down on us from the walls—who were accustomed to a different sort of relationship between our two countries—would have been surprised and, in their hearts, pleased."[16] In her memoirs, she recalls Giscard gazing at the portraits and remarking upon the irony. "I replied that it was no less ironic that I should have to look at portraits of Napoleon on my visits to Paris. In retrospect, I can see that this was not quite a parallel. Napoleon lost."[17]

The summits grew progressively more acrimonious and were marked each time by greater rudeness. Giscard would ostentatiously read his newspaper while Thatcher banged on and on about the budget; Helmut Schmidt would close his eyes and pretend to snore. Once, apparently, as Thatcher was raving about "my oil" and "my fish," she punctuated her comments with the words "my God!" Someone in attendance loudly replied, "Oh, not *that*, too." According to legend, during a 1984 summit meeting, she slammed her handbag on the table and screeched, "*I want my money back!*" This did not actually happen, but again, it is one of those anecdotes that suggests something about the mood of these encounters.

Finally, exhausted, François Mitterrand gave way. At the Fontainebleau Summit in 1984, the EEC agreed to give an annual rebate to the United Kingdom, amounting to 66 percent of the difference between Britain's contributions and its receipts. Powell recalls the "electric tension" when Mitterrand said, at last, "Mrs. Thatcher should have what she wants."

Thatcher won the fight, but the love affair was never the same. It is so often that way.

---

16. Speech at dinner for French President Giscard d'Estaing, November 19, 1979, Thatcher MSS (digital collection), doc. 104172.

17. Thatcher, *The Downing Street Years*, p. 24.

Despite these conflicts, says Powell, Thatcher at this point still fundamentally believed that "Europe was on balance where Britain should be. It was OK. There were things like common fisheries policies that needed to be changed, improved, but she made this great campaign for the single market in Europe, and it was one of the great successes of Europe. It was certainly very much in our interests." The Single European Act of 1986, a Thatcher initiative, established a European market, without frontiers, in which goods, services, people, and capital might move freely. This was, of course, consistent with the economic principles she stood for.

"What tipped her over the edge against Europe was really two things," Powell says. "One was when they started to go to the single currency. She believed that was eroding national sovereignty to a point which was just unacceptable." A single currency, Thatcher believed, necessarily entailed something very like a single economic policy: Britain would no longer be able to set its own interest rates or make adjustments to its exchange rates. In other words, it would no longer have access to the key economic instruments normally available to sovereign governments. Instead, these decisions would be made centrally, in the context of a huge federal European budget. To Thatcher, this idea was for obvious reasons anathema.

The second provocation came in the form of Jacques Delors, the socialist president of the EEC Commission. Delors was, in Thatcher's words, on "the federalist express." By 1988, she writes, "he had slipped his leash as a *fonctionnaire*." Delors in that year announced to the European Parliament that in the coming five years, the European Community would become responsible for 80 percent of all legislation: An "embryo" European government, he said, might emerge.

To Europeans who had "no real confidence in the political system or political leaders of their own country," Thatcher later wrote, it might be tolerable to have "foreigners" like Delors "telling you how to run your affairs." But not to a proud Briton. "To put it more bluntly," she sniffs, "if I were an Italian I might prefer rule from Brussels too."[18]

As if this wasn't enough, Delors then pitched up in Britain to address the Trades Union Conference. "He used words to the effect that in a couple years' time all important decisions about Britain will be taken in Brussels, not here," Powell recalls. "And that just infuriated her, politically, I mean, made her just *angry.* She just thought, *Well, now, they've really come clean on what the elite in Europe are really after. They're after the extinction of national sovereignty.*"

Delors won the trade unions over. Originally wary, their members became persuaded that the European unification project might well be a way to roll back Thatcherite reforms, particularly since the ballot box certainly wasn't doing the trick. Ron Todd, the head of the Transport and General Workers' Union, heard Delors's speech and emerged, inspired, declaring, "We have not a cat in hell's chance of achieving [our goals] in Westminster, but we may have it in Brussels."[19] The Labour Party agreed.

Thatcher remained committed to the overarching principle that anything the Labour Party wanted must be bad for Britain: If they were now for Europe, she was against it. "From then on," recalls Powell, "she was determined to start a fight back."

This is where the story gets ugly. Her clashes with Jacques Chirac in the European Council were, as Powell chastely puts it, "memorable." In one of them, "He used a word about her so vulgar that all the interpreters screeched to a halt—she was totally unaware of it, not speaking any French at all. She didn't—"

"And the word was?"

---

18. Thatcher, *The Downing Street Years*, p. 742.
19. Craig R. Whitney, "Pressed at Home, British Unions Are Looking to Europe for Gains," *New York Times*, September 11, 1988.

Powell blushes. "I wouldn't dream of repeating it with your recorder on."

"I'll switch it off."

"I wouldn't say it even then. Um, but um—"

"Is there some way I can find out? Was it reported anywhere else?"

"I don't think anyone's put it in any book, no, but it's famous for being a vulgarism which would not normally be used in any sort of society, let alone what was supposed to be a polite—I mean, this is because he got very angry with her, this was about agriculture, his desire to protect the French farmers and so on—"

"And really, truly, the interpreters all screeched to a halt?"

"Yes, you could hear the brakes going on!"

"And how was the word translated in the end?"

"It wasn't. There was just sort of, you know, this embarrassed pause."

I couldn't find anyone who would tell me what Chirac said, and I still do not know, but judging from Powell's uncomfortable squirming—he was clearly mortified just thinking of it—it must have been quite something.

Chirac: Frappe mon cul poilu, sacrifice de putain, tu me casses les couilles! Retournez à la pute qui t'a accouchée!

Translator 1: [*Whispers*] Oh-là-là! . . .

Meanwhile, the obsessively regulatory character of the European project was becoming increasingly apparent. At one stage, directives on transport safety threatened to consign London's famous double-decker buses to oblivion. The commission objected to calling Cadbury bars "chocolate" because they didn't contain the regulation measure of cocoa solids. Thatcher, said Powell, "was pretty rapidly reaching the view that actually Britain should withdraw from the European Union. Now, she never said that publicly in a speech, but she came close to it."

On September 20, 1988, Thatcher made her infamous speech to the College of Europe at Bruges. She began with a few pleasantries, then briskly offended everyone present by reminding them of the debt they owed to Britain:

> Over the centuries, we have fought to prevent Europe from falling under the dominance of a single power. We have fought and we have died for her freedom. Only miles from here in Belgium lie the bodies of 120,000 British soldiers who died in the First World War. Had it not been for that willingness to fight and to die, Europe would have been united long before now—but not in liberty, not in justice . . .
>
> It was British support to resistance movements throughout the last War that helped to keep alive the flame of liberty in so many countries until the day of liberation . . .
>
> It was from our island fortress that the liberation of Europe itself was mounted.

She professed her commitment to European cooperation. "I want to see us work more closely on the things we can do better together than alone." She then defined this as a distinctly more narrow category than envisioned by Delors:

> . . . working more closely together does not require power to be centralized in Brussels or decisions to be taken by an appointed bureaucracy.
>
> Indeed, it is ironic that just when those countries such as the Soviet Union, which have tried to run everything from the center, are learning that success depends on dispersing power and decisions away from the center, there are some in the Community who seem to want to move in the opposite direction.

> We have not successfully rolled back the frontiers of the
> state in Britain, only to see them re-imposed at a European
> level with a European super-state exercising a new domi-
> nance from Brussels.

She concluded by warning against Utopian goals: "Utopia never comes," she said. "We should not like it if it did."[20] Subtext: *You lot have certainly got yourself in trouble every time you've tried to create Utopia, haven't you?*

The Bruges speech seems eminently reasonable now, in the fullness of hindsight. It hardly appears to be an expression of fulminating xenophobia—or, for that matter, incipient madness and overweening pride. In 2000, Tony Blair returned to Belgium and allowed that many of Thatcher's concerns had been justified. But at the time her words had the effect of a thunderclap.

"The Bruges speech was really like Martin Luther nailing his theses to the church door," says Powell. "For the first time someone set out the limits of Europe and where it should go. It accepted most of what Europe had done up to that point, but it said: 'Thus far and no further.'" Indeed, the profoundly offended audience responded with about as much enthusiasm as the Catholic church responded to Martin Luther. "Frankly, I am shocked," said one European commissioner. "Maybe all her speech at Bruges was intended to keep her nationalist-minded right-wingers happy while the serious business in Europe is done more discreetly," sniffed another.[21]

To those who subscribed to the view—not long ago Thatcher's own—that in a unified Europe lay the solution to the long tradition of European carnage, Thatcher might as well have delivered this speech in a gas mask while calling for the immediate renewal

---

20. Speech to the College of Europe ("The Bruges Speech"), September 20, 1988, Thatcher MSS (digital collection), doc. 107332.
21. "Thatcher Sets Face Against United Europe," *Guardian*, September 21, 1988.

of hostilities on the Western Front. The Belgian prime minister in-dignantly replied that European unification "is not based on a utopian concept but rather on some very practical considerations: the preservation of peace and prosperity on a continent torn by fratricidal strife."[22]

This view was emphatically shared by Thatcher's foreign secre-tary. In his memoirs, Geoffrey Howe describes Thatcher's descrip-tion of a Europe ruled by an appointed bureaucracy and through endless regulation as "sheer fantasy." Listening to the Bruges speech was, he wrote, "a little like being married to a clergyman who had suddenly proclaimed his disbelief in God."[23]

To those who saw European unification as inevitable, Thatcher's intransigence seemed strategically witless: By alienating her Euro-pean counterparts, they believed, she would ensure nothing but a diminished role for Britain. Neil Kinnock swiftly seized upon this point:

> If we are to get a square deal or even a fair change in the
> Single Market we need a Government in Britain . . . that
> will participate in the development of Europe, that will play
> a direct influential role in fashioning the institutions and re-
> lationships of the Market within which our economy must
> work in order to prosper. Mrs. Thatcher's failure to accept
> co-operation and to exert Britain's sovereignty in a positive
> way is creating the threat of a two-tier Europe, with Britain
> firmly stuck in the second rank—passed by Italy in the
> 1980s, likely to be passed by Spain in the 1990s. We cannot
> afford that. We mustn't afford it.[24]

---

22. Speech by Wilfried Martens, September 28, 1988, Brussels, in *Europe: Documents* 1527 (December 10, 1988): 7–8, Agence Europe S.A.
23. Geoffrey Howe, *Conflict of Loyalty* (St. Martin's Press, 1994), pp. 537–538.
24. Speech in Wales, April 28, 1989, Archives historiques des Communautés européennes, Florence, Italy.

For a change, Kinnock found a great deal of sympathy for this view—if not for him—in the Conservative Party.

___◦ ◦──

"Do you think her sentiments about Europe were at the heart of her downfall?" I ask Powell.

"No. They were part of it, but they weren't at the heart of it. They were the tactical excuse for it, unleashing Geoffrey Howe to start a process which led to a fear among many conservative MPs that the poll tax was going to prevent their re-election. And her increasingly high-handed treatment of her closest political colleagues probably cost her more votes, or combined to a much greater vote."

"When you say 'her increasingly high-handed treatment'—"

"Well, she used to *berate* Geoffrey Howe in cabinet—"

"When you say 'berate'—"

"Well, just sort of slap him down or overrule him. She got very dismissive, in the end. Impatient. You know, after ten, eleven years in government, head of government when the military went to victories—she had the answers and wasn't really interested in listening to reservations."

"What kind of language did she use?"

"She didn't use bad language, never used bad language. 'Forceful' and 'strident' are the sort of words that come to mind. She could behave—it was pretty embarrassing at times to listen to it, frankly. You know, that she could treat someone like that. Because it was bound to have an effect, really, bound to."

Enter now Geoffrey Howe, who until this point has not figured largely in my story not because he was insignificant—he was Thatcher's first chancellor and her longest-serving cabinet minister—but because, honestly, he is boring. Mild-mannered. Bland. Unconfrontational. In 1978, Labour Chancellor Denis Healey said that being challenged by Howe in debate was "like being savaged by a dead sheep."

There is a sequel to this anecdote. When in 1983 Healey congratulated Howe upon his appointment as foreign secretary, Howe told the House that it was "like being nuzzled by an old ram." A nice riposte. But think about that: Howe had been stewing over that insult and storing up that response for *five years*.

Nigel Lawson writes that Thatcher found Howe's "quiet, dogged manner intensely irritating. Increasingly, over the years, she felt compelled—to the acute embarrassment of everyone else present—to treat him as something halfway between a punchbag and a doormat . . . she went out of her way to humiliate him at every turn."[25] When I spoke to Lawson, I asked him just why, exactly, Howe's manner irritated her so. "She bullied people who she thought were bully-able," he said tersely. "Which is not a very attractive characteristic, but you know, nobody's perfect."

Howe was not the only one she had bullied. The list of those she had aggrieved was long. Lawson, by this point, was among them, and so was her former defense secretary, Michael Heseltine. She had enemies everywhere. But she did not believe they would dare rise up against her.

ARTEMIDORUS
Caesar, beware of Brutus; take heed of Cassius;
come not near Casca; have an eye to Cinna, trust not
Trebonius: mark well Metellus Cimber: Decius Brutus
loves thee not: thou hast wronged Caius Ligarius.
CAESAR
What, is the man insane?

Thatcher's popularity declined in 1989. Inflation was once again rising. She blamed Nigel Lawson. She claimed that her chancellor

---

25. Lawson, *The View from No. 11*, pp. 659, 956.

had been following an economic policy in preparation for monetary union without her knowledge and against her wishes. The story does not reflect well on her. If he was doing this without her knowledge, she was not in control; if he was doing this against her wishes, she was not in command. In either case, she was not accepting responsibility.

At the Madrid European summit, Lawson and Howe threatened to resign unless Thatcher agreed, at a minimum, to state the circumstances under which she would join the European Exchange Rate Mechanism. Thatcher saw the Exchange Rate Mechanism as the precursor to monetary union. She capitulated to their ultimatum because she had no choice, but she took revenge. She demoted Howe to leader of the House—a position he rightly saw as ceremonial—and from then on permitted her economic advisor Alan Walters, a caustic Euroskeptic, to eclipse Lawson.

When Howe first rose to speak in his new, diminished capacity, Lawson recalled,

> A loud and long spontaneous cheer rose from the massed Conservative benches of a kind that is rarely heard. It was a tribute to the affection with which Howe was held within the Party. But more than anything else, it was a clear warning to Margaret. No experienced Tory Member could have failed to get the message—except perhaps one: Margaret Hilda Thatcher.[26]

Lawson resigned from Thatcher's cabinet that October, stating—correctly—that Thatcher's reliance on Walters had undermined him.

Lawson's resignation came as a great shock to her. This in itself indicates that her uncanny political judgment had begun to fail her. Shortly after Lawson's resignation, Thatcher was interviewed

---

26. Ibid., p. 936.

for ITV by Brian Walden. It is a remarkable exchange: It is clear that Thatcher is losing her grasp not only politically, but emotionally. It is the only interview I can recall watching in which Thatcher's interlocutor pulverizes her. She appears bewildered, off-balance, flustered, and insane.

Walden: Prime Minister, it is fairly clear, is it not, what was getting up Nigel's nose. It was not that you had an economic adviser who very quietly and silently whispered things to you in the still watches of the night. He felt that you were not seen to be united because Professor Alan Walters, a very able man, was making absolutely clear to anybody who cared to listen to him, fundamental disagreements that he had with the Chancellor. . . . Now surely he put that point to you and what did you say to that?

Prime Minister: Alan Walters is part-time as my adviser. He has only just recently returned . . . It is just not possible that this small particular thing could result in this particular resignation . . . I am very sad that [Lawson] has gone. But he has and now we must turn to the future. The same policies will continue because they are sound and we shall carry on in precisely the same way.

Walden: I want to ask you about that of course Prime Minister. But let us come back to Professor Alan Walters . . . [*Thatcher says the same inane things*] All right, well let us consider Lawson. I have to take it the way you have put it, Prime Minister, that you blame Nigel for the resignation, not yourself? . . . [*Thatcher repeats herself*] Of course, so let me ask you again, why did Nigel resign? You say he knew that he was unassailable, he knew that you loved him and that everything that he did was marvelous, but he resigned . . . [*Thatcher repeats herself, voice rising*] He was unassailable, you say; you were in agreement, you say; everything was going well, you say; and he said to you: "Margaret, you have got to get rid of Alan Walters!" Why didn't you and keep your Chancellor? . . . [*Thatcher repeats herself, voice hysterical, and begs him to change the subject*] Do you deny Nigel would have stayed if you had sacked Professor Alan Walters? . . .

Prime Minister: [*Nearly shrieking*] I do not know!

Walden: You never even thought to ask him that?

Prime Minister: I do not know! Nigel had determined that he was going to put in his resignation. I did everything possible to stop him! I was not successful! No! *You are going on asking the same question!*

Walden: [*Calmly*] Of course, but that is a terrible admission, Prime Minister.

Prime Minister: I do not know! Of course I do not know!

Walden: You *do not know* you could have kept your Chancellor, possibly, if you had sacked your part-time adviser? . . . Let me sum you up so far. You do not accept blame for the resignation of the Chancellor of the Exchequer, you do not know why he resigned, he is to tell me himself, you can offer no guidance on that. And you do not accept that the other resignations from your government, or the other sackings from your government, have arisen because you cannot handle strong men . . . You come over as being someone who one of your Back Benchers said is "slightly off her trolley," authoritarian, domineering, refusing to listen to anybody else . . .

Prime Minister: Nonsense, Brian! I am staying my own sweet reasonable self, . . . reasonably, firmly, strongly—

Walden: Prime Minister, I must stop you there!

Prime Minister: No, you must not!

Walden: I must! Thank you very much indeed![27]

---

27. October 28, 1989, *The Walden Interview*, Thatcher MSS (digital collection), doc. 107808.

In November 1989, Thatcher was challenged for the leadership of the Conservative Party by Anthony Meyer, an unknown backbencher. She defeated him handily, but it was now clear that the knives had been unsheathed. She did not seem to sense it. Asked by an interviewer where she stood, she replied, "In the lead, I am the Leader, I am Prime Minister. That is where I am and I shall just carry on as I have always carried on." Did that mean she would go on ad infinitum? he asked. "No, no, no," she said blithely. "I did not say ad infinitum—no-one can go on ad infinitum . . . One is, after all, finite."[28]

> CAESAR
> Cowards die many times before their deaths;
> The valiant never taste of death but once.
> Of all the wonders that I yet have heard.
> It seems to me most strange that men should fear;
> Seeing that death, a necessary end,
> Will come when it will come.

By the fall of 1990, the Conservative Party had come to see Thatcher as a liability. Europe was not the only reason for this. The introduction of the so-called Community Charge—a fixed-rate tax for local services—was intended to expose the wastefulness of Labour-controlled local governments. It replaced a tax pegged to the notional rental value of a taxpayer's house. Thatcher hoped that voters would at last realize how much the Labour councils were really spending and throw the bums out. But unsurprisingly, a tax that appeared to penalize the poor at exactly the same rates

---

28. TV Interview for TV-AM, November 24, 1989, Washington, D.C., Thatcher MSS (digital collection), doc. 107829.

as the rich was not well-received. In March, a demonstration in London against the poll tax turned into the worst riot seen in the city for a century. Millions refused to pay. Protestors resisted the bailiffs and disrupted the court hearings of the debtors. At Balliol— a very left-wing college—students were constantly organizing and marching against the poll tax. All through that autumn they were making banners and passing around leaflets and petitions. I watched this with puzzlement: It seemed to me that for a change they were right. The poll tax was insanity. I couldn't figure out what Thatcher was thinking.

Thatcher refused to compromise or change the tax.

CAESAR

Know, Caesar doth not wrong, nor without cause
Will he be satisfied.

But I am constant as the northern star,
Of whose true-fix'd and resting quality
There is no fellow in the firmament.

The economy was headed toward recession. The Conservatives were trailing in the polls. The Conservative Party is not known for loyalty. In 1975 Thatcher herself had studied the omens, then challenged and vanquished Ted Heath.

"The most tearing blow," Neil Kinnock recalls, "was the fact that we were 14, 16 points ahead on the day she went through the door. And an objective assessment of the reasons for her departure will take account of her arrogance, the distance that she developed between herself and her party, the poll tax—but really, what lit the fuse was that month after month after month we were way ahead in the opinion polls, and the Tories were starting to worry about their own security. Political security. So a group said, rightly, 'If she stays there, we're going to lose the next election.' They were right about that."

It is impossible to say if they were right about that. She never had the chance to put the matter to the test. "You might not like it," says Powell, "but for eleven years, every time the British people were given a chance to express a view on it"—"it" being Thatcherism and Thatcher—"they supported it, voted for it, and I think she would have won the election in 1992 as well, had she stayed in. She was always a pragmatist. She always knew how to retreat sometimes. She was very good in Europe. You had to adjust, obviously, you could never have outright victory on anything in Europe, and she was very good at blowing smoke and retreating behind the smokescreen . . . on the poll tax, the community charge, she would have done exactly what John Major did, that is, loan some of the costs off of central taxation and make some changes, and I think would have won the 1992 election on the back of it. You always have to remember she was dislodged by a coup d'état, not by any democratic procedure."

At the end of October 1990, upon returning from a European Council meeting in Rome, Thatcher again made it clear to the Commons that she was vehemently opposed to the idea of a European single currency and the development of a federal Europe. "The President of the Commission, Mr. Delors, said at a press conference the other day that he wanted the European Parliament to be the democratic body of the Community, he wanted the Commission to be the Executive and he wanted the Council of Ministers to be the Senate." With this, she sucked in a great lungful of air, and then with all the drama of a concert soprano hitting the high note of a tragic aria cried out: "NO! NO! NO!"[29]

This spectacle pushed the long-suffering Howe over the edge. On November 1, 1990, he resigned.

---

29. October 30, 1990, Hansard HC [178/869–92].

It was obvious now to everyone—but her—that the rats were briskly paddling away. "I don't think she realizes what a jam she's in," Alan Clark wrote in his diary. "It's the bunker syndrome. Everyone around you is clicking their heels. The saluting sentries have highly polished boots and beautifully creased uniforms. But out at the Front it's all disintegrating . . . whole units are mutinous and in flight."[30]

On November 13, Howe plunged the first dagger. His resignation speech was by far the best of his career. It was, in Thatcher's words, "cool, forensic, light at points, and poisonous."[31] He would from then on be remembered, she predicted, "not for his staunchness as Chancellor, nor for his skilful diplomacy as Foreign Secretary, but for this final act of bile and treachery. The very brilliance with which he wielded the dagger ensured that the character he assassinated was in the end his own." The evaluation is bitter, to be sure, but not unfair.[32] No one remembers Howe for anything but this speech.

It was essential, he warned,

> . . . not to cut ourselves off from the realities of power; not to retreat into a ghetto of sentimentality about our past and so diminish our own control over our own destiny in the future . . .
>
> It would have spared us so many of the struggles of the last 20 years had we been in the Community from the outset; had we been ready, in the much too simple phrase, to "surrender some sovereignty" at a much earlier stage. If we had been in from the start, as almost everybody now acknowledges, we should have had more, not less, influence over the Europe in which we live today. We should never

---

30. Clark, *Diaries: In Power,* pp. 342–343.
31. Thatcher, *The Downing Street Years,* p. 839.
32. Ibid., p. 840.

forget the lesson of that isolation, of being on the outside looking in, for the conduct of today's affairs . . .

As Thatcher had done years before, Howe summoned to arms the spirit of Winston Churchill:

I have to say that I find Winston Churchill's perception a good deal more convincing, and more encouraging for the interests of our nation, than the nightmare image sometimes conjured up by my right hon. Friend, who seems sometimes to look out upon a continent that is positively teeming with ill-intentioned people, scheming, in her words, to "extinguish democracy," to "dissolve our national identities" and to lead us "through the back-door into a federal Europe." . . .

The tragedy is—and it is for me personally, for my party, for our whole people and for my right hon. Friend herself, a very real tragedy—that the Prime Minister's perceived attitude towards Europe is running increasingly serious risks for the future of our nation. It risks minimizing our influence and maximizing our chances of being once again shut out. We have paid heavily in the past for late starts and squandered opportunities in Europe. We dare not let that happen again. If we detach ourselves completely, as a party or a nation, from the middle ground of Europe, the effects will be incalculable and very hard ever to correct.

He concluded on an ominous note. "I have done what I believe is right for my party and my country. The time has come for others to consider their own response to the tragic conflict of loyalties with which I myself have wrestled for perhaps too long."[33]

---

33. You may watch highlights of the speech here: www.youtube.com/watch ?v=f1C2hieHKgA. Note that John Major—Thatcher's chancellor—is sitting to Thatcher's left and nodding sagely in seeming approval of Howe's remarks.

These words were widely interpreted as they were meant: They were an invitation to Michael Heseltine, Thatcher's longtime adversary, to force a leadership election.

> **BRUTUS**
> If there be any in this assembly, any dear friend of
> Caesar's, to him I say, that Brutus' love to Caesar
> was no less than his. If then that friend demand
> why Brutus rose against Caesar, this is my answer:
> —Not that I loved Caesar less, but that I loved
> Rome more. Had you rather Caesar were living and
> die all slaves, than that Caesar were dead, to live
> all free men? As Caesar loved me, I weep for him;
> as he was fortunate, I rejoice at it; as he was
> valiant, I honour him: but, as he was ambitious, I
> slew him. There is tears for his love; joy for his
> fortune; honour for his valour; and death for his
> ambition. Who is here so base that would be a
> bondman? If any, speak; for him have I offended.
> Who is here so rude that would not be a Roman? If
> any, speak; for him have I offended. Who is here so
> vile that will not love his country? If any, speak;
> for him have I offended. I pause for a reply.
> **ALL**
> None, Brutus, none.

—◦ ⦿ ◦—

Heseltine: Big hair. An oily charisma. A self-made millionaire with eight gardeners and a personal arboretum. The press called him "Tarzan." On *Spitting Image* they depicted him in a superhero cape: *By day, Michael Heseltine is a suave millionaire MP. By night, he is a vain, ambitious little weasel. "The Tory Party Leadership? This is a job for Blondeman! Into the Blondemobile!"*

Heseltine was more than ready to strike the coup de grâce. After months of declaring that he could "foresee no circumstances" under which he would challenge the prime minister, he suddenly saw them clearly.

On November 20, 1990, Heseltine was defeated, 204–152, in the first ballot for the party's leadership. But according to the party's rules, this was not sufficient to give Thatcher an outright victory. Thatcher was at the time at a summit in Paris. She did not return to campaign for the second round.

A fatal misjudgment.

She underestimated the seriousness of the challenge. She did not cajole or reassure her wavering supporters. "It's absolute madness," wrote Clark in his diary. "There's no Party mileage whatever in being at the Paris summit. It just makes her seem snooty and remote. And who's running the campaign? Who's doing the canvassing? Who's putting the pressure on?"[34]

Charles Powell understands her decision thus: "A lot of people say, 'Well, why wasn't she in London for her reelection as Party leader instead of sitting in Paris at this great conference on the end of the Cold War?' And in her view, *of course* they were going to reelect her as leader of the Party after all she'd done for them. Why should she be groveling in the House of Commons' tea room soliciting votes from people who she created, got elected, had given ten years in government? I mean, they *owed* it to her, her right place was representing Britain in the triumphal conclusion of the Cold War, and it never occurred to her to go. I think that attitude—it's perfectly easy to understand, but that's what brought her down."

CAESAR
[To the Soothsayer] The ides of March are come.
SOOTHSAYER
Ay, Caesar; but not gone.

---

34. Clark, *Diaries: In Power,* p. 349.

"The whole house is in ferment," wrote Clark. "Little groups, con-
claves everywhere . . . in the corridors it is all whispering and
glancing over shoulders . . . a great basket of bitterness, thwarted
personal ambition and vindictive glee. Talk of country, or loyalty, is
dismissed as 'histrionics.'"[35]

In the end, one of Thatcher's great strengths—her ability to stand
remote from the men around her—became her great liability. "One
of the qualities that men tend to have," Nigel Lawson says to me, "or
Englishmen, you know, from the sort of background that most of
the cabinet came from, is clubbability. They're extremely clubbable.
And there's a kind of men's club atmosphere. She had no element of
clubbability in her at all. Now, I say this is both a strength and a
weakness. It was a strength because it disconcerted the men. They
didn't quite know how to deal with a leader who was unclubbable.
And this therefore made it easier for her to exert the power she
wished to exert and the leadership she wished to exert.

"It was a disadvantage because it did rather, and increasingly,
separate her from the rest of her cabinet, all of whom were men
. . . So it was an all-male cabinet and she became separated because of this lack of clubbability, not merely from the people she
may have not minded being separated from, but also from her actual supporters within the cabinet. And this contributed to her
downfall in two ways. The most important way is that she did become rather out of touch, and she didn't—obviously, she thought
she was completely self-sufficient—she didn't need anybody else.
She also didn't interact, after a time. She did in the beginning,
when she first came in, but less and less so . . . and that made her
less sure-footed. And the other thing of course is that it meant that
there wasn't, when she stood for the leadership . . . there wasn't
the degree of emotional support from her colleagues that I think
she thought she deserved."

---

35. Ibid, p. 351.

_∞ ⇌ ∞_

Before she even returned to London, it was already over.

On the evening of November 21, a series of ministers visited her in Downing Street. They told her, one by one, that she had lost the support of the party. She would not win the second round.

"She looked calm, almost beautiful," wrote Clark.

> "Ah, Alan . . . "
>
> "You're in a jam."
>
> "I know that."
>
> "They're telling you not to stand, aren't they?"
>
> "I'm going to stand. I have issued a statement."
>
> "That's wonderful. That's heroic. But the Party will let you down."
>
> "I am a fighter."
>
> "Fight, then. Fight right to the end, a third ballot if you need to. But you lose."
>
> There was quite a little pause.
>
> "It'd be so terrible if Michael won. He would undo everything I have fought for."
>
> "But what a way to go! Unbeaten in three elections, never rejected by the people. Brought down by nonentities!"
>
> "But Michael . . . as *Prime Minister.*"
>
> "Who the fuck's Michael? No one. Nothing. He won't last six months. I doubt he'd even win the election. Your place in history is towering . . . "
>
> Outside, people were doing that maddening trick of opening and shutting the door, at shorter and shorter intervals.
>
> "Alan, it's been so good of you to come and see me . . . "[36]

Clark was the only one who encouraged her. The others hewed to their script. "As I well realized," Thatcher writes, "they had been

---

36. Ibid., p. 366.

feverishly discussing what to say in the rooms off the Commons Cabinet corridor above my room. Like all politicians in a quandary, they had sorted out their 'line to take' and they would cling to it through thick and thin. After three or four interviews, I felt I could almost join the chorus."

Of course I support you, they told her, one by one. *This is a travesty. You have my complete loyalty. But we're outnumbered—you're going to lose. You must step down, so that we can defeat Heseltine, who will destroy everything you've worked for . . .*

"I was sick at heart," Thatcher remembers. "I could have resisted the opposition of opponents and potential rivals and even respected them for it; but what grieved me was the desertion of those I had always considered friends and allies and the weasel words by which they had transmuted their betrayal into frank advice and concern for my fate."

ANTONY

This was the most unkindest cut of all;
For when the noble Caesar saw him stab,
Ingratitude, more strong than traitors' arms,
Quite vanquish'd him: then burst his mighty heart;
And, in his mantle muffling up his face,
Even at the base of Pompey's statua,
Which all the while ran blood, great Caesar fell.

After the last visitor left, she dictated a brief statement. She would resign.

—⟋⟍ ⟅⟆ ⟍⟋—

"They demonstrated the ruthlessness of the officer class," says Kinnock. "It was quite an operation, but they got rid of her. And I had to tell my people, 'Celebrate, and get drunk tonight, and then wake up in the morning and know that we have just lost our greatest political asset.' Which is the truth."

It is said that Ted Heath cried "Rejoice! Rejoice!" when he heard the news. When later he was asked whether he had indeed said this, he replied no: He hadn't said "rejoice" twice, he'd said it *three* times.

> BRUTUS
> People and senators, be not affrighted;
> Fly not; stand stiff: ambition's debt is paid.

I remember where I was when I heard. Everyone who lived in Britain then would. I was in Holywell Manor, the graduate annex of Balliol College. There had been rumors all week that she might resign, that Heseltine would challenge her, but truly, no one believed it would really happen. It was inconceivable. I had never known a Britain in which Margaret Thatcher wasn't the prime minister.

A student burst through the door, shouting: *She's resigned!*

> CINNA
> Liberty! Freedom! Tyranny is dead!
> Run hence, proclaim, cry it about the streets.

Everyone knew who "she" was. Almost everyone in earshot began cheering, punching the air. The elderly porter in the porter's lodge looked stricken. We raced to the lone television set in the building to follow the story. The college bar was opened early. All day long there were choruses of "Ding, dong, the witch is dead!" That night, at least a dozen students were found passed out or vomiting in the rose bushes.[37]

> FIRST CITIZEN
> This Caesar was a tyrant.

---

37. I don't wish to be misleading: They were often found that way. A good handful would have been in those bushes on any given evening.

THIRD CITIZEN

Nay, that's certain:

We are blest that Rome is rid of him.

On November 28, the prime minister tendered her resignation to the Queen. One week later, she was driven away from Downing Street.

She was in tears.

ANTONY

O mighty Caesar! dost thou lie so low?

Are all thy conquests, glories, triumphs, spoils,

Shrunk to this little measure? Fare thee well.

—◦— ⇒ —◦—

Kinnock called for a motion of no confidence in the Conservative government. In defeat, Thatcher seized the opportunity to deliver one of her most astonishing performances. "Each sentence," she recalls, "was my testimony at the bar of History. It was as if I were speaking for the last time, rather than merely for the last time as Prime Minister."

She began by recalling Nicholas Henderson's famous missive from Paris describing the state of Britain when she took power: "We talk of ourselves without shame as being one of the less prosperous countries of Europe," she quoted from the dispatch. The prognosis for Britain in 1979, she reminded those present, was terminal decline.

"Conservative government has changed all that," she reminded the House. "Once again, Britain stands tall in the councils of Europe and of the world, and our policies have brought unparalleled prosperity to our citizens at home."

For Brutus is an honorable man.

"The average pensioner now has twice as much to hand on to his children as he did 11 years ago . . . "

So are they all, all honorable men—
"We are no longer the sick man of Europe . . . "
And Brutus is an honorable man.
"Britain no longer has an overmanned, inefficient, backward manufacturing sector, but modern, dynamic industries . . . "
And Brutus is an honorable man.
"We have worked for our vision of a Europe which is free and open to the rest of the world, and above all to the countries of eastern Europe as they emerge from the shadows of socialism . . ."
In the middle of this speech, an immortal moment:

The Prime Minister: I am *enjoying* this!

This is the astonishing thing: She genuinely *does* appear to be enjoying this. I would swear she is having a simply splendid time. It is a bravura performance. Sheer arrant pride, bustling about as if she hadn't a single care, chest out, immaculately powdered and lacquered, not a trace of self-pity. If ever I am thus humiliated, I pray I could put on a face like that.

They knew it, too, the House. They were in the presence of an indomitable spirit. You can see it and you can hear it—they are watching her and thinking, *My God, she's magnificent.* And a heartbeat later: *My God, what have we done?*

Mr. Michael Carttiss: Cancel it! You can wipe the floor with these people!
The Prime Minister: Yes, indeed.

"Under our leadership, Britain has been just as influential in shaping the wider Europe and the relations between East and West. Ten years ago, the eastern part of Europe lay under totalitarian rule, its people knowing neither rights nor liberties. Today, we have a Europe in which democracy, the rule of law and basic human rights are spreading ever more widely, where the threat to our security from the overwhelming conventional forces of the Warsaw pact has been removed: where the Berlin wall has been torn down and the Cold War is at an end."

And sure he is an honorable man.

"There is something else which one feels. That is a sense of this country's destiny: the centuries of history and experience which ensure that, when principles have to be defended, when good has to be upheld and when evil has to be overcome, Britain will take up arms.

"It is because we on this side have never flinched from difficult decisions that this House and this country can have confidence in this Government today!"[38]

The House was stunned.

The motion of no confidence was defeated, 367 to 247.

But it was too late: She was gone.

      FIRST CITIZEN
      O piteous spectacle!
      SECOND CITIZEN
      O noble Caesar!
      THIRD CITIZEN
      O woeful day!
      FOURTH CITIZEN
      O traitors, villains!

      WHAT HAVE THEY DONE?
      —Daily Express

---

38. November 22, 1990, HC S: [Confidence in Her Majesty's Government], House of Commons Speech, Hansard HC [181/445–53].

Why Margaret Thatcher Matters

The title of this book implies a doubt. A book called *Why Hitler Matters* would be inherently absurd; no one doubts that he mattered and no one needs to be told why. But the title of this book also implies a conviction. No one would write a book called *Why John Major Matters*. We know full well that he doesn't.

You picked up this book because you know already that Thatcher is significant. But how significant is she, and why?

I do not propose to appeal to judgments only time can make. No one now asks whether Hitler, Lenin, Stalin, Churchill, and Roosevelt were historical figures of enduring significance. They were judged as massive during their lifetimes; these judgments proved correct. But we should remember that a similar assessment was once made of Chiang Kai-shek. He was believed by his contemporaries to be—I quote now from the Chiang Anthem, and I reckon I would lose no money by betting that this is not on your iPod—"the savior of mankind, the greatest person in the whole world, the lighthouse of freedom, the Great Wall of democracy." He bustled and strutted over the world stage; he was the darling of American conservatives and a fulcrum of great power politics.

Nonetheless, professional historians of China apart, no one now thinks of Chiang as one of the pivotal figures of human history. No one today would write a book titled *Why Chiang Matters*. I assume that quite a number of my readers will need to go to Wikipedia to remind themselves who he was.

Will Margaret Thatcher be placed among the pantheon of politicians with enduring significance? Or will she pass, like Chiang, into the fog of history? I cannot tell you. No one can.

I can only tell you why she matters to us now.

⚯

Begin with a broader question: What do political figures who matter have in common? Why, as I asked at the beginning of this book, do some of them become larger than life?

Here is my answer. The political figures who matter have two rare gifts. First, they are able to perceive the gathering of historical forces in a way their contemporaries are unable to do. What do I mean by "the gathering of historical forces"? I mean, they are able to *sense the big picture*. Lenin was able to discern a convergence of trends in Czarist Russia—the migration of the peasants, the rise of revolutionary consciousness, the weakness of the Czarist government, the debilitation inflicted upon Russia by the First World War—and to recognize what this convergence implied: The old order could now be toppled—not merely reformed, but destroyed. Czar Nicholas II could not perceive this. It is thus that Lenin now matters and Nicholas II does not.

Second, when promoted to power, those who matter are able to *master* these historical forces. Chiang understood perfectly that China was vulnerable to communism and understood as well precisely what communism in China would mean. He perceived the forces of history. But he was unable, for all his energy and efforts, to master them. And so, tragically, he does not matter.

Churchill perceived the forces of history and then mastered them. In 1933, Hitler was widely regarded outside of Germany as no more than a buffoon. Churchill knew better. His assessment of Hitler was at the time astonishingly prescient and singular. He perceived the unique danger of Nazism when others could not see it or refused to believe it. He was steadfast in his warnings. When at last Churchill acquired power, he discharged his responsibilities in such a fashion as to gain him immortality.

When politicians matter, they matter because of these gifts.

Thatcher had these gifts. She perceived—as did many of her contemporaries—that Britain was in decline. She perceived that the effects of Marxist doctrine upon Britain had been pernicious. But unlike her contemporaries, she perceived that Britain's decline was not inevitable. And she perceived too that socialism was not—as widely believed—irreversible.

Simultaneously, she sensed a wider and related tide in history that no other leader in the Western world, apart from Reagan, sensed at all. She understood that the Soviet Union was far from

"It is easy to forget the state of the country . . . in the years which led up to 1979," remarked Michael Howard, leader of the Conservative Party from 2003 to 2005. "The air of defeatism which was the prevailing climate of the time was the economic and social equivalent of Munich . . . from the beginning she displayed the resolve and determination which made her, to my mind, the peacetime counterpart of Churchill." *(Courtesy of the family of Srdja Djukanovic)*

the invulnerable colossus it was imagined to be. She sensed, in fact, that it was unable to satisfy the basic needs of its own population. It was corrupt, moribund, and doomed.

Having perceived the gathering of historical forces, she mastered them. She reversed the advance of socialism in Britain, proving both that a country can be ripped from a seemingly overdetermined trajectory and that it takes only a single figure with an exceptionally strong will to do so. She did not single-handedly cause the Soviet empire to crumble, but she landed some of the most devastating punches of the Cold War and, extraordinarily, emerged unbloodied from the fight.

There is an even larger sense in which Margaret Thatcher perceived and mastered the forces of history.

Since the eighteenth century, two views of political life have vied for dominance in the Western world. They are views about the hypothetical state of nature—the condition of mankind in the absence of government. The first view is that of Thomas Hobbes: The life of man in the state of nature, he wrote, is "solitary, poor, nasty, brutish and short." The second is that of Jean-Jacques Rousseau: "Man is born free, but he is everywhere in chains."

Hobbes wrote *Leviathan* during the English civil wars of the seventeenth century. Such horrors as he had seen, he believed, arose because of the absence of government, and in particular, the absence of a government powerful enough to overawe men who would otherwise be fractious and dominated by self-interest.

Leviathan is a defense of a central and commanding power in political life. It is sometimes understood, for this reason, as an argument for totalitarianism. A close study of Hobbes suggests little to encourage this view. The form of this central power was to Hobbes largely a matter of indifference. He favored a monarchy, but this is not his key point. His key point is that there is a choice between anarchy and a powerful state. And since, as he could plainly see, anarchy was awful, he chose a powerful state.

This powerful state is the Leviathan, and it is a Leviathan because it possesses—in theory, at least—a monopoly on violence. *Leviathan* to this day remains a critical justification for the existence and the primacy of the nation-state. This was a primacy Thatcher sought instinctively and ferociously to preserve.

It is perverse that Hobbes is widely seen as providing a defense of absolutism in political life, for the historical trail between his thought and the unspeakable evils of the twentieth century is almost impossible to map. Neither Lenin, nor Stalin, nor Hitler, nor Mao thought in his terms; they did not justify their rule by an appeal to a state of nature in which men would find themselves enemies to one another.

These were men, instead, who had read Rousseau.

It is Rousseau's view of the state of nature, not Hobbes's, to which the great and awful events that began with the Terror and ended with the Gulag may be traced. In Rousseau's view, man is born both good and noble; if he finds himself in chains, it is because these chains have been imposed by government. A syllogism is implied. If these chains have been imposed by government, these chains must be snapped. If these chains must be snapped, violence must be employed—otherwise, men would free themselves. If violence must be employed, it must be employed without restraint. Every revolutionary movement from the eighteenth century to the twenty-first has seen the logic of this position. It is inexorable.

I do not believe Margaret Thatcher was a careful student of Hobbes—or of Rousseau, for that matter. To judge from her autobiography, she too misunderstood Hobbes's point. Raisa Gorbachev, apparently, displayed an interest in the copy of *Leviathan* on Thatcher's bookshelf during her visit to Chequers; Thatcher worried this might signify that Mrs. Gorbachev was a particularly hard-line communist. But while she did not properly understand what Hobbes had written, she was, nonetheless, in instinctive agreement with his views. Political life, Thatcher believed, must be organized around nation-states. These states must possess a monopoly on violence. The authority of the nation-state must not be compromised from the outside, by transnational bodies such as the European Union, or from the inside, by groups such as the National Union of Mineworkers.

Thatcher's career may be viewed as a series of rebukes to those who would seek to diminish the authority of the nation-state and to reduce its monopoly on violence. She is thus not only one of the greatest enemies of socialism the world has known, but one of the greatest enemies of anarchy, as well. Again, she perceived the forces of history, and again, she mastered them.

If you need to be reminded why anarchy is awful, one word will suffice: Iraq.

That word brings me to my next point. Thatcher was enormously prescient. But she was not supernaturally prescient, and it is a mistake to assign to her the status of a secular saint. On some issues, she was simply wrong. Iraq was one of them. By "wrong," I do not mean the invasion of Iraq was ultimately wrong. I don't know yet whether it was, and this is not the place for this debate. I mean that she did not weigh properly the real risk that invading Iraq would lead to anarchy, and she did not foresee what would be required to contain that anarchy. In this sense, she was wrong.[1]

On other issues—critical issues—she was bizarrely oblivious. This is often the case, even among the political figures who matter most. If some politicians are given the gift of seeing into the loom of time, they are rarely given the gift of seeing it whole. Churchill

---

1. I was wrong too, but my opinions are obviously of less historical significance.

saw with astonishing prescience the danger posed by the Nazi regime; in 1946, he saw with the same prescience the descent of the Iron Curtain. About India, however, he was blind, and he was blind again in thinking the call for social reform in postwar Britain could be ignored.

The world's attention now is focused on the conflict with radical Islam. Rightly so. But let us be frank: About this, Margaret Thatcher was blind. In this regard, she doesn't matter. I looked everywhere for evidence that she had even considered the issue carefully. I could not find it.

CB: There's not a single mention in your book, and not a single mention in any memoir from the time, of anyone being concerned by the growing threat of Islamic extremism—

Bernard Ingham: No.

CB: Were there *no* indications at the time that this was an issue that would preoccupy Britain so greatly in the next decades?

BI: Well, I suppose our objective was to keep them on our side because of the oil . . . and I suppose that perhaps in trying to keep them on our side because of the oil we did exacerbate the problem. Because we did play up to some pretty reprehensible regimes . . . Where were the indications coming from, apart from OPEC, which was really a business response, a monopolist response, where were the indications coming from of Islamic extremism at the time?

CB: Well, the Iranian revolution, for one thing. The rise of the Muslim Brotherhood, in Egypt. The rise of the Taliban, which of course we contributed to—

BI: Yes, but we'd put up—let me plead our history, we'd put up with so many sects in our time! HAH! HAH! I mean, we put up with *India!* HAH! I mean, what was another *sect?!* HAH! HAH! . . . But you're quite right . . . who the hell had ever heard of Islamic extremism in 1979? I didn't. I'd heard of oil.

Who the hell had ever heard of Islamic extremism in 1979? I had, for one: I was only eleven years old, but I had seen newscasts about American hostages with hoods over their heads. Yet by all accounts, these images made a bigger impression on me than they did on Thatcher and those around her.

CB: During the time that you were working with Margaret Thatcher, do you remember anyone asking the question, "Are we nurturing a problem with Islamic fundamentalism, here and abroad?"

John Hoskyns: It wasn't in the air. It wasn't in the air at all.

I asked this question again and again; the response was always the same.

CB: When you were working with Mrs. Thatcher, was there any anticipation of the conflict with radical Islam?

Peter Walker: No, not really, no.

CB: It was really not anticipated—

PW: I never heard a murmur.

However much this appears to be the crucial conflict of the modern world, it truly does seem that Thatcher had nothing to say about it.

Thatcher's vision and her accomplishments were considerable—immense, even—but this business of venerating her as an infallible living god is intellectually indefensible and slightly idolatrous. It simply isn't plausible, however often it is asserted, that if she were still in charge, we wouldn't be in this mess—"this mess" being whatever has recently gone wrong.

In March 2007, when British sailors were seized, held hostage, and humiliated by the Iranian navy, you could scarcely open a newspaper without reading that this would never have happened if Thatcher were in power.

CB: How do you think she would have handled the Iranian seizure of the British sailors? And I know you can't answer that definitively, but—

Charles Powell: Yes, well, I mean, it's hard to—she was shocked, to the degree that she understood what had happened, she really was. Well, first of all, I find it so hard to believe it would have happened in those days. I mean, her armed forces were just better-equipped and everything . . . once it had happened, I think she would have been very strong in her rhetoric about absolutely no bargaining . . . we wouldn't have surrendered to blackmail, there would have been no giving in to the Iranians, for the hostages . . . and they would certainly not have been treated in any way as heroes when they got back. But that's all speculation.

Perhaps that is just what would have happened—no bargaining, no giving in, and no one would have dared to do that to her in the first place. Or perhaps not. A small but relevant point: On April 17, 1984, a group of anti-Gadhafi demonstrators gathered in front of the Libyan embassy in London. Gadhafi loyalists opened fire on the demonstrators from the second floor of the embassy, striking and killing a young British policewoman. Shortly afterward, the murderers were permitted quietly to leave the country. They were not arrested and tried, despite howls of outrage from the British press. Why not? Because Thatcher feared reprisals against British citizens in Libya. This is precisely the sort of thing that would *never* have happened if Thatcher were still in power, except that in this case, Thatcher was in power.

In other words, as Powell rightly says, it is all speculation.

It is likewise often said that if Thatcher were still in power, we would never have gone into Iraq so unprepared to cope with the aftermath of the invasion.

CB: I wonder how you think she would have handled Iraq . . . The overwhelming feeling I get is that this is a woman who picks her battles very, very carefully—

John Hoskyns: Yes.

Miranda Hoskyns: You always said she was quite cautious about quite a lot of things—

JH: She was, *rightly.* Everyone said she was very cautious, but one would say that was sensible. Sensibly so. She realized how things can go wrong. And also, certainly, once she'd been prime minister for five or six years, she also realized how absolutely crucial it was—and this was what I was always going on about, with my business experience and indeed my military experience, little though that was—that there really are only a *few* things that you're going to be able to do, and they've *got* to be related to whatever the great purpose is, small in number, and they've got to be worked out like *mad* before you do them. And even then, one out of three will probably go disastrously wrong. This you've seen in all her domestic policy. So I can imagine her intuitively saying, you know . . . *the question is, how do we get out again?* . . . I can imagine that she would have been basically pretty sympathetic to the war, as I was . . . I didn't think, "Oh, this is a wonderful idea. This is the best thing we've ever done," but what I could see was, and I think people over here were very short-sighted about it, was if you had had 9/11 in the middle of London, you do realize that you've got to do *something*—electorally, politically, and in terms of sort of material force . . . What it is you do, I don't know, but you can't just sort of say, "We must all stay very calm and play 'The Stars and Stripes' and hope for the best." Because all the Arabists say, or many of them say, the one thing Islamic fundamentalism says is that the West is depraved, disintegrating, collapsing, corrupt, and all we really have to do is give one push and the whole thing will implode. So you bet-

ter make sure that they don't get that presumption confirmed . . . She might easily have listened, she might have
talked to one of the top generals or soldiers offline, nobody
knowing, and they would have said, "I'm sure we can win
that little war, but we really do have to know what happens
after that." . . . And I would have thought her caution
would have said, "We really *do* have to know." Because
again, she's intuitive! She isn't stupid! And one feels now,
which I *didn't* at the time, because I *didn't* believe it, but
you know, that Rumsfeld and others were—almost *mad!*
They must have been! . . . I feel that if she'd been there,
she wouldn't have had those sort of people, she wouldn't
have been that stupid herself, and she'd have had cleverer
people 'round her, and there's a *chance* she would have said
. . . "I think this Rumsfeld fellow's got it wrong. I don't
think he really understands what he's doing. And he should
certainly not, as your Secretary of Defense, be telling Colin
Powell to go away and shut up. Because the State Department is going to have to pick up these pieces." I can't believe she would have been that stupid. Whereas it seems to
me that Blair thought, "This is wonderful. I'm going to ride
behind the mighty colossus of American military power, we
put in a few thousand jolly good British troops, just to show
we're willing, and my name will be in lights! Isn't this fun!"
You know?

That she would have exhibited greater caution about Iraq is an
extremely common point of view; no one to whom I spoke dis-
sented from it.

CB: Just as a hypothetical—had she been in power, how do you
think she would have dealt with the second, the most recent, Iraq War? Do you think she would have offered the
kind of support Tony Blair offered—

Peter Walker: Um, I mean, it's a guess, obviously—

CB: Absolutely, of course it is—

PW: I would have guessed that she would have given much more thought to what happens when the initial battle is over. I mean, the extraordinary thing about the whole affair, two really bad things, is that both George Bush and Tony Blair, well, first, they misled people about the reason, and both tried to doctor the intelligence services' advice, and they gave no thought to—after you won the military battle, what the hell do you do? And I think, if she had had the caliber of foreign secretary of Peter Carrington, he would have said, "Look, when this is over, there'll be civil war in Iraq. You've got these two groups that hate each other, despise each other, and no matter how nasty the present president has been, he's stopped that civil war taking place."

Not only would Thatcher have had the foresight to prevent the Iraq debacle, her admirers say, it wouldn't have been an issue in the first place if only she had remained in power:

Bernard Ingham: I tell you, the situation would not have arisen if she'd have been in office in '91. She'd have gone straight through to Baghdad. She wouldn't have stopped. The turkey shoot—straight through to Baghdad. No, she would have had to persuade George Bush, but she was a fairly formidable persuader. And she would have simply said, "Well, we're not leaving our job half-done."

CB: Really? You think she would have had the ability to persuade him? Because he was so reluctant. *Really* reluctant.

BI: Well, what you don't know is what kind of diplomatic efforts she would have mounted to secure that, do you? I mean, damn it, they were defeated, weren't they? What you don't know is what kind of aftermath we would have had to cope with—nobody knows that.

CB: You have to imagine the aftermath would have been pretty similar to what we're seeing now.

BI: Could have been, yes.

CB: And that was precisely the problem Bush Senior didn't want.

BI: Could well be. But I think she was of the view, admittedly she was out of office, that we should have gone through to Baghdad and finished the job.

CB: You *think* she was of the view, or have you *heard* her say that?

BI: I've heard her say that.

Now let's look at the facts; they are a matter of public record. In 2002—in her last significant public speech, delivered to an American audience—this is what she said:

> Our purpose must be to strike the other centers of Islamic terrorism wherever they are. And we must act equally strongly against those states which harbor terrorists and develop weapons of mass destruction that might be used against us or our allies.
>
> The recent shameful European reaction to President Bush's State of the Union Speech reminds me of nothing so much as that which greeted President Reagan's words two decades ago. Americans shouldn't take too much notice. Fear masquerading as caution, pique posing as dignity, words substituting for thought—we have been there many times before. Whatever the protests of the faint-hearts, it is high time to take action against the rogue states which are arming against us.
>
> In particular, Saddam Hussein constitutes unfinished business. And he now needs to be finished—for good. First rate intelligence, the support of opposition elements within Iraq, and overwhelming force will probably all be required.

But the risks of not acting far outweigh those of allowing
Saddam to continue developing his weapons of war. I hope
and trust that Britain will support to the hilt the action your
president decides to take.[2]

I see no evidence in these remarks that she would have shown
any greater prescience about Iraq than those who were, in fact, in
power.[3] She was certainly correct to note that first-rate intelligence, the support of opposition elements within Iraq, and overwhelming force would be required. Perhaps if she had been in
power, she would have noticed the absence of all three elements in
the plan. But we simply cannot know.

So that is *not* why she matters. She matters enough for what she
really did perceive and what she really did achieve that there is no
need to exaggerate. It does not diminish her much to note that as
idols generally do, she has feet of clay.

_⟡ ⟡ ⟡_

A final point. She matters *now* because her battles are not over. For
a brief, perishable moment during the 1990s, it was possible to
imagine that the great questions of history had been settled. But
history did not, as Francis Fukuyama predicted, come to an end.
Quite the contrary.

Socialism was buried prematurely. This fact has been little remarked, precisely because the world's attention has in recent
times been focused on the dramatic rise of Islamic extremism.
Amid this anxiety it has been forgotten that the appeal of socialism as a political program is ultimately far wider, more seductive,
and more enduring than political Islam. To the vast majority of the

---

2. Speech paying tribute to Ronald Reagan, Washington, D.C., March 1,
2002, Thatcher MSS (digital collection), doc. 109306.

3. Again, my own judgment on this issue was no better at all. I was in full
agreement with this speech.

secular world, Islam is alien and will always be alien. Islamic law is widely and correctly perceived as a recipe for immiseration. This is *not* so of socialism, a political movement that like fascism embodies the religious impulse in secular form, and is thus an ideology destined to rise again and again from the grave, skeletal claws outstretched and grasping for the instruments and subjects of labor.

Wherever men are miserable—and that is almost everywhere—they will be vulnerable to those who promise Utopia, for if Hobbes expressed some portion of the truth, Rousseau expressed some portion of the truth as well. There is no inconsistency between the declaration that life in the state of nature is solitary, poor, nasty, brutish and short and the declaration that man is everywhere in chains. That this observation is bleak is no reason not to think it correct. If for no other reason, I doubt the promises of socialism will ever lose their capacity to inspire.

Throughout Central America, the Middle East, and Africa, policies Thatcher would deplore remain or have recently been put in place. One need only look at the Iraqi constitution, which assumes that it is the business of the state and not the individual to create jobs, to see that this is so. Socialism is again on the ascendant in Latin America. It is a commonplace of American political discourse that we must reduce our dependence upon Saudi oil, given the Saudi kingdom's pernicious tendency to export Islamic extremism. We import almost as much Venezuelan oil as we do Saudi oil. Venezuela is now exporting socialist extremism every bit as energetically as the Saudis export Islamic extremism. Cuba appears for now to have won the stand-off with the United States. Socialist dogma and practice remain solidly entrenched throughout Africa and the Middle East. Socialism is again on the march throughout Europe, especially in France. *France, you say? But Sarkozy won.* Indeed he did. And the first thing he did upon taking office—because he had no choice—was pack his government with socialists. He even married one.

According to a poll conducted in 2005, only 36 percent of French citizens support the free-enterprise system. In Germany,

47 percent of the population claims to embrace socialist ideals.[4] Chancellor Angela Merkel, once described as Germany's Thatcher, has abandoned plans for free-market reforms. She has instead imposed new taxes and restrictions on the labor market. She has promised new efforts to "regulate" globalization.

American academics remain enthralled by socialism. You will not find many college students wearing Osama bin Laden T-shirts, but Che Guevara T-shirts are campus favorites. Socialism is the real message of the anti-globalization movement: The forces Thatcher confronted are one and the same as the forces that in 1999 led to the imposition of martial law in Seattle.

I live in Istanbul, and I am regularly asked by concerned Americans whether secularism in Turkey is under threat. Do I fear, they ask, that the Turkish government has fallen under the control of Islamic crypto-fundamentalists? My standard answer to this question is that this is a legitimate concern, but so far I am not excessively alarmed. In fact, the only political violence I've seen here has nothing to do with Islam. On May Day 2008, just as I was finishing this book, the Turkish security forces used tear gas and water cannons to prevent crowds of trade unionists, communists, and anarchists from marching to Istanbul's Taksim Square. Turkey's three main trade union confederations, which bitterly oppose the government's efforts to implement free-market reforms, claimed to have mobilized half a million marchers. The demonstrators showed up with gas masks and Molotov cocktails, throwing rocks at the police. The police beat them indiscriminately. They fired gas bombs into the crowd and shot water cannons into the trade union headquarters. Hundreds were arrested. Dozens were injured. I was proofreading the chapter of this book titled "I *Hate* Communists" when the police chased some 500 wet, coughing communists right down the street in front of me.[5]

4. See Stefan Theil, "Europe's Philosophy of Failure," *Foreign Policy*, January/February 2008.

This conflict, even more than the divide between religion and secularism, will be the fault line of the coming century. How could it not be? It has been the fault line of political life since the French Revolution.

I cannot promise it (remember Chiang!), but I do strongly suspect that Margaret Thatcher's ideas and personality will assume an even greater significance with time. Recognizing what she achieved in Britain—and coolly appraising the cost of these victories, which was considerable—is as essential for our generation as for hers. Every society confronting these historical forces will inevitably arrive at a place much like the one Margaret Thatcher found herself upon her ascent to 10 Downing Street.

She perceived these forces, and for a time she mastered them. This is why she matters to history.

These forces are still at work; they must again be mastered.

This is why she matters to you.

---

5. I mention this as evidence that this is still one of the world's most active political conflicts. I do not mean these remarks to be construed as any kind of approval of the excessive force used by the Turkish police. Under Thatcher, the police did *not* tear gas people sitting peacefully in cafes, and they did *not* tear gas women and children who were caught in the melee, and they did *not* tear gas leukemia patients in hospitals.

EPILOGUE

It has been more than fifteen years since I last took an exam that counted for anything. But I still have the dream. I have it all the time. I am sitting down to take my final exams, but when I open the exam booklet I realize, with dawning horror, that I haven't studied at all. I have never opened the book. In fact, I haven't been to class once the entire term.

I mention this to Neil Kinnock as our conversation draws to a close. I ask him whether he still dreams about facing Margaret Thatcher at Prime Minister's Questions. "No," he says. "But I do dream about my exams, and it's forty-odd years since I sat any! I know exactly what you mean."

We marvel briefly at the weird ubiquity of this dream. I have no idea why so many people have it.

But Kinnock insists he never dreams about Thatcher. "No, no," he says. "I don't. Maybe, I'll tell you, because of this factor: She went through the door because we were beating Margaret Thatcher and were going to inflict a terminal defeat on her. So maybe I don't dream about it because of that."

"Right."

"And secondly, when I failed to beat John Major—much more narrowly, of course, but I failed to beat him in 1992—I decided the curtain was coming down on that. Because I just could not live on a diet of memories. I mean, I was fifty years of age. And that was—if the worst decision I ever made was not to denounce Scargill, and demand a ballot, and say publicly they couldn't win without one, that was my worst decision—then my best—politically, I mean, my best decision ever was to ask my wife to marry me—maybe my best political decision was to bring that curtain down and stick to it."

"Yeah. Absolutely. I completely understand that."

And I do. How well I do.

"I'd probably be dead now. I probably would have corroded myself to death."

The art of bringing down the curtain is hard to master. It has not been easy for Margaret Thatcher. Nigel Lawson remarks to me that she had no interests outside of politics. "I mean, she was interested in ideas, and religion, and so on, but she wasn't interested in sports, she wasn't . . . "

His voice trails off. I finish his sentence for him. "She wasn't the woman you'd go to for a good game of snooker."

"Absolutely not."

He chuckles bloodlessly. It is the only time I hear him laugh.

It has been more than eighteen years since her precipitous tumble from power. Thatcher's former friends and allies are still grudging with their praise, eager to appropriate credit for her achievements, smoldering with petty resentments. In part, of course, this is inevitable—proximity to power is not known for making men more generous in spirit.

Margaret Thatcher herself is ill, and deeply lonely. Denis Thatcher died in 2003. She had cooked his breakfast every morning until the end. She would let no one else do it.

Carol Thatcher, her daughter, says that her mother has never fully recovered from her betrayal. "Treachery," said Carol, "festers in your DNA."

A full-time assistant cares for the former prime minister now. Of course, her friends still visit her. Gorbachev, in particular, has been kind. "One of the nicest things about him," Charles Powell tells me, "is he does come to see her now when he comes to the UK. And he knows she doesn't really make sense now, and there are days when she doesn't even really remember who he is, but he comes along, and usually brings a daughter, or a granddaughter, and a nice present, and sits . . . he sits and talks to her, and she repeats herself, or says the same question three times. He doesn't mind, goes over it, and it's really nice to see. Actually, he's one of the people who's treated her most kindly, most courteously, since she's had troubles."

Not long ago, while touring an animal shelter to which she had made a donation, Margaret Thatcher—now Baroness Thatcher—encountered Marvin, an elderly and abandoned tabby cat. She and Marvin saw in each other's eyes a flicker of understanding.

She adopted him on the spot.

PHOTOGRAPH
ACKNOWLEDGMENTS

The photographer Graham Wiltshire and the family of the photographer Srdja Djukanovic permitted me to reproduce the photographs in this book simply because they are generous and for no other reason. I acknowledge their remarkable kindness to me with special gratitude.

ACKNOWLEDGMENTS

I extend a lifetime of gratitude to a prince among archivists, Andrew Riley, the ever-patient, ever-droll, ever-helpful, ever-tactful Thatcher Papers Archivist and Public Services Manager at the Churchill Archives Centre in Cambridge. I am more indebted to him than anyone who has not written a book about Margaret Thatcher could possibly understand. For his efforts, Andrew would in a just world receive from me bouquets of hothouse orchids, magnums of champagne, crates of chocolate truffles, tins of Beluga caviar, a solid-gold watch, a month-long vacation in the Caribbean, and my firstborn child. Over the past year I've asked Andrew a billion questions (more or less) about the documents he lovingly curates. He has patiently and learnedly answered every one of them, usually within minutes. He introduced me to many of the men and women I interviewed, spent hours helping me find and secure the rights to all the photos in this book (and did so at the very last minute, without a word of complaint), and read every word I wrote, in multiple drafts. I suspect there is nothing he would not do to help a researcher. I implore others never to take advantage of his good will as I have.

Andrew tsked-tsked (very tactfully) when he came across passages that he found insufficiently respectful of Margaret Thatcher or her friends. The concern in his voice when he said, "She might not like that!" was touching and a great tribute to the loyalty Margaret Thatcher inspires. I hope she appreciates that in Andrew, she has a servant as hardworking and energetic as she is, and as devoted to her as she deserves. I can promise her that any word in this book that displeases her remains despite Andrew's strenuous objections. Many words were removed as a result of them.

I'd also like to thank Andrew's colleague Sophie Bridges, who spent many hours combing through the archives in search of the perfect photos for me.

Then there is Chris Collins, editor of the official Web site of the Margaret Thatcher Foundation. The site, www.margaretthatcher.org, is the most useful resource of its kind I've seen, all thanks to his industry and energy. There is far more material about Ronald Reagan on this site, for example, than on the Reagan Library's and Foundation's sites put together. I could not have written this book while living in Istanbul without Chris's determination to make these documents available to researchers around the world. Chris too went far beyond the call of duty in answering questions, reading draft material, granting me the rights to use the material I cite from the Foundation archives, and helping me to make the book generally better. I thank him gratefully.

I suspect that my editor, Bill Frucht, may be a man of the Left. He has hinted as much in our phone conversations. Nonetheless, he acquired this book and gave me the freedom to say precisely what I wished to say, proof of his admirable intellectual confidence and tolerance. Bill has been particularly kind to me personally. When I signed the contract for this book the dollar was strong. By the time I finished it, it was not. Having just written a spirited defense of free markets operating in the context of robust contract law, I could hardly make an intellectually credible case to Bill that he should give me more money simply because I didn't have enough of it. All the same, I *didn't* have enough of it. Bill found a creative way to interpret our contract and to cut my advance check ahead of the stipulated date. "The free market," he wrote to me, "does not always yield the optimal solution. Unless it's balanced by reason and compassion, it can, like any machine or algorithm, go off course." Given the circumstances, these struck me as remarks of godlike sagacity. I hereby qualify this book with his wise words. If only everyone who was tempted to tamper with the free market possessed his reason and his compassion.

I extend my thanks as well to my industrious production editor, Annie Lenth, whom readers must imagine as this book's drill sergeant, responsible for maintaining good unit order and discipline. I also thank my meticulous copy editor, Antoinette Smith.

My friends Damian Counsell, Norah Vincent, Kristen Erickson, Judith Wrubel-Levy, Martin Davies, Bill Walsh, Elizabeth Pisani, Justin Hintzen, Zia Rahman, and David Gross all read chapters or full drafts of this book, in some cases several drafts, and every one of them made it better. Zia, in particular, devoted days to the manuscript while visiting Istanbul, setting aside his own work to do so. I am lucky to have friends like these.

As always, my father and brother were my unofficial collaborators. I particularly thank my brother for calling me one evening to say, "You know what you should write, Claire? A book about Margaret Thatcher." And I thank my father, as always, for showing me how it should be done.

It hardly needs to be said—but I will say it anyway—that I am grateful to my mother and my stepfather for their unfailing support.

The people I interviewed in this book were extraordinarily generous with me. They were to the last gracious about my questions, even when less good-humored subjects might have thrown me out of their homes or offices. I hope that it is clear that even when I did not agree with them, I had a wonderful time with each and every one of them. I would especially like to thank Brian Lewis for his superb hospitality in Yorkshire and for his wonderful gifts of Thatcher memorabilia and books about the miners' strike, which I treasure. I'd also like to convey my affection and gratitude to Andrew Graham, the Master of Balliol, not only for his help with this book but for his warmth and patience with me when I was his student.

A number of people who were close to Margaret Thatcher spoke to me off the record, and in doing so greatly helped me to form a more complete mental picture of her. I thank them all for their time and insight.

For all the reasons I've named in this book, the world owes Margaret Thatcher a great debt. Historians are more indebted to her still. Lady Thatcher was under no obligation to give her personal papers to anyone. Indeed, she could have sold them to the highest bidder or burnt them had she thought it prudent. She instead donated them to the British people. This is proof of the depth of her commitment to the ideal of an open society, not to mention an extraordinary testimony to her confidence in her own character. You do not hand over to historians and journalists 3,000 boxes of papers, many of which you have not seen since the day they crossed your desk, if you are not *certain* that you have always conducted yourself with irreproachable integrity. Think about it: Would you?

A final word for my agent, Daniel Greenberg. For reasons that will be obvious to him, I acknowledge his work on my behalf with particularly profound feeling. No words are quite adequate to express what needs to be said, so I will choose the simplest ones. Thank you, Daniel. Not a day has passed when you have not been in my thoughts.

A GUIDE TO FURTHER READING

The scholarly literature about Thatcher and Thatcherism is vast. I've not endeavored here to provide a complete guide to it. These are merely a few suggestions for readers who are now on fire to deepen their acquaintance with Thatcher and her epoch.

If you're looking for a more traditional biography of Margaret Thatcher, John Campbell's two volumes are the gold standard. *The Grocer's Daughter* covers the years from 1925 to 1979. *The Iron Lady* treats her life until 2003. I particularly recommend the first seven chapters of *The Grocer's Daughter*. This is an unauthorized biography, but Campbell has received excellent cooperation from the key players.

Charles Moore, formerly the editor of the *Daily Telegraph*, is now working on Thatcher's authorized biography. He has had access to all of her papers. No one else has. His book will be published upon her death. I would say that I cannot wait to read it, but given what this implies, I would prefer to wait for a very long while.

Thatcher's memoirs—again, two volumes—are wonderful. *The Path to Power* treats her life until 1979; *The Downing Street Years* covers her premiership. If you have time for only one, read *The Downing Street Years*. Critics have been snotty about her memoirs, as indeed they are snotty about her generally, but they are snotty for no reason: These books are lively, revealing, arch, wise, and beautifully written. Also invaluable is *Statecraft: Strategies for a Changing World*, her treatise on international affairs.

As for other memoirs of this period, no one should shuffle off this mortal coil before reading Alan Clark's diaries. There are three volumes: *Into Politics, In Power,* and *The Last Diaries.* I'm not sure that you'll come away from them with a much deeper understanding of Margaret Thatcher, but you'll certainly better understand the environment in which she was obliged to maneuver. (Clark describes Michael Heseltine, for example, as the kind of person "who bought his own furniture"—a remark from which an entire book about the British class structure could be derived.)

The View from No. 11, by Nigel Lawson, is the most important memoir of economic policymaking during this period. No one ever wished it longer, but you'll have no further questions about the Exchange Rate Mechanism dispute after you finish it.

Although it is now hard to come by, I also recommend John Hoskyns's diary, *Just in Time: Inside the Thatcher Revolution.* Shrewd, detailed, and too rarely read. On Thatcherism as an ideology, Shirley Robin Letwin's *The Anatomy of Thatcherism* is unusually sophisticated and interesting.

If you'd like to know more about Arthur Scargill, Paul Routledge has written an excellent eponymous biography. It is of course unauthorized. Scargill is apparently now preparing his own autobiography. I expect his perspective on the miners' strike will be different from mine.

For the Falklands, nothing comes close to Sir Lawrence Freedman's two-volume *Official History of the Falklands War.* It's the best, most thoroughly sourced, and most comprehensive work extant on the subject.

On Thatcher's role in the Cold War, I suggest John O'Sullivan's book, *The President, the Pope and the Prime Minister: Three Who Changed the World.* I would argue that the book should have had half as much pope and twice as much prime minister, but in O'Sullivan's defense, he has already written a great deal for and about Margaret Thatcher. He was her speechwriter and subsequently played a large hand in the writing of her memoirs.

For a sturdy academic account of Thatcher's economic policy, try *Mrs. Thatcher's Economic Experiment* by William Keegan. It is accessible but critical. Martin Holmes's *The First Thatcher Government* is somewhat more sympathetic. David Smith's *From Boom to Bust* deals with the later period. Robert Skidelsky's anthology, *Thatcherism*, contains a useful selection of essays about her economic policies, both for and against.

The Margaret Thatcher Foundation offers free access to thousands upon thousands of source documents on its Web site, as well as many interesting photos and video clips. If you are at all curious about this epoch, you'll pass many happy hours there. Likewise, if you're seeking a comprehensive, up-to-date bibliography, check there. The Foundation is preparing one right now. It will probably be ready by the time you read this.

INDEX

Able Archer, 266
Accents, 211–212
Afghanistan: Soviet invasion of, 271;
    Soviet withdrawal from, 304;
    United States and, 303
Africa, 271, 296, 357
Alcoholism, 239, 247, 250
American Constitution, 307
Anarchy, 346–347
Andropov, Yuri, 266, 281
Argentina: communications of,
    162–164; coup in, 160; Falkland
    Islands ownership by, 157–158;
    Falklands War popularity in,
    160, 170; *General Belgrano* and,
    76–77, 174; navy of, 162;
    surrender of, 177. *See also*
    Falklands War
Armament: in Europe, 296;
    Gorbachev, M., on, 284, 297;
    Soviet Union, 276–277, 286, 289,
    292–293, 297, 303; Thatcher, M.,
    on, 277; United States, 276–277,
    288, 289. *See also* Disarmament;
    Exocet missile; Nuclear arms;
    Satan missile
"Arthur Scargill Walks on Water,"
    193
Ascension Island, 172
Asia, 6, 271
Atlantic Conveyor, 175
Attractiveness, Thatcher's, 21–22;
    Graham, A., on, 81–84;
    Hoskyns, J., on, 98, 99; Kinnock
    on, 90–91; Mitterand on, 81, 91

Australia, 203, 260
Austria, 305, 312

Baghdad, 354, 355
Bank of England, 137
BBC News, 186, 220
BBC World Service, 175
Belgrano. See General Belgrano
Benn, Anthony, 24, 42–43, 209
Berlin Wall, 40, 305
Berlinski, Claire, 310, 311
Big Bang, 148
bin Laden, Osama, 358
Birmingham, 185, 242
Blair, Tony: on EEC, 322; Iraq War
    and, 353–354; legacy of
    Thatcherism on, 7, 146, 322;
    Walker on, 353–354; at World
    Economic Forum, 146;
    Yorkshire miners on, 258
BNP. *See* British National Party
Bordeaux, Michael, 268
Boudicea, 76–80, 82–85, 103–105,
    232–233
Brezhnev, Leonid, 113, 121, 194,
    281, 283, 293
Britain, 210; agriculture in, 316;
    Central Intelligence Agency on,
    273; economy of, 13, 24, 32,
    35, 37, 39, 41, 42, 57,
    128–155, 203–204, 238–239;
    in EEC, 313–322; Europe and,
    276, 309, 313–322; Falkland
    Islands ownership by, 157–158,
    159; foreign policy of, 313;

Britain *(continued)*: Germany and,
36; Gorbachev, M., on, 295, 300;
Grantham, 15–16; identity of,
313, 314; investments in,
148–149; Iran and, 350–351;
Kissinger on, 10; Libyan embassy
in, 229, 275, 351; navy of, 162,
172; Paris and, 34; Post Office of,
140, 143–144; postwar census
in, 10; power of, 9–10; in sixties,
96; stagflation in, 126–127;
strikes in, 11–12, 234; subsidies
in, 316; trains in, 142; underclass
in, 146; unemployment in, 22,
37, 39, 130, 136; United States
and, 140–141, 273–274, 275. *See
also* Birmingham; British
Disease; London; Orgreave,
South Yorkshire; Yorkshire
British Disease, 56–57
British National Party (BNP),
257–258
British Nationality Act, 159–160
Brize Norton Air Force base, 280
Brown, Gordon, 7
Bruges, Belgium, 321–323
Brussels, Belgium, 319
Bush, George: Ingham on, 354;
State of the Union speech by,
355; Thatcher, M., and, 290;
Walker on, 354

Callaghan, James "Jim," 31, 52–53
Capitalism: miners and, 206–207;
Scargill on, 192–194
Carlton Club, 2, 187
Carter, Jimmy, 275
Castro, Fidel, 194
Central Intelligence Agency (CIA):
on Britain, United States
relationship with, 273; on
Soviet Union, United States
relationship with, 271
Centre for Policy Studies, 27
Chamberlain, Neville, 170
Charisma, 71, 105; Hoskyns, J., on,
64, 102; Hoskyns, M., on, 98,
99–100, 104; Kinnock on,
106–108

Chequers: Gorbachev, M., meeting
at, 279–284; Sovietologists'
meeting at, 268–270
Chernenko, Konstantin, 279, 281,
288
Chiang Kai-shek, 343–344
China: democracy in, 343–344;
mining in, 203, 205
Chirac, Jacques, 319–320
Churchill Room, 187
Churchill, Winston: Hitler
assessment by, 344–345;
Howard on, 345; Howe on, 333;
perception of, 349; Thatcher,
M., on, 314
Civil Contingencies Unit, 208
Clark, Alan: affairs of, 91; on Class
War, 206; on Gow, 73, 98; on
Thatcher, M., downfall, 332,
335, 336, 337
Class, 251–252
Clause 4, 6, 189
Clement, Tony, 221–222
Clinton, Bill, 16, 84, 105–106
Clinton, Hillary, 71, 84
Coal. *See* Miners; Mining
Coal and Electricity Generating
Board, 209
Coal strike, 1984, 40; end of, 230,
232, 234; government
preparation for, 208, 210;
Lawson's mine openings during,
218–219; miners' dissent from,
215–216, 217; miners'
impoverishment in, 223; mining
after, 234, 235, 239; pit closures
after, 200, 217, 235; police in,
219; Scargill's Soviet Union
tours during, 194–195; Soviet
Union support of, 194–195;
stockpiling for, 224–225, 227,
229; timing of, 199, 211, 224;
violence in, 229–230; Walker's
alternative to, 214–216. *See also*
Flying pickets; National Coal
Board; National Union of
Mineworkers; Nottinghamshire;
Orgreave, South Yorkshire;
Scargill, Arthur "King Arthur"

Cold War: end of, 7, 295, 304–305;
Powell, Charles, on, 298; Reagan
on, 272; SDI and, 293;
Thatcher, M., on, 273; Thatcher,
M., Soviet visit and, 295; in
United States, 48
College of Europe at Bruges,
321–323
Committee to Celebrate the
October Revolution, 194
Common Market, 313, 323
Communist Party of Great Britain,
189, 192
Community Charge. *See* Poll tax
Congress of Europe, 314
Conservative Group for Europe,
314
Conservative Manifesto, 1979, 48,
49
Conservative Party:
communications strategy of,
53–54; on EEC membership,
314; free-market economics
proposal of, 22–23; Howe's
resignation from, 309–310,
326, 331, 332–333; Kinnock
on, 330; on miners, 207;
research department of, 65, 67;
Thatcher, M.'s resignation from,
23, 340; Thatcher, M.'s
unpopularity in, 329–330;
women and, 92. *See also*
Conservative Manifesto, 1979
Constitution: American, 307;
European, 307, 308; of Iraq,
357
Containment, 272
Contract law, 127
Council houses, 39, 44, 142, 243
Crime, 148, 250
Cuba, 171, 194, 296, 303, 357
Currency: British, 34, 128–129;
European, 318, 331; Soviet,
272, 303

Delors, Jacques, 318–319, 331
Department of Health and Social
Security (DHSS), 131
d'Estaing, Valéry Giscard, 316–317

Disarmament: Gorbachev, M.,
proposal for, 180–181,
292–294; Labour Party
demands for, 274, 277;
Thatcher, M., on, 180–181,
293
Diva, 76, 99–100, 110
"Dress to Kill" (Izzard), 177–178
Dublin European Council, 316

Eastern Europe, 305; destabilization
of, 272, 304; Soviet missiles in,
270
Economics: of Britain, 13, 24, 32,
35, 37, 39, 41, 42, 57, 128–155,
203–204, 238–239;
contractionary, 128; free-
market, 22–23, 115–122, 148;
Keynesian, 128; Kinnock on,
152; Labour Party, 137; of
Scargill, 195–196; of Socialism,
116; of Soviet Union, 269, 270,
272–273, 288, 303, 304;
specialization in, 144–145;
supply-side, 139–141, 146; of
Thatcher, M., 52, 114; of
Thatcherism, 114–115, 148,
240; of United States, 249
Economists: Hoskyns, J., on, 55;
Howe on, 136; inflation and,
137; Keynesian, 37, 41–42; on
money measurement, 134; on
readjustment period, 141;
Thatcher, M., criticism by, 135,
136, 144, 249–250
Education, 249–252
El Salvador, 275, 276
Electrician's union, 220
Electricity industry, 203–204
Emergency, state of, 23
Employment Act (1982), 209–210
Endurance, 159, 161
Energy: coal alternatives, 208, 209;
globalization of, 203; mining
importance for, 203; state of
emergency on, 23; subsidization
of, 203–204. *See also* Oil;
Walker, Peter
Equality, 147

Europe: armament in, 296; Britain
  and, 276, 309, 313–322; Howe
  on, 323. *See also* Eastern
  Europe; France; Germany; Italy;
  Madrid; Netherlands
European Commission, 308
European Constitution:
  referendums on, 307; rejection
  of, 308
European Economic Community
  (EEC), 313; Blair on, 322;
  Britain in, 313–322; Chirac and,
  319–320; Conservative Party
  on, 314; Delors and, 318–319,
  331; Germany in, 316; Kinnock
  on, 323; Labour Party on, 314,
  319; Mitterand and, 317;
  Powell, Charles, on, 316,
  317–318, 319, 320–321;
  subsidies in, 316; Thatcher, M.,
  on, 313, 314–316, 317,
  318–319, 320–322
European Exchange Rate
  Mechanism, 134, 326
European Union, 238; Berlinski on,
  311; financial aid from,
  240–241; Thatcher, M., on, 310,
  311
Euroskepticism, 311, 313, 326
"Evil Empire" (Reagan), 265
Exclusion zone, 76, 172, 174
Exocet missile, 82, 162, 175
Expansionary policy, 124

Fabian Society, 43
Falkland Islands, 39; land mines in,
  181–182; oil in, 181; ownership
  of, 157–158, 159
Falklands War, 76, 82, 110;
  Argentinean communications
  in, 163–164; Argentinean
  popularity of, 160, 170;
  Argentinean surrender, 177;
  British naval response to, 167,
  172; East Falkland battle in,
  175–176; effects of, 177–178,
  179–181; Mitterand on, 166;
  peace plan for, 175; Powell,
  Charles, on, 230; Reagan's
  response to, 171, 174, 176; ships

sunk in, 76–77, 174; start of,
  160–162; Thatcher, M., on,
  77–80, 158–159, 164–166, 168,
  171–172, 173–174, 176; United
  Nations response to, 166;
  United States response to,
  169–170, 171, 174, 176
FCO. *See* Foreign and
  Commonwealth Office
Female roles, 72; Boudicea, 76–80,
  82–85, 103–105, 232–233; diva,
  76, 99–100, 110; flirt, 81–82,
  90–91, 282, 297; housewife, 52,
  136, 205–206; matron, 85,
  92–94; shrew, 86–87, 106–108,
  324, 325
Financial aid: from Britain, 240,
  242; from European Union,
  240–241; Lewis on, 240–241;
  for miners, 195, 260; Thatcher,
  M., on, 241
Fiscal policy, 124, 137
Flying pickets: Ingham on, 225–226;
  interview with, 253–254; in
  Nottinghamshire, 216, 253,
  254; pay of, 254; at Saltley coke
  depot, 185; Scargill on, 196
Foreign and Commonwealth Office
  (FCO), 268–269
Foreign exchange controls, 133, 134
Fountainebleau Summit, 317
France, 145; Britain and, 34;
  European Constitution rejection
  in, 308; Paris, 34; Socialism in,
  357; Thatcher, M., on, 313, 314
Free-market economics, 117–120,
  122; Conservative Party
  campaign for, 22–23; Thatcher,
  M., on, 115–116, 121, 148; in
  Thatcherism, 240
Friedman, Milton, 24, 125, 126;
  article by, 134–135; Joseph and,
  135–136; unemployment fix of,
  138–139
Frost, David, 77–79

Galtieri, Leopoldo, 39; arrest of,
  181; Haig and, 171; strategy of,
  160; on Thatcher, M., 210
Gandhi, Indira, 71

Gandhi, Sonia, 72
Gates, Robert, 271–272
Gender, 13–14; in politics, 71–72, 92. *See also* Female roles; Women
General Belgrano, 76–77, 174
Geneva, 279, 288
Germany: Britain and, 36; in EEC, 316; Socialism in, 357–358; Thatcher, M., and, 310, 311, 312–313, 314. *See also* West Germany
Goose Green, 175
Gorbachev, Mikhail, 347; on armament, 284, 297; Brezhnev letter to, 283; on Britain, 295, 300; Chequers meeting of, 40, 279–284; disarmament proposal of, 180–181, 292–294; election of, 288; on food prices, 121; Howe on, 280; Intermediate-Range Nuclear Forces Treaty signing by, 302; Kinnock on, 300–301; Kremlin meeting of, 295–302; Powell, Charles, on, 279–282, 295–298; Reagan and, 284–285, 287–289, 292–293, 297, 302; at Reykjavik summit, 292–293; role in ending Cold War, 302–303; Scargill on, 194; on Solidarity movement, 305; Thatcher, M., and, 279–285, 288, 290, 291, 302
Graham, Andrew, 81–82; on inflation, 132–133, 135–136, 138; on money supply, 134; on privatization, 141–143; Wilson and, 80
Grantham, Britain, 15–16, 312–313
Great Depression, 130
Greenham Common, 277
Grenada, 278, 303
Guevara, Che, 358

Hahn, Frank, 114, 136
Haig, Alexander: on Galtieri, 171; peace plan endorsement by, 175; Thatcher, M., meeting with, 169–170
von Hayek, Friedrich, 8, 24

Healey, Denis, 30, 324–325
Heath, Edward "Ted": free-market campaign of, 22–23; Scargill and, 185; on Thatcher, M., election, 28; on Thatcher, M., resignation, 339; U-turns by, 23
Henderson, Nicholas, 34–35, 145, 340
Hennessy, Peter, 87
Herald of Free Enterprise, 107
Heseltine, Michael, 40–41, 325, 334–335
Hitler, Adolph, 344–345
HMS *Sheffield*, 82
Hobbes, Thomas, 346–347, 357
Holocaust, 129
Hong Kong, 159
Hoskyns Group, 140
Hoskyns, John: on British Disease, 56–57, 140–141, 143–144; communication strategy of, 53–54; Conservative Party on economists, 55; Ingham on, 55–56; on Iraq, 352–353; on Islamic extremism, 350, 352; on Labour Party, 61–62; on miners, 207; on mining, 207–208, 210; resignation of, 208; on Rumsfeld, 353; on Scargill, 188–189, 210–211; on Socialism, 57, 60–62; "Stepping Stones" by, 52–53, 54–55, 57, 60; on stockpiling, 209; on Thatcher, M., attractiveness, 98, 99; on Thatcher, M., charisma, 64, 102; on Thatcher, M., courage, 105; on Thatcher, M., humor, 100–101; on Thatcher, M., leadership style, 64–65, 352–353; on Thatcher, M., Reagan friendship with, 275; on United States, 275; on Whitelaw, 98; wife of, 95; wiring diagram of, 57, 63–64
Hoskyns, Miranda: on British Disease, 140–141, 144; husband of, 95; on Thatcher, M., charisma, 98, 99–100, 104; on Thatcher, M., conservatism, 96; on Thatcher, M., courage, 97, 105

Hoskyns, Miranda *(continued)*: on Thatcher, M., humor, 101–102; on Thatcher, M., leadership style, 352; on Thatcher, M., women and, 97–98
Housewife, 52, 136, 205–206
Howarth, Alan, 67–68
Howe, Geoffrey, 37, 40, 85, 87; on Churchill, 333; demotion of, 326; on economists, 136; on Europe, 323; on Gorbachev, M., 280; on Healey, 325; Healey on, 324; Lawson on, 325, 326; Powell, Charles, on, 324; resignation of, 309–310, 326, 331, 332–333; on Soviet Union, 279; Thatcher, M., on, 324
Hungary: elections in, 304, 305; invasion of, 192
Hussein, Saddam, 355–356

Ilford Conservative Club, 61
Immigration, 261
"Implementing Our Strategy" (Patten), 65
Income: inequality in, 147, 148; per capita, 145; rise in, 148; tax, 140–141, 147
Independent, 309
India, 349
Inflation: in 1989, 325–326; economists and, 137; Graham on, 132–133, 135–136, 138; Lawson on, 129, 137; lowering of, 129–130; Phillips Curve and, 124; price and, 127; Thatcher, M., on, 127–129; unemployment and, 125–126, 127–131, 136, 138, 145–146. *See also* Non-Accelerating Inflation Rate of Unemployment
Ingham, Bernard, 2; on British extremism, 70; on British Left, 41–42; on Bush, 354; on flying pickets, 225–226; on Hoskyns, J., 55–56; on Iraq, 354–355; on Islamic extremism, 349–350;

political start of, 19–20; on Scargill, 196, 225–226, 233–234; on Thatcher, M., class challenge of, 44; on Thatcher, M.'s honesty, 293; on Thatcher, M.'s infirmity, 3–4; on Thatcher, M.'s upbringing, 20–21; on Thatcherism, 27, 28; upbringing of, 42–43; on Walker, 233–234
Institute of Directors, 2–3
Interest rates, 124, 137
Intermediate-Range Nuclear Forces Treaty, 40, 302
International Money Fund, 12
Intervention, 24
Interviews: coal miner, 243–244, 245–248, 249–250, 253–262; Soviet, 298–299; Thatcher, M., on Lawson, 326–328
Investment, 127, 141, 148–149
IRA bombing, 104–105
Iran: Britain and, 350–351; Powell, Charles, on, 351; United States hostages in, 270–271
Iraq, 348, 351; Blair and, 353; constitution of, 357; Hoskyns, J., on, 352–353; Ingham on, 354–355; Thatcher, M., and, 351–356; Walker on, 354
Iron Curtain, 349
"Iron Lady," 32, 89, 178, 232, 263
Islamic extremism: Hoskyns, J., on, 350, 352; Ingham on, 349–350; oil and, 349; secular perception of, 356–357; Thatcher, M., and, 349–351, 355; Walker on, 350
Islas Malvinas. *See* Falkland Islands
Italy, 313, 323
ITV, 327
Izzard, Eddie, 177–178

Japan, 271
Jaruzelski, Wojciech, 102–103
Johnson, William Samuel, 178
Joseph, Keith "Mad Monk," 43; Friedman and, 135–136; as mentor, 23–24, 108; on Socialism, 25; speech on

eugenics, 26–27; Upminster speech of, 42

KAL. *See* Korean Airlines Flight 007
Keynesian economics, 37, 41–42, 124
Kinnock, Neil, 87–88; on Conservative Party, 330; on economics, 152; on EEC, 323; on Gorbachev, M., 300–301; on Grenada, 278; Labour Party changes due to, 234–235; loyalties of, 226; no confidence motion of, 340; on Orgreave riots, 186–187; on pit closures, 200; Powell, Charles, on, 88; Prime Minister's Questions and, 87–90; Reagan and, 274–275; on Scargill, 197–200, 211, 216–217; Sheridan on, 200–201; on stockpiling, 224–225, 227; on Sweden, 151–152, 154; on Thatcher, M., attractiveness, 90–91; on Thatcher, M., charisma, 106–108; on Thatcher, M., class challenges, 211–213; Thatcher, M., conflict with, 89–90; on Thatcher, M., downfall, 309, 339; on Thatcher, M., Kremlin meeting, 300–302; on Thatcher, M., matron role, 92–94; Thatcher, M., on, 232; on Thatcher, M., Reagan friendship with, 278
Kissinger, Henry, 10
Kohl, Helmut, 311
Korean Airlines Flight (KAL) 007, 263–264, 267; Scargill on, 194–195; Thatcher, M., on, 265–266
Kuril Islands, 159

Labour aristocracy, 193
Labour Party: Clause 4 of, 6, 189; disarmament demands of, 274, 277; economic changes by, 137; on EEC membership, 314, 319;

Hoskyns, J., on, 61–62; Kinnock's changes in, 234–235; Reagan and, 275; strike support by, 232; Thatcher, M., on, 196, 315; Thatcher, M, Soviet Union diplomacy and, 298; Trade unions link with, 62, 196–197. *See also* Fabian Society; New Labour
"The Lady's Not for Turning" (Thatcher), 37, 127
Lawson, Nigel: on Howe, 325, 326; on inflation, 129, 137; inflation and, 325–326; on Powell, Charles, 73; resignation threat of, 326; on Scargill, 208, 218; on Socialism, 66; on Soviet Union, 291; on Thatcher, M., 290, 291, 326, 335–336; Thatcher, M., on, 327–328; on Thatcher, M., Reagan friendship with, 290, 291; on Thatcherism, 114–115; "Thoughts on the Coming Battle" by, 65–66
Leadership, style of, 64–65, 335–336, 352–353
Lenin, Vladimir, 344
Leviathan (Hobbes), 346–347
Lewis, Brian: on development schemes, 240–241; on industry change, 248, 249; on Orgreave, 255; on Scargill, 243; on Scargill's Soviet Union tour, 259–260; on Thatcher, M., 258, 260–261; upbringing of, 242–243; on Yorkshire, 238–240, 243–244, 255
Libya, 229, 275, 351
Liverpool, 130
Lockerbie, Scotland, 106–107
London, 149, 261

M3, 132
Macmillan, Harold, 21, 109
MAD. *See* Mutual Assured Destruction
Madrid, 326
Major, John, 88, 138, 331

Manufacturing industry:
competitiveness of, 155; jobs in,
148; reduction of, 130; service
industry replacement of,
144–145
"Margaret Thatcher Talking about
Sinking the *Belgrano*," 76
Marriage, 101
Marshall, Walter, 209, 233
Marxism: appeal of, 243; of Scargill,
188, 192, 213–214; Thatcher,
M., on, 47–48, 68, 69
Marxist-Leninism, 300, 301
Matron, 85, 92–94
Menace in Europe (Berlinski), 310,
311
MI5. *See* Military Intelligence,
Section 5
Midlands, 216, 218
Military Intelligence, Section 5
(MI5), 183, 220–221
Miners: in 1981, 208; capitalism to,
206–207; coal strike dissent of,
215–216, 217; as communists,
204; Conservative Party on,
207; financial aid for, 195, 260;
Hoskyns, J., on, 207;
impoverishment of, in coal
strike, 223; interviews with,
243–244, 245–248, 249–250,
253–262; OPEC and, 203;
Scargill loyalty of, 224–226;
Walker on, 227; work ethic of,
246–247; in Yorkshire, 238–239
Miners' Federation of Great Britain,
203
Mining: after coal strike, 234, 235,
239; in Britain, 203–205, 239; in
China, 203, 205; conditions in,
204, 252–253; cost of, 203;
dependency culture from, 239;
energy importance of, 203;
history of, 203; Hoskyns, J., on,
207–208, 210; Lawson's
proposal for, 218; nationalization
of, 203; new, 218; pit closure in,
205–206, 210, 217, 235;
privatization of, 203; safety in,
204–205, 227–228; Socialism
and, 206–207; stockpiling and,

208–209, 210, 224–225, 227,
229; subsidization of, 203–204;
union politics with, 244; in
United States, 203; under
Wilson, 205. *See also*
Employment Act (1982);
Midlands; Nottinghamshire;
Yorkshire
Ministry of Defense, 162
"Misc. 101," 217
Mitterand, François: at EEC
summit, 317; on Falklands War,
166; on Thatcher, M.,
attractiveness of, 81, 91
Monetarism, 124–127, 133;
application of, 37, 135; success
of, 136; Thatcher, M., and,
135–136; in Thatcherism, 123,
138–139
Monetary aggregates, 132
Monetary policy, 124, 137; in
Thatcherism, 138–139
Money, 12, 132–133
Money supply, 132; Graham on, 134;
measurement of, 133, 134, 135
Monopolies and Mergers
Commission, 203
Mulroney, Brian, 288
Mutual Assured Destruction
(MAD), 270, 272; Thatcher, M.,
on, 285–286

NAIRU. *See* Non-Accelerating
Inflation Rate of
Unemployment
Narcissism, 83
National Coal Board: founding of,
203; MacGregor at, 210; pit
closures by, 205; strike response
of, 217
National Security Agency, 264
National Security Council, 289
National Union of Mineworkers
(NUM), 38; founding of, 203;
MI5 in, 183; at Orgreave riots,
183–186; Scargill's rise in, 189,
199; strike ending by, 230;
Walker's proposal to, 214–216.
See also Union of Democratic
Mineworkers

Nation-state, 348
Natural gas, 303
Nazis, 312, 349
Netherlands, 308
New Labour, 41, 227
Nicaragua, 270
Nicholas II (Czar), 344
Non-Accelerating Inflation Rate of
 Unemployment (NAIRU), 126,
 138–139, 146
North Atlantic Treaty Organisation
 (NATO), 270; Britain in, 274;
 Intermediate-Range Nuclear
 Forces treaty and, 302
North Vietnam, 270
Northern Ireland, 90–91
"This Is Not the Time to Be Mealy-
 Mouthed: Intervention Is
 Destroying Us" (Joseph) 24, 25
Nott, John, 159, 161, 173
Nottinghamshire: flying pickets in,
 216, 253, 254; mine closure at,
 235; strike refusal of, 215, 216,
 223; union politics in, 216, 219,
 244
Nuclear arms: demonstrations
 against, 277; Gorbachev, M., on,
 284; of Soviet Union, 270,
 298–299; Soviet Union scare
 with, 267; in United States, 270
Nuclear winter, 281, 284

Oil: in Falkland Islands, 181; Islamic
 extremism and, 349; mining
 and, 203; in Soviet Union, 270,
 303
Organisation for Economic Cooperation and Development,
 136
Organization of the Petroleum
 Exporting Countries (OPEC),
 203
Orgreave, South Yorkshire: flying
 pickets at, 254; Kinnock on,
 186–187; Lewis on, 255; NUM
 at, 183–186; police at,
 183–186, 255; rioting at,
 183–187, 221; Scargill at, 183,
 186
Orwell, George, 92, 202

Ostpolitik, 270
Oxford, England, 17–18, 49, 80, 84,
 237

Pall Mall, 2
"La Pasionaria of Middle Class
 Privilege," 30
Perón, Eva, 71
Persian Gulf, 203
Phillips Curve, 124, 125, 145
Pit closures: after coal strike, 200,
 217, 235; Kinnock on, 200; by
 National Coal Board, 205;
 Scargill on, 195–196, 210;
 strikes and, 206; under
 Thatcher, M., 205–206; under
 Wilson, 205
Pitmatic, 199
Poland, 303; free elections in,
 304–305; Thatcher, M., visit to,
 102–103. *See also* Solidarity
 movement
Police: brutality of, 244; in coal
 strike, 219; at Orgreave,
 183–186, 255
Politburo, 281
Poll tax, 40, 329–330
Port Stanley, 174
Post Office, 143–144
Powell, Charles: background of, 72;
 on Bruges speech, 322–323; on
 Chirac, 319–320; on Cold War,
 298; on EEC, 316, 317–318,
 319, 320–321; on Falklands
 War, 230; on Fountainebleu
 Summit, 317; on Gorbachev,
 M., meetings, 279–282,
 295–298; on Howe, 324; on
 Iran, 351; on Kinnock, 88;
 Lawson on, 73; power of, 73; on
 Socialism, 111; on strike,
 230–232; on Thatcher, M.,
 downfall, 335; on Thatcher, M.,
 '87 election, 298; on Thatcher,
 M., German antipathy of, 311;
 on Thatcher, M., popularity,
 331; on Thatcher, M., Reagan
 friendship with, 290, 291; on
 Thatcher, M., Soviet interview,
 298, 299; on trade unions, 231

Powell, Colin, 353
Prices, 118–120; inflation and, 127;
in Soviet Union, 121. *See also*
Retail price index
Privatization, 3, 27; Graham on,
142–143; of mining, 203;
Thatcherism and, 123, 141,
144; in United States, 7

QE2. *See Queen Elizabeth 2*
Queen Elizabeth 2 *(QE2)*, 167
Quintus Fabius Maximus, 43

Railway workers, 217, 234
Reagan, Ronald, 2; on armament,
277, 292–294; on Cold War,
272; election of, 271; "Evil
Empire" speech by, 265;
Falklands War response of, 171,
174, 176; Faulds on, 277; funeral
of, 292; Gates on, 271–272;
Gorbachev, M., and, 284–285,
287–289, 292–293, 297, 302;
Hoskyns, J., on, 275;
Intermediate-Range Nuclear
Forces Treaty signing by, 302;
Kinnock and, 274–275, 278; on
Korean airliner downing, 265;
Kremlin and, 266–267; Labour
party and, 275; Lawson on, 290,
291; Powell, Charles, on, 290,
291; at Reykjavik summit,
292–293; SDI and, 39, 286–287,
292–294; on Socialism, 8; on
Soviet Union, 271–272, 280;
Soviet Union economy effect of,
303, 304; Thatcher., M., and,
269, 273, 274–275, 284–288,
289–292, 293, 294
Recession, 138, 146
Referendum: on EEC, 314; on
European Constitution, 307
Regeneration schemes, 241–242
Rentschler, James, 169–170, 171
Resolution 502, 166
Retail price index, 131, 139
Reykjavik summit, 40, 292–293
Riley, Andrew, 49–50
Rimington, Stella, 220–221, 222

Riots: at Orgreave, 183–187, 221; in
Turkey, 358–359;
unemployment-related, 130;
Whitelaw on, 130
The Road to Wigan Pier (Orwell),
202
Romney, Mitt, 1, 2
Rotary Club, of Grantham, 312
Rousseau, Jean-Jacques, 346, 347, 357
Royal, Ségolène, 71, 84, 86
Rumsfeld, Donald, 353
Russia. *See* Soviet Union

Safety, in mining, 204–205,
227–228
Sakharov, Andrei, 296
Saltley coke depot, 185
Sandinistas, 270
Sarbanes-Oxley Act, 148–149
Sarkozy, Nicolas, 86, 111
Satan missile, 270, 276–277
Saudi Arabia, 303, 357
Scargill, Arthur "King Arthur," 40;
on capitalism, 192; economics
of, 195–196; on flying pickets,
196; funding of, 229, 259–260,
283; on Gorbachev, M., 194;
government blame by, 235;
Harry on, 256, 257; Heath and,
185; history of, 189; Hoskyns, J.,
on, 188–189, 210–211; Ingham
on, 196, 225–226, 233–234;
Johnny on, 256–257, 258–259;
Kinnock on, 197–200, 211,
216–217; on Korean Airlines
Flight 007, 194–195; Lawson
on, 208, 218; Lewis on, 243,
259–260; loss without limit
declaration by, 246; Marxism of,
188, 192, 213–214; miners'
loyalty to, 224–226; NUM rise
of, 189, 199; at Orgreave, 183,
186; on pit closures, 195–196,
210; at Saltley coke depot, 185;
Sheridan on, 201–202; on
Soviet Union, 193–195; Soviet
Union tours of, 194, 258–259;
spying on, 220–223; as Stalinist,
193–194; stockpiling and, 225,

227, 229; strike insistence of, 215–216; on Trade unions, 192; Walker on, 195, 197, 213–214. *See also* "Arthur Scargill Walks on Water"; Sheridan, Linda; "There's only one Arthur Scargill"

Schmidt, Helmut, 317

Scotland, 189

Scowcroft, Brent, 73

Seattle, 358

Second Cold War, 179

Shakespeare, William, 70, 310

Shame, 60–62

Sheffield, 175

Sheridan, Linda, 189–191; on Kinnock, 200–201; on Scargill, 201–202; on strike, 216–217; on Thatcher, M., 190, 191

Shrew, 86–87, 106–108, 324, 325

Shultz, George, 288, 292–294

Silver Fox, 220, 222, 223

Single European Act, 318

Sixties, 96

Socialist Labour Party, 189

Solidarity movement, 102, 103, 194; election of, 304–305; Gorbachev, M., on, 305; political support of, 272

"Some Suggestions for Strategic Themes" (Howarth), 67

South Africa, 203

South Georgia, 160–161, 172–173

South Korea. *See* Korean Airlines Flight (KAL) 007

South Yorkshire. *See* Orgreave, South Yorkshire

Soviet Union: Afghanistan invasion of, 271; Afghanistan withdrawal of, 304; armament of, 276–277, 286, 289, 292–293, 297, 303; Berlin Wall and, 305; Britain and, 179–180; Central Intelligence Agency on, 271; coal strike support by, 195; collapse of, 7, 302–303; Eastern Europe and, 270, 304; economy of, 269, 270, 272–273, 288, 303, 304; Howe on, 279; KAL

attack response by, 265; Kuril Islands and, 159; Labour Party and, 298; Lawson on, 291; Lewis on, 259–260; nuclear arms in, 270, 298–299; nuclear scare in, 267; oil in, 270, 303; plane attack by, 195; Powell, Charles, on, 298, 299; prices in, 121; Reagan and, 266–267; 271–272, 280, 303, 304; Scargill and, 193–195, 258–259; SDI effect on, 286–287, 288, 293; Thatcher, M., meeting in, 295–302; Thatcher, M., meeting about, 268–270; Thatcher, M., on, 31–32, 266, 322; Thatcher, M., visit to, 103, 294–302; Trade unions and, 195; United States and, 179, 268, 270–271, 288; Walker on, 195. *See also* Chernenko, Konstantin; Gorbachev, Mikhail

Sovietologists, 268–270

Spain, 323

SS-18 missile, 270

SS-20 missiles, 277

Stagflation, 125, 126

Stalin, Joseph, 109, 193

Stalin Society, 193

State of the Union speech, 355

Statecraft (Thatcher, M.), 310, 311

Steel industry, 203–204

"Stepping Stones" report (Hoskyns, J.), 52–53, 54–55, 57, 60; Socialism in, 60–62

Stockpiling, of coal: Hoskyns, J., on, 209; Kinnock on, 224–225, 227; plans for, 208–209, 210; Scargill and, 225, 227, 229; Walker and, 224, 229

Strasbourg, 316–317

Strategic Arms Reduction Treaty, 279

Strategic Defense Initiative (SDI), 285; Cold War and, 293; Reagan and, 39, 286–287, 292–294; Reykjavik summit proposal for, 292–293; Soviet effect of, 286–287, 288, 293; Thatcher, M., on, 286–287, 288

Strategy and Tactics Committee, 66–67

Strikes: Britain, 11–12, 234; end of, 230, 232, 234; history of, 206; pit closures and, 206; railway workers threat of, 217, 234; regularity of, 246; scab death in, 229–230; supervisor's threat of, 217–218; union votes on, 215, 216. *See also* Coal strike, 1984

Subsidies, 316

Such, Such Were the Joys (Orwell), 92

Suez, 158

Suicide, 238

Supply side, 139–141, 146

Sweden, 151–152, 154

Tax, 124; fixed-rate, 329–330; income, 140–141, 147; lowering of, 139; poll, 40, 330; subsidized mining as, 204; Value Added, 147

Thatcher, Denis, 19, 85, 100, 101

Thatcher, Margaret: 2002 speech of, 355–356; accent of, 211–212; on armament, 277; assassination attempt on, 104–105; attractiveness of, 21–22, 81–82, 90–91, 98, 99; Bible references of, 26; as Boudicea, 76–80, 82–85, 103–105, 232–233; on British identity, 313, 314; Bruges speech of, 321–323; on Bush, 290; charisma of, 64, 71, 98, 99–100, 102, 104, 105–108; Chirac and, 319–320; on Churchill, 314; Clark on, 332, 335, 336, 337; class challenges of, 31, 43–44, 206; on coal strike alternative, 214–215; coal strike and, 214–216; coal strike speech of, 233; on coal strike violence, 229–230; Cold War and, 273, 295; on Common Market, 313; on communists, 47–48, 296; Conservative Party conference speeches of, 37, 68–69; Conservative Party resignation of, 23, 340; courage of, 97, 104–105; on Delors, 318–319, 331; d'Estaing and, 316–317; on disarmament, 180–181, 293; in diva role, 76, 99–100, 110; economic criticism of, 135, 136, 144, 249–250; economics of, 52, 114; on EEC membership, 313, 314–316, 317, 318–319, 320–322; as emasculating, 248–249; equality speech of, 147; on European Union, 310, 311; on Falklands War, 77–80, 158–159, 164–166, 168, 171–172, 173–174, 176; father figure for, 290; female roles of, 52, 72, 76–80, 81–85, 86–87, 89, 90–91, 92–94, 99–100, 103–105, 106–108, 110, 136, 205–206, 232–233, 282, 297, 324, 325; on financial aid, 241; first years of, 37–39; as flirt, 81–82, 90–91, 282, 297; on France, 313, 314; on free-market economics, 115–116, 121, 148; Galtieri on, 210; Germany and, 310, 311, 312–313, 314; Gorbachev, M., and, 279–285, 288, 290, 291, 302; Haig meeting of, 169–170; Heath on, 28, 339; honesty of, 293; Hoskyns, J., on, 64–65, 98, 99, 100–101, 102, 105, 275, 352–353; Hoskyns, M., on, 96–102, 104, 105, 352; in housewife role, 52, 136, 205–206; Howe and, 324; humor of, 100–102; on Hussein, 355–356; on inflation, 127–129; Ingham on, 3–4, 20–21, 44, 293; on Iranians, 351; Iraq and, 351–356; Islamic extremism awareness of, 349–351, 355; ITV interview of, 327–328; on Kinnock, 232; Kinnock conflict with, 89–90; Kinnock on, 89–91, 92–94, 106–108, 211–213, 278, 300–302, 309, 339; on Korean airplane attack, 265–266; Kremlin meeting of,

295–302; Labour Party and, 196, 298, 315; on Lawson, 327–328; Lawson on, 290, 291, 326, 335–336; leadership style of, 64–65, 335–336, 352–353; at Lockerbie, 106–107; marriage of, 101; on Marxism, 47–48, 68, 69; matron role of, 85, 92–94; mentor of, 23–24, 108; mining issue for, 206; Mitterand and, 81, 91, 317; monetarism and, 135–136; on nation-states, 348; negativity towards, 41–42, 89–90; papers of, 49–52; pit closures under, 205–206; Polish visit of, 102–103; political start of, 18–19, 21; popularity of, 329–330, 331; Powell, Charles, on, 74–76, 85, 86–87, 108–111, 279–282, 290, 291, 295–298, 299, 311, 322–323, 331, 335; power loss by, 309, 332, 335–338, 339; Reagan and, 269, 273, 274, 275, 284–288, 289–292, 293, 294; re-election of, 39; resignation of, 40–41, 339–342; second election of, 309; in Second World War, 312–313; Sheridan on, 190, 191; as shrew, 86–87, 106–108, 324, 325; Single European Act of, 318; on Socialism, 5–8, 13, 25–26, 49, 68–69, 117, 196, 206–207; on Soviet Union, 31–32, 266, 322; Soviet Union interview for, 298–299; Soviet Union visit of, 103, 294–302; *Statecraft* by, 310, 311; temperament of, 74–76, 82–85; third election of, 40; Trade unions and, 248; transformation of, 108–109; United Nations address of, 179–181; upbringing of, 15–18, 20–21, 43–44, 109; Walker's appointment by, 187–188; on Walters, A., 327; Winter of Discontent speech of, 11–12; women as threat to, 97–99; as xenophobe, 310, 311,

312; Zamyatin on, 283. *See also* Thatcherism
Thatcher Revolution, 53; Falklands War and, 158; wiring diagram as start of, 64
"Thatcher the Milk-Snatcher," 23, 96
Thatcherism: criticism of, 42; economics of, 114–115, 148, 240; free markets in, 240; Ingham on, 27, 28; Lawson on, 114–115; monetarism in, 123, 138–139; Socialism in, 54–55
"There's only one Arthur Scargill," 193
Third Way, 146
Thompson, Fred, 1–2, 4
"Thoughts on the Coming Battle" (Lawson), 65–66
Tory Party. *See* Conservative Party
Trade unions: 1982 Employment Act and, 209–210; government and, 231; Labour Party link with, 62, 196–197; Powell, Charles, on, 231; Scargill on, 192; Soviet Union and, 195; Thatcher, M., 248. *See also* Coal strike, 1984; Electrician's union; National Union of Mineworkers; Transport and General Workers Union; Union of Democratic Mineworkers
Trades Union Conference, 319
Training, 152
Trains, 142, 217, 234
Transport and General Workers Union, 224, 319
Travellers Club, 63
Treasury, 137
Turkey, 358–359

UB40, 131
Underclass, 146
Unemployment, 124; in Britain, 22, 37, 39, 130, 136; Friedman's ideas about, 138–139; inflation and, 125–126, 127–131, 136, 138, 145–146; rioting due to, 130; in Sweden, 151–152, 154; in Yorkshire, 238, 241–242

Unemployment Benefits 40, 131
Union of Democratic Mineworkers,
    219
United Nations: Falklands War
    response of, 166; Thatcher, M.,
    address to, 179–181
United States: Afghanistan and, 303;
    armament of, 276–277, 288,
    289; Britain and, 140–141,
    273–274, 275; Central
    Intelligence Agency on, 271,
    273; in Cold War, 48;
    communism and, 48, 272;
    economics of, 249; Falklands
    War response of, 169–170, 171,
    174, 176; Grenada invasion of,
    278; Hoskyns, J., on, 275;
    hostages from, 270–271; mining
    in, 203; in North Vietnam, 270;
    nuclear power of, 270;
    privatization in, 7; Sarbanes-
    Oxley Act in, 148–149; Soviet
    Union and, 179, 268, 270–271,
    288

Vale of Belvoir, 218
Value Added Tax, 147
Venezuela, 357
"Vote Yes" campaign, 314

Wakefield. *See* Yorkshire
Walden, Brian, 327–328
Walesa, Lech, 103
Walker, Peter: on Blair, 354; on
    Bush, 354; Ingham on,
    233–234; on Iraq, 354; on
    Islamic extremism, 350; on
    miners, 227; on Scargill, 195,
    197, 213–214; on Soviet Union,
    195; stockpiling and, 224, 229;
    strike alternative of, 214–216;
    Thatcher, M., appointment of,
    187–188

Warsaw Pact, 270
"Wedgie" Benn. *See* Anthony Benn
Weinberger, Caspar, 287
Welfare, 139, 148, 154–155; mining
    as, 204
Wellington Room, 187
West Germany, 145, 270, 271
Wham!, 131
Whitelaw, William, 87; Hoskyns, J.,
    on, 98; on rioting, 130
"Who Governs Britain?", 23
Wilson, Harold: EEC referendum of,
    314; election of, 23; Graham
    and, 80; mining under, 205;
    resignation of, 31
Winter of Discontent, 11–12, 33
Wiring diagram, 57, 63–64
Women: Conservative Party and, 92;
    Kinnock and, 87–94; Thatcher,
    M., and, 97–99
Woodward, John, 172
World Economics Forum, 146
World Trade Organization (WTO),
    358
World War II, 311–313
Wreford-Brown, Chris, 174
WTO. *See* World Trade Organization

Xenophobia, 310–312

Yorkshire: miner interviews in,
    243–244, 245–248, 249–250,
    253–262; miners in, 238–239;
    unemployment in, 238,
    241–242. *See also* Orgreave,
    South Yorkshire
Yorkshire Miner, 194
Young Communist League, 189

Zamyatin, Leonid, 282, 283
Zeebrugge harbor, Belgium, 107
Zulu, 254–255